Aḥmad al-Ghazālī, Remembrance, and the Metaphysics of Love

SUNY series in Islam

Seyyed Hossein Nasr, editor

Aḥmad al-Ghazālī, Remembrance, and the Metaphysics of Love

JOSEPH E. B. LUMBARD

SUNY PRESS

Published by State University of New York Press, Albany

Printed in the United States of America

For information, contact State University of New York Press, Albany, NY
www.sunypress.edu

Production, Eileen Nizer
Marketing, Michael Campochiaro

Library of Congress Cataloging-in-Publication Data

Names: Lumbard, Joseph E. B., 1969–
Title: Aḥmad al-Ghazālī, remembrance, and the metaphysics of love / Joseph E. B. Lumbard.
Description: Albany : State University of New York Press, [2016] | Series: SUNY series in Islam | Includes bibliographical references and index.
Identifiers: LCCN 2015010183 | ISBN 9781438459653 (hardcover : alk. paper) | ISBN 9781438459646 (pbk. alk. paper) | ISBN 9781438459660 (e-book)
Subjects: LCSH: Ghazzālī, Aḥmad ibn Muḥammad, –1126. | Ghazzālī, Aḥmad ibn Muḥammad, –1126. Savāniḥ. | Islamic philosophy—History. | Sufism—History.
Classification: LCC BP189.26.G44 L86 2016 | DDC 181/.5—dc23
LC record available at http://lccn.loc.gov/2015010183

10 9 8 7 6 5 4 3 2 1

For Alexis

"Love is not love
which alters when it alteration finds,
or bends with the remover to remove."

Contents

Acknowledgments

This book derives from a doctoral dissertation submitted to Yale University's Department of Religious Studies. I am deeply indebted to my dissertation advisor, Gerhard Böwering, who first suggested this topic and saw the project through to completion. I must also thank Seyyed Hossein Nasr, under whom I completed an MA thesis on Abū Ḥāmid al-Ghazālī and who first introduced me to the fields of Islamic Studies and Sufi Studies. Beatrice Gruendler served as a meticulous reader for the dissertation and provided the overall structure that I have maintained in the final book. As a reader for the dissertation, William Chittick provided many excellent suggestions. His thorough critique of the revised manuscript many years later was invaluable.

Neither the dissertation nor this book would have been possible without Mohammed Musavi, who spent many hours guiding me through the allusive works of Aḥmad Ghazālī and other luminaries of the Persian Sufi tradition. Mohammed Faghfoory's guidance in first approaching these works was also invaluable. Nasrollah Pourjavady has served as an excellent sounding board for various ideas over the years. Without the foundations he established, this book would not have been possible. James Morris has been a source of insight and encouragement for many years.

Ryan Brizendine, Caner Dagli, Atif Khalil, Shankar Nair, Mohammed Rustom, Walid Saleh, and Laury Silvers all provided valuable input at various stages along the way. Three anonymous reviewers from SUNY Press made excellent suggestions and caught many mistakes. Any errors that remain are of course my own.

Last but not least, my heartfelt thanks go to my family. My mother has supported me through every success and every failure. My grandfather provided an atmosphere for study and contemplation when this project first began. My father instilled in me a love for poetry that led to this study and enriched my life in many ways.

My sister has endured the peculiarities of having an academic for a sibling and done her part to keep me in touch with "the real world." My daughters Layla, Rayhan, and Tasneem have successfully delayed this project many times over, giving me much time to reconsider and deepen my understanding. My wife Alexis has made innumerable sacrifices to support me and has improved my writing in many ways. This book is dedicated to her.

Introduction

The name al-Ghazālī rings through the annals of Islamic intellectual history. Many who know little about the Islamic tradition have heard of al-Ghazālī, and most whose professional lives are dedicated to the study of Islam, especially its intellectual sciences, have encountered this name in one form or another. For the vast majority, it is the name of Imām Abū Ḥāmid Muḥammad b. Muḥammad al-Ghazālī (d. 505/1111) with which they are familiar. Imām Abū Ḥāmid al-Ghazālī had an enduring influence on philosophy, theology, and jurisprudence that forever changed the course of these disciplines. Muslims of different eras and varying ethnicities have seen in his writings the tools for a revival of the basic piety of Muslim life.[1] Given the extent of his influence, Abū Ḥāmid al-Ghazālī is arguably the most eminent intellectual in Islamic history. All of the attention received by Imam Abū Ḥāmid al-Ghazālī has, however, overshadowed the contributions of his younger brother, Shaykh Aḥmad b. Muḥammad al-Ghazālī (d. 517/1123 or 520/1126), who, as an influential Sufi Shaykh and important figure in the early development of Persian Sufi literature, is more renowned for his spiritual attainment and instruction than for his achievements in the religious sciences.

Why Study Aḥmad al-Ghazālī?

Aḥmad al-Ghazālī's *Sawāniḥ* (Inspirations) is one of the earliest extant Persian treatises to be written on Sufism, preceded only by the *Sharḥ-i taʿarruf li-madhhab-i taṣawwuf* (Explanation of the Introduction to the Sufi Way) of Ismāʿīl b. Muḥammad al-Mustamlī (d. 434/1042–3), the *Kashf al-maḥjūb* (Unveiling of the Veiled) of ʿAlī b. ʿUthmān al-Hujwīrī (d. 465/1073 or 469/1077), and several works of Khwājah ʿAbdallāh

Anṣārī (d. 481/1089). There is clear evidence that Sufism was discussed extensively in Persian before these treatises. Many scholars whose native tongue was Persian, such as Abū ʿAbd ar-Raḥmān as-Sulamī (d. 412/1021), Abū Saʿīd b. Abi'l-Khayr (d. 440/1049), and Abu'l-Qāsim al-Qushayrī (d. 465/1072), were among the most influential Sufis before Aḥmad al-Ghazālī. But just as Arabic was at this time the only language in which Islamic law and theology were presented, so too did it dominate the textual presentation of Sufism. It was, however, only a matter of time before the Persians availed themselves of the natural poetic nature of their language to express the subtlest of Islamic teachings. As William Chittick observes, "Persian pulls God's beauty into the world on the wings of angels. Persian poetry, which began its great flowering in the eleventh century, shines forth with this angelic presence."[2] Along with ʿAbdallāh Anṣārī a generation earlier, and his younger contemporaries Sanāʾī of Ghaznah (d. 525/1131), Aḥmad b. Manṣūr as-Samʿānī (d. 534/1140), author of *Rawḥ al-arwāḥ fī sharḥ asmāʾ al-malik al-fattāḥ* (The Repose of Spirits Regarding the Exposition of the Names of the Conquering King), and Rashīd ad-Dīn al-Maybudī (*fl.* sixth/twelfth century), author of the ten-volume Quran commentary, *Kashf al-asrār wa ʿuddat al-abrār* (The Unveiling of Secrets and the Provision of the Pious), Aḥmad al-Ghazālī stands at the forefront of the Persian Sufi tradition.

Written in the first decade of the sixth Islamic century, the *Sawāniḥ* is the first recorded treatise in the history of Islam to present a full metaphysics of love, in which love is seen as the ultimate reality from which all else derives and all that derives from it is seen as an intricate play between lover and beloved, who are themselves laid to naught before love.[3] For this reason, Leonard Lewisohn refers to the *Sawāniḥ* as "the founding text of the School of Love in Sufism and the tradition of love poetry in Persian,"[4] and Leili Anvar affirms that the *Sawāniḥ* is "justly considered as the founding text of the School of Love in Sufism and the tradition of love poetry in Persian."[5] The centrality of love for the Sufi way was in many ways inaugurated a generation before al-Ghazālī in the works of ʿAbdallāh Anṣārī, *42 Chapters* (Chihil u du faṣl), *Intimate Discourses* (Munājāt), and *Treatise on Love* (Maḥabbat-nāma). Nonetheless, the manner in which love can also be envisioned as the ultimate origin of all that exists is stated more directly in the *Sawāniḥ*.[6] While the precise origins of this complete metaphysics of love may never be known, what is clear is that Aḥmad al-Ghazālī was among the generation of authors who inaugurated the Persian Sufi literary tradition as we know it today. As such leading scholars of this tradition continue to declare,

Aḥmad al-Ghazālī is "one of the greatest expositors in Islam of the meaning of love."[7]

Initiatic Influence

In addition to his literary influence, Aḥmad al-Ghazālī is said to have received many disciples; among those mentioned are influential political figures such as the Saljūq leader Mughīth ad-Dīn al-Maḥmūd (r. 511–525/1118–1131), who ruled Iraq and western Persia, and his brother Aḥmad Sanjar (r. 513–552/1119–1157), who ruled Khurāsān and northern Persia. But Aḥmad al-Ghazālī's influence as a Sufi shaykh is more important for the initiatic chains (*silsilah*s) of the Sufi orders. As regards the initiatic history of Sufism, Shaykh Ḍiyā' ad-Dīn Abu'n-Najīb as-Suhrawardī (d. 563/1186) is his most important disciple.[8] It is not known just how much contact al-Ghazālī had with as-Suhrawardī, but it appears that al-Ghazālī held him in high regard and appointed him as his representative (*khalīfah*) while they were together in Iṣfahān.[9] Abu'n-Najīb's most famous disciple is his nephew Abū Ḥafṣ ʿUmar as-Suhrawardī (d. 632/1234), author of the famous *ʿAwārif al-maʿārif* (Gifts of the Gnostics), which is employed as a manual of Sufi practice to this day, and the founder of the Suhrawardiyyah Sufi order, which spread throughout the Muslim world.[10] The Suhrawardiyyah gave rise to other orders such as the Zayniyyah, which spread throughout the Ottoman Empire among other places and still exists in Turkey. Along with the Chishtiyyah, Naqshbandiyyah, and Qādiriyyah, the Suhrawardiyyah is one of the most influential orders in the history of India and Pakistan.[11] While it has died out in most parts of the Arab world, the Suhrawardiyyah is still active in Iraq and Syria.[12]

Three of Abu'n-Najīb as-Suhrawardī's disciples, Ismāʿīl al-Qaṣrī (d. 589/1193), ʿAmmār b. Yāsir al-Bidlīsī (d. 582/1186), and Rūzbihān al-Wazzān al-Miṣrī (d. 584/1188), are said to have collaborated in the spiritual development of the eponymous founder of the Kubrāwiyyah Sufi order, Najm ad-Dīn Kubrā (d. 618/1221).[13] This order spread throughout the region of Khwārazm into Persia, Afghanistan, India, and China. The Kubrāwiyyah still exists with *khānqāh*s in present day Iran, though its influence has diminished substantially. Among the Sufi orders that issued from the Kubrāwiyyah are the Firdawsiyyah, the Hamadāniyyah, and the Yaʿqūbiyyah, all of which still exist in India, as well as the Dhahabiyyah in Iran.[14]

Among the later luminaries of the Kubrāwiyyah are such figures as Najm ad-Dīn Dāya Rāzī (d. 654/1256), who either revised or extended Kubrā's Quran commentary, *ʿAyn al-ḥayāt* (The Spring of Life),[15] which goes to the seventeenth and eighteenth verses of *Sūrah* 51 (*adh-Dhāriyāt*) under the title of *Baḥr al-ḥaqāʾiq* (The Ocean of Realities). Rāzī also wrote *Mirṣād al-ʿibād min al-mabdaʾ ila'l-maʿād* (The Path of God's Bondsmen from the Beginning to the Return), an influential Persian Sufi treatise that is still in use both in Iran and India as a guide for Sufi adepts.[16] The *ʿAyn al-ḥayāt* was later completed from *Sūrah* 52 (*aṭ-Ṭur*) under the title *Najm al-Qurʾān* (The Star of the Quran) by another renowned shaykh of the Kubrāwiyyah order,[17] ʿAlāʾ ad-Dawlah as-Simnānī (d. 736/1336), who had many disciples in his *khānqāh* outside of Simnān, two hundred kilometers east of Tehran, and is known for opposing Ibn al-ʿArabī's doctrine of the oneness of being (*waḥdat al-wujūd*) and proposing a perspective in which is found the germ of the oneness of witnessing (*waḥdat ash-shuhūd*),[18] which later became prevalent among the Mujaddidī branch of the Naqshbandiyyah Sufi order.[19]

Another disciple of Aḥmad al-Ghazālī who is important for the initiatic history of Sufism is Abu'l-Faḍl al-Baghdādī (d. 550/1155). One *silsilah* of the Niʿmatallāhī order founded by Shāh Niʿmat Allāh Walī (d. 834/1331) comes seven generations through al-Baghdādī.[20] This order has had great influence in Turkey and continues to have new waves of influence in the growing Muslim communities of Europe and America. Although the historical validity of this *silsilah* cannot be substantiated, it nonetheless demonstrates that later adherents of the Niʿmatallāhī order recognized the spiritual authority of both Aḥmad al-Ghazālī and al-Baghdādī.

The only *silsilah* given by Shams ad-Dīn Aflākī (d. 761/1360) in his *Manāqib al-ʿārifīn* (The Feats of the Knowers of God) for the Mavlavī Sufi order founded by Jalāl ad-Dīn Rūmī (d. 672/1123) records Aḥmad al-Ghazālī as the shaykh of Aḥmad Khāṭibī al-Balkhī (d. 516/1123), upon whom he conferred the practice of remembrance (*dhikr*). Balkhī in turn conferred the *dhikr* upon Shams al-Aʾimma as-Sarakhsī (d. 571/1175), who was the Shaykh of Rūmī's father, Bahā ad-Dīn Walad (d. 628/1231). Burhān ad-Dīn at-Tirmidhī (d. 638/1240) was then the next Shaykh in this line, and was followed by Jalāl ad-Dīn Rūmī.[21] That later followers of the Mavlavī order recognized Aḥmad al-Ghazālī's spiritual authority is demonstrated by a passage attributed to Jalāl ad-Dīn Rūmī:

> Imām Muḥammad Ghazālī, may God have mercy on him, has dived into the ocean of the universe, attained to a world of dominion, and unfurled the banner of knowledge. The

> whole world follows him and he has become a scholar of all the worlds. Still . . . If he had one iota of love (*ʿishq*) like Aḥmad Ghazālī, it would have been better, and he would have made known the secret of Muḥammadan intimacy the way Aḥmad did. In the whole world, there is no teacher, no spiritual guide, and no unifier like love.[22]

Despite the presence of Aḥmad al-Ghazālī in Rūmī's *silsilah* and the respect he is accorded, he does not appear to have been as much of a direct literary influence upon Rūmī as was Ḥakīm Sanāʾī, whose *Ḥadīqat al-ḥaqīqah* (Garden of Reality) was the prototype for Rūmī's *Mathnawī*. Aflākī reports that Rūmī said of the *Ḥadīqat al-ḥaqīqah*, "By God this is more binding [than the Quran] because the outer form of the Koran is analogous to yoghurt, whereas these higher contents are its butter and cream."[23] Of the spiritual efficacy of Sanāʾī's writings, Aflākī reports that Rūmī said, "Whoever reads the words of Sanāʾī in absolute earnestness will become cognizant of the secret of the radiance (*sanā*) of our words."[24] Whereas Aḥmad al-Ghazālī's *Sawāniḥ* has had an extensive literary influence and he is accorded initiatic influence through several Sufi orders (*ṭuruq*), Sanāʾī's influence has come only through his writings.

Literary Influence

Given the importance of Sanāʾī and the still unexamined influence of figures such as Samʿānī and Maybudī, the importance of Aḥmad al-Ghazālī's *Sawāniḥ* for the history of Persian literature is a matter of debate. Like his younger contemporaries Samʿānī and Maybudī, he receives almost no mention in either Jan Rypka's *History of Iranian Literature* or in E.G. Browne's *A Literary History of Persia*.[25] This omission stands in stark contrast to Nasrollah Pourjavady's assertion that "the greatest Iranian Sufis and gnostics after him came under the influence of the special teaching which appeared from his beliefs about love (*ʿishq*) and his manner of expression."[26] Although it might be more accurate to say that Aḥmad al-Ghazālī was a pivotal figure among a generation of authors that forever changed the course of Persian Sufi literature, he nonetheless forms a crucial link in what some scholars have called "the path of love" or "the school of love." This "school" is not a direct succession of Sufi initiates marked by a definitive spiritual genealogy like the Sufi orders (*ṭarīqahs*) discussed above, but rather designates a significant trend within Sufi thought in which all aspects of creation and spiritual aspiration are presented in an allusive imaginal language fired by love for God. As Omid Safi observes, "The Path of Love may be described as a loosely affiliated group of Sufi mystics and poets who throughout the centuries have propagated a highly nuanced teaching focused on passionate love (*ʿishq*)."[27] ʿAbdallāh Anṣārī, Aḥmad al-Ghazālī, Aḥmad Samʿānī, Ḥakīm Sanāʾī, and Maybudī are among the first to have written in this vein.

The most direct evidence of Aḥmad al-Ghazālī's literary influence can be found in the commentaries on the *Sawāniḥ* written in both Persia and India, as well as the many extant manuscripts of the *Sawāniḥ*.[28] His theory of love that presents all the stages of the spiritual path as an interplay between love, the lover, and the beloved became central to Persian Sufism in later generations, while his literary style, blending poetry and prose in one seamless narrative, was employed in many later Sufi treatises. Given the degree to which Aḥmad al-Ghazālī's literary style and teachings are reflected in later Sufism, his influence must be reconsidered. It is, however, a subject that can be done justice only through extensive comparative textual analysis of the entire Persian Sufi tradition. Here I will touch on some of the most important traces.

As the goal of al-Ghazālī's writings is to facilitate traveling the spiritual path, his literary influence is intrinsically bound to his perceived spiritual and initiatic influence. All of his extant Persian writings are in fact addressed to his disciples. He never writes as a scholar of love or as a theoretician attempting to dissect love with the rational faculties; rather, his is an attempt to guide and encourage others who are on the path, helping them realize the Ultimate Reality that he considers to be inexpressible. The first traces of Aḥmad al-Ghazālī's literary influence are found in the works of his disciple ʿAyn al-Quḍāt Hamadānī (d. 526/1131), to whom al-Ghazālī addressed his Persian treatise *ʿAyniyyah* and perhaps nine other letters.[29] Hamadānī's letters and his *Tamhīdāt* take up many of the same themes expressed in al-Ghazālī's writings, such as the sincerity of Satan, the limitations of religious law, and the all-encompassing nature of Love. In many instances, the *Tamhīdāt* can be read as a commentary that expands on the central themes of the *Sawāniḥ*. In particular, the sixth chapter, "The Reality and States of Love," examines both the written and unexpressed dimensions of al-Ghazālī's teachings.[30] The *Tamhīdāt* has had an extensive influence on the Persian and Indian Sufi traditions and has been the subject of several commentaries.[31] ʿAyn al-Quḍāt instructed many students, teaching seven or eight sessions a day, and had many disciples,[32] but he is not recorded in any major *silsilah*s.

In addition to his influence on ʿAyn al-Quḍāt, al-Ghazālī likely had a continued influence on the aforementioned writings of both the Kubrāwiyyah and Suhrawardiyyah orders. Among those whom Pourjavady mentions are Abu'n-Najīb as-Suhrawardī and Abū Ḥafṣ ʿUmar as-Suhrawardī, as well as Najm ad-Dīn Rāzī. But such influence is not as evident as that which he had on the writings of Farīd ad-Dīn ʿAṭṭār (d. 617/1220) and Fakhr ad-Dīn ʿIrāqī (d. 688/1289). The latter's *Lamaʿāt* (Divine Flashes) is indebted to al-Ghazālī's *Sawāniḥ* for both its style and content. ʿIrāqī expresses a subtle metaphysics that gives an intellectual architecture to the question of love in Sufi thought. As ʿIrāqī writes in the beginning of the *Lamaʿāt,* it is intended to be "a few words explaining the levels of love in the tradition of the *Sawāniḥ,* in tune with the voice of each spiritual state as it passes."[33] Like al-Ghazālī, ʿIrāqī bases the entirety of his metaphysical discourse on the idea that "the derivation of the lover and the beloved is from Love,"[34] and sees all of reality as an unfolding of Love wherein none but Love is the lover or the beloved. Like al-Ghazālī's *Sawāniḥ,* Irāqī's *Lamaʿāt* is both a work of art and a sublime metaphysical treatise. The *Lamaʿāt* continues to be regarded as a treasure of Persian Sufism, and ʿAbd ar-Raḥmān Jāmī's (d. 833/1477) commentary on it, *Ashiʿʿat al-Lamaʿāt* (Rays of the Flashes), is still used as an introductory text for the study of the science of *ʿirfān* (recognition) in Iran.[35]

Aḥmad al-Ghazālī's *Dastān-i Murghān* (Ar. *Risālat aṭ-ṭayr;* The Treatise of the Birds) most likely provided the outline for ʿAṭṭār's famous *Manṭiq aṭ-ṭayr* (The Conference of the Birds).[36] Both works begin with a gathering of the birds, which, despite their differences, recognize their mutual need for a sovereign and set out to find one; for, as the birds say in *Dastān-i Murghān,* "If the shadow of the King's majesty is not upon our heads, we will not be secure from the enemy."[37] Both works describe a journey of many trials by which the birds find their sovereign, the Simurgh. But being of much greater breadth, Aṭṭār's *Manṭiq aṭ-ṭayr* deals with the theme of spiritual wayfaring in greater detail. As Seyyed Hossein Nasr writes:

> He [ʿAṭṭār] uses the Ghazzalean theme of suffering through which the birds are finally able to enter the court of the celestial King. But he passes beyond that stage through the highest initiatic station whereby the self becomes annihilated and rises in subsistence in the Self, whereby each bird is able to realize who he is and finally to know him-Self, for did not the Blessed Prophet state, "He who knows himself

> knows his Lord"? In gaining a vision of the Simurgh, the birds not only encounter the beauty of Her Presence, but also see themselves as they really are, mirrored in the Self which is the Self of every Self.[38]

Like Rūmī, ʿIrāqī and ʿAṭṭār are both said to have received initiations that flowed from the initiatic chains attributed to Aḥmad al-Ghazālī's disciples. ʿAṭṭār was a disciple of Majd ad-Dīn al-Baghdādī (d. 616/1219),[39] a disciple of Najm ad-Dīn Kubrā,[40] and ʿIrāqī was a close disciple of Bahāʾ ad-Dīn Zakariyyā (d. 659/1262), a disciple of Abū Ḥafṣ ʿUmar as-Suhrawardī.[41]

As Persian was the language of discourse for educated Muslims in India until the colonial period, the influence of the Persian masters of love in the subcontinent has been extensive. Among the many masters who are indebted to Aḥmad al-Ghazālī and his pupil ʿAyn al Quḍāt are Niẓām ad Dīn Awliyāʾ (d. 1325), Naṣīr ad-Dīn Chirāgh-i Dihlī (d. 757/1356), Burhān ad-Dīn Gharīb (d. 738/1337), Rukn ad-Dīn Kāshānī (d. after 738/1337), and Gīsū Darāz (d. 825/1422),[42] the last of whom is reported to have taught the *Sawāniḥ* and to have compared his own treatise, *Ḥāẓāʾir al-Quds*, to it.[43] When the Sufi poet, musician, and scholar Amir Khusraw (d. 1325) catalogued the nine literary styles of his day, the first that he listed was the style of the Sufis, for which he names two varieties. The first variety is that of "the people of gravity and stations," and the second variety is that of "the people of states," for which he gives the works of Aḥmad Ghazālī and ʿAyn al-Quḍāt Hamadānī as examples.[44] In addition, the Mughal prince Dara Shikuh (d. 1659) states that his treatise *Ḥaqq numā* should explain all of the wisdom from the great writings on the subject, among which he lists the *Sawāniḥ*, Ibn al-ʿArabī's *Fuṣūs al-ḥikam* and *Futuḥāt al-Makiyyah*, ʿIrāqī's *Lamaʿāt*, and Jāmī's *Lawāmiʿ* and *Lawāʾih*.[45] Such references demonstrate the high regard in which the *Sawāniḥ* was held in the Indian subcontinent. Nonetheless, despite the respect accorded to the *Sawāniḥ*, the *Tamhīdāt* of ʿAyn al-Quḍāt played a more prominent role in Indian Sufism.[46]

Studies on Aḥmad al-Ghazālī

Despite Aḥmad al-Ghazālī's extensive influence, little information was available in the scholarly literature until 1979. This oversight was amended by the appearance of three monographs in Persian: *Majmūʿāh-ye āthār-i fārsī-ye Aḥmad Ghazālī* (Compendium of the

Persian Works of Aḥmad Ghazālī) by Aḥmad Mujāhid, *Sulṭān-i ṭarīqāt* (The Master of Sufi Paths) by Nasrollah Pourjavady, both in 1979, and *Āyāt-i ḥusn va-ʿishq* (Signs of Beauty and Love) by Hishmatallāh Riyāḍī in 1989.[47] The studies by Mujāhid and Pourjavady made solid contributions to the study of Persian Sufism in general and of Aḥmad al-Ghazālī in particular. Mujāhid presented critical editions of all the extant Persian writings attributed to Aḥmad al-Ghazālī. His extensive introduction documents the majority of the available resources for the life and work of Aḥmad al-Ghazālī and thus proves to be an invaluable resource. But Mujāhid provides no analysis of either the literary works or of the historical information. For this one must look to Pourjavady, who provides a biography of Aḥmad al-Ghazālī and then examines his teachings. Pourjavady's insightful study does not, however, analyze the historical accuracy of the available biographical information, and his examination of Aḥmad al-Ghazālī's teachings includes *Baḥr al-ḥaqīqah* (The Ocean of Realities) and *Bawāriq al-ilmāʿ fi'r-radd ʿalā man yuḥarrimu's-samāʿ bi'l-ijmāʿ* (Glimmers of Allusion in Response to Those who Forbid Sufi Music),[48] works whose attribution to Aḥmad al-Ghazālī has since been disproven. As Pourjavady himself has observed, this significantly undermines the value of the analyses in *Sulṭān-i ṭarīqāt*.[49] Riyāḍī's study shows a great appreciation for Aḥmad al-Ghazālī, but seems to borrow from Mujāhid and Pourjavady more than build on them. The works of Mujāhid and Pourjavady provide a solid foundation for studies of Aḥmad al-Ghazālī, and this study is greatly indebted to them.

Aḥmad al-Ghazālī's introduction to Western audiences came in 1936 through James Robson's translation of *Bawāriq al-ilmāʿ*, a treatise that defends the use of music in Sufi gatherings and provides guidance for its implementation. As will be demonstrated in Chapter 1, the attribution of this text to Aḥmad al-Ghazālī is erroneous. Many scholars still believe him to be the author of this work and thus count him among the chief defenders of Sufi music (*samāʿ*). The inclusion of this text in his oeuvre has led to misunderstandings about Aḥmad al-Ghazālī that persist to this day.[50]

Aside from a minor article by Helmut Ritter in the *Encyclopaedia of Islam*,[51] it was not until almost forty years later that Aḥmad al-Ghazālī was reintroduced to Western audiences through the translation of his *Sawāniḥ* into German by Richard Gramlich.[52] The *Sawāniḥ* was translated into German a second time by Gisela Wendt two years later.[53] It was then introduced to the English-speaking public through a translation by Nasrollah Pourjavady published in 1986.[54] Aḥmad al-Ghazālī's most substantial Arabic treatise, *at-Tajrīd fī kalimat at-tawḥīd* (Abstract

Regarding the Expression of Testifying to Unity), was translated into German by Gramlich in 1983 and into French by Muhammad ad-Dahbi in 1995.[55] Only the translations of the *Sawāniḥ* by Gramlich and Pourjavady provide substantial introductory material, but neither is intended to be comprehensive. Pourjavady also provides a brief insightful commentary for the *Sawāniḥ* to accompany his translation.

The Goal of this Book

This study provides the first full examination of the life and work of Aḥmad al-Ghazālī in any European language. It builds on the foundations established by Mujāhid and Pourjavady, but adds to their invaluable contributions by fully ascertaining the authenticity of works attributed to Aḥmad al-Ghazālī and critically evaluating the biographical literature regarding him. The first chapter provides an extensive analysis of all extant primary-source material on Aḥmad al-Ghazālī. It examines the Arabic and Persian sources for his life and teachings, both the works attributed to him and the writings about him in the extensive Islamic biographical tradition. The authenticity of works attributed to him is examined. Then the biographical traditions are evaluated to see which authors provide new material, which authors borrow from previous authors, what are the dominant ideological trends in the biographical presentation of Aḥmad al-Ghazālī, and how these trends change over time, moving from biography to hagiography. Examined in this light, many of the accounts regarding Aḥmad al-Ghazālī appear to be hagiographical embellishments that developed over time. When one accounts for the sources, motivations, and historicity of these accounts, almost one hundred pages of extant biographical material boils down to less than two pages of raw historical data.

Chapter 2 draws on the biographical sources and other primary historical sources to reconstruct the life and times of Aḥmad al-Ghazālī in the early Saljuq period. The biographies of Aḥmad al-Ghazālī in and of themselves do not provide enough information to thoroughly reconstruct his life. But through an examination of the period in which he lived and references to his brother's life in the biographical literature, we can gain important insights into this period of Saljuq history and the nature of his position within it. This was a period of great intellectual fervor in all of the Islamic sciences. Abū Ḥāmid al-Ghazālī came to be a central figure in several substantial developments in jurisprudence (*fiqh*) and theology (*kalām*). His intellectual gifts brought him favor in the court, and he advanced to the highest academic position in the land as the head of the Niẓāmiyyah *madrasah* (college). Aḥmad al-Ghazālī also found favor at court. He too was actively engaged in many different aspects of the thriving intellectual culture of the era and also attained a high degree of proficiency in *fiqh* and *kalām*. But from an early age, his primary focus was Sufism.

The central focus of Aḥmad al-Ghazālī's life and teachings is the Sufi path, and he spent all of his adult life engaged in devotional and spiritual exercises. Nonetheless, this aspect of his teachings has not been discussed in any of the secondary literature devoted to him. Chapter 3 endeavors to reconstruct this practice. Aḥmad al-Ghazālī did not provide any explicit Sufi manuals in the manner of some of his spiritual descendants. Nonetheless, his Arabic treatise *at-Tajrīd fī kalimat at-tawḥid* provides an extended discussion that portrays the spiritual path as various stages and degrees of remembrance and discusses the process whereby one becomes ever more immersed in *dhikr*, remembrance or invocation. For al-Ghazālī, as for most Sufis before and after him, *dhikr* is the central axis of Sufi life and practice. He envisions three way stations for the spiritual traveler: the first is the world of annihilation (*fanā'*) wherein one's blameworthy attributes predominate and one should invoke "No god, but God." The second way station is the world of attraction (*jadhabiyyah*) wherein one's praiseworthy attributes predominate and one should invoke the name *Allāh*. In the third way station, the world of possession (*qabḍ*), praiseworthy attributes have vanquished blameworthy attributes and one invokes *Huwa, Huwa* (He, He), subsisting in God alone. This chapter also draws on al-Ghazālī's occasional advice scattered throughout his writings and sessions (*majālis*), as well as the works of his contemporaries and his spiritual descendants in order to flesh out the nature of his spiritual practice. The majority of his extant writings appear to come from the later period of his life when he was already an established Sufi shaykh, and the biographical tradition provides only vague allusions to his spiritual practice. It is therefore difficult to trace the development of these practices over time. But it is clear that some form of supererogatory spiritual practice played a central role in al-Ghazālī's life from an early age.

The final two chapters turn from the life and practice of Aḥmad al-Ghazālī to his central teachings, especially his understanding of love (*'ishq*). After briefly examining his controversial teachings regarding Satan, Chapter 4, "The Roots of al-Ghazālī's Teachings" provides an in-depth examination of the historical development of the Sufi understanding of love and the place of al-Ghazālī's *Sawāniḥ* within it. A broad examination of the various Sufi teachings regarding love before the *Sawāniḥ* demonstrates that although traces of Aḥmad al-Ghazālī's ideas regarding love can be found in the Sufi tradition preceding him, there is no text before the *Sawāniḥ* that expresses a full metaphysics of love in which all aspects of creation are presented as manifestations of Love and all phases of spiritual wayfaring are defined in relation to Love.

Chapter 5 delves into the ocean of Aḥmad al-Ghazālī's *Sawāniḥ*. In his writings and sermons, the Shaykh is always aware of the shortcomings inherent in language—because a signifier can never be the same as that which it signifies. This chapter thus begins by examining his attitude toward the medium he must use to convey his message. It first surveys his allusions to the relativity of language in the *Sawāniḥ* and in the recorded public sessions (*majālis*) that he held in Baghdad. Then it discusses his relation to the secular literary tradition, particularly the *ʿudhrī ghazal* (longing love) and the *khamriyyah* (wine) traditions, arguing that, like many Sufis before and after him, Aḥmad al-Ghazālī borrowed themes from these traditions but transferred them to a Sufi context. This is followed by a brief examination of Aḥmad al-Ghazālī's use of Quran, ḥadīth, and poetry as a means to incite his audience to seek love and recognition (*ʿirfān*). The last half of the chapter is devoted to a close reading of the teachings of love in the *Sawāniḥ*. It begins by considering the central terms for Aḥmad al-Ghazālī's discussion of love, *ʿishq, rūḥ* (spirit), *qalb* (heart), and *ḥusn* (beauty). Then it examines the stages of spiritual wayfaring whereby the heart is brought to complete maturity until it is immersed in the ocean of love, beyond duality, separation, and union.

Part I

Life and History

Chapter 1

Sources for the Aḥmad al-Ghazālī Tradition

In the primary biographical sources of the Islamic tradition, Aḥmad al-Ghazālī is usually listed as Aḥmad b. Muḥammad b. Muḥammad b. Aḥmad al-Ghazālī, Abu'l-Futūḥ aṭ-Ṭūsī. But at times he can be found under one of his honorifics (*alqāb*, sg. *laqab*), Abu'l-Futūḥ (The Father of Victories), which in some sources is mistakenly recorded as Abu'l-Fatḥ, or Majd ad-Dīn (The Glory of Religion). In the early biographical (*ṭabaqāt*) tradition, he is known as a preacher (*wāʿiẓ*), a Sufi, and a jurisprudent (*faqīh*). He is also recorded as a scholar of the exoteric sciences and the esoteric sciences (*ʿālim wa ʿārif*) and as a master of miracles and allusions (*ṣāḥib al-karāmāt wa'l-ishārāt*). Though many later Sufis saw Aḥmad al-Ghazālī as an accomplished spiritual master, in the earlier *ṭabaqāt* literature he is often viewed in light of his more celebrated brother, Abū Ḥāmid al-Ghazālī. All biographies mention that he is the brother of Imām Abū Ḥāmid, and in several works his biography is presented as an addendum to that of his brother. But from the eighth/fourteenth century onward, Aḥmad is given pride of place in the Sufi hagiographical tradition; his biographies are more extensive than Abū Ḥāmid's, and he is consistently portrayed as the spiritual superior of his older, more famous brother. The prevailing opinion conveyed in the biographical works comes to be that which was attributed to Jalāl ad-Dīn Rūmī (d. 672/1273) by his biographer Shams ad-Dīn Aḥmad al-Aflākī (d. 761/1360): "If he [Abū Ḥāmid] had one iota of love (*ʿishq*) like Aḥmad al-Ghazālī, it would have been better, and he would have made known the secrets of Muḥammadan intimacy the way Aḥmad did."[1]

Whereas in the earlier *ṭabaqāt* works Aḥmad al-Ghazālī is recognized as a scholar (*ʿālim*), a jurisprudent (*faqīh*), and a preacher (*wāʿiẓ*), in later sources he is referred to as Shaykh, and even as the

Shaykh of shaykhs (*shaykh al-mashāyikh* or *shaykh ash-shuyūkh*). The attribution of such honorifics is part of a larger trend in which a complex hagiography develops to compensate for a lack of historical details, not only for Aḥmad al-Ghazālī, but for many luminaries of the Sufi tradition. In order to properly detail the course of Aḥmad al-Ghazālī's life and the nature of his teachings, we must first examine the authenticity of his works, their interrelationship with other textual sources, and the development of the biographical and hagiographical traditions. This is essential for differentiating his teachings from those that have been attributed to him, and distinguishing those anecdotes that develop and perpetuate a legendary image from the stories which provide details of an historical person who forever changed the face of Persian Sufi literature.

Works by Aḥmad al-Ghazālī

In both Western academia and the modern Islamic world, even in his native Iran, Aḥmad al-Ghazālī is usually known only as the younger brother of Abū Ḥāmid. Some have a deeper appreciation of his accomplishments and are familiar with his place in the initiatic chains of several Sufi orders. But Aḥmad al-Ghazālī is best known for his sublime treatise on Love, *Sawāniḥ*, the most read of his works.[2] The *Sawāniḥ* was widely read throughout the Persian speaking world and has exerted an influence on Persian literature that has carried through to this day. As noted in the introduction, it has been the subject of several Persian commentaries and has been translated into both German and English. But all of the attention received by the *Sawāniḥ* may have obscured other writings that are also fundamentally important for obtaining a full picture of Aḥmad al-Ghazālī as an individual, as a Sufi shaykh, and as a literary and historical figure.

Aḥmad al-Ghazālī composed several other works in Persian, all of which have been critically edited, and three works in Arabic, two of which have been printed, but only one of which has been critically edited. In addition, several works have been incorrectly attributed to him. The content and style of his authentic works will be discussed in Chapters 3, 4, and 5; here the authentic will be separated from the spurious. Among the Persian works that are definitely of his hand are the aforementioned *Sawāniḥ* on mystical love (*ʿishq*), *Dastān-i murghān* (The Treatise of the Birds) on the symbolism of spiritual flight,[3] *Risālah-yi ʿAyniyyah* (Treatise for ʿAyn al-Quḍāt), written in response to a letter from his most celebrated disciple, ʿAyn al-Quḍāt

Hamadānī,[4] on many aspects of the spiritual life,[5] and several letters, most of which are believed to have been written for ʿAyn al-Quḍāt, though the authenticity of the letters is not fully established.[6] All of Aḥmad al-Ghazālī's Persian treatises are distinguished by concise, yet allusive prose, interspersed with frequent citations of *ḥadīth*, Quran, and both Arabic and Persian poetry.

Two other Persian works attributed to Aḥmad al-Ghazālī in Brockelmann's *Geschichte der arabischen Litteratur* (*GAL*) are *ʿIshqiyyah* and *Baḥr al-ḥaqīqah* (The Ocean of Reality).[7] The former appears to be another title for the *Sawāniḥ,* and the latter appears to be spurious. There is only one extant manuscript of *Baḥr al-ḥaqīqah,* from 877/1472, and it is attributed to Aḥmad al-Ghazālī.[8] The date of the manuscript and internal evidence, however, shows it to be highly unlikely that this is a work of his hand, though it may have been inspired by his teachings, thus explaining its attribution to him. The two leading scholars of Aḥmad al-Ghazālī, Aḥmad Mujāhid and Nasrollah Pourjavady, have considered it a part of the Ghazālian corpus, and both have edited it.[9] As Pourjavady observes, "Though the ideas expressed in this book can very well be considered to belong to Aḥmad al-Ghazālī, the style and composition of the book are somewhat different from those of the *Sawāniḥ,* the *Risālat aṭ-ṭayr,* and the letters."[10] It is this very difference of style and composition that make the authenticity of this work more dubious than probable. The treatise is divided into an introduction and seven chapters, each about one of the seven oceans of spiritual realization. It is this seven-ocean scheme that represents its closest relation to the Ghazālian corpus, for in his sessions he cites a story from the famous Sufi Abu'l-Ḥusayn an-Nūrī (d. 295/908), who was asked, "How does one arrive at recognition (*maʿrifah*)?" To which he responded, "It is seven oceans of light and fire."[11] Nonetheless, the fact that this is a well-ordered text distinguishes it from all of Aḥmad's writings; the style of his authenticated works resembles the immediate inspiration of a preacher more than the systematic exposition of a scholar. Though Aḥmad al-Ghazālī's writings have an internal order, it is not readily accessible and must be discerned by close reading. Furthermore, the content and method of citation in *Baḥr al-ḥaqīqah* is completely different from that of his authentic writings. From forty-seven pages in Mujāhid's edition of *Baḥr al-ḥaqīqah* only seventeen citations of Quran and *ḥadīth* can be gleaned, whereas in just over four pages of *Dastān-i murghān* there are twenty such citations. The difference is even more striking in the *ʿAyniyyah,* which is woven almost entirely of citations from Quran and *ḥadīth*. In addition, the poetry in *Baḥr al-ḥaqīqah* is limited to four verses of Persian poetry at the end of each chapter, and no Arabic poetry is cited. Such an orderly fashion of citing poetry is not found in any of Aḥmad al-Ghazālī's Persian or Arabic writings, and such a limited use of poetry is not part of any of his Persian writings. Arabic poetry is absent from only a few of his letters and the shortest of his treatises, *Dastān-i murghān*. These stylistic inconsistencies, coupled with the late date of the unicum, disaffirm the attribution of this text to Aḥmad al-Ghazālī.

Among the Arabic works, the most widely received has been *at-Tajrīd fī kalimat at-tawḥīd*, a treatise on the levels of spiritual development and the corresponding modes of remembrance (*dhikr*), which for Ahmad al-Ghazālī and most Sufis before and after him is the central axis of the spiritual life and practice.[12] In accordance with the teaching of the Quran, *The remembrance of God is far greater* (29:45), and its exhortations to remember God: *And remember the name of your Lord morning and evening* (76:25), Sufis of all ages have regarded remembrance as the central pivot of the spiritual life. In one of his sessions Aḥmad goes so far as to say, "There is no occupation but the remembrance of God,"[13] and in a letter he tells a disciple that it is a necessary part of being human: "Just as there is something in man which lives by bread and water, so, too, there is something which lives by the remembrance of God."[14] As will be seen in Chapter 3, *at-Tajrīd* is a text that examines the method whereby the spiritual aspirant can advance toward the perpetual remembrance (*dhikr*) that penetrates every aspect of one's being.

There are at least thirty extant manuscripts of *at-Tajrīd* and two printed editions.[15] This is a valuable treatise for understanding al-Ghazālī's spiritual practice, as it outlines what was most likely the method of remembrance he practiced and provides his views on sanctity (*wilāyah*), the qualifications for being a spiritual guide (*murshid*), and other issues central to the Sufi way. In addition to these works of Aḥmad's own hand there is one collection of public sessions entitled *Majālis Aḥmad al-Ghazālī* (The Sessions of Aḥmad al-Ghazālī). These were delivered in Baghdad and recorded by one Saʿīd b. Fāris al-Labbānī, regarding whom no biographical information remains. They were originally arranged in two volumes comprising eighty-three sessions of which only some twenty recorded sessions remain.[16] As with the Persian treatises, the style of *at-Tajrīd fī kalimat at-tawḥīd* and the sessions lean more toward the exuberant sermons of a preacher than the didactic lessons of a scholar.

In addition to the works mentioned above, several Arabic works have been incorrectly attributed to Aḥmad al-Ghazālī. Among these is a summary of his brother's *Iḥyāʾ ʿulūm ad-dīn* (The Revival of the

Religious Sciences), entitled *Lubāb min al-Iḥyā'* (The Kernels of the Revival), which is attributed to Aḥmad by several biographers, but in most manuscripts is attributed to Abū Ḥāmid al-Ghazālī.[17] Elements of a commentary on Chapter 12 of the Quran, "Joseph," entitled *Baḥr al-maḥabbah fī asrār al-mawaddah fī tafsīr sūrat Yūsuf* (The Ocean of Love Regarding the Secrets of Affection: A Commentary on Sūrat Yūsuf),[18] appear similar to Aḥmad al-Ghazālī's other works, especially his esoteric understanding of Satan, wherein he is seen as the foremost of those who testify to God's unity (*muwaḥḥid*) and as the greatest lover of God because he refused to bow to anything other than God. This position is attributed to al-Ghazālī by several biographers, and an account in his sessions is very similar to that in *Baḥr al-maḥabbah*. The fact that al-Ghazālī makes several references to the story of Joseph in his sessions would also appear to support the attribution of this commentary to him. But as with *Baḥr al-ḥaqīqah*, internal stylistic evidence makes this attribution dubious. This is most evident in the citation of poetry. *Baḥr al-maḥabbah* is replete with poetry from the Sufi tradition, but in his writings and sessions al-Ghazālī rarely cites Sufi poetry, and instead relies heavily on the famous figures of the Arabic literary tradition, such as Abū Nuwās (d. ca. 197/813) and al-Mutanabbī (d. 354/965). Furthermore, the manner of expressing Sufi ideas lacks the immediacy that characterizes his other writings. In all of his authenticated writings and in his recorded sessions, he is a preacher exhorting his audience to follow the path, but *Baḥr al-maḥabbah* reads more like a disjointed exposition of Sufi ideas. It is possible that *Baḥr al-maḥabbah* precedes his other writings, representing an inchoate intellectual and spiritual outlook and an undeveloped literary style. But its authenticity is further disaffirmed by the fact that of the fourteen known manuscripts the earliest is dated 929/1523, over four hundred years after Aḥmad al-Ghazālī's death.[19] Thus, until more evidence is available, it should not be counted among his works.

The most famous Arabic text to have been incorrectly attributed to Aḥmad al-Ghazālī is the aforementioned *Bawāriq al-ilmāʿ fī'r-radd ʿalā man yuḥarrimu as-samāʿ bi'l-ijmāʿ* (Glimmers of Allusion in Response to Those who Forbid Sufi Music), a treatise that defends the legitimacy and spiritual efficacy of employing song and dance in Sufi gatherings and provides instruction regarding its implementation. It is not attributed to al-Ghazālī by any biographers until the modern period, when it is mentioned by Khayr ad-Dīn az-Ziriklī.[20] As it was the first of the works attributed to Aḥmad al-Ghazālī to be edited and translated into a Western language, it is the one most often mistaken by scholars and students of Islam for one of his works, leading many to maintain that

Aḥmad al-Ghazālī was a "keen supporter of the practice of samāʿ."[21] The style and content of the *Bawāriq* are unlike those of any known works by Aḥmad al-Ghazālī. It is well argued and systematic and oriented more toward jurisprudence than Sufism. But a detailed analysis of the style and content is not necessary, for as Aḥmad Mujāhid has shown, the attribution to Aḥmad al-Ghazālī is clearly incorrect. Mujāhid has identified fifteen manuscripts of the *Bawāriq*, of which only three actually state that this is a text by al-Ghazālī, all three of which are from the twelfth century *hijrī* or later. Two of these manuscripts were employed by James Robson in his critical edition.[22] The third manuscript used by Robson is dated 714 *hijrī* and does not attribute the text to Majd ad-Dīn Aḥmad b. Muḥammad b. Muḥammad aṭ-Ṭūsī al-Ghazālī, but rather to Najm ad-Dīn Aḥmad b. Muḥammad b. Muḥammad aṭ-Ṭūsī,[23] who in most manuscripts is recognized by the honorific Shihāb ad-Dīn, rather than Najm ad-Dīn.[24]

It is surprising that Robson chose to follow the two later manuscripts in attributing the *Bawāriq* to al-Ghazālī, as the author of the *Bawāriq* clearly refers to the *Tadhkirat al-awliyā'* of Farīd ad-Dīn ʿAṭṭār (d. 627/1230): "And the people of all times agreed about the soundness of the sainthood of al-Junayd, ash-Shiblī, Maʿrūf al-Karkhī, ʿAbdallāh b. Khafīf, and others of those who are mentioned in *Tadhkirat al-awliyā'*."[25] Robson was aware of this difficulty but chose to maintain the attribution to al-Ghazālī. As he explains in a footnote:

> The only book of this name with which I am familiar is the Persian work by ʿAṭṭār (d. 627/1230). As Majd ad-Dīn died in 520 (1126), one can only conclude that, if this is the book referred to, the passage is not a part of Majd ad-Dīn's original work. The saints mentioned are all dealt with in ʿAṭṭār's work. If this passage is part of Majd ad-Dīn's work, one must assume that he is either referring to some unknown book, or using the phrase in a general sense with reference to the biographies of saints. But it is possible that the whole paragraph has been added by a later hand, as it is in the style of pp. 87–90, and so does not seem in place here.[26]

Despite Robson's efforts to explain the citation, the manuscript evidence and the inner stylistic evidence, combined with reference to *Tadhkirat al-awliyā'*, clearly disaffirm the attribution of this text to Aḥmad al-Ghazālī.

One account in the *Tamhīdāt* of Aḥmad al-Ghazālī's foremost disciple, ʿAyn al-Quḍāt Hamadānī, indicates that both attended Sufi sessions of *samāʿ*.[27] And an account in the *Lisān al-mīzān* of Ibn Ḥajar al-ʿAsqalānī (d. 853/1449) attributes miraculous powers to al-Ghazālī where he spun upon his head in a Sufi gathering "until he had no feet upon the ground."[28] Nonetheless, the systematic defense of *samāʿ* found in the *Bawāriq* can no longer be attributed to Aḥmad al-Ghazālī, but rather to the still unknown Shaykh Shihāb ad-Dīn Aḥmad aṭ-Ṭūsī, most likely of the late seventh Islamic century, regarding whom I can find no extant biographical information. This finding necessitates that we rethink the historical development of formalized sessions of *samāʿ*, since some features, such as the recitation of the Quran before and after sessions of *samāʿ*, had previously been thought to have been incorporated by the sixth/twelfth century but may in fact have been later developments.[29]

The most perplexing of the texts attributed to Aḥmad al-Ghazālī is *adh-Dhakhīrah fī ʿilm al-baṣīrah* (Treasure Regarding Knowledge from Insight).[30] The first to attribute this text to Aḥmad al-Ghazālī is Ibn al-Mustawfī al-Irbilī (d. 637/1239) in his *Taʾrīkh Irbil* (The History of Irbil).[31] It is later attributed to him by at least six other biographers of the classical period, as well as three cataloguers and biographers of the premodern and modern periods. Two extant manuscripts are recorded by Brockelmann, one in Berlin and the other at the Qarawiyyīn library in Fez, Morocco.[32] The latter is in fact another manuscript of *at-Tajrīd fī kalimat at-tawḥīd*, under the title of *Risālah fī lā ilāha illa'llāh*. The Berlin manuscript is under the title *adh-Dhakhīrah li ahl al-baṣīrah*. A stylometric analysis reveals that the text in this manuscript is most likely not authored by Aḥmad al-Ghazālī. Like the *Bawāriq* and *Baḥr al-ḥaqīqah*, it is far more systematic than any of Aḥmad al-Ghazālī's authenticated writings. It is divided into four chapters on knowledge of the soul, knowledge of God, knowledge of the world, and knowledge of the hereafter. The central thesis, that knowledge of oneself is the key to the knowledge of all else, is similar in some aspects to Aḥmad al-Ghazālī's thought, and many of the same general teachings of Sufism are conveyed, such as the need for *dhikr* (remembrance), but whereas al-Ghazālī couches his discussion in the technical vocabulary of early Sufism and employs the allusive and emotive style of a preacher, the author of the *adh-Dhakhīrah li ahl al-baṣīrah* is far more reliant on the technical vocabulary of Peripatetic Islamic philosophy and develops his arguments in a systematic and, at times, repetitive fashion. Furthermore, the term *ʿishq*, which is so central to Aḥmad al-Ghazālī's teachings, is used here as a negative term referring to the vice of passionate desire for what is lower. The text also relies heavily on the writings of Abū Ḥāmid al-Ghazālī, repeatedly stating that one should learn the Islamic sciences from him. In none of his extant texts does Aḥmad ever mention his older brother.

The most conclusive evidence that the Berlin manuscript is not the text of the *adh-Dhakhīrah fī ʿilm al-baṣīrah* is that the following passage from the text cited by Ibn al-Mustawfī al-Irbilī is not in the Berlin manuscript and is not at all similar in style to the manuscript:

> It is forbidden for a heart filled with love of the world to find the sweetness of remembrance, and it is forbidden for a heart filled with passions to have a connection with eternity (*al-qidam*). You are only commanded to leave what you are in. As for the magnificence of eternity, do not refrain from what contains the rank of servitude and the path of belovedness. You have no report from them and no news from them. You are in a valley and they are in a valley.[33]

This citation is very similar in both style and content to the writings and sessions of Aḥmad al-Ghazālī in that it provides an allusive directive to spiritual action, leaving the reader to deduce the full meaning behind the exhortation. While the same sentiment is expressed in parts of *adh-Dhakhīrah li ahl al-baṣīrah*, it is clearly not the same text as the one cited by al-Irbilī. Thus the Berlin manuscript entitled *adh-Dhahkīrah li ahl al-baṣīrah* provides no conclusive evidence regarding *adh-Dhakhīrah fī ʿilm al-baṣīrah*. Until more manuscripts become available, no conclusions regarding the authenticity of *adh-Dhakhīrah fī ʿilm al-baṣīrah* can be reached.

Other texts that have been catalogued in a manner that attributes them to Aḥmad al-Ghazālī are *Sirr al-asrār fī kashf al-anwār* (The Secret of Secrets Concerning the Unveiling of Lights),[34] *Laṭā'if al-fikr wa-jawāmiʿ ad-durar* (The Subtle Graces of Contemplation and the Gatherings of Pearls),[35] *Natā'ij al-khalwah wa lawā'iḥ al-jalwah* (The Effects of Spiritual Retreat and the Regulations of Spiritual Disclosure),[36] *Manhaj al-albāb* (The Way of Hearts),[37] and *Mukhtaṣar as-salwah fi'l-khalwah* (A Synopsis of the Delight in Spiritual Retreat).[38] I still know nothing of *Natā'ij al-khalwah*, but the other texts appear to be written by the same author, one Aḥmad b. Muḥammad b. Muḥammad aṭ-Ṭūsī, as is reported at the beginning of each.[39] He is also referred to in each as "the poor servant" (*al-ʿabd al-faqīr*). That Aḥmad b. Muḥammad b. Muḥammad aṭ-Ṭūsī is not another name for Aḥmad b. Muḥammad b. Muḥammad b. Aḥmad aṭ-Ṭūsī al-Ghazālī is evident for several reasons. First, Aḥmad al-Ghazālī is only referred to as aṭ-Ṭūsī without al-Ghazālī in one biographical work, and he is never referred to as only aṭ-Ṭūsī by Sufi writers or in his own writings. Were these to have been his authentic works, those in his spiritual lineage would most likely have sought to claim and disseminate them. Second, as with the *Bawāriq*, *Baḥr al-ḥaqīqah*, and *adh-Dhakhīrah*, stylometric analysis reveals a far more didactic and systematic style than that found in any of Aḥmad al-Ghazālī's extant writings. The content, though focused on Sufism, is also markedly different, and a different technical vocabulary is employed. Third, the most distinguishing feature of these works is a central emphasis on spiritual poverty (*faqr*), which could be said to be the defining characteristic of Aḥmad aṭ-Ṭūsī's writings, wherein he defines every existent thing in terms of poverty. As he writes in *Sirr al-asrār*:

> Know that the meaning (*maʿnā*)[40] of poverty is concealed in the substance of every existent thing, except the Highest Principle (*al-mabdaʾ al-aʿlā*), the One Who pours forth upon existences—glory be to Him alone—because He is perpetually self-disclosing in existent things through the general existence-bestowing mercy (*ar-raḥmah al-ʿāmmah al-ījādiyyah*), in order to give everything the strength and power for which it is fit. That thing thus needs a capacity for receiving that mercy. This is the capacity that necessitates turning towards Him perpetually in all states and utterances, so that one does not receive an outpouring from anything other than Him and does not attach any affair to anything other than Him. The Prophet alluded to this meaning in his saying, "Poverty is my pride and I take pride in it."[41] Meaning, on the Day of Resurrection my pride will be that I am in need of God and of nothing other than Him.
>
> In so far as man is the most noble and perfect of existent things, as according to His saying, *And we have honored the children of Adam* (17:70), his poverty has become more perfect and more complete than that of any other. In regards to man, poverty is divided into three: poverty of the essence, poverty of attributes, and poverty of actions. As for the poverty of essence, all men share in it; it is the confirmation of oneness, because everyone—believer and unbeliever—when he is obliged in his states and utterances, returns to God completely and remembers Him with his tongue and heart. That return is the poverty of the essence.
>
> As for the poverty of attributes, that is the poverty of the friends (of God); for when they travel the path of

> disengaging from the world, withdrawing from the hereafter, and reach the world of testifying to unity, all the attributes adjoined to them, such as desire, cupidity, love of dignity and leadership, and the vision of the soul, fall away from them. So they become like the clipped bird, unable to fly. They are thus in need of attributes from the direction of God, such that they are described by them in the experience of making the effects of the great friendship (*al-wilāyah al-kubrā*) manifest. These are the discerning sciences and the lordly wisdoms and other than that.
>
> As for the poverty of actions, it is the poverty of the prophets because they are in need of God for permission regarding deeds, proper conduct (*al-ādāb*), and other things. So whoever is described by one of these actions is poor (*faqīr*).[42]

This is a unique interpretation of poverty with no precedents in Sufi thought. It is central to all of aṭ-Ṭūsī's writings. In *Manhaj al-albāb* this tripartite division of poverty is expanded into five: poverty pertaining to essence, poverty pertaining to attributes, poverty pertaining to actions, poverty pertaining to prophets, and poverty pertaining to creation.[43] Though poverty is discussed by Aḥmad al-Ghazālī in many passages from his sessions and writings, there is no instance in which the same emphasis is found, wherein poverty is "concealed in the substance of every existent thing," nor is the three-fold or five-fold division of poverty found in the known writings of any other Sufis, let alone Aḥmad al-Ghazālī.[44]

It is also evident that aṭ-Ṭūsī had a different vision of *dhikr*, or remembrance. As will be seen in Chapter 3, in *at-Tajrīd fī kalimat at-tawḥīd* al-Ghazālī sees three degrees of *dhikr*—*lā ilāha illa'llāh, Allāh,* and *huwa huwa* (He is He)—which correspond to different degrees of the spiritual path. Aṭ-Ṭūsī, however, sees four degrees, to which correspond three formulas of remembrance. The formulas are similar to those of al-Ghazālī, but aṭ-Ṭūsī places them in a different ascending order: *lā ilāha illa'llāh, yā huwa,* and *Allāh*.[45] Other aspects of his writings that clearly distinguish them from those of al-Ghazālī are the use of terminology specific to later, more doctrinal, Sufism and a science of the soul that employs the Avicennan understanding of the soul that influenced so many medieval thinkers.[46]

As with Shihāb ad-Dīn Aḥmad b. Muḥammad aṭ-Ṭūsī, the exact identity of the Aḥmad aṭ-Ṭūsī who authored these works cannot be determined. The best indication is a chain of transmission found in the introduction to one manuscript of *Risālah fī faḍl al-faqr wa'l-fuqarā'*, wherein the text is said to have been received by Shaykh Aḥmad b. Muḥammad b. Muḥammad aṭ-Ṭūsī from ash-Shaykh al-Ḥājj Aḥmad b. al-Ḥasan b. al-Ḥusayn, from Shaykh ʿĪsā b. al-Ḥasan as-Silafī al-Kurdī, from Shaykh Ḥāfiẓ Ḥāfiẓ al-Ḥuffāẓ Abū Ṭāhir Aḥmad b. Muḥammad b. Muḥammad b. Aḥmad b. Ibrāhīm as-Silafī al-Iṣfahānī, who is reported to have said that, in the port of Alexandria, in the *madrasah* known as al-ʿĀdiliyyah, during the middle ten days of the month of Ramaḍān in the year 600, he heard this from al-Qāḍī as-Saʿīd ʿAbd ar-Raḥmān b. al-Imām Aḥmad b. Ḥanbal, who transmitted this from his father al-Imām Aḥmad b. Ḥanbal, whose chain of transmission comes directly from Jaʿfar aṣ-Ṣādiq, through the Shīʿite Imāms from the Prophet Muḥammad.[47] This chain of transmission appears, however, to be a fabrication. Al-Ḥāfiẓ as-Silafī died in the year 576/1180–81, and the text says that he heard this text in the year 600. Furthermore, al-Ḥāfiẓ as-Silafī was born in 472/1076 and thus lived almost two hundred years after the death of ʿAbd ar-Raḥmān b. Imām Aḥmad b. Ḥanbal (d. 290/903). In addition the latter's father, Imām Aḥmad b. Ḥanbal (d. 241/855), was not a contemporary of Imām Jaʿfar aṣ-Ṣādiq (d. 148/765). Nonetheless, we must take what indications we can from this *silsilah*. The presence of al-Ḥāfiẓ as-Silafī and the mention of the year 600 tell us that Aḥmad aṭ-Ṭūsī is most likely separated by three generations from Shaykh Aḥmad al-Ghazālī, and was thus active in the late seventh/thirteenth century.[48]

There are four other Arabic works attributed to Aḥmad al-Ghazālī, regarding which little information is available. Both Pourjavady and Mujāhid list *Faraḥ al-asmā'* (The Joy of the Names).[49] There is one manuscript of this text in Lucknow, which, however, no Ghazālī scholars have been able to obtain. In addition, Mujāhid lists *al-Ḥaqq wa'l-ḥaqīqah* (The Real and the Reality), *Fī ṣūrat ash-shajarah aṭ-ṭayyibah fi'l-arḍ al-insāniyyah* (Regarding the Good Tree in the Human Earth), *Risālah nūriyyah* (Epistle on Light), and *Kīmiyā' as-saʿādah* (The Alchemy of Happiness) as texts mistakenly attributed to Aḥmad al-Ghazālī. The last is obviously not by Aḥmad al-Ghazālī. It is a mistaken attribution in one manuscript of his brother's famous treatise. It is not, however, clear as to which manuscript Mujāhid refers.[50] Mujāhid also gives no indication for the sources that attribute *al-Ḥaqq wa'l-ḥaqīqah* or *Risālah nūriyyah* to al-Ghazālī. There is one manuscript of *Fī ṣūrat ash-shajarah aṭ-ṭayyibah* listed among the Persian manuscripts in Medina,[51] which is reported to be a short treatise based on *ar-Risālah al-laduniyyah* of Abū

Ḥāmid al-Ghazālī.[52] The attribution of these three texts appears dubious, but until further manuscript evidence is available a full evaluation cannot be made.

Primary Sources for al-Ghazālī's Vita

While supplemented by his writings and recorded sessions, the biography presented in Chapter 2 will be based on accounts related in Sufi texts and on the hagiographical *ṭabaqāt* literature of the Sufi tradition, the more general *ṭabaqāt* literature of the Islamic tradition, and local *ṭabaqāt* works from Baghdad, Irbil, and Qazwīn, which are among the cities in which Aḥmad al-Ghazālī preached. Here our task is to sift through the biographical material so as to better extract information about the historical person from the hyperbole of both his opponents and supporters. The primary sources for Aḥmad al-Ghazālī's biography provide more information about how he was interpreted and portrayed than they do about the historical details of his life. Nonetheless, the glimpses of his character and of the impression that his personality made on others are a valuable resource.

Accounts from Individual Sufis

Aḥmad al-Ghazālī is mentioned in many Sufi hagiographies, in the poetry of Farīd ad-Dīn ʿAṭṭār,[53] and in several Sufi texts from both Iran and the Indian subcontinent. Nonetheless, there are only four Sufi texts that provide valuable material. The first story transmitted by his most famous disciple, ʿAyn al-Quḍāt Hamadānī, is the most valuable historical account among all biographical materials because it was recorded during Aḥmad al-Ghazālī's life. In his *Zubdat al-ḥaqāʾiq* (The Cream of Realities), ʿAyn al-Quḍāt speaks of the influence that the books of Abū Ḥāmid al-Ghazālī and the presence of Aḥmad al-Ghazālī had on his intellectual and spiritual development. After his initial study of Abū Ḥāmid's *Iḥyāʾ ʿulūm ad-dīn* and other texts, a state of spiritual doubt remained, which was then relieved by Shaykh Aḥmad:

> I remained like that for almost a year, yet I did not arrive at the truth of what had happened to me in that year until destiny sent to my hometown of Hamadān my Master and Lord, the Shaykh, the most splendid Imām, master of the spiritual path and interpreter of reality, Abu'l-Futūḥ Aḥmad b. Muḥammad b. Muḥammad al-Ghazālī—may

> God grace the people of Islam with his continued presence and grant him the best reward. Through his service the veil of bewilderment was withdrawn from the face of that event in less than twenty days, such that I saw clearly what had happened. Then I was given insight into an affair wherein nothing of me nor of what I sought other than Him remained, except what God willed. It has now been several years that I have occupied myself with nothing but seeking to pass away in that affair.[54]

This is the only historical account in Hamadānī's writings, but Aḥmad al-Ghazālī is also mentioned four times in the *Tamhīdāt* and once in his letters. These passages offer little biographical information, but they do convey the high regard ʿAyn al-Quḍāt had for Aḥmad, counting him and Abū Ḥāmid as two of only ten people who were experts in both the exoteric and esoteric sciences.[55] Another passage of the *Tamhīdāt* recounts that ʿAyn al-Quḍāt's father saw Aḥmad dancing with them in a Sufi gathering,[56] and two passages attribute verses to Aḥmad that are not found in his extant writings.[57]

The next Sufi text to provide information regarding Aḥmad al-Ghazālī is the *ʿAwārif al-maʿārif* (Gifts of the Gnostic Sciences) of Shihāb ad-Dīn Abū Ḥafṣ ʿUmar as-Suhrawardī (d. 632/1234), whose uncle and spiritual master, Shaykh Ḍiyāʾ ad-Dīn Abu'n-Najīb as-Suhrawardī (d. 563/1186), had been a disciple of Aḥmad al-Ghazālī. This account is valuable not only for information about the relationship between two great Sufi shaykhs, but also for insight into Aḥmad al-Ghazālī's method of spiritual guidance:

> I heard our Shaykh (Abu'n-Najīb) [i.e., the author's uncle] say, "A man came to Shaykh Aḥmad al-Ghazālī while we were in Iṣfahān, seeking the *khirqah* (Sufi mantle) from him. The Shaykh said to him, "Go to so-and-so—indicating me—in order that he may tell you the meaning of the *khirqah*. Then come for me to bestow the *khirqah* upon you." So he came to me and I told him the rights of the *khirqah*, what the custody of its right requires, the proper conduct of one who wears it, and who is qualified to wear it. The man regarded the rights of the *khirqah* as great and shrank from wearing it. So I told the Shaykh what came about for the student from my speaking to him. He summoned me and reproached me for what I had said to him, saying, "I sent him to you in order to tell him what would increase

> his desire for the *khirqah,* then you told him what caused his determination to abate. All that you told him is true and it is what is necessitated by the rights of the *khirqah,* but if we were to require that of the beginner, he would flee and be incapable of upholding it. So we bestow the *khirqah* upon him in order that he becomes like unto the people [i.e., the Sufis] and dons their attire; for that brings him close to their gatherings and meetings. Through the grace of his consorting with them and looking upon the states of the people and their journey, he wants to travel their path and through that he arrives at something of their states."[58]

Another of al-Ghazālī's spiritual descendants in the same lineage, Najm ad-Dīn Rāzī (d. 654/1256), provides a very brief account of a young Aḥmad al-Ghazālī sitting and eating with his own Shaykh, Abū Yūsuf Hamadānī, and some companions. After al-Ghazālī went into a trance, he came to his senses and then related a vision: "I have just seen the Prophet, peace be upon him. He came and put a morsel of food in my mouth." This is not, however, taken as an indication of Aḥmad al-Ghazālī's spiritual attainment, since Shaykh Hamadānī is reported to have replied, "These are imaginings by which the infants of the path are nurtured."[59] The few other citations of Aḥmad al-Ghazālī in Rāzī's *Mirṣād al-ʿibād min al-mabdaʾ ila'l-maʿād* do, however, indicate that Rāzī held him in high esteem, since when citing verses from the *Sawāniḥ* he refers to him as "Shaykh" and bestows upon him honorifics, such as, "May God's mercy be upon him" and "May God sanctify his spirit" that are reserved for revered Sufi masters.[60]

The fourth Sufi text to provide information on Aḥmad al-Ghazālī is the *Tabṣirat al-mubtadiʾ wa-tadhkirat al-muntahī,* attributed to Ṣadr ad-Dīn al-Qūnawī (d. 673/1274). Here the story is less historical; rather, al-Ghazālī is used as a mouthpiece to clarify the Sufi ideal of detachment. He is asked by a disciple, "Every day you scorn the world, praise poverty, and enjoin people to cut ties [with the world], yet you have many horses and donkeys. How can you proclaim this?" In response he replies, "I have placed a long stake in the ground. I have not placed it in the heart. 'Verily God—transcendent is He—does not look at your forms, nor at your deeds, but He looks at your hearts.'"[61] With this account it appears that anecdotes of Aḥmad al-Ghazālī in Sufi texts cease to be empirical historical accounts and become a matter of historical fiction, wherein he is used as a symbol for advancing particular lessons or ideals pertaining to the Sufi way.

Though this and other anecdotes may be based on the transmission of actual events, it is more likely that they represent tropes developed out of impressions derived from his writings and sessions.

Aḥmad al-Ghazālī is referred to as "The Sultan of all Notables" in the *Maqālāt* of Shams ad-Dīn Tabrīzī (d. 638/1241),[62] the fourth and last Sufi text to provide original information regarding Aḥmad's life. With over seven pages of stories about Aḥmad al-Ghazālī, the *Maqālāt* provides more details than any other source and would appear to be an essential resource. It is the only account to mention a third brother, ʿUmar al-Ghazālī, whom Shams ad-Dīn claims was a successful merchant whose generosity matched the knowledge of Abū Ḥāmid al-Ghazālī.[63] He also claims that Abū Ḥāmid al-Ghazālī was the true author of *adh-Dhakhīrah fī ʿilm al-baṣīrah* and *Lubāb al-Iḥyāʾ* and that Aḥmad saw no use in these books.[64] He further claims that Aḥmad was "untrained in these outward sciences,"[65] did not write, and did not engage in the practice of seclusion (*khalwah*),[66] an assertion that appears to be contradicted by the biographical tradition and by Aḥmad al-Ghazālī's own writings.

Shams ad-Dīn provides the first biographical account to discuss the controversial practice of *shāhid-bāzī*, or "witness play," also known as "gazing upon beardless young men."[67] The best-known account is one that is also told of another famous Sufi Shaykh, Rūzbihān Baqlī (d. 606/1209) in the *ʿUshshāq Namah*, a text incorrectly attributed to Fakhr ad-Dīn ʿIrāqī.[68] In both accounts it is reported that the Atabeg was informed of Aḥmad al-Ghazālī (or Rūzbihān Baqlī) lying with his leg next to a young boy in the bathhouse. When the Atabeg came to look through the window, "The Shaykh shouted out. 'You little Turk, look carefully!' Then he turned his gaze toward him, lifted up his other foot, and placed it in the middle of the burning brazier. The Atabeg was astonished and asked forgiveness. He went back astonished."[69] A similar account states that people objected to the Atabeg: "He spends a whole week in the bath-house, night and day, one leg next to a servant and the other next to the son of the headman. He's set up a brazier and is making kabob. He takes a kiss from this one, and a kiss from that one! What is left?" When the Atabeg went to investigate, he witnessed the same miracle described in the previous account.[70] This is a very stylized account. As Nasrollah Pourjavady observes, "His foot, lowered into the hot coals, does not burn, demonstrating that he is not captive to the flames of lust but has already conquered this internal fire."[71]

In another instance, it is reported that the Shaykh refused to preach until the same young boy was brought before him to sit in the front row.[72] Lest someone think that these were instances of lust or lasciviousness, Shams ad-Dīn states, "He didn't incline to these beautiful forms out of appetite. He saw something that no one else saw. If they had taken him apart piece by piece, they would not have found an iota of appetite." Rather it appears that *shāhid-bāzī* was a practice that served two functions. First and foremost, the Shaykh would witness the self-disclosures of Divine beauty in their most perfect configuration in the human being. Second, it would serve to combat the blaming nature of the lower soul, such that those who were not able to abide such acts would be turned away from the path for which they were not qualified. The place of *shāhid-bāzī* in Shaykh Aḥmad's spiritual practice will be examined in greater depth in Chapter 3.

The main element of Shams ad-Din's accounts that resonates with other hagiographies is the claim that Aḥmad was far superior to Abū Ḥāmid in spiritual attainment. Like many of the hagiographers examined below, Shams ad-Dīn Tabrīzī used the relationship between the Ghazālī brothers as an example of the superiority of spiritual knowledge—knowledge by presence—to all other forms of knowledge, a theme that runs throughout the *Maqālāt*. This is most evident in the following passage:

> After all, look at that great man [Abū Ḥāmid Ghazālī] in relation to Aḥmad Ghazālī. His crime was simply that he sent books to him,[73] for the sake of repelling the denunciation of the people: "Sometimes you should quote from this book, so it will stop the tongues of the criticizers." He [Aḥmad] didn't let his brother into his *khānqāh*. One report is that Aḥmad commanded him to travel for seven years, another that it was fifteen years. He was saying, "Is this a pigsty so that, as soon as a state overmasters you, you come in here?"
>
> "I mean, I have no wish from these companions. First, I don't gain any knowledge from you. On the contrary, you will grasp my words well when you make yourself totally present through need and when you empty yourself of your own knowledge. Even then, you may not grasp my words."[74]

Here, as in Shams ad-Dīn Tabrīzī's words regarding Aḥmad al-Ghazālī, there is nothing historical. Judging from the context, he is likely transmitting from an oral tradition regarding Aḥmad al-Ghazālī that was particular to the region of Tabrīz. In one account, Shams ad-Dīn Tabrīzī is said to have received an initiation from one Rukn ad-Dīn Sujāsī Maḥmūd at-Tabrīzī (d. 595/1199), who was initiated by Quṭb ad-Dīn al-Abharī (d. 577/1181), who received initiation from Abu'n-Najīb as-Suhrawardī.[75] It may be that Shams ad-Dīn's understanding of Aḥmad al-Ghazālī reflects an oral tradition that came through this Sufi lineage. In any event, it seems that, as with the story in *Tabṣirat al-mubtadi'*, such accounts reflect embellishments that accrued over several generations.

Biographical Literature

While to some it may seem evident that the hagiographical literature of the Sufi tradition would provide a more partisan view than the general and local biographical literature, which espouses a different historiographical aim, in fact, almost all medieval and even modern biographical works of the Islamic tradition must be interpreted in light of shifting institutional interpretations and appropriations. Not only must the hagiographies of such works as ʿAbd ar-Raḥmān Jāmī's (d. 833/1477) *Nafaḥāt al-uns* (Breaths of Intimacy) and Ibn al-Mulaqqin al-Miṣrī's (d. 804/1402) *Ṭabaqāt al-awliyā'* (Biographies of the Saints) be treated with caution,[76] so, too, all the biographies should be examined with an eye toward the purposes for which they were written and the predilections of their authors. This is especially true with Abu'l-Faraj ʿAbd ar-Raḥmān Ibn al-Jawzī's (d. 597/1201) *al-Muntaẓam fi't-ta'rīkh al-mulūk wa'l-umam* (The Classification of Kings and Nations) and *Kitāb al-quṣṣāṣ wa'l-mudhakkirīn* (The Book of Storytellers and Preachers),[77] which, because of their early dates, written within seventy years of Aḥmad al-Ghazālī's death, and the tremendous importance of their author, have influenced many subsequent biographers.

Although the Arabic and Persian biographical literature provides over twenty biographies of Aḥmad al-Ghazālī, totaling more than seventy pages, less than a third of these pages contain original material. Since many of these entries derive some of their information from previous biographical sources, and some derive all of their information from previous sources, they fall naturally into three categories: original sources that provide all or mostly original material in relation to the extant biographical tradition; middle sources that contain some new information or original interpretations but also repeat information from earlier biographies; and derivative sources based entirely on previous biographies.

Seven biographers, most writing within a century of Aḥmad al-Ghazālī's death, provide significant information that is either particular to their biographical entries or enters the extant biographical tradition through them. They are Ibn al-Jawzī, ʿAbd al-Karīm al-Qazwīnī (d. 623/1226), Ibn an-Najjār al-Baghdādī (d. 634/1238), Abu'l-Barakāt Ibn al-Mustawfī (d. 636/1239), Ibn aṣ-Ṣalāḥ ash-Shahrazūrī (d. 643/1246), Zakariyyā b. Muḥammad al-Qazwīnī (d. 682/1283–84), and Ibn Ḥajar al-ʿAsqalānī (d. 853/1449). To these must be added Ibn Abi'l-Ḥadīd (d. 656/1258), whose *Sharḥ Nahj al-balāghah* (Commentary on the Path of Eloquence) marks the first extant citation of certain episodes from al-Ghazālī's sessions, and Abū Saʿd ʿAbd al-Karīm as-Samʿānī (d. 561/1166),[78] whose *Dhayl ta'rīkh Baghdād* (Addendum to the History of Baghdad) is probably the single most important influence in the biographical tradition for Aḥmad al-Ghazālī. As-Samʿānī is cited directly by all of the above biographers save Ibn al-Jawzī and Zakariyyā b. Muḥammad al-Qazwīnī, but his influence on Ibn al-Jawzī is evidenced by the fact that several accounts that appear in Ibn al-Jawzī's *Muntaẓam* and *Kitāb al-quṣṣāṣ* are transmitted on the authority of as-Samʿānī in later biographies. But since no printed edition of *Dhayl ta'rīkh Baghdād* is available, we cannot determine its exact contents.

In what follows, I will first examine the major structural features of the original biographies listed above. I will then examine eleven middle-source biographies that are partially dependent upon previous biographies but which offer some new information or have had extensive influence on subsequent works. Then I will briefly review the derivative works that offer no new information but are nonetheless important for a full understanding of the reception and interpretation of Aḥmad al-Ghazālī through the ages.

ORIGINAL SOURCES

As the first to include Aḥmad al-Ghazālī in an extant *ṭabaqāt* work, the famous Ḥanbalī *faqīh,* historian, and preacher Ibn al-Jawzī provides much valuable biographical information. But due to Ibn al-Jawzī's harsh condemnations of Sufis and preachers, two categories in which Aḥmad al-Ghazālī can be included, these contributions must be seen as particular evaluations rather than objective historical presentations. This is especially important because verbatim repetitions and traces of Ibn al-Jawzī can be found in almost half of the later biographies, both attributed and unattributed.

Ibn al-Jawzī's reports draw on Aḥmad al-Ghazālī's public sessions, oral reports transmitted from Qāḍī Abū Yaʿlā b. al-Farrā' (d. 560/1165), and transmissions from Muḥammad b. Ṭāhir al-Maqdisī (d. 507/1113 or 14), a Sufi and a Hadith specialist whom Ibn al-Jawzī criticizes in his *Muntaẓam* for transmitting amazing and laughable stories in his *Ṣafwat at-taṣawwuf* (The Quintessence of Sufism), and for not practicing the proper methods in weighing *ḥadīth* (*jarḥ*).[79] The stories of Aḥmad al-Ghazālī may have been in *Ṣafwat at-taṣawwuf,* as Ibn al-Jawzī clearly had access to this work, but in *al-Muntaẓam* they are related through the transmission of one Muḥammad b. Nāṣir al-Ḥāfiẓ (d. 550/1155). Although the stories that Ibn al-Jawzī selects from al-Ghazālī's public sessions have not been preserved in the one extant manuscript of his sessions, comparison with what has been preserved in both this manuscript and other *ṭabaqāt* works reveals that Ibn al-Jawzī selected the more scandalous passages. He appears to have taken them out of their greater context to present a picture of al-Ghazālī's preaching that supports the claim of Ibn Ṭāhir al-Maqdisī, transmitted by Ibn al-Jawzī, that "Aḥmad al-Ghazālī was a sign among the signs of God in lying, gaining access to worldly goods through preaching."[80] Ibn al-Jawzī's accounts must thus be read both as an historical biography and as an effort to protect institutional orthodoxy against perceived innovations. As ʿAbd ar-Raʾūf al-Munāwī (d. 1030/1621) writes of Aḥmad al-Ghazālī in *al-Kawākib ad-durriyyah* (The Brilliant Stars), "Ibn Ṭāhir and Ibn al-Jawzī have accused him of things following the custom of the *muḥaddithūn* and the jurists."[81] The main complaints found in the *Muntaẓam* regard Aḥmad al-Ghazālī's controversial teachings regarding Satan that will be examined at the beginning of Chapter 4 and reports that he was given to the controversial spiritual practice of *shāhid-bāzī*, sitting with young men and gazing upon them as a means of witnessing the manifestation of God's beauty.[82]

The second earliest source is the more balanced: ʿAbd al-Karīm al-Qazwīnī's *at-Tadwīn fī akhbār Qazwīn* (The Registry Regarding Reports from Qazwīn).[83] Al-Qazwīnī reports through Abū Saʿd as-Samʿānī that Aḥmad al-Ghazālī took to the practice of Sufism at an early age. Al-Qazwīnī has not had any influence on the biographical tradition in Arabic, as is evidenced by the fact that his account of Abū Ḥāmid's praise for Aḥmad, "Glory be to God! We search and Aḥmad finds,"[84] does not resurface until ʿAbd ar-Raḥmān Jāmī's *Nafaḥāt al-uns,*[85] and the date al-Qazwīnī gives for Aḥmad's death, Rabīʿ al-Ākhir 517 (May 1123), though more precise than any of the Arabic accounts, is also not repeated until *Nafaḥāt al-uns* and Khwāndamīr's (d. 942/1535–36) *Taʾrīkh ḥabīb as-siyar.*[86] Furthermore, the one verse of Arabic poetry cited is not repeated in any other accounts. Nonetheless, this account is important for two reasons. On the one hand, it marks the point at which Arabic and Persian sources diverge; all other Arabic accounts mark 520 as the date of death, whereas most Persian sources follow al-Qazwīnī. On the other hand, it marks the beginning of a trend in which Aḥmad is recognized as the spiritual superior of his older brother. This trend is not exhibited in many other Arabic works, but it resurfaces in the *Nafaḥāt al-uns* and becomes an important aspect of the Persian hagiographical tradition.

Dhayl ta'rīkh Baghdād was composed by the historian and foremost Shāfiʿī *ḥadīth* authority of his day, Muḥibb Allāh Abū ʿAbdallāh Muḥammad b. Maḥmūd al-Baghdādī, known as Ibn an-Najjār.[87] It provides new and valuable information regarding Aḥmad al-Ghazālī's time in Baghdad and extols his virtues as an eloquent preacher. Much of this account appears to rely on the history of Baghdad by Abū Saʿd as-Samʿānī. Some of Ibn an-Najjār's influence is thus an extension of as-Samʿānī's influence. Ibn an-Najjār has had almost as much influence as his erstwhile teacher Ibn al-Jawzī on the biographical tradition. He is the first to record several verses of poetry that come to be the most cited in the Ghazālian *ṭabaqāt* tradition. Similar versions of one poem are repeated in five subsequent biographies:

> I am an ardent lover,
> And my sorrow is great.
>
> My night extends with no dawn;
> My eye wakes while they sleep.
>
> My eye sleeps not, due to lightning;
> And we drank it while they abstained.
>
> I have burning thirst, am one ailing,
> An adversary, and am infatuated.
>
> So my heart belongs to my rebuker,
> The handmaid of passionate love.[88]

The following account is repeated in seven subsequent biographies, thus constituting the most oft-repeated account of the Ghazālian *ṭabaqāt* tradition:

> One day the reciter read in front of him [al-Ghazālī], "*O My servants who have been prodigal to the detriment of their own souls! Despair not of God's Mercy. [Truly God forgives all sins. Truly He is the Forgiving, the Merciful]*" [Quran: 39:53].[89]

Then he said, "He honored them with the *yā'* of the *iḍāfah* by saying *'O My servants'"* [*yā 'ibādī*]. And then he recited:

Blame became easy for me [to bear] near to her love,
And the chain of my enemies, "Verily he is profligate."

I am deaf when called by my name, but verily
when I am told, "O slave of her," I listen.[90]

Though the first two pages of Abu'l-Barakāt al-Mubārak b. Aḥmad Ibn al-Mustawfī's *Ta'rīkh Irbil* (The History of Irbil) are a verbatim repetition of the biographical entry from Ibn al-Jawzī's *Muntaẓam,* with minor textual variations, the next three pages provide valuable details available in no other account. Like Ibn an-Najjār, accounts of Aḥmad al-Ghazālī's stay in Baghdad are reported on the authority of as-Sam'ānī. But the accounts reported through Shaykh Abu'l-Ma'ālī Ṣā'id b. 'Alī (d. 625/1128) provide far more detail. Abu'l-Ma'ālī also transmits verses from al-Ghazālī through Qāḍī Abū Ya'lā b. al-Farrā' (d. 560/1165) that are not recorded by any other biographers.[91] Al-Mustawfī is the first to attribute the works *Lubāb al-Iḥyā'* and *adh-Dhakhīrah fī 'ilm al-baṣīrah* to Aḥmad al-Ghazālī. We thus know that unless these were added by a later hand, within a hundred years of his death al-Ghazālī was considered to have authored these two treatises. These are the only two works mentioned in the Arabic *ṭabaqāt* literature until the modern period. Not until Jāmī is there any account of his Persian writings, and only the *Sawāniḥ* and the *'Ayniyye* are mentioned, and not until az-Ziriklī and al-Kaḥḥālah in the twentieth century is there any mention of other Arabic works such as *at-Tajrīd fī kalimat at-tawḥīd* and the erroneously attributed *Bawāriq al-ilmā' fī radd 'alā man yuḥarrimu as-samā'*.[92] But although *Ta'rīkh Irbil* is the first extant source to mention *Lubāb al-Iḥyā'* and *adh-Dhakhīrah fī 'ilm al-baṣīrah,* it is not likely that this reflects Ibn al-Mustawfī's influence, since none of the other material that is original to this account is repeated by later biographers.

The first of the Shāfi'ī *ṭabaqāt* works to include a biography of al-Ghazālī, *Ṭabaqāt al-fuqahā' ash-shāfi'iyyah* (Biographies of the Shāfi'ī Jurists),[93] by the famous Shāfi'ī *ḥadīth* scholar Taqī ad-Dīn Abū 'Amr 'Uthmān b. 'Abd ar-Raḥmān ash-Shahrazūrī, known as Ibn aṣ-Ṣalāḥ, begins with a negative evaluation of Aḥmad al-Ghazālī's sessions. Ibn aṣ-Ṣalāḥ writes: "They comprise the ramblings and speculations of preachers, and the insolences of backward Sufis, as well as their obfuscations."[94] This is followed by several pages of episodes and quotations from al-Ghazālī's sessions which, along with those related by Ibn al-Jawzī and Abū Yaʿlā, expose other dimensions of the *Majālis* not preserved in the extant manuscript. Other than the hagiographical accounts in works such as Jāmī's *Nafaḥāt al-uns* and Maʿṣūm ʿAlī Shāh Shīrāzī's *Ṭarāʾiq al-ḥaqāʾiq* (The Paths of Realities), this is the only biography to list Abū Bakr an-Nassāj (d. 487/1094) as al-Ghazālī's shaykh. In two accounts, al-Ghazālī is said to relate stories from an-Nassāj's shaykh, Abu'l-Qāsim al-Kurrakānī (d. 469/1076), though Ibn aṣ-Ṣalāḥ expresses doubt as to their authenticity. Again the influence of as-Samʿānī is present, as it is on his authority that Ibn aṣ-Ṣalāḥ attributes to al-Ghazālī the saying, "He who is destroyed in God, his vicegerency is for God" (*man kāna fi'llāhi talafuhu kāna ʿala'llāhi khalafuhu*),[95] which is also cited by al-Ghazālī in *at-Tajrīd fī kalimat at-tawḥīd*.[96] This is the first occurrence of this saying in the extant biographical material. Several slight variations are transmitted in the biographies written by al-Kutubī (d. 764/1362),[97] aṣ-Ṣafadī (d. 765/1363),[98] as-Subkī (d. 771/1368),[99] al-Miṣrī (d. 804/1402),[100] and al-Munāwī (d. 1030/1621).[101] But as with Ibn al-Mustawfī, it is more likely that later biographers took this information from as-Samʿānī than Ibn aṣ-Ṣalāḥ, since none of Ibn aṣ-Ṣalāḥ's other material on Aḥmad al-Ghazālī is repeated in later sources.

The one work that seems to have drawn from a completely independent source for all of its information is Zakariyyā b. Muḥammad al-Qazwīnī's *Āthār al-bilād wa-akhbār al-ʿibād*, completed in the year 674/1276. Qazwīnī shows great deference to Aḥmad al-Ghazālī, referring to him as the King of the substitutes (*malik al-abdāl*), denoting a high rank within the invisible hierarchy of the spiritual elite whom many Sufis believe govern the world.[102] Like ʿAbd al-Karīm al-Qazwīnī before him, Zakariyyā al-Qazwīnī relates a story of Abū Ḥāmid's recognition of Aḥmad's attainments: "What has come to us through the path of devotion to study is what has come to Aḥmad through the path of spiritual exercises."[103] He also tells us that the two were praying together and upon completion Aḥmad said to Abū Ḥāmid, "Repeat your prayer because during your prayer you were considering the price of a donkey."[104] Such stories mark the beginning of a trend that, as will be seen, begins to flourish in the ninth/fourteenth century.

Qazwīnī also relates a story that would appear to confirm Aḥmad al-Ghazālī's practice of *shāhid-bāzī*, which occupies much of Shams ad-Din Tabrīzī's account, and is mentioned by Ibn al-Jawzī. He writes that Sultan Malik Shāh was a spiritual disciple (*murīd*) of Aḥmad al-Ghazālī and that one day when Sanjar b. Malik Shāh visited the Shaykh he kissed Sanjar on the cheek. Upon hearing of this, Malik Shāh told Sanjar, "You have come to possess half of the earth. Had he kissed your other cheek, you would have come to possess the whole of the earth."[105] In addition to allusions to controversial practices, this account portrays Aḥmad al-Ghazālī in the role of Sufi guarantor of worldly power, a function often attributed to Shaykh Abū Saʿīd b. Abi'l-Khayr and other famous figures, but rarely associated with Aḥmad al-Ghazālī. This work is thus significant for exposing a mode of interpretation that is not revealed by the other original sources, and rarely found in other primary sources.

Though not a *ṭabaqāt* work, the most famous composition of the *uṣūlī* jurist Ibn Abi'l-Ḥadīd, his commentary on the famous collection of sayings, speeches, and letters of Imām ʿAlī b. Abī Ṭālib (d. 40/661) compiled by ash-Sharīf ar-Raḍī, *Sharḥ Nahj al-balāghah*,[106] is included among the original sources because it marks the first extant occurrence of several accounts from Aḥmad's sessions that are later perpetuated by other biographers. All of the original accounts concentrate on al-Ghazālī's "extolling Iblīs for refusing to prostrate to Adam,"[107] an inclination for which Ibn Abi'l-Ḥadīd repudiates al-Ghazālī, "In his preaching he followed an abominable path, extolling Iblīs and declaring that he is the master of those who testify to unity (*al-muwaḥḥidūn*)."[108] The first two accounts are also cited by Ibn Ḥajar al-ʿAsqalānī, and the third, which closely resembles an account in the extant sessions,[109] is taken up by al-Kutubī, aṣ-Ṣafadī, and al-Munāwī:

> On another occasion he said, "Moses and Iblīs met on the road of Sinai, so Moses said, 'O Iblīs, why did you not prostrate to Adam—peace be upon him?' He said, 'Never! It is not for me to prostrate to a man. How could I testify to His unity then turn to one other than Him? But you, O Moses, you asked for the vision of Him, then you looked to the mountain. So I am more sincere than you in testifying to unity.'"[110]

The remainder of the entry is drawn from Ibn al-Jawzī's *Muntaẓam*, with the exception of the last line and one poem attributed to Bāyazīd al-Bisṭāmī (d. 262/875), which is said to be an example of the many sayings Ibn Abi'l-Ḥadīd claims Aḥmad al-Ghazālī transmitted from him:

> Who is Adam meanwhile,
> And who is Iblīs if not for You?
>
> You try all, yet despite the trial
> All love You.[111]

It is important to note that Ibn Abi'l-Ḥadīd takes al-Ghazālī to task for his teachings on Satan, yet does not cite other Sufis known for this view, such as Manṣūr al-Ḥallāj (d. 309/922) or al-Ghazālī's disciple, ʿAyn al-Quḍāt Hamadānī. This reveals one of the ways in which al-Ghazālī was perceived and received by later Islamic thinkers.[112]

Though *Lisān al-mīzān*, written by the jurisprudent historian and *ḥadīth* specialist Shihāb ad-Dīn Ibn Ḥajar al-ʿAsqalānī, is sometimes noted for providing little original material, this is not the case with Aḥmad al-Ghazālī.[113] There are in fact many original stories that are not repeated in any extant biographies. Much of this biography is based on stories transmitted from as-Samʿānī. But it is the only biography to transmit an account from one Abū Faḍl Masʿūd b. Muḥammad aṭ-Ṭirāzī. Both of the accounts from as-Samʿānī and aṭ-Ṭirāzī record the opinions of the Sufi shaykh and *ḥadīth* specialist Yūsuf b. Ayyūb al-Hamadānī (d. 535/1140) that al-Ghazālī was of a low spiritual rank and inspired more by Satan than by God: "His words are like blazing fire, but his support is Satanic not Lordly."[114] Al-ʿAsqalānī also cites Ibn Abi'l-Ḥadīd's *Sharḥ Nahj al-balāghah* as a source for al-Ghazālī's *taʿaṣṣub li-Iblīs* (Zeal for Iblīs), in an account that resembles that of Ibn al-Jawzī's *Kitāb al-quṣṣāṣ wa'l-mudhakkirīn*,[115] but is not reported by Ibn Abi'l-Ḥadīd. Another story is attributed to Ibn al-Jawzī's *Muntaẓam*, but it is not found in any of the printed editions.

MIDDLE SOURCES

Among the works that draw on earlier sources but also provide new information, the *Wafayāt al-aʿyān wa-anbāʾ abnāʾ az-zamān* (The Passing of Notables and Tidings of the Sons of Time) of the Shāfiʿī judge Shams ad-Dīn Aḥmad b. Muḥammad Ibn Khallikān (d. 681/1282) is the earliest.[116] Though no important new information is transmitted, this biography is significant for its influence on later biographies. The first paragraph is repeated verbatim, or almost verbatim, by aṣ-Ṣafadī, al-Kutubī, al-Khwānsārī, and Shīrāzī, while parts of it are repeated by Ibn Kathīr, al-Isnawī, and Ibn al-Mulaqqin al-Miṣrī:

> He was an eloquent preacher, beautiful to behold, the master of miracles and allusions, and he was among the jurisprudents, although he inclined to preaching, such that it overcame him. He taught at the Niẓāmiyyah university [*madrasah*], replacing his brother, Abū Ḥāmid, when he left teaching, abstaining from it. He summarized his brother's *Iḥyāʾ ʿulūm ad-dīn* in a single volume and called it *Lubāb*

> *al-Iḥyā'*, and he has written another book that he called *adh-Dhakhīrah fī 'ilm al-baṣīrah*. He traveled the country, dedicated himself to Sufism, and inclined to isolation.[117]

Ibn Qāḍī Shuhbah also appears to have based the introduction to his entry on Aḥmad al-Ghazālī on this paragraph, and he in turn is cited by Ibn al-'Imād.[118] Thus, after as-Sam'ānī, Ibn al-Jawzī, and Ibn an-Najjār, Ibn Khallikān's account of Aḥmad al-Ghazālī has had the most direct influence on later *ṭabaqāt* works.

The biographical entries from the *'Uyūn at-tawārīkh* (The Sources of History) of the Syrian historian Muḥammad Abū 'Abdallāh b. Shākir al-Kutubī (d. 764/1362) and *Kitāb al-wāfī bi'l-wafayāt* (The Full Account of Those Who Have Passed) of the Shāfi'ī biographer Ṣalāḥ ad-Dīn Khalīl b. Aybak aṣ-Ṣafadī (d. 765/1363) are almost identical.[119] They differ only slightly in the last paragraph, where aṣ-Ṣafadī ends with a story from Ibn al-Jawzī's *Muntaẓam* and the opinions of Ibn al-Jawzī, Ibn Ṭāhir, and a Sufi shaykh identified as ash-Shaykh Shams ad-Dīn regarding al-Ghazālī's heterodoxy, whereas al-Kutubī skips the story and provides the same opinions in a more summary fashion. The fact that aṣ-Ṣafadī's account is more detailed in this last paragraph implies that his account precedes al-Kutubī's. But as the two lived at the same time and died within a year of each other, the exact relation is difficult to determine. Both accounts begin with a verbatim repetition of Ibn Khallikān's introduction and cite all the poetry first transmitted by Ibn Najjār, with slight variations in two of the three poems. Another verse of poetry is transmitted that is first cited by Ibn Abi'l-Ḥadīd:

> Laylā and I were ascending in passion,
> When we became complete, I stood firm and she slipped.[120]

A slight variation of this poem, in which the "I" is replaced with "we," is the only poetry from Aḥmad al-Ghazālī transmitted by Ibn al-Jawzī.[121] Like Ibn aṣ-Ṣalāḥ ash-Shahrazūrī, aṣ-Ṣafadī and al-Kutubī transmit excerpts from al-Ghazālī's sessions that are not found in the extant sessions and are not present in earlier *ṭabaqāt* works:

> When the story of Adam was mentioned, and that he granted his son David long life, then refused it, he said, "The angel of death came to him and he resisted it, and it was as if the tongue of the situation addressed the spirit, 'You are the one who lamented yourself when you were

> commanded to enter this body and you said, "It is a dark, impure house." So what difficulty is there for you in leaving it?' And it was as if it responded with the tongue of the state:
>
> We descended to it reluctantly but when
> Habituated, we left it reluctantly.
>
> It is not the abode we love; but the bitterest of life
> is still separation from whom we love."[122]

Compared to the extant sessions, such accounts show a concern for some of the same themes and the citation of similar *aḥādīth* and Quranic verses, though the words attributed to al-Ghazālī are not as perspicacious. The emergence of such accounts in the biographical tradition thus indicates that the sessions may have been more widely available than is indicated by the one extant manuscript.

The historical work *Mir'āt al-janān* (Mirrors of the Soul) by the famous Yemeni Sufi scholar ʿAfīf ad-Dīn ʿAbdallāh b. Asad al-Yāfiʿī (d. 768/1367) includes a short entry on Aḥmad al-Ghazālī.[123] All of the historical information is repeated from the first paragraph of either al-Kutubī or aṣ-Ṣafadī. Nonetheless, it is regarded as a middle source because it is the first extant biographical source to follow the aforementioned Sufi texts in referring to Aḥmad al-Ghazālī as Shaykh, and as the Shaykh of shaykhs (*Shaykh ash-shuyūkh*), a trend that comes to predominate in later works.

The *Ṭabaqāt ash-shāfiʿiyyah* (Biographies of the Shāfiʿīs) of Tāj ad-Dīn Abū Naṣr ʿAbd al-Wahhāb b. ʿAlī as-Subkī also refers to Aḥmad as Shaykh, but provides mostly unoriginal material.[124] As-Subkī cites as-Samʿānī, Ibn an-Najjār, Ibn aṣ-Ṣalāḥ, and Ibn Khallikān and transmits one account from the sessions that is also found in aṣ-Ṣafadī and al-Kutubī:

> In one of the gatherings for his sessions he was asked about the saying of ʿAlī—may God be pleased with him and bless his face—"If the veil were removed I would not increase in certainty," and the saying of Abraham, the intimate of God—peace be upon him—"'Show me how You bring the dead to life.' He said, 'Do you not believe?' He said, *'Of course, but so that my heart may be tranquil'*" (2:26). So he (al-Ghazālī) said, "Denial overcomes certainty, and denial does not overcome tranquility. God said, *'And they denied*

them, though their souls acknowledged them wrongfully and out of pride"' (27:14).[125]

Nonetheless, as-Subkī provides one original account from the noted *Ḥadīth* specialist al-Ḥāfiẓ as-Silafī al-Iṣfahānī (d. 576/1180–81), who reports that he attended a gathering in the *ribāṭ* of Hamadān where "there was intimate friendship and affection between us; and he was the most intelligent of God's creation, the most capable of them in speech, an outstanding scholar in jurisprudence and other matters."[126] As-Subkī's most important contribution is to provide the name of one of the compilers of al-Ghazālī's sessions in Baghdad, Ṣāʿid b. Fāris al-Labbānī, and he is the only author to tell us that there were eighty-three sessions contained in two volumes.[127] Ibn aṣ-Ṣalāḥ marks the number of volumes at four, but gives no indication of the number of sessions.[128] As the one extant manuscript only contains a little over twenty sessions, as-Subkī's account is important for establishing the potential veracity of the excerpts provided by other biographers. As-Subkī is also the first biographer to cite these two lines of poetry from al-Ghazālī, the last of which is also found in the extant sessions:

When you attend kings, then wear
The clothes of most powerful protection;

And when you enter, enter blind,
And when you leave, leave mute.[129]

Though the *Ṭabaqāt al-awliyāʾ* (Generations of the Saints) of Ibn al-Mulaqqin Sirāj ad-Dīn Abū Ḥafṣ ʿUmar b. ʿAlī al-Miṣrī (d. 804/1401) contains sentences from Ibn Khallikān and as-Samʿānī, most of the material provided is not available in any other biographies.[130] A commentary on the *ḥadīth qudsī*, "He is a liar who claims love for me then sleeps when the night comes,"[131] followed by the verse of the Quran, *Verily God is a guardian over you* (4:1), is also transmitted.[132] These citations are also found together in the extant sessions, and although the general meaning of al-Ghazālī's commentary is the same, the words are not.[133]

The first Persian biographical entry for Aḥmad al-Ghazālī is found in the hagiographical *ṭabaqāt* work *Nafaḥāt al-uns min ḥaḍarāt al-quds* by the famous Sufi author Nūr ad-Dīn ʿAbd ar-Raḥmān Jāmī (d. 883/1477). Little new information is provided here, but it is the first biography to list the *Sawāniḥ* among al-Ghazālī's works and to cite some of its passages. In his entry for ʿAyn al-Quḍāt, Jāmī extols al-Ghazālī's *ʿAyniyye*: "In eloquence, elegance, fluidity, and facility, one can say that it has no peer."[134] Jāmī's biography marks the first point at which the information from al-Qazwīnī's *Taʾrīkh Qazwīn* re-enters the biographical tradition. But whereas Qazwīnī relates one story that implies the spiritual superiority of Aḥmad over Abū Ḥāmid, Jāmī uses the two brothers to imply the superiority of the Sufi way over that of jurisprudence, the superiority of the inward sciences (*ʿilm-i bāṭinī*) over the outward sciences (*ʿilm-i ẓāhirī*). In response to an inquiry of his brother's whereabouts, Jāmī has Aḥmad reply, "He is in blood"; when his words are conveyed to Abū Ḥāmid, he responds, "He spoke the truth; I was pondering one of the many issues pertaining to menstruation."[135] Here the mode of interpretation that is most apparent in Shams ad-Dīn Tabrīzī's *Maqālāt* enters the biographical/hagiographical tradition.

This is an interpretive trend that continues throughout the Persian hagiographical tradition. The history of Persian Sufism, *Rawḍāt al-jinān wa-jannāt al-janān* (The Meadows of Paradise and the Gardens of the Soul) of Ḥāfiẓ Ḥusayn Karbalāʾī Tabrīzī (d. 11th/16th century) and the *Jawāhir al-asrār* (The Pearls of Secrets),[136] a commentary on Jalāl ad-Dīn Rūmī's *Mathnawī* by Ḥusayn b. Ḥasan Sabzawārī (d. 1212/1797–98) discussed below, continue this trend by repeating the stories of Aḥmad taken from Jāmī and providing previously unrecorded accounts. Though their late occurrence calls the veracity of these and other such stories into question, it is important to take full account of them because they demonstrate how the historical relationship between Aḥmad and Abū Ḥāmid came to be seen as a reflection of the predominance of Sufi knowledge, or presential knowledge (*al-ʿilm al-ladunī*), over all other forms of knowledge, be they transmitted (*naqlī*) or rational (*ʿaqlī*), a position that Aḥmad maintained throughout his life and which Abū Ḥāmid clearly advocates, especially in some of his later writings.[137]

Nafaḥat al-uns also reintroduces the practice of *shāhid-bāzī* that predominates in Shams ad-Dīn Tabrīzī's accounts of Shaykh Aḥmad. Although the practice is not referred to in his entry on Aḥmad al-Ghazālī, elsewhere Jāmī states, "A group among the leading figures, such as Shaykh Aḥmad Ghazālī and Awḥad ad-Dīn ʿIrāqī[138] occupied themselves with contemplating the beauty of sensory loci in forms. In those forms they witnessed the Absolute Beauty of the Real—may He be exalted—though they were not attached to sensory form."[139] Thus, like Shams ad-Din Tabrīzī and in contrast to Ibn al-Jawzī, Jāmī saw this practice in a positive light.

Tabrīzī's *Rawḍāt al-jinān* is the only biography to refer to Aḥmad al-Ghazālī as "the one whom the saints give the appellation of the 'Second Junayd.'"[140] Though he does not transmit any new material, Tabrīzī is considered a middle source because he is the first to bring certain writings from other Sufis, as well as certain of Aḥmad al-Ghazālī's writings into the *ṭabaqāt* tradition. Among the former he cites the passage from ʿAyn al-Quḍāt Hamadānī's *Zubdat al-ḥaqāʾiq,* translated above, and the passage from the *Tabṣirat al-mubtadiʾ wa'tadhkirat al-muntahī.*[141] Tabrīzī is the only biographer to note the correspondence that transpired between al-Ghazālī and ʿAyn al-Quḍāt. He cites a long passage from the most extensive of these correspondences, the *Risāla-yi ʿAyniyye,* written by Shaykh Aḥmad in response to questions posed by ʿAyn al-Quḍāt.[142] The remainder of the entry is comprised of direct citations from Jāmī's *Nafaḥāt al-uns* and Yāfiʿī's *Mirʾāt al-janān.*

Al-Kawākib ad-durriyyah of ʿAbd ar-Raʾūf al-Munāwī (d. 1030/1621) is an important source because it is the first to directly defend Aḥmad al-Ghazālī against his accusers, most notably Ibn al-Jawzī.[143] Most likely in response to the accusations begun by Ibn al-Jawzī, Ibn Ṭāhir al-Maqdisī, and Yūsuf b. Ayyūb al-Hamadānī, al-Munāwī maintains that al-Ghazālī "spoke without affectation."[144] As noted above, he writes, "Ibn Ṭāhir and Ibn al-Jawzī have accused him of things following the custom of the *muḥaddithūn* and the jurists."[145] He thus provides the most decisive demonstration of how later interpretations of Aḥmad al-Ghazālī not only turn toward the positive but also oppose some previous interpretations. Most of al-Munāwī's biographical information was copied from either al-Kutubī or aṣ-Ṣafadī. The only original information is one quote: "The jurists are the enemies of those who are privy to spiritual realities (*maʿānī*)."[146]

Though presented as a commentary on Rūmī's *Mathnawī,* the beginning of *Jawāhir al-asrār* of Ḥusayn b. Ḥasan Sabzawārī functions as a hagiographical *ṭabaqāt* work. Sabzawārī transmits more passages from the *Sawāniḥ* than any biographer and, as noted above, he continues the trend of Jāmī in relating stories that demonstrate the spiritual superiority of Aḥmad to Abū Ḥāmid. Indeed, this is the richest source for stories of the spiritual relationship between the two brothers. In several stories Aḥmad reprimands Abū Ḥāmid for a lack of spiritual depth and focus. But the *Jawāhir* goes beyond the *Nafaḥāt* to present Aḥmad as the primary catalyst in his brother's conversion to Sufism. The penultimate account is of a dispute between the siblings regarding which of them had a greater claim to knowledge of the truth:

One day his brother, the famous Imām Abū Ḥāmid al-Ghazālī, said to him, "What a jurisprudent you would be if you strived more than this in [the study of] the religious law." So Shaykh Aḥmad said to him, "What a knower you would be if you were to go to greater lengths than this in [the study of] reality (*al-ḥaqīqah*)." Abū Ḥāmid said, "I can claim that I have precedence in the field of reality (*miḍmār al-ḥaqīqah*)." The Shaykh replied, "The goods of conceptualization (*at-taṣawwur*) and accounting (*al-ḥisāb*) do not have much currency in the market of secrets." He replied, "Let there be a judge between us!" The Shaykh said, "And the judge of this path is the Messenger of God." The Imām said, "And how can he be so for us unless we see his place and hear his declaration (*bayān*)?" Aḥmad replied, "When someone finds a share of his reality, who does not see him as he wants and does not hear from his secrets and his realities?" From the effect of this rebuke, the fire of jealousy was set ablaze within Imām Abū Ḥāmid. The two of them appointed the Messenger of God as judge between them and separated until night came and each undertook his own manner of worship.

The Imām was overcome with begging, crying, and pleading such that his eyes became warm. Then he saw the Messenger of God come to him with one of his companions and he brought him good tidings and the eminence of recognition (*ma ʿrifah*) in this matter. In the hands of that companion there was a plate of fresh dates, then he offered him a portion of it and gave him those dates. When the Imām awoke, he saw those dates in his palm, so he set out with joy and delight to his brother's room and began knocking on the door vigorously. Then Aḥmad said from behind the door, "The like of this does not require wonder," indicating the dates. The Imām's perplexity increased from amazement at these words. When he entered his brother's room he said, "And how did you know what came to me from this honoring?" The Shaykh replied, "The Messenger of God did not give to you until he had appeared to me seven times. If you do not believe me, then go to the shelf of the room and look at what you see." When the Imām went, he saw that plate which had been in the hands of the companion and it had decreased by a portion which was the measure of these dates [in his hand]. Thus he knew that

> what had come to him from that plate was also from the blessings of the breaths of the Shaykh. So he undertook the path of [spiritual] traveling, comportment, and the unveiling of the secrets of realities, such that he became a follower of the companions of the path without a word, except that he admitted the excellence of the Shaykh and saw himself next to him as a child next to his older teacher.[147]

This trend is also found in the *Itḥāf as-sādah,* the most famous commentary on Abū Ḥāmid al-Ghazālī's *Iḥyā' ʿulūm ad-dīn* by Muḥammad al-Murtaḍā (d. 1205/1790):

> The reason for his [Abū Ḥāmid's] traveling and asceticism is that one day he was preaching to the people and his brother entered and recited:
>
> You helped them when they stayed back,
> Yet have yourself been kept behind while they went ahead.
>
> You have taken the role of guide,
> Yet you will not be guided; you preach but do not listen.
>
> O whetstone, how long will you whet iron,
> Yet not let yourself be whetted?[148]

The last work of this middle category is the *Rawḍāt al-jannāt fī aḥwāl al-ʿulamā' wa's-sādāt* (The Paradise of Gardens Regarding the States and Joys of Those Who Know) of the great Shīʿī *mujtahid* Sayyid Mirzah Muḥammad Bāqir al-Khwānsārī (d. 1313/1895).[149] The beginning of this biography is taken directly from Ibn Khallikān's *Wafayāt al-aʿyān,* and this is followed by an Arabic translation of the story cited above from Sabzawārī's *Jawāhir al-asrār*.[150] It is considered a middle source because it transmits this account to Arab speakers and ends with two Persian poems, the first of which is not found in any of al-Ghazālī's extant writings, nor cited in any other sources, and the second of which is only cited in Khwāndamīr's *Ḥabīb as-siyar*:

> What we have written cannot be taken away.
> What we have picked up cannot be put down.
>
> What we believed has been but an illusion.
> What a shame that we wasted life in vain.[151]

With poverty, if I desire the kingdom of Sanjar,
May my face be black like the parasol of Sanjar.

I will not buy a hundred kingdoms of Khurāsān for a
barley [seed],
Since my soul found the news of tasting in the middle of
the night.[152]

DERIVATIVE SOURCES

Among the accounts that are based entirely on extant previous works, and thus offer no new information or interpretation, are the contributions from Sibṭ Ibn al-Jawzī (d. 654/1257), Naṣrullāh b. Muḥammad Ibn al-Athīr (d. 636/1239), Shams ad-Dīn Muḥammad b. Aḥmad adh-Dhahabī (d. 748/1347), ʿAbd ar-Raḥmān al-Isnawī (d. 772/1370), Ismāʿīl b. ʿUmar Ibn Kathīr (d. 775/1373), ʿAbd al-Ḥayy Ibn al-ʿImād (d. 1089/1678), and Muḥammad Maʿṣūm Shīrāzī (d. 1344/1926). To these could be added the *Muʿjam al-muʾallifīn* of ʿUmar Riḍā Kaḥḥālah,[153] *al-Aʿlām* of Khayr ad-Dīn az-Ziriklī, and the *Kashf aẓ-ẓunūn* of Ḥajjī Khalīfah Kātip Çelebī (d. 1067/1657), though these three works offer few historical details as they are more bibliographical records than biographical accounts. There is also brief mention of Aḥmad al-Ghazālī as one of the luminaries of Ṭūs in ʿAbdallāh Yāqūt ar-Rūmī's description of Ṭūs in *Muʿjam al-buldān*.[154]

The information regarding Aḥmad al-Ghazālī in Sibṭ Ibn al-Jawzī's *Mirʾāt az-zamān* and Ibn al-Athīr's *al-Kāmil fi't-taʾrīkh* is based entirely on Ibn al-Jawzī's *Muntaẓam*,[155] as are adh-Dhahabī's accounts in *Taʾrīkh al-Islām, al-ʿIbar fī khabar man ghabar*, and *Mīzān al-iʿtidāl*.[156] But in his entry for Tarkān Khātūn, a wife of the Saljūq Sultan Malik Shāh, Sibṭ Ibn al-Jawzī tells us that Aḥmad al-Ghazālī was one of two people to preach at her funeral in Baghdad in 515/1121.[157]

Al-Isnawī's *Ṭabaqāt ash-shāfiʿiyyah* paraphrases information from Ibn Khallikān's *Wafayāt al-aʿyān* and transmits one saying previously reported in ash-Shahrazūrī's *Ṭabaqāt al-fuqahāʾ ash-shāfiʿiyyah*.[158] The first two-thirds of Ibn Kathīr's *al-Bidāyah wa'n-nihāyah fi't-taʾrīkh* are taken directly from Ibn al-Jawzī and the last third is from Ibn Khallikān.[159] Ibn al-ʿImād's *Shadharāt adh-dhahab* repeats sections of adh-Dhahabī's *ʿIbar* and Ibn an-Najjār's *Dhayl taʾrīkh Baghdād* verbatim.[160] And Muḥammad Maʿṣūm Shīrāzī's *Ṭarāʾiq al-ḥaqāʾiq*,[161] though more extensive than any other biography, offers no new information as it is based on citations from the *Sawāniḥ* and verbatim repetition and translation from ten biographical sources: Ibn Khallikān, Ibn an-Najjār, ʿAbd ar-Raḥmān Jāmī, Qazwīnī, Ibn al-Athīr, Sabzawārī, al-Khwānsārī, and Khwāndamīr, all of whom are mentioned above, as well as *Taʾrīkh-i Guzideh* and *Riyāḍ al-ʿārifīn*. Although such works provide no new material, they are important for tracing the influence of other works and for examining al-Ghazālī's position in relation to other Sufis and scholars whose biographies are recorded in particular works. These factors help us to evaluate how the understanding of Aḥmad al-Ghazālī evolved from one generation of scholars to the next.

Summary

Viewed in historical succession, it is apparent that interpretations of Aḥmad al-Ghazālī's persona differed from the very beginning. The most important source for understanding his beliefs is obviously his own writings and sessions. Therefore, the greatest service provided by the biographers is to preserve many fragments from his public sessions. But through their interpretation, commentary, and selective presentation the biographers can sometimes obfuscate more than clarify. These interpretations represent a history of attitude and opinion more than detailed historiography. They must therefore be viewed in relation to one another in order to obtain a broader understanding of the context in which they are transmitted.

The only first-hand accounts, those of ʿAyn al-Quḍāt, present Aḥmad al-Ghazālī as an accomplished spiritual master and praise him as both a scholar (*ʿālim*) and a "recognizer," or gnostic (*ʿārif*), of the highest rank. His merit as a Sufi master is affirmed by the most reliable second-hand account, namely that transmitted from Shaykh Abu'n-Najīb as-Suhrawardī by his nephew, Abū Ḥafṣ ʿUmar as-Suhrawardī. His abilities as a *faqīh* and a preacher are then extolled by the renowned *ḥadīth* scholar al-Ḥāfiẓ as-Silafī, as recorded in *aṭ-Ṭabaqāt ash-shāfiʿiyyah*. At the same time, the negative opinion of Ibn Ṭāhir al-Maqdisī and the scathing attack of Shaykh Yūsuf b. Ayyūb al-Hamadānī, presenting al-Ghazālī as a seducing charlatan, are transmitted by Ibn al-Jawzī and Ibn Ḥajar al-ʿAsqalānī, respectively. These conflicting opinions may reflect a divide along Shāfiʿī and Ḥanbalī lines, as ʿAyn al-Quḍāt, as-Suhrawardī, as well as Ibn Ḥajar, al-Ḥāfiẓ as-Silafī, and the transmitter of his account, as-Subkī, hailed from the Shāfiʿī school, whereas al-Maqdisī, Yūsuf b. Ayyūb al-Hamadānī, and the transmitters of their accounts hailed from the Ḥanbalī school. Though there may be merit to this perspective, the division is not so clear, for the famous Shāfiʿī *Ḥadīth* specialist Ibn aṣ-Ṣalāḥ also took exception to the content of Aḥmad al-Ghazālī's sessions. What is clear is that Aḥmad al-Ghazālī was a controversial figure whose words gave rise to both the deepest of spiritual aspirations and the most vitriolic of condemnations.

The differences among biographers most likely represent both individual interpretations and institutional and sectarian divisions. Al-Ghazālī was first presented by al-Qazwīnī and Ibn an-Najjār in a positive light; his orthodoxy was not questioned, and his dedication to the Sufi way and eloquence as a public preacher were extolled:

> He was among the best of people in words he preached and among the most eloquent in expression, displaying a beautiful disposition in all that he conveyed. He was gifted in his citations [of Quran, *Ḥadīth*, and poetry], the most gracious of the people of his age and the gentlest of them in nature.[162]

At the same time, Ibn al-Jawzī condemned him in the harshest of terms and conveyed the opinion that Aḥmad al-Ghazālī was a heterodox charlatan, scoffing at al-Ghazālī's claim to have seen the Prophet in a waking vision and writing in response to his discussions of Satan:

> I have indeed been astonished at the like of such absurdities and abominable lies. How is it that such things can take place in the City of Peace [Baghdad] and be passed over in silence? If these things had been mentioned in a small village, [its people] would have disowned such strange fanatic devotion to the Devil and rejected the claim that he professes *tawḥīd* on the basis of the words of God [to Satan]: *Surely My curse shall be upon thee till the Day of Judgment* (38:78), as well as the claim that he is frequent in the performance of divine worship. It has been known all along that he [Satan] occupies himself with nothing except opposing the good and urging people to disbelieve and commit acts of rebellion [against God].[163]

Due to the extensive influence of Ibn al-Jawzī on subsequent authors, many biographers over the next three hundred years reflected some aspect of this attitude, though not with such vitriol. During this time, there are two fundamental strands: one is a negative evaluation, as exhibited by Ibn al-Jawzī and Ibn aṣ-Ṣalāḥ; the other is a more even-handed approach which deals mostly with historical details, such as is found in adh-Dhahabī and as-Subkī.

In the early period, there are few favorable accounts to balance the scales. That of al-Qazwīnī stands alone in attributing to Aḥmad al-Ghazālī a spiritual station superior to that of Abū Ḥāmid. But in the late ninth/fourteenth century, starting with Jāmī, the praise for Aḥmad al-Ghazālī exhibited in the hagiographical perspective begins to grow, and soon comes to predominate. Most later sources refer to him as "Shaykh," whereas as-Subkī and al-Yāfiʿī are the only biographers of the early middle period to do so. In the eleventh/seventeenth century, Ibn al-Jawzī's interpretation of Aḥmad al-Ghazālī is directly challenged by ʿAbd ar-Raʾūf al-Munāwī. All subsequent biographers until the twentieth century then take the more hagiographical approach. The initial thrust of this hagiographical approach comes through Persian sources and is carried forward by both Persian and Arabic authors. It is possible that with these Persian sources we witness the translation of an oral Sufi tradition into written works, as also occurred in the accounts of Aḥmad al-Ghazālī provided by Shams ad-Dīn Tabrīzī. This would explain how several stories presenting Aḥmad's spiritual superiority to Abū Ḥāmid enter into the *ṭabaqāt* tradition for the first time in Jāmī's *Nafaḥāt al-uns* and especially Ḥusayn b. Ḥasan Sabzawārī's *Jawāhir al-asrār*. But we have no means by which to measure the full content of the oral tradition or its veracity. This change in perspective is not an isolated event; it is part of a major historical trend wherein Sufism came to play an increasingly central role in shaping the understanding of the Islamic sciences.[164] As a result, there was a need to perpetuate the legendary images of many Sufi figures to compensate for the lack of historical detail.

The true Aḥmad al-Ghazālī is thus not to be found in either the hagiographical appropriations of Jāmī, al-Munāwī, Sabzawārī, and others, nor in the institutional condemnations of Ibn al-Jawzī and Ibn aṣ-Ṣalāḥ, nor at a convenient middle point. Rather, these biographies should be taken as multiple refractions and reflections of Aḥmad al-Ghazālī's personality through the personalities of his biographers and the agendas behind their works. While we can sketch the bare bones of Aḥmad al-Ghazālī's life, the events that flesh out the skeleton to provide the picture of a living person are conveyed to us by individuals who have continued to fashion the form in which such stories are transmitted. Some anecdotes may retain the trace of an authentic memory, but it is more likely that they are fictions, extrapolated from impressions derived from his writings and sessions. What comes through this centuries-long process thus represents a collage of visceral reactions, institutional interpretations, and personal opinions which, when viewed in light of one another, may capture the person of Aḥmad al-Ghazālī better than mere historiography.

Chapter 2

The Life and Times of Aḥmad al-Ghazālī

Abū Ḥāmid and Aḥmad al-Ghazālī were natives of Ṭūs, a small region in Khurāsān just fifteen kilometers northwest of present-day Mashhad. The region of Ṭūs was known to have three major cities, Ṭābarān, Nūqān, and Rādkān, the first often being identified as the city or town of Ṭūs. It is most likely that the Ghazālī brothers grew up in a township of Ṭūs/Ṭābarān named Ghazāl, hence the name al-Ghazālī. The Ṭūs of the 6th/11th century in which they lived was destroyed in 618/1221 during the Mongol invasion. It was rejuvenated in 637/1239, only to be decimated once again in 791/1389 by the armies of Tīmūr Lang. Though rebuilt again in 809/1406–07, Ṭūs was never to regain its former size, as it was eventually eclipsed by the greater splendor of nearby Mashhad, which grew around the tomb of the seventh Shiite Imām, ʿAlī ar-Riḍā (d. 203/818), as it became a prominent site of pilgrimage.

Though of modest size, Ṭūs produced some of the most influential scholars of Islamic history. Not only did the Ghazālī brothers hail from this now deserted town, so too did the famous Firdawsī (d. 411/1020), who is credited with single-handedly reviving and preserving the Persian language through his *Shah-nāmah*. Naṣīr ad-Dīn Ṭūsī (d. 672/1274), the great reviver of Ibn Sīnā's philosophy and perhaps the greatest philosopher and astronomer of the thirteenth century, also claimed Ṭūs as his home town, as did the famous Abū Naṣr as-Sarrāj aṭ-Ṭūsī (d. 378/988), author of *Kitāb al-Lumaʿ fi't-taṣawwuf*, one of the most important handbooks of early Sufism. Not least among the influential scholars of Ṭūs was the famous Saljuq vizier Abu'l-Ḥasan b. ʿAlī aṭ-Ṭūsī, known as Niẓām al-Mulk (455–85/1063–92), whose policies helped to fund and encourage many generations of scholars.

With such an array of famous scholars, Ṭūs was among the most intellectually influential regions per capita of classical Islam.

The Ghazālī brothers lived at a time when political instability was giving way to a period of remarkable intellectual fervor. The instability had been marked by the last phase of the "Daylamī interlude" in which the Ziyārids (315–483/927–1090) controlled the Caspian provinces down to Iṣfahān,[1] with only a small mountain province for the last sixty years of their rule, the Būyids (320–454/932–1062) ruled in most of Persia and Iraq, and the Musāfirids (304–483/916–1090) ruled in northern Persia and Azerbaijan. This was followed by several waves of Turkic tribes, such as the Sāmānids (204–395/819–1005), who ruled Transoxiana and Khurāsān, and the Ghaznavids (365–431/976–1040), who controlled Khurāsān, Khwārazm, and Afghanistan and went as far west as Ray and Hamadān. Extensive disputes between Shīʿīs and Sunnīs, followed by major disputes between the Ḥanafī and Shāfiʿī schools of law, had also contributed to the instability of late fourth- and early fifth-century Iran. But this then gave way to a period of stability under the vast centralizing rule of the Turkic Saljuqs, who ruled Iraq, Iran, and Khurāsān from 429/1038 to 552/1157, though their historical influence extends far beyond these 123 years.

The Saljuqs

In the absence of the genealogical claim to legitimacy similar to that of the ʿAbbasid caliphate, the Saljuqs proved adept in establishing other modes of legitimization.[2] An integral component of their claim to legitimacy was the defense of the ʿAbbāsid caliph al-Qāʾim bi-Amr Allāh (422–67/1031–75) by the Turkish warlord Ṭughril Beg (431–55/1040–63) in 450/1058. It is reported that under siege by Fāṭimid-backed forces, the Turkish general Basāsīrī, who had captured Baghdad, made the *khuṭbah* in the name of the Fāṭimid caliph, Abū Tamīm al-Mustanṣir (427–87/1036–94), exiled the ʿAbbāsid caliph to ʿĀnā, and killed many of his administrators. Al-Qāʾim bi-Amr Allāh then begged the Saljuqs for help, there being no other place to turn. Many sources record this desperate plea: "O God! O God! Save Islam! The cursed enemy has overcome us, and the Qarāmaṭī propaganda has spread!"[3] Ṭughril is then said to have heeded the call, responding through the language of revelation: *Return unto them! For we shall come unto them with hosts they cannot withstand, and we shall expel them hence, abased, and they shall be humbled* (Q 27:37). Ṭughril is further depicted as having restored the caliph, re-established social order, and defended a normative interpretation of Islam. As C.E. Bosworth writes:

> Ṭoghril's march to Baghdad has often been viewed as a Sunnī crusade to rescue the caliph from its Shīʿī oppressors. . . . We can only guess at Ṭoghril's inner motives, but it is surely relevant to note that his Iranian advisers include many officials from Khurāsān, the most strongly Sunnī part of Iran.[4]

Whatever the particular motives of Ṭughril and the Saljuqs may have been, their rule served to sustain the ʿAbbāsid caliphate and consolidate Sunnī orthodoxy. As Francis Robinson observes:

> The caliphate was given another lease on life as the Turks freed the Abbasids from their Buyid thralldom and created a new institution, the universal sultanate. Henceforth the caliph bestowed legitimacy on the effective holders of power as he did when he crowned the first Seljuq sultan in 1058, while it was now the sultan's duty to impose his authority on the Islamic community, defending it against attacks from the outside and denials of God's word within.[5]

Though the Saljuqs outwardly paid homage to the ʿAbbāsid Caliph and were in need of his blessings to sustain the legitimacy of their sultanate, they would at times remind the Caliph where the power now resided, as evidenced by the Saljuq Sultan Malikshāh's (465–85/1073–92) insistence that the Caliph leave Baghdad in 485/1092, and his refusal to give the Caliph any reprieve.[6] Indeed, Malikshāh seemed bent upon joining the power of the sultanate to that of the caliphate.

In addition to the political mechanisms to legitimize their rule, the Saljuqs sought to undergird their claims to Islamic legitimacy by supporting scholars and other religious figures. This was not done through direct political action but through the establishment of *waqf*s (endowments) that benefitted men of religion in all spheres, particularly within Sunnī Islam and among Sufis. Just as *waqf*s served to consolidate and perpetuate legal schools, chiefly the Ḥanafī and Shāfiʿī, so too did they serve to cultivate and perpetuate the influence of Sufism.[7] Saljuq rulers, their wives, and their viziers sought the counsel of Sufi masters and in several cases provided ample support for the establishment of Sufi *ribāṭ*s and *khānqāh*s. While this period is often known as one of Sunnī revival in which theology (*kalām*) and jurisprudence (*fiqh*) were reformulated in ways that buttressed the "consolidation of Sunnī authority as the dominant ethos of rule,"[8] it also saw the broad development in Sufi thought and the reemergence of Sufism as an influential component of Islamic life and thought.

The main architect behind this dimension of Saljuq legitimization was the aforementioned Saljuq vizier, Niẓām al-Mulk (455–85/1063–92), who was so central to Saljuq rule that his period of service is referred to by Ibn al-Athīr as "the Niẓāmiyyah state" (*ad-dawlā an-niẓāmiyyah*).[9] Niẓām al-Mulk proved remarkably effective in creating a vast system of education that served to bolster the Saljuq reputation by providing support for Sunnī orthodoxy. Though the central component of this movement was madrasahs, the Saljuq vizier also patronized the Sufis and was said to have funded many *khānqāhs*. He was not the first to establish madrasahs, as some have claimed,[10] but he was the first to establish fixed stipends and to recognize the value to the state of supporting scholars and establishing an intricate educational system.[11] These efforts to support both scholars and Sufis served in many ways to define the arena in which the Ghazālī brothers came to maturity. Abū Ḥāmid al-Ghazālī played a defining role in buttressing Sunnī orthodoxy and in reintroducing Sufi ideas into mainstream Sunnī Islam.[12] Aḥmad al-Ghazālī's role was focused on Sufism, where he appears to have also been the beneficiary of the *waqf*s given by both the men and women of the Saljuq regime. During their lives, the Saljuq empire was at its peak, and though Abū Ḥāmid traveled beyond its heartland to Damascus and Jerusalem, Aḥmad al-Ghazālī lived his entire life in the central lands of the Saljuq empire; they controlled every region he is known to have traveled, from Khurāsān in the northeast to Baghdad in the south and Tabrīz in the northwest.

The Stages of Aḥmad al-Ghazālī's Life

Though the historically accurate information in the primary sources may be scant and not all of it can be corroborated, there is nonetheless enough information to trace the course of Aḥmad al-Ghazālī's life through five periods: (1) a period of childhood and education in Ṭūs and perhaps Jurjān; (2) a period of spiritual training under Shaykh Abū Bakr an-Nassāj (d. 487/1094) in Nishapur; (3) a period of preaching and teaching in Baghdad; (4) a period in which he attended to his brother's family in both Baghdad and Ṭūs; and (5) a period of itinerant preaching, which came to an end with his death in Qazwīn in either 517/1123 or 520/1126. Unfortunately, this is only a rough outline and the exact dates for each period are difficult to identify.

As many details of Aḥmad's life can be brought into full relief only by examining the treatment of Abū Ḥāmid in the primary sources, an accurate historical examination of the former's life will necessarily cast him in the shadow of the latter. This is somewhat unavoidable, as it reflects the focus of the primary source material. In Chapters 3, 4, and 5, Aḥmad al-Ghazālī will be seen in his own light as a preacher and a Sufi Shaykh. In relation to these functions, it is Abū Ḥāmid who must stand in the shadow of Aḥmad.

Education and Training

ṬŪS

Aḥmad al-Ghazālī's earliest years were inextricably tied to those of Abū Ḥāmid. Thanks to the interest of many Muslim biographers in Abū Ḥāmid's education, we are thus able to trace the early years of Aḥmad's life more closely than we might otherwise expect. Both brothers were born in Ṭūs. The exact date of Aḥmad's birth is not known, but it is said that he was born a few years after Abū Ḥāmid. Most scholars have maintained that Abū Ḥāmid was born in 450/1058, but as Frank Griffel demonstrates, internal evidence in the letters of Abū Ḥāmid Ghazālī indicates that he was born circa 448/ 1056–57.[13] Based on the date of 450/1058 for Abū Ḥāmid's birth, Nasrollah Pourjavady argues that Aḥmad was born in 453, about three years after Abū Ḥāmid,[14] while Aḥmad Mujāhid maintains that Aḥmad was born in either 451 or 452.[15] Taking Griffel's recent findings into account, 450 or 451 would appear to be the most accurate date.

We know nothing of their mother and little about their father, both of whom passed away while the boys were in their youth. Several biographers, such as as-Subkī, Ibn Najjār, and adh-Dhahabī,[16] relate that their father was a weaver who sold his wares in the markets of Ṭūs. But this account likely results from the effort to explain the name *al-Ghazzālī,* rather than *al-Ghazālī,* as a *nisbah* deriving from the occupation of the *ghazzāl,* meaning "spinner" in Arabic.[17] As most biographers accept that the name derives from Ghazālah, one of the villages of Ṭūs, this is at best a suspect piece of information.

In Islamic lore, the divergent roles and talents of the Ghazālī brothers are said to be prefigured in the prayers of their pious father.

As Tāj ad-Dīn as-Subkī reports in an account that is likely more hagiographical than biographical:

> [Their father] would frequent the jurisprudents, sit with them, undertake to serve them and strive to do good for them and provide for them as much as he was able, and when he heard their discourse he cried. So he implored God and asked Him to provide him with a son and make him a jurisprudent. In addition, he attended sessions of preaching, and when the experience was joyous for him, he cried and asked God to provide him with a son who was a preacher. So God answered his supplication. As for Abū Ḥāmid, he was the best jurisprudent (*faqīh*) of his generation and the leader of the people of his time, the master of his domain, whom both those who agreed with and opposed him would cite . . . As for Aḥmad, he was a preacher whose admonitions would cleave solid granite and whose calls to recollection would shake the descendants of those present.[18]

Before his death, their father is reported to have entrusted them to the care of a friend, who is reported to have been a pious man and a follower of the Sufi tradition;[19] some speculate that he was their first Sufi instructor. He undertook to care for the boys and attend to their education. But when he had exhausted the funds provided by their father, it became impossible for him to provide for them. He thus enjoined them to go to the madrasah in Ṭūs as if they were students of jurisprudence (*fiqh*), that they might thereby obtain food. As Abū Ḥāmid is reported to have said, "We came to a madrasah seeking jurisprudence with no goal other than obtaining food. Our study was for that, not for God."[20] In another account, Abū Ḥāmid is reported to have said, "We sought knowledge for reasons other than the sake of God; but knowledge refuses to be for anything other than the sake of God."[21] As Frank Griffel observes, many aspects of this account seem highly stylized.[22] This is most evident in the prayer of their father, which supports the perception of the distinction between the brothers in the later biographical tradition. Nonetheless, the historical kernel, that the brothers' father died while they were young and provided them with little inheritance, and that financial circumstances led them to seek provisions from the local madrasah, is most likely accurate. Despite their ulterior motives, the brothers excelled in their studies. There is no mention of Aḥmad al-Ghazālī's educational biography in the sources, but it is likely that he followed a path similar to that of Abū Ḥāmid. While in Ṭūs, Abū Ḥāmid is reported to have begun his study of the religious sciences under Aḥmad ar-Radhakānī, about whom little is known.[23]

JURJĀN

In his late teenage years, Abū Ḥāmid left Ṭūs to study with Imām Abū Naṣr al-Ismāʿīlī (d. 488/1095) in the city of Jurjān on the Caspian Sea, some 350 kilometers west of Ṭūs.[24] Jurjān had served as a capital for the Ziyārids (319–483/931–1090) during the first part of their rule and had flourished as a center for the arts while under the Ziyārids, the Sāmānids, and the Būyids. Abū Ḥāmid's move to Jurjān demonstrates the importance this city had come to attain once again under the Saljuqs, being rebuilt as a center of Islamic culture. Some believe this to be the first time the brothers were separated,[25] but as there is no information regarding Aḥmad's life at this time, it is also possible that he accompanied his older brother to Jurjān. As Aḥmad's later career and the accounts regarding the extent of his knowledge from ʿAyn al-Quḍāt Hamadānī and al-Ḥāfiẓ as-Silafī indicate that he must have received extensive training in *fiqh* and *kalām*, it is not unlikely that the younger Ghazālī joined his older brother on this journey.

Although madrasahs had become an integral component of intellectual development, there were many other institutions of higher learning. As Roy Mottahedeh observes, "Even in the Saljūq period, as a glance at the biographical dictionaries will show, large numbers of people outside the madrasah system were considered ulema."[26] George Makdisi has noted that among these institutions were the *jāmiʿ*, the mosque, and the *mashhad*.[27] To these we should add the Sufi *khānqāhs*, as they appear to have been an important place of education for scholars of many predilections. But despite the existence of these many institutes of higher learning, the increased funding for madrasah education assured that many scholars were in some way attached to the state. This extensive network of educational institutions provided seekers of knowledge many opportunities to advance their studies. Though we do not know exactly which type of institutes they studied in, it does appear that the Ghazālī brothers took full advantage of the plethora of educational venues, the funding for students, and the fertile intellectual soil that the two provided.

The eleventh century was not a time of intellectual stagnation in which Muslims "turned in a horizontal spiral around their techniques,"[28] as has too often been maintained. By no means was the dynamism of legal development stifled, as some have declared, in following the scholarship of Goldziher, Schacht, and Hurgronje.[29] Rather, this was a time of tremendous development in which the teachings of fiqh, *kalām*, philosophy, and Sufism were all to find new modes of expression. As Marshall Hodgson observes:

> In the tenth and eleventh centuries, all the different intellectual traditions were well matured. . . . Each tradition was ready to look beyond its own roots. Now, in particular, the Hellenists and the ʿulamāʾ fully confronted each other and the result was as stimulating in the intellectual field as the confrontation of the adībs with the Sharʿism of the ʿulamāʾ had been frustrating in the social field.
>
> On the level of imaginative literature, we find the expression of a human image that was relatively secular. . . . Then in more explicit speculation, where the assumption of Sharʿī dominance was more pressing, we find a growing pattern of free esoteric expressions of truths.
>
> By the end of the eleventh century, the political milieu was no longer Shīʿī. (And fewer of the intellectuals were of the old Shīʿī families.) Moreover, pressure for conformity on a Jamāʿi-Sunnī basis was gaining governmental support. But the confrontations had borne fruit. And just as in the social and political life the various elements of urban society had worked out effective patterns consistent in the supremacy of the iqṭāʿ-amīrs, so in intellectual life by then, ways had been found to accommodate in practically all fields of thought a certain intellectual supremacy that had to be accorded the madrasah-ʿulamāʾ. So was ushered in the intellectual life of the Middle Periods, in which the intellectual traditions were relatively interdependent. The graduates of the madrasahs themselves eventually tended to blur the lines between the kalām of the ʿulamāʾ, the various sciences of the Faylasūfs, and even the adab of the old courtiers. The Faylasūfs, in turn, adjusted their teachings, at least in secondary ways, to the fact of Sharʿī supremacy. And speculative Sufism penetrated everywhere.[30]

The Ghazālī brothers were both among that class of "madrasah ʿulamāʾ" to which Hodgson refers, if not exemplars of it. As such, they underwent an intense training in *uṣūl al-fiqh* (the roots of jurisprudence) and *furūʿ al-fiqh* (the branches of jurisprudence), these being the backbone of the madrasah education. But the very fact that this was a period of intense development and intellectual cross-fertilization makes it difficult for us to determine just what would have been the specific course they studied. Unlike a century and a half later, the exact texts being studied at this time are difficult to determine. In his *Tahdhīb al-asmāʾ waʾl-lughāt,* the famous Shāfiʿī scholar Imām Abū Zakariyyā an-Nawawī (d. 676/1277) lists what he believes to have been the most influential texts of jurisprudence in the Shāfiʿī madhhab, but of these only one, the *Mukhtaṣar* of ash-Shāfiʿī's pupil Abū Ibrāhīm Ismāʿīl al-Muzanī (d. 264/877), precedes the fifth Islamic century. Nonetheless, a view of the intellectual activity of the fourth/tenth century can give us some insight into the figures whose influence would have to some degree determined the subject matter and materials studied by the Ghazālī brothers in their mastery of jurisprudence.

The most important figure for the development of *uṣūl al-fiqh* in the early fourth/tenth century was Abuʾl-ʿAbbās Ibn Surayj (d. 306/918), who was known to some as the "Young Shāfiʿī" for his work in establishing the methodology of *uṣūl al-fiqh* and spreading the Shāfiʿī madhhab. There is no evidence that Ibn Surayj left extensive writings for subsequent generations, but his students were the first generation to author works that treated *uṣūl* proper, especially Abū Bakr aṣ-Ṣayrafī (d. 330/942), who is sometimes regarded as "the most knowledgeable scholar on *uṣūl al-fiqh* after ash-Shāfiʿī,"[31] and al-Qaffāl ash-Shāshī (d. mid. 4th/late 10th century), who authored the influential book on *uṣūl* titled *at-Taqrīb,* and of whom it is said "the *fuqahāʾ* of Khurāsān issued from him."[32] Aḥmad and Abū Ḥāmid thus came at an exciting moment, when the methodology of *uṣūl* was taking shape. They would most likely have studied the writings of aṣ-Ṣayrafī, the *Taqrīb* of ash-Shāshī, and others who, according to Wael B. Hallaq, comprised the first multigenerational collection of scholars to have at their disposal the combination of traditionalist and rationalist approaches to *fiqh* necessary for developing a fully formed science of *uṣūl*[33]—a science to which Abū Ḥāmid gave another form of expression in his *al-Mustaṣfā, Shifāʾ al-ghalīl* and *al-Wasīṭ al-wajīz,* works that shaped the study of *uṣūl al-fiqh* for generations to come.

ṬŪS AND NISHAPUR

Abū Ḥāmid did not study in Jurjān for more than two years. He then returned (perhaps with Aḥmad) to Ṭūs, where he is reported to have remained for the next three years, memorizing all he had previously studied.[34] Afterward, he traveled to the city of Nishapur, the political, intellectual, and spiritual hub of Khurāsān, about a hundred kilometers southwest of Ṭūs, to study with the famous scholar Imām al-Ḥaramayn Abuʾl-Maʿālī al-Juwaynī (d. 478/1085), a noted Shāfiʿī jurisprudent and the leading Ashaʿrite theologian of his day.[35]

It appears that Aḥmad either traveled with Abū Ḥāmid or followed shortly thereafter, but it is also possible that his arrival in Nishapur preceded that of Abū Ḥāmid. It is not clear whether Aḥmad came to study theology and jurisprudence like his brother, or whether the goal of his journey was to be with Abū Bakr b. ʿAbd Allāh aṭ-Ṭūsī an-Nassāj (d. 487/1094), a Sufi shaykh whose spiritual heritage traces back through four generations to the famous Sufi master al-Junayd al-Baghdādī (d. 298/910). Whatever the original intention may have been, Aḥmad kept the company of an-Nassāj and appears to have kept Nishapur as his home until an-Nassāj's death. He was then named an-Nassāj's successor and thus became a spiritual master in his middle thirties, remaining so throughout his life. The nature of the spiritual practices in which he may have participated at this time will be examined in Chapter 3.

It is likely that the brothers had previously been exposed to Ashʿarite *kalām*, perhaps along with other forms of *kalām*. While in Nishapur they both had their first opportunity to study with true experts, people at the forefront of developing new expressions of this science. That Abū Ḥāmid was thoroughly versed in theology is evident from his tremendous impact on its development, especially through his *al-Iqtiṣād fiʾl-iʿtiqād* (Moderation in Creed).[36] Aḥmad's exposure to *kalām* is, however, undocumented. In his sermons there are several allusions to Ashʿarite positions, while the fact that he favored Ashʿarism is attested to by a passage in the *Tajrīd* in which he criticizes many schools of theology, but spares Ashʿarism:

> The tree of testifying to unity (*tawḥīd*) is neither of the east nor of the west, it does not deny God's attributes nor does it multiply them. It is neither materialistic (*dahriyyah*) nor dualistic, neither Jewish nor Christian, neither anthropomorphic nor Muʿtazilite, neither Qadarite nor predestinarian (*jabariyyah*), rather it is Muḥammadan, heavenly.[37]

Though this passage can by no means demonstrate the full breadth (or lack thereof) of his learning, it does demonstrate that like his brother he most likely identified with the Ashʿarite school of theology.

Shaykh Aḥmad and Imām Abū Ḥāmid

NISHAPUR

Though several biographers, beginning with as-Samʿānī, write that Aḥmad al-Ghazālī took to the Sufi practice at an early age, implying that he had begun to follow the spiritual path while in Ṭūs,[38] the period in Nishapur marks the first point at which we can identify his definite adherence to a particular Sufi lineage. It is also the first point at which there is a definite divergence in the lives and pursuits of Aḥmad and Abū Ḥāmid. Abū Ḥāmid was dedicated to theology and jurisprudence and provided instruction in these subjects in Nishapur until he left to join the scholarly circle that Niẓām al-Mulk had assembled in his camp. In 484/1091 he was appointed lecturer in *fiqh* and *kalām* at the Niẓāmiyyah madrasah in Baghdad and was soon recognized as the premier scholar of his day. Al-Kātib al-Iṣfahānī writes, with some hyperbole: "The wonders of his knowledge radiated to the East and West."[39] Aḥmad, meanwhile, spent these years in adherence to the Sufi path, devoted, as best we can tell, to the practices of remembrance (*dhikr*), seclusion (*khalwah*), and solitude (*ʿuzlah*) that many Sufis maintain are necessary for disciplining the soul and cultivating the heart until it yearns for none but God. Nonetheless, Aḥmad clearly continued his studies of the religious sciences (*al-ʿulūm ad-dīniyyah*) alongside his devotional practices; otherwise he would not have been qualified to teach at the Tājiyyah madrasah in Baghdad, or to fill his brother's position at the Niẓāmiyyah madrasah several years later.[40] Furthermore, Abū Ḥāmid's association with Sufi teachings did not begin in Baghdad. While in Nishapur, he studied with the Sufi shaykh Abū ʿAlī al-Fārmadhī (d. 477/1084),[41] who was himself regarded by many as the Shaykh of Shaykhs (*shaykh ash-shuyūkh*) in the region of Khurāsān.[42] As both al-Fārmadhī and an-Nassāj had studied with many of the same Sufi masters, such as Imām Abu'l-Qāsim al-Qushayrī (d. 465/1072), author of the famous *Qushayrī Epistle* (*ar-Risālah al-Qushayriyyah*), Abu'l-Qāsim al-Jurjānī (d. 469/1076), and the tremendously influential Abū Saʿīd b. Abi'l-Khayr (d. 440/1049), it is more than likely that the two brothers traveled in the same circles and sat together at the feet of masters of both the esoteric and exoteric religious sciences. Indeed, posterity has viewed both brothers as men of great achievement in each domain. As ʿAyn al-Quḍāt al-Hamadānī writes:

> O Friend! For some time nine scholars who are firm in knowledge have been known to me, but tonight, which is Friday night, the day for writing, a tenth became known to me. That is Khwājah Imām Muḥammad al-Ghazālī [God's mercy upon him]. I knew about Aḥmad, but I did not know about Muḥammad. He is also one of us.[43]

That this was ʿAyn al-Quḍāt's position is confirmed by a passage in one of his letters: "Those who are among the wayfarers (*sālikūn*) and have knowledge of the outward are very few, save ten people. Among these ten people I do not know for certain of anyone who exists now. Khwājah Abū Ḥāmid Ghazālī and his brother Aḥmad are among this group."[44]

According to ʿAbd ar-Raḥmān Jāmī, an-Nassāj was Aḥmad's shaykh, and al-Fārmadhī was Abū Ḥāmid's shaykh.[45] It is most likely that an-Nassāj and al-Fārmadhī provided spiritual instruction for both brothers,[46] but that al-Fārmadhī's role in Aḥmad's life was more intellectual than spiritual, such that Aḥmad may have studied the *Epistle* of al-Qushayrī and other Sufi texts with al-Fārmadhī, while an-Nassāj attended to his spiritual training.[47] Thus, al-Fārmadhī was likely more responsible for Abū Ḥāmid's spiritual training, while Aḥmad followed an-Nassāj and received the Sufi mantle (*al-khirqah*) from him.

That the Ghazālī brothers were students of both the inward and the outward sciences is emblematic of the relationship between these fields, which were joined together by a membrane that simultaneously separated them. Analyses of Sufism in this period must thus avoid a simplistic bifurcation between the *fuqahāʾ*/*ʿulamāʾ* and the Sufis such as that found in Hamid Dabashi's work on ʿAyn al-Quḍāt. Dabashi argues that the Sufis were subverting both the "nomocentrism of the clerical establishment" and the political authority of the Saljuqs,[48] and maintains that Sufism and Islamic law represent

> a reflection of two fundamentally opposed interpretations of the Koranic revelation and the Muḥammadan legacy. The positive nomocentricity of Islamic law found the language of Islamic mysticism as quintessentially flawed in nature and disposition. The feeling was mutual. The Sufis, too, rejected the rigid and perfunctory nomocentricity of the jurists as quintessentially misguided and a stultification of the Koranic message and the Prophetic traditions.[49]

Nothing could be further from the reality of the manner in which Sufism, law, and theology were intertwined in the lives of the Ghazālī brothers. As Aḥmad states in one of his sessions, "The Shariah and the *ṭarīqah* (Sufi path) are two conditions for you to perform one cycle of prayer according to what you have been commanded."[50] This attitude is expressed by many Sufis of this period. As al-Ghazālī's younger contemporary Samʿānī writes, "You must devote your outer aspect to the Shariah and your innner aspect to the *ḥaqīqah* (reality)."[51] This symbiosis between training in *taṣawwuf* and law was by no means new to this period. A generation earlier, ʿAbdallāh Ansārī counsels,

"Make the Shariah the sultan of your acts and the *ṭarīqah* the sultan of your character traits. Then you may perfect the noble character traits with the *ṭarīqah* of the Men [i.e., the Sufis] and arrange the character traits of submission and faith by observing the Shariah."[52] In the generations before them, such luminaries as al-Junayd al-Baghdādī and Abu'l-Qāsim al-Qushayrī are also known to have combined training in jurisprudence (*fiqh*) with adherence to the Sufi path. As Marshall Hodgson observes in discussing the relationship between the Sufis and the *Ahl al-ḥadīth* more than a century earlier, "In some cases it is hard to draw a line between what was Sufi mystical self-examination and what was Ḥadīthī moralism."[53] Many Sufis not officially recognized as *ḥadīth* scholars had some knowledge of both fiqh and *ḥadīth*. The biographical dictionaries of the Sufis, in which are recorded the companions and sayings of many famous representatives, also serve as repositories of *ḥadīth* known to have been transmitted by them. A close examination of these sources reveals that the proponents of Sufism drew on the same materials as other scholars and constituted an integral component of the scholarly community as a whole. The *Ahl al-ḥadīth* movement, the jurisprudents, and the Sufis comprised intertwining circles whose methods, interests, and members overlapped. Whereas the jurisprudents, the Quran reciters, and the *Ahl al-ḥadīth* transmitted knowledge in a way that could properly be called teaching (*ta ͑līm*), the Sufis put more emphasis on inner training (*tarbiyyah*) for the sake of purification (*tazkiyyah*). But *ta ͑līm* and *tarbiyyah* were by no means mutually exclusive. They were in fact complementary parts of a greater whole. By observing how closely connected the Sufis were with the *Ahl al-ḥadīth* we can see that *tarbiyyah* and *tazkiyyah* were not just individual spiritual practices but an important aspect of early Islamic pedagogy and intellectuality.

A study of the biographies of early Sufis demonstrates that the sayings of the Prophet Muḥammad were an integral component of their discourse and thus of their self-understanding. Well-established Sufis also reached a high degree of competency in other fields. A noted *ḥadīth* scholar and one of the foremost authorities on Sufism, Abū ͑Abd ar-Raḥmān as-Sulamī (d. 412/1021) compiled the biographies and teachings of over one hundred Sufis from the early Islamic period in his *Generations of the Ṣūfīs* (*Ṭabaqāt aṣ-ṣūfiyyah*). Among those he recorded as companions of the Sufis and of the *Ahl al-ḥadīth* are men such as Abu'l-͑Abbās as-Sayyārī (d. 342/953–54), a Sufi shaykh, jurist, and noted *ḥadīth* scholar. According to as-Sulamī, all the *Ahl al-ḥadīth* were as-Sayyārī's companions.[54] Ruwaym b. Aḥmad al-Baghdādī (d. 303/915) was among the most revered Sufi masters of Baghdad. He is recorded by as-Sulamī as a practicing jurist, a noted reciter of the Quran, and a scholar of Quranic exegesis (*tafsīr*).[55] The most famous of the early Sufis, al-Junayd al-Baghdādī (d. 298/910), was also a practicing jurist who studied with many scholars known to be directly aligned with the *Ahl al-ḥadīth*. Foremost among his teachers were Abū Thawr (d. 241/855), the pre-eminent jurist of his day in Baghdad, and the aforementioned Abu'l-ʿAbbās Ibn Surayj, heralded by many as the leading scholar of *uṣūl al-fiqh* in his day. One disciple said of al-Junayd: "His words were connected to the texts [i.e., the Qurʾān and the *ḥadīth*]."[56] These few examples demonstrate that any theory that posits the *fuqahāʾ* and the Sufis as diametrically opposed camps in a struggle for the heart of Islam is based on disregard for the primary sources.

The notion that Sufi practitioners of this period opposed the *fuqahāʾ* and represented a challenge to state authority is at odds with the historical reality. Saljuq leaders, their viziers, and their family members were known to have supported and even frequented Sufi masters.[57] Niẓām al-Mulk frequented Sufis and *fuqahāʾ* alike. He also established both madrasahs and Sufi *khānqāh*s, as did other less famous individuals, such as Abū Saʿd al-Astarābādī (d. 440/1048–49) and Abū Saʿd al-Kharkūshī (d. 1013 or 1016).[58] Abū ʿAlī ad-Daqqāq (d. 405/1015), renowned as a Sufi master, founded a madrasah in the city of Nasā.[59] He and his more famous son-in-law, Abu'l-Qāsim al-Qushayrī, are said to have taught in a madrasah that later became known as the Qushayriyyah madrasah.[60] Shaykh Abū ʿAlī al-Fārmadhī professed a love for his shaykh that inspired him to move from the madrasah to the *khānqāh*.[61] Given this environment, it is most likely that both Ghazālī brothers traveled freely between madrasah and *khānqāh*. It is reported that after leaving his teaching position, Abū Ḥāmid later returned to his homeland, where he spent his last days providing instruction in a "*khānqāh* for the Ṣūfīs, and in a madrasah for the sake of those who seek knowledge."[62]

The interconnections between practitioners of both the inward and outward sciences, as well as the free movement of such intellectuals between the *khānqāh* and the madrasah demonstrate that there was no clear divide between the Sufis and the *ʿulamāʾ*, nor between the madrasah and the *khānqāh*. The lines that have been drawn by secularist and revivalist Muslim interpreters,[63] as well as Orientalists, are more a result of the modern mind in which Enlightenment and Protestant Christian notions of mysticism are imposed upon the classical Islamic world.[64] As in any healthy social environment, the intellectuals of this period frequently criticized one another's predilections, but they all participated in the same discourse. Their particular interests and resulting identities often differed, but still overlapped.

This aspect of the early middle period is essential for understanding the intellectual and spiritual environment in which the Ghazālī brothers came to maturity. Though we are unable to determine the precise details, it appears that while the intellectual and spiritual paths of Imām Abū Ḥāmid al-Ghazālī and Shaykh Aḥmad al-Ghazālī did take different courses, they often crossed. Aḥmad excelled in the gnostic sciences, or sciences of recognition (*al-maʿārif*),[65] while maintaining his studies of the religious sciences (*al-ʿulūm ad-dīniyyah*), and his brother rose to the height of Ashʿarī theology and Shāfiʿī jurisprudence, while developing an understanding of the sciences of recognition—one that eventually turned him toward a path more akin to that of his younger brother.

BAGHDAD

After Abū Ḥāmid al-Ghazālī moved to Baghdad, it appears that the brothers may have remained in close contact; for when Abū Ḥāmid underwent his now famous spiritual crisis,[66] it was Aḥmad who took his place at the Niẓāmiyyah madrasah and cared for his family so that he could travel and devote himself to the Sufi path. Whether Aḥmad was already in Baghdad at this time or if he came to Baghdad expressly to assist his brother is difficult to discern. As several of Aḥmad's later biographers would have it, he was in Baghdad sometime before his brother's decision to leave the Niẓāmiyyah, as he allegedly served as the catalyst for his brother's spiritual conversion.[67] But such accounts reflect an interpretation of events that is not available in any of the earlier sources. The political realities of Baghdad may account for some of the factors that influenced the movements of the Ghazālī brothers. This is especially important because they lived in an age when the institutions of knowledge and education were closely tied to the political powers.[68]

Before his tenure at the Niẓāmiyyah, Aḥmad had also served for some time at the Tājiyyah madrasah in Baghdad, which had been established by Tāj al-Mulk Abu'l-Ghanāʾim Pārsī [Fārsī] (d. 486/1093), the vizier of Tarkān Khātūn, a wife of the Saljuq Sultan Malikshāh, and Niẓām al-Mulk's main rival to the vizierate of the Saljuq empire. According to C.E. Bosworth, this was around 480 to 482.[69] Tāj al-Mulk most likely established the madrasah named after him in order to make an important political statement, as he built it next to the tomb of Shaykh Abū Isḥāq ash-Shīrāzī (d. 476/1083–84), the first chair of the Niẓāmiyyah in Baghdad, whose tomb was also constructed through his patronage. Though the duration of Aḥmad's appointment and his exact responsibilities are not known, the fact that he served at the Tājiyyah may be of some importance for understanding the political inclinations of both brothers, for the Tājiyyah and the Niẓāmiyyah madrasahs represented rival claims to state control. Though not all who studied or taught at these institutions would necessarily be involved in, or even fully aware of, these divisions, Aḥmad al-Ghazālī had clearly found favor with the caliph and his wife, as is attested by the fact that he preached at the funeral of Tarkān Khātūn,[70] and that several of the Saljuq rulers are recorded among his disciples. The political conflict between Tāj al-Mulk and Niẓām al-Mulk may therefore be of some importance for fully understanding the positions of the Ghazālī brothers.

According to most of the earliest sources, Tarkān Khātūn had been conspiring to have Malikshāh replace Niẓām al-Mulk with Tāj al-Mulk by casting aspersions on Niẓām al-Mulk and searching for any fault for which he might be held accountable.[71] While Niẓām al-Mulk was still in power, the sultan awarded Tāj al-Mulk the vizierate of his children and entrusted to him the affairs of the harem. He further appointed him head of the *ṭughrā* (royal seal) and the *inshā'* (royal correspondence).[72] Omid Safi postulates that the increasing power of Tāj al-Mulk, and especially these appointments, was the impetus behind Chapter 41 of Niẓām al-Mulk's famous manual of statecraft,[73] *Siyāsat-nāmah,* entitled "On not giving two appointments to one man," which begins:

> Enlightened monarchs and clever ministers have never in any age given two appointments to one man or one appointment to two men, with the result that their affairs were always conducted with efficiency and lustre. When two appointments are given to one man, one of the tasks is always inefficiently and faultily performed; and in fact you will usually find that the man who has two functions fails in both of them, and is constantly suffering censure and uneasiness on account of his shortcomings.[74]

These words appear to indicate a tension that had been brewing within the Saljuq court, one that may well have been the cause of Niẓām al-Mulk's assassination. In most secondary sources, such as Bernard Lewis's *The Assassins,* it is commonly accepted that Niẓām al-Mulk was removed from this world through the machinations of the *fidāʾī* Ismāʿīlīs.[75] But the earliest primary sources offer an alternative account—that the assassination of Niẓām al-Mulk was the result of inner Saljuq rivalries, not outer sectarian strife.

Tāj ad-Dīn as-Subkī offers both the theory of Ismāʿīlī accountability and Saljuq accountability. While he openly maintains that the theory that lays responsibility at the feet of the Ismāʿīlīs is "closer to the truth," he devotes only one paragraph to the discussion of this theory, and several pages to how the soured relations between the sultan and the vizier may have led to the latter's assassination. As-Subkī writes:

> There are those who claim that the sultan is the one who arranged the assassin for him. In support of that they mention that estrangement (*waḥshah*) had arisen between them. As we mentioned before, Niẓām al-Mulk honored the [ʿAbbāsid] caliph, and whenever the sultan wanted to remove the caliph he prevented him from that and secretly sent a message to the caliph informing him of it and directing him to attempt to win over the favor of the sultan.[76]

As-Subkī goes on to mention that in 485/1092 the sultan "set out from Iṣfahān to Baghdad, intending to change the *khalīfah*, and he knew that would not come to him so long as Niẓām al-Mulk was alive. So he worked to have him killed before his arrival in Baghdad, as we have explained."[77]

As-Subkī is by no means the only historian to offer this "alternative theory." Ibn Khallikān writes, "It is said that the assassin was suborned against him by Malikshāh, who was fatigued to see him live so long, and coveted the numerous fiefs he held in his possession."[78] However, he also mentions another theory, which has nothing to do with the Ismāʿīlīs:

> The assassination of Niẓām al-Mulk has been attributed also to Tāj al-Mulk Abu'l-Ghanāʾim al-Marzubān Ibn Khosrū Fīrūz, surnamed Ibn Dārest; he was an enemy of the vizier and in high favor with his sovereign Malikshāh, who, on the death of Niẓām al-Mulk, appointed him to fill the place of vizier.[79]

Whether the assassination was planned by Tāj al-Mulk or not, he was clearly held responsible for it by others: "Ibn Dārest was himself slain on Monday night, 12th Muḥarram, 486 (February A. D. 1093); having been attacked and cut to pieces by the young mamlūks belonging to the household of Niẓām al-Mulk."[80]

It is evident that both Malikshāh and Tāj al-Mulk had something to gain from the elimination of Niẓām al-Mulk: the latter would rise in position, as he did for a short time, and the former would have his main obstacle to the dethronement of the ʿAbbāsid caliph removed. The Ismāʿīlīs, on the other hand, had little to gain, knowing that such an act would raise the ire of the Saljuqs, and they certainly did not have the strength to overthrow them. The most plausible account of Niẓām al-Mulk's assassination would thus seem to be that proferred by Rāwandī and Ẓāhir ad-Dīn Nīshāpūrī, who state that the sultan abandoned Niẓām al-Mulk to Tāj al-Mulk, and according to whom the assassination was committed by the Ismāʿīlīs through the instigation of Tāj al-Mulk.[81]

The most comprehensive account of all the intricate factors that brought this incident to a head is provided by Nīshāpūrī:

> Niẓām al-Mulk was extremely powerful and possessed great authority and dominion. Tarkān Khātūn, the daughter of Tamghāj Khān of Samarqand, was the sultan's wife, having the utmost beauty, elegance, high lineage, and inherited grandeur. She was domineering without limit, and she had a vizier from the regions of Fars named Tāj al-Mulk Abu'l-Ghanā'im who understood both the surface and the inner nature of things and was known for his competence, learning, and magnanimity. He was also the keeper of the Sultan's Wardrobe. Tarkān wanted to advance him over Niẓām al-Mulk, and she insisted that the Sultan give him the vizierate. She continually defamed Niẓām al-Mulk in private and recounted his offences, until, finally, she caused the Sultan to change his attitude toward him. The cause of this enmity was that Tarkān Khātūn had a son named Maḥmūd. She wanted the Sultan to make him crown prince, and he was very small and a child. Barkyaruq was from Zubaydah Khātūn, the daughter of Amir Yāqūtī, sister of Malik Ismāʿīl, and the eldest of the children of the Sultan. Niẓām al-Mulk inclined toward him, since he saw the mark of kingship and the aura of rulership in his face, and he encouraged the Sultan to make him crown prince and bestow the reins of the kingdom on him. And the Sultan was more agreeable to making Barkyaruq his deputy. In

sum, when they had filled the ear of the Sultan with the offences of Niẓām al-Mulk, one day the Sultan gave a message to him, saying "Evidently it appears that you share in my rule, for you give governorates and fiefs to your sons, and, whatever you wish to control in the realm, you take without consulting me. Do you want me to order that they take the pen-box from in front of you and remove the turban from your head?" Niẓām al-Mulk answered, "My pen-box and your crown are bound together and are twins, but the command belongs to the latter." To the satisfaction of Tarkān, the tellers of tales added embellishments to that. The rage and anger of the Sultan increased as a result of this statement. He gave him into the hands of Tāj al-Mulk. He had contacts and acquaintance with the deviationists in secret, and the Sultan knew nothing about this. It happened about that time that they set out from Isfahan for Baghdad. When they reached Nihāwand, the accursed deviationists stabbed Niẓām al-Mulk, also at the instigation of Tāj al-Mulk.[82]

It appears that Niẓām al-Mulk had been well aware of these machinations and may even have had some premonition of where they were leading. As he writes in these eerily prescient words of the *Siyāsat-nāmah*:

> There are certain persons who on this very day hold privileged positions in this empire. . . . They try to persuade The Master of the World to overthrow the house of the ʿAbbāsids, and if I were to lift the lid from the top of that pot—oh! the disgraceful things that would be revealed! But—worse than that—as a result of their representations The Master of the World has become weary of his humble servant, and is not prepared to take any action in the matter, because of the economies which these people recommend, thereby making The Master of the World greedy for money. They make out that I am interested in my private advantage and so my humble advice finds no acceptance. One day The Master will realize their iniquity and treachery and criminal deeds—when I have disappeared.[83]

The theory that Niẓām al-Mulk was disposed of in order to make way for Malikshāh's assault on the ʿAbbāsid caliph is supported by the fact that the sultan wasted no time in carrying out his ambitions. When he arrived in Baghdad just shortly after the death of the Niẓām al-Mulk, he asked the caliph to remove his designation from his son Mustaẓhir and designate his son Jaʿfar as the crown prince (*walī al-ʿahd*).[84] As Jaʿfar's mother was Malikshāh's daughter, this was a clear attempt to join the sultanate and the caliphate in one bloodline. But as Malikshāh died within forty days of Niẓām al-Mulk, Jaʿfar's ascension to the caliphate was not to be. In the absence of both Niẓām al-Mulk and Malikshāh, Saljuq power waned and the ʿAbbāsid caliphate was able to regain some of its political prestige.

This short analysis of Saljuq intrigue demonstrates that Aḥmad al-Ghazālī's position at the Tājiyyah and Niẓāmiyyah madrasahs may have had political implications. If he was appointed before the death of Tāj al-Mulk, it was perhaps as a foil to his brother's appointment at the Niẓāmiyyah, but if he was appointed after the death of Tāj al-Mulk, it may have been as an effort to re-incorporate this madrasah into the central power structure. His move to the Niẓāmiyyah madrasah in 488/1095 implies that he was aligned with his brother, as the events described above occurred two years prior. Some have interpreted Abū Ḥāmid al-Ghazālī's flight from the Niẓāmiyyah as one of political expediency, fearing that he may have been the target of another assassination.[85] But this theory is predicated on the belief that the Ismāʿīlīs were solely responsible for the death of the vizier, and Abū Ḥāmid, like the vizier, had indeed been their staunch opponent, taking them to task in works such as *Faḍāʾiḥ al-bāṭiniyyah wa-faḍāʾil al-mustaẓhiriyyah* (The Disgraces of the Esoterists and the Merits of the Exoterists) and *Ḥamāqah ahl al-ibāḥah* (The Folly of the Libertines). But in light of the facts detailed above, it seems that if indeed there were any external political motivations, one could speculate that as a result of the conduct of Malikshāh, Tarkān Khātūn, and Tāj al-Mulk, and the subsequent deterioration of the Saljuq state, Abū Ḥāmid had come to see the true nature of his position as a servant of the empire and was alienated by the politics of his day. This in turn may have brought on a profound spiritual dilemma as he came to realize that in his "quest for knowledge" he had come to serve a coercive state institution, and this then turned him to a life of asceticism and contemplation. As Kenneth Garden states,

> Al-Ghazālī's famous spiritual crisis of 488/1095 had a very worldly context. It must be understood at least partially as a response to the political events of his age, both because he felt morally compromised by his political involve-

> ment . . . and because he despaired of the role of the regime in establishing a stable and just worldly order.[86]

Thus, while the political situation most likely influenced his decision, that his motivations were primarily political is highly unlikely, for given his reputation, he could easily have gone elsewhere to continue his teaching career. It is, however, impossible to determine his exact motivations and Aḥmad's role, other than that of replacing him for a short time at the Niẓāmiyyah.

The duration of Aḥmad's tenure in Abū Ḥāmid's position at the Niẓāmiyyah is a matter of some debate. Nasrollah Pourjavady believes he was there for about six months, until Abū ʿAbd Allāh aṭ-Ṭabarī (d. 495/1102) came to fill the position in 489/1096,[87] while Aḥmad Mujāhid maintains that he held this position for ten years.[88] The issue is further complicated by the fact that as-Subkī writes that aṭ-Ṭabarī was already in Baghdad teaching at the Niẓāmiyyah madrasah when Abū Ḥāmid al-Ghazālī felt compelled to leave his position.[89]

However long the duration of Aḥmad's tenure at the Niẓāmiyyah and Tājiyyah madrasahs may have been, his career in the religious sciences was neither as illustrious nor as extensive as that of his brother. For Aḥmad, the sciences of law and theology, though necessary, take a backseat to the sciences of the spirit (Ar. *rūḥ*; Per. *jān*), to which he devoted his life. In his view, exoteric knowledge (*ʿilm*) is important but pertains only to the heart and does not penetrate to the spirit, the cultivation of which is the purpose of all learning. It is only recognition (*maʿrifah*) that pertains to the spirit. In this vein, Shaykh Aḥmad states in one of his sessions, "Fleeting thoughts pertain to the soul and have no path to the heart; knowledge pertains to the heart and has no path to the spirit; and recognition is in the spirit."[90] As will be detailed in Chapters 3 and 5, such sayings imply a psychology wherein the soul designates the baser human elements that are overcome by forgetfulness and dispersion. The heart refers to a subtler faculty that fluctuates between the soul and the spirit. And the spirit refers to that part of the human being that inclines fully to God. As Samʿānī puts it, "The spirit is luminous and heavenly, the soul terrestrial and dark, while the heart fluctuates and is bewildered. The attribute of the spirit is all conformity [to God]. The attribute of the soul is all opposition [to God]. And the attribute of the heart is fluctuating in the midst."[91] Seen in this light, Aḥmad viewed the knowledge obtained through madrasah studies as a potential support that could pull the heart away from the fleeting thoughts of the soul and orient it toward the spirit. Nonetheless, the knowledge obtained by such learning ultimately fell short of the spirit. As all of Aḥmad's extant writings are dedicated to the sciences of recognition (*ʿirfān*), rather than knowledge (*ʿilm*), this time at the Tājiyyah and Niẓāmiyyah madrasahs should not be regarded as the defining feature of his life. His spiritual instruction and itinerant preaching were the means by which he advanced the teachings of recognition. It is thus through his function as a Sufi teacher and as a preacher that his fame and influence spread.

Travels of Aḥmad al-Ghazālī

AFTER BAGHDAD

It is difficult to trace the steps of Aḥmad al-Ghazālī between the years 489/1096 and his brother's death in 505/1111. It appears that at some point after fulfilling his duties at the Niẓāmiyyah, he escorted Abū Ḥāmid's family to Nishapur and then to Ṭūs, where they were reunited with Abū Ḥāmid several years later. One manuscript of *Lubb al-iḥyāʾ* states that this work was written by Aḥmad, but that the manner of summarizing the work was dictated by Abū Ḥāmid.[92] If this report is accurate, the two brothers spent at least some time together in either Ṭūs or Nishapur after Abū Ḥāmid's years of travel and devotion. It is clear that they were in close contact, for Abū Ḥāmid al-Ghazālī's *al-Maḍnūn bihi ʿalā ghayr ahlihi* (That Which is Withheld from Those Who are Unqualified) is devoted and addressed to Aḥmad.

According to as-Subkī, Aḥmad al-Ghazālī was with his brother in Ṭūs on 12 Jumādā al-ākhirah, 505/16 December, 1111, when the latter passed away. The only account of Abū Ḥāmid's last moment is that related by his younger brother:

> When it was Monday morning, my brother Abū Ḥāmid performed his ablution, prayed, and said, "Give me my shroud." He took it, kissed it, and placed it over his eyes and said, "Obediently, I enter into the kingdom." Then he stretched out his feet, faced the *qiblah*, and died before sunrise.[93]

ITINERANT PREACHING

After his brother's death, Aḥmad continued his itinerant preaching, traveling to Baghdad and many of the major cities of Persia, such as Iṣfahān, Nishapur, Marāgheh, Tabrīz, Qazwīn, and Hamadān. This of course means that he paid short visits to many of the smaller villages between these major centers. There are, however, only a few accounts of where he may have been at particular times. The first indication of al-Ghazālī's whereabouts is provided by Ibn al-Jawzī, who, as noted above, cites Muḥammad b. Ṭāhir al-Maqdisī's polemic against al-Ghazālī.[94] As al-Maqdisī died in 507/1113 and relates several events that transpired in Hamadān, it is clear that Aḥmad al-Ghazālī spent some time in Hamadān before the year 507/1113. The second indication is provided by one of the manuscripts of the *Sawāniḥ*, which states that Aḥmad wrote this treatise in the towns of Marāgheh and Tabrīz, both of which are located in the northwest of present-day Iran, in the year 508/1114.[95]

The next indication comes from ʿAyn al-Quḍāt Hamadānī, who writes in *Zubdat al-ḥaqāʾiq* that during one of Aḥmad al-Ghazālī's visits to Hamadān, located almost halfway between Baghdad and present-day Tehran, he became ʿAyn al-Quḍāt's shaykh and helped him to advance on the Sufi path.[96] As ʿAyn al-Quḍāt, born in 492/1099, wrote this book at twenty-four years of age, recounting a spiritual awakening that had begun three years earlier, we can surmise that this meeting occurred sometime between the years 513/1119 and 516/1122.[97] There were several other meetings between them in Hamadān and Qazwīn, but the dates are not given by either Hamadānī or al-Ghazālī.

Another account of Aḥmad's whereabouts is related by Ibn al-Jawzī in *al-Muntaẓam*, wherein, during a celebration at the court of the Saljuq sultan Maḥmūd b. Muḥammad b. Malikshāh, the sultan gave Aḥmad al-Ghazālī 1,000 dinars, whereupon al-Ghazālī took the horse of the vizier, which was richly mounted with a saddle of gold. When informed of this, the sultan ordered that he not be pursued.[98] As Maḥmūd ruled from 511/1117–18 until 525/1131, for this event to have occurred, it must have taken place between 511/1117 and Aḥmad's death in either 517/1123 or 520/1126. It may have occurred in 515/1121, when al-Ghazālī reportedly dwelt at the sultan's court in Baghdad[99] and preached at the funeral proceedings of Tarkān Khātūn. But given the favor he seems to have found with Tarkān Khātūn, it is likely that he visited the court on more than one occasion.

Two other cities in which Aḥmad al-Ghazālī is reported to have appeared are Iṣfahān, located 340 kilometers south of present-day Tehran, and Irbil, 670 kilometers west of Tehran, but we cannot even conjecture as to when he may have been in either of these places. According to a brief note in Shaykh Abū Ḥafṣ ʿUmar as-Suhrawardī's *ʿAwārif al-maʿārif*, his shaykh and uncle, Abu'n-Najīb as-Suhrawardī, was in Iṣfahān with his shaykh, Aḥmad al-Ghazālī, serving as his representative.[100] As for al-Ghazālī's presence in Irbil, in his *Taʾrīkh Irbil*

(History of Irbil) the historian Ibn al-Mustawfī al-Irbilī (d. 637/1239) reports that Shaykh Abu'l-Yaman Sabīh told of Aḥmad al-Ghazālī preaching to the people in the *ribāṭ* of Irbil.[101]

While exact dates cannot be obtained, Aḥmad al-Ghazālī traveled extensively, preaching in many towns and villages and calling people to remember and worship their Lord. Despite his itinerant lifestyle, it appears that Aḥmad al-Ghazālī did not travel very widely. There is no account of his having made the pilgrimage to Mecca, and nothing tells of his venturing any further than Baghdad to the south and west, nor further than Tabrīz to the north, and no further than his native region of Khurāsān in the east.

Last Years, Death, and Tomb

The last years of Aḥmad's life were spent in the city of Qazwīn, located about 175 kilometers northwest of present-day Tehran, then a stronghold of the Ismāʿīlī sect. Exactly when he settled here is unknown. He may have come to Qazwīn just after his brother's death in 505/1111 and spent most of his time providing instruction and seeking seclusion in a Sufi *khānqāh,* occasionally traveling to preach in other cities.[102] Alternatively, he may have settled here toward the last days of his life, after an itinerant life, moving from one Sufi *khānqāh* to another, preaching in one town and then the next.

If one takes the account in *Tabṣirat al-mubtadiʾ wa'tadhkirat al-muntahī* literally, it appears that al-Ghazālī spent these last years living in relative opulence, possessing a stable with many horses. But, as observed in Chapter 1, this account appears to be more an ideological representation than a historical transmission. Nonetheless, it is a possibility: supporting influential Sufis had long been a policy of the Saljuq rulers, and al-Ghazālī was said to have several high-ranking disciples. As noted in Chapter 1, Zakariyyā b. Muḥammad al-Qazwīnī counts Malikshāh among Shaykh Aḥmad's disciples.[103] Furthermore, Mughīth ad-Dīn al-Maḥmūd (511–25/1118–31), who ruled Iraq and western Persia, and his brother Aḥmad Sanjar (513–52/1119–57), who ruled Khurāsān and northern Persia, are both recorded as disciples of Aḥmad al-Ghazālī. Given that his more famous brother had continued interactions with the Saljuq rulers even when he had ostensibly tried to avoid them,[104] it is not unreasonable to think that Aḥmad al-Ghazālī also rubbed elbows with them on occasion. Nonetheless, the exact nature of this relationship will never be fully known.[105]

Shaykh Aḥmad al-Ghazālī most likely died in Qazwīn in Rabīʿ al-Ākhir 517/May 1123 517/1123 since this is the earliest and most detailed record of his death provided.[106] Nonetheless, most biographers list 520/1126 as the year of Aḥmad al-Ghazālī's death.[107] His tomb was at first located just outside Qazwīn. During the Safavid period, Shāh ʿAbbās (995–1038/1587–1629) expressed dissatisfaction with this location. A new tomb was thus constructed within the city, and several *murīds* (seekers) of a Sufi order whose *silsilah* was connected to al-Ghazālī transferred the remains.[108] The tomb remains to this day in a small mosque by the name of the Aḥmadī Mosque. It is a humble, well-kept structure, rarely recognized as a site of pilgrimage. A small courtyard bedecked with grape vines leads to the tomb in a basement underneath the mosque. The Qurʾānic verse *Everything perishes save His face* (28:88) adorns the wall of the tomb, followed by an Arabic inscription from the year 1362/1943:

> This is the tomb of the shaykh of shaykhs and the pole of poles, Majd ad-Dīn Abu'l-Futūḥ Aḥmad b. Muḥammad aṭ-Ṭūsī al-Ghazālī—may his inmost being be hallowed—who died in the year 520. He wore the mantle of poverty from the hand of Shaykh Abū Bakr an-Nassāj, and he via Abu'l-Qāsim al-Garakānī, he via Shaykh Abū ʿAlī al-Kātib, from Shaykh Abū ʿAlī ar-Rudabārī, from the head of the orders al-Junayd al-Baghdādī, from Sarī as-Saqaṭī, from Maʿrūf al-Karkhī, from the sultan of the friends of God ʿAlī b. Mūsā ar-Riḍāʾ—peace be upon him—and nine of the twenty-four known *silsilah*s wear the mantle at the hand of the one whose tomb this is.[109]

Part II

Practice and Teachings

Chapter 3

Aḥmad al-Ghazālī's Spiritual Practice

As seen in Chapter 2, Aḥmad al-Ghazālī's central focus was the sciences pertaining to recognition (*ʿirfān*) and following the path by which they are realized, what many refer to as Sufism. As seen in Chapter 1, as Sufism became more institutionalized, Aḥmad al-Ghazālī's connection to it became more stated in the hagiographical tradition. In order to separate the real Aḥmad from many of these ideological representations, it is best to study his particular spiritual discipline without the complications of identifying him with terms such as *Sufism* and *mysticism* that have come to assume very different meanings for people of varying ideologies. This chapter will examine Aḥmad al-Ghazālī's view of the prescriptions and proscriptions of the Shariah and identify the elements of his spiritual practice. Each practice will first be examined in light of its precedents within the Quran and the *ḥadīth*. Then Shaykh al-Ghazālī's own views will be presented. As the precedents for the practices of seclusion (*khalwah*) and audition (*samāʿ*) in the foundational sources of Islam are not as strong as other practices, they will be examined in relation to other authors of the Sufi tradition. It appears that supererogatory practices were an integral part of Aḥmad al-Ghazālī's life from his early years in Ṭūs until his death. Although his perception of spiritual discipline and practice may have changed over time, his authenticated writings do not provide enough information to discern such developments.

As noted by many of Aḥmad al-Ghazālī's biographers, both past and present, he is chiefly regarded as a Sufi. But what he may have understood by this term, what various biographers have understood by this term, and what many modern readers understand by this term varies to such an extent as to render the term problematic. Scholars such as Annemarie Schimmel, Margaret Smith, R.A. Nicholson, and

A.J. Arberry have identified Sufism as "the mystical dimension of Islam" or as "Islamic mysticism," and many have followed in their footsteps. But the words "mystical" and "mysticism" are part of the very problem. As Leigh Eric Schmidt observes, "There is hardly a more beleaguered category than 'mysticism' in the current academic study of religion."[1] Compounding the problem is the fact that other pietistic movements of the early middle Islamic period, such as the Karrāmiyyah, the Malāmatiyyah, the Sālimiyyah, and the Ḥakīmiyyah were incorporated into the Sufi movement.[2] Other individuals and factions in medieval Islam are also deserving of the term *mysticism*—as plastic as the moniker may be. The Ikhwān aṣ-Ṣafā᾿, or Brethren of Purity, Ismāʿīlī philosophers such as Abū Yaʿqūb as-Sijistānī (d. 361/971) and Ḥamīd ad-Dīn Kirmānī (d. ca. 412/1021), as well as such figures as Shihāb ad-Dīn Yaḥyā as-Suhrawardī (d. 587/1191) and Afḍal ad-Dīn Kāshānī (d. 610/1213–14) certainly have mystical tendencies, but they cannot be identified as part of the Sufi movement. To describe Sufism in a manner that neither incorporates the problematic cultural assumptions of the word *mysticism,* nor excludes other groups who had similar interests, perhaps the best one can say is that Sufism is a "powerful tradition of Muslim knowledge and practice bringing proximity to or mediation with God."[3] It was the most widespread pietistic movement of premodern Islam, and one that still exerts extensive influence in the modern period.

Spiritual Practice

As discussed in Chapter 1, several biographical dictionaries mention that Aḥmad al-Ghazālī took to the Sufi path at an early age, and that he practiced seclusion (*khalwah*) and isolation (*ʿuzlah*). But little more about his spiritual training and practice can be gleaned from these sources. Nonetheless, the outline of a spiritual practice comprised of adherence to the Shariah, *dhikr,* remembrance of death, night vigil (*tahajjud*), seclusion, and audition (*samāʿ*) can be constructed from his writings, especially the sermons and letters. Such practices were common among several pietistic movements at his time. Situated in relation to other Sufi writings, the writings of Aḥmad al-Ghazālī and about him are most notable for the fact that there is no mention of asceticism (*zuhd*) or of supererogatory fasting (*ṣawm*). It is most likely that the practices Aḥmad al-Ghazālī discusses are the ones in which he himself was engaged during his time in Nishapur and perhaps before; for in *at-Tajrīd fī kalimat at-tawḥīd* he indicates that one cannot be a guide on the spiritual path unless one has followed it oneself:

> The likeness of the wayfarer (*sālik*) on the path of the Hereafter is like a man who wayfares the path of the desert, witnessing it and knowing its way stations and its phases, its plains and its mountains. He knows them inch-by-inch; he knows them and is certain in both knowledge and experience. Just as it is suitable for this man to be a guide on the path of the desert, so, too, it is suitable for the wayfarer to be a guide on the path of the Hereafter.[4]

Given this assertion, the methods of wayfaring he prescribes in other writings most likely pertain to the path he himself had traveled. As is apparent from his letters, he clearly saw himself as an accomplished wayfarer fit to guide others on this path:

> Listen to these words with the ear of the heart and write them on the tablet of the soul and know me as a sincere intermediary and a sincere inheritor; for among the people [i.e., the Sufis] are those who when asked are inspired, granted success, and guided, and "encountering the people of good supports hearts."[5] Their words are a gift from the unseen, and their advice is free of faults. How can one prosper who has not seen one who prospers?[6]

The belief that his are the words of one who is inspired, guided, and qualified to teach others is also transmitted in the *Majālis*: "Whoever comes to me with the ears of the spirit, I shall transmit to him the secrets of the empyreal realm (*asrār al-malakūt*)."[7]

Shariah

Despite this emphasis on the unseen and the empyreal realm and occasional vituperations against mere legalism in religion, Aḥmad al-Ghazālī prescribes diligent observance of the Shariah for one who wishes to follow the *ṭarīqah*: "If you believe, then accept the outer holy law (*ash-sharʿ aẓ-ẓāhir al-muqaddas*) with all that you are."[8] As he advises a disciple in a letter, "Everyone who puts his foot on the path must make the edicts (*fatāwā*) of the religious law applicable to him."[9] This is in following a principle that he applies to all aspects of being human: "Giving oneself permission and interpreting for oneself is one thing, and finding permission from the source is another."[10] The Shariah is what gives permission pertaining to one's outer worldly affairs, while the *ṭarīqah* gives permission pertaining to one's inner spiritual journey; "for the Shariah and the *ṭarīqah* are two conditions for you to perform one cycle of prayer according to what you have been commanded: *And they are not ordered but to worship God, purifying for Him the religion* (Quran 98:6)."[11] Thus, although the realities (*ma'ānī*) perceived by traveling the spiritual path betray the limitations of the Shariah, on the level of the Shariah itself they do not supplant its prescriptions or diminishes its proscriptions. Given his training, the fact that he was qualified to teach at both the Tājiyyah and Niẓāmiyyah madrasahs, and that he was counted by 'Ayn al-Quḍāt Hamadānī as one of only ten people qualified in both the outward and inward sciences, al-Ghazālī likely held a position similar to that articulated by Abu Naṣr as-Sarraj, "The Sufis agree with the jurists and the traditionists regarding their teachings; they accept their disciplines (*'ulūm*) and do not oppose them as regards their meanings and methods, since they avoid innovation and following caprice, while conforming to the established pattern and example of tradition. They are allied with them in their assent to an affirmation of all aspects of their disciplines."[12]

Aḥmad al-Ghazālī often rails against the inadequacy of a religion confined to superficial legalisms. He is adamant in maintaining the need for sincerity that goes beyond the perfunctory performance of prescribed rituals, citing a famous *ḥadīth*: "How many fast, yet receive nothing from fasting but hunger and thirst? How many pray, yet receive nothing from prayer but exhaustion and trouble?"[13] Through his own words he indicates the vacuity of mere observance:

> How many a harvest of obedience which at the moment of death—*We shall advance upon what work they have done and make it as scattered dust* (25:23)—is given to the wind of needlessness. How many an exalted breast which in the throes of death—*And there appeared to them from God what they had not been reckoning* (39:47)—they destroy.[14]

Although the foundation of Aḥmad al-Ghazālī's spiritual practice and wayfaring is the standard Islamic practice, for him, like many Sufis before, the law in and of itself is a dead husk. To experience its vitality the wayfarer must penetrate into the reality (*ma'nā*) of that which the law enjoins; for where the jurist enjoins the performance of actions, the seeker enjoins the purification of hearts. Aḥmad illustrates this principle in the *Majālis* by transmitting an apocryphal account of an old madman who was questioned by Imām ash-Shāfiʿī (d. 205/820) and Imām Aḥmad b. Ḥanbal (d. 241/855) as to what a man must do when he has missed the five daily prayers:

> The old man said, "This is a heart with bad character; opposition has clouded it, and the rust of sins has blackened it. If he enters the furnace of the fires of grief and the burning of regret, perhaps he will return." Aḥmad [b. Ḥanbal] fell unconscious before him, amazed by his words. When wisdom falls upon the ears of pure hearts, they are drawn to it. The jurist says, "Perform the five prayers," and they say, "Treat the forgetfulness of the heart."[15]

From this perspective, the outer actions enjoined by the Shariah and the inner sincerity cultivated by the Sufi path are both essential. As ʿAbdullāh Ansārī puts it, "Without the reality (*ḥaqīqah*) the Shariah is useless; and without the Shariah, the *ḥaqīqah* is useless. Anyone who does not act in accord with both is useless."[16] Employing this same dichotomy between Shariah and *ḥaqīqah*, Maybudī sees an allusion to this relationship in the Quran, when it states, *For each among you We have appointed a road and a way* (5:48):

> The road is the Shariah and the way is the *ḥaqīqah*. The road is the customs of Shariah, and the way is the road toward the Real. The road is what Muṣṭafā [i.e., the Prophet Muhammad] brought, and the way is a lamp that the Real holds next to the heart. The road is following the Shariah, and the way is gaining access to the light of that lamp. The road is that message that you heard from the Prophet. The way is that light that you find in the secret core. The Shariah is for everyone. The *ḥaqīqah* is for some.[17]

For Aḥmad al-Ghazālī, the obligatory prayer is essential for following both the Shariah and the Sufi path, not simply because it is enjoined but because it has a reality that pertains to the inner dimensions of the human being:

> "The first thing for which man is called to account is prayer."[18] "The coolness of my eye is made in prayer."[19] Do you not have a body, a spirit, and a heart? Likewise

> for the prayer there is a body, which is the movements and the action, a heart, which is presence (*al-ḥuḍūr*), and a spirit, which is being absent from remembrance (*dhikr*) in the witnessing of The Remembered, and that is "the coolness of the eye."[20]

From this perspective, the ritual prayer is a mode of that practice and principle that is most central to Aḥmad al-Ghazālī's teachings, the remembrance of God (*dhikr Allāh*). As he says in a sermon, "Perform remembrance perpetually, for it is the hard cash of the ritual prayer."[21] Like remembrance, prayer has levels and degrees of participation. In one sense, the goal of the Sufi path could be seen as the performance of the ritual prayer with complete sincerity (*ikhlāṣ*). For according to al-Ghazālī, when prayer is performed with sincere intention and a pure heart, "the cover is lifted and one sees the unseen from the beauty of the worshipped, then the prayer employs him, he does not perform the prayer."[22] At this level of realization wherein one prays with full presence of heart, prayer becomes an act that serves not only the worshipper but serves also to sustain the world: "two light rounds of prayer in the middle of the night are accepted, sufficing for the people of the earth."[23]

Dhikr

Dhikr, which indicates remembrance of God and the invocation of God, has long been considered the axis around which all other dimensions of Sufi practice rotate. As Ibn ʿAṭāʾillāh as-Skandārī (d. 709/1309) writes, "The remembrance of God is the key to prosperity and the luminary of spirits . . . it is the fundamental support of the Sufi path and sustenance for the people of truth."[24] This central idea follows on the injunction to remember God or remember or invoke the name of God that is found throughout the Quran. In some verses it is joined to specific acts, as when one is told to invoke the name of God over sacrificial animals (e.g., 5:4, 6:118–119), or when one is told to "remember God" upon hearing the Quran recited (7:204–205). But it more often appears as a general injunction, as in 73:8: *So remember the Name of thy Lord and devote thyself to Him with complete devotion;* 76:25: *And remember the Name of thy Lord morning and evening* (cf. 3:41); and 33:41: *Remember God with frequent remembrance*. From a Quranic perspective, *dhikr* engenders happiness in this life and the next—*and remember God much, that haply you may prosper* (62:10)—and is that through which human beings can find peace: *Truly God leads astray whomsoever He will and guides to Himself whosoever turns in repentance—those who believe and whose hearts are at peace in the remembrance of God. Are not hearts at peace in the remembrance of God?* (13:27–28). In contrast, the hearts of disbelievers are said to be *hardened to the remembrance of God* (39:22).

In accord with this central Quranic message, Aḥmad al-Ghazālī, like most adherents of Sufi Islam before and after him, saw remembrance as the axis of the spiritual life. In one of his sessions he goes so far as to say, "There is no occupation but the remembrance of God. It is the sword of God encircling the hearts of the prophets and saints, cutting their hearts off from what He does not love to be joined to them."[25] And in a letter he tells a disciple that *dhikr* is a necessary part of being human: "Just as there is something in man that lives by bread and water, so, too, there is something in man that lives by the remembrance of God."[26] He thus enjoins his followers to remember God at all times, since it is the heart of prayer. From this perspective, *dhikr* entails a degree of belief or sincerity that is beyond the injunctions followed by most believers. Long before al-Ghazālī, *dhikr* had become a complex term through which the whole of the Sufi path was described. As al-Kalabādhī writes, "*Dhikr* is divided into several kinds: The first is the remembrance of the heart, which is that the Remembered not be forgotten, but remembered. The second is remembering the attributes of the Remembered and the third is witnessing the Remembered, such that one is annihilated from remembrance because the attributes of the Remembered annihilate you from your attributes and you are annihilated from remembrance."[27]

Dhikr and spiritual love (*ʿishq*) can be understood as the two central themes of al-Ghazālī's teachings. The whole of the *Sawāniḥ* can be read as a commentary on the mysteries of spiritual love and divine love and the whole of *at-Tajrīd fī kalimat at-tawḥīd* can be read as a guide to the levels of *dhikr*. *Dhikr* is also discussed extensively in the *Majālis*. It is of such importance for al-Ghazālī that all other dimensions of his spiritual practice can be seen as supports for *dhikr* or as extensions of it, as demonstrated in his discussion of ritual prayer. For those who can be identified as adherents to the school of love, love and the remembrance are intimately intertwined. In this respect, Maybudī speaks of drinking "the wine of love from the cup of *dhikr*."[28]

In general discussions regarding the practice of *dhikr*, Aḥmad al-Ghazālī implores one to go beyond the remembrance and the rememberer (*dhākir*) to the Remembered (*al-madhkūr*). In one of his sessions, he responds to a question regarding how one remembers, "Say 'Allāh' until He says 'My servant.' Oh Muslims! We do not cease saying 'Allāh' until we forget saying 'Allāh,' for this is His word, *And remember thy Lord when thou dost forget* (18:25). That is, when you forget the name remember the Named." The questioner then said, "But I have forgotten remembrance." To which Aḥmad responded, "It is incumbent upon you to forget the rememberer (*dhākir*), for the remembrance of the rememberer is mixed with his remembrance of the Remembered (*al-madhkūr*)." To which the man responded, "I have forgotten the remembrance and the rememberer." Shaykh Aḥmad replied:

> The entire point remains, it remains for you to forget that you are one who forgets. For your knowledge of forgetting is the joy of the expression of unity (*kalām at-tawḥīd*). So when one hears one is silent, for his silence is the forgetting of forgetting. If one says, "I forgot," that is the remembrance of forgetting. In faith there is a taste that does not cease to say "Allāh" until the event (*al-khuṭṭah*) is spread before him, and when the event is spread, the locus of remembrance envelops him and the tear is expanded instantly.[29]

Here, the event refers to the realities of the grave and the Day of Judgment and other matters pertaining to the Hereafter that are described in the Quran and the Hadith. Most Muslims understand the punishments and blessings described in such accounts as being experienced after corporeal death. But for many Sufis they are realities that lie within the human being and are realized as one travels the path toward God. In describing this aspect of the path, ʿAyn al-Quḍāt writes, "The first thing that becomes known to the wayfarer concerning the world of the Hereafter is the states of the grave. . . . These are all in the interior of man, since they arise from him. No doubt, they are connected to him."[30]

The stage of forgetting everything and remembering only the Remembered can be understood as the highest level of remembrance, which in the *Tajrīd* corresponds to "the provision of the secret core" of the spiritual wayfarer. As Najm ad-Dīn Kubrā (d. 618/1221), a spiritual descendant of Aḥmad al-Ghazālī, writes in speaking of the stages of remembrance as degrees of immersion (*istighrāq*), "The third immersion is the descending of remembrance into one's secret core. This is the disappearance of the rememberer from the remembrance in the Remembered."[31] But whereas al-Ghazālī emphasizes forgetting everything because it is nothing next to the Remembered, Kubrā emphasizes the immersion of what is less real in what is the Real Itself.

The stages of the path whereby one reaches this degree of *dhikr* are alluded to in al-Ghazālī's letters and sessions, but more extensive details are provided in the *Tajrīd.* In one of his sessions, al-Ghazālī states that when Abu'l-Ḥusayn an-Nūrī was asked, "How does one arrive at recognition (*ʿirfān*), he answered, "It is seven oceans of fire and light. When you cross it 'a fish swallows you'; it swallows the first and the last."[32] In another session, al-Ghazālī speaks of the stages of creation as seven, basing this on the Quranic testimony that God created seven heavens: *Have you not considered how God created the seven heavens one upon another, and made the moon a light therein and made the sun a lamp?* (Quran 75:15–16; cf. e.g. 2:29, 41:12, 65:12, 67:3, 71:15). The Shaykh says,

> Encounter the stages of your created nature as seven skies. The moon of the stages of your created nature is your heart and its sun is your spirit. The first thing to come to the Muslim in *dhikr* is a light appearing on the horizon of his heart, that is the crescent moon. Where is its night? He does not cease to increase in *dhikr* and his heart inclines to the encounter (*al-muwājahah*) with His saying, *"I have turned my face"* (6:79).[33] Then when he becomes the son of fourteen [stages], he says, "My heart has seen my Lord." So he becomes a witnesser and one witnessed."

The number seven also defines al-Ghazālī's vision of the spiritual path in the *Tajrīd*, where he divides the types of being into praiseworthy and blameworthy. The praiseworthy being of man corresponds to bounty (*faḍl*) and the blameworthy being corresponds to justice (*ʿadl*). These correspond to the dimensions of the human being that manifest different aspects of God's Attributes. Thus the praiseworthy dimension of the human being manifests the names pertaining to God's Bounty or Mercy, while the blameworthy dimension of the human being manifests God's Justice or Wrath. The process of spiritual purification is thus one wherein the Divine Attributes of Bounty and Mercy come to predominate over the Attributes of Justice and Wrath in accordance with the *ḥadīth qudsī*:"Verily My Mercy takes precedence over My Wrath."[34] Both the dimension of bounty and the dimension of justice can be considered to correspond to different categories of believers in accord with which attributes they may manifest more fully. According to Shaykh Aḥmad, what separates them is that the people of bounty take the form and meaning of "No god but God," while the people of justice take the expression of "No god but God" "in its form without its meaning. They adorn their outward natures with saying and their inward natures with disbelief, and their hearts are blackened, darkened."[35] To be a person of bounty is for Aḥmad al-Ghazālī the beginning of the Sufi path. It requires that one seek intimacy with none but God, relying only on Him. At this level, *dhikr* dwells in "the kingdom of the spirit." Al-Ghazālī refers to wayfarers at this level as the lovers (*al-ʿāshiqūn*) beyond whom are the elect of the elect who are the unveilers (*kāshifūn*) for whom *dhikr* dwells in the secret core.[36]

The first two-thirds of *at-Tajrīd* focus on making sharp distinctions between the people of justice and the people of bounty. But in the last third of the text, al-Ghazālī embarks on a technical explanation of the process by which the wayfarer employs different formulas of *dhikr* as he travels the path. His presentation is based on a delineation of the oppositions between bounty and justice within the human being. Bounty comprises eight parts: sense perception, understanding, intellect, outer heart, heart, spirit, secret core, and aspiration, while justice comprises seven parts: sense perception, preoccupation, caprice, murkiness of soul, the soul, humanness, and nature. Justice represents the anticipated fire, and bounty represents the light of *tawḥīd*. The seven attributes of justice stand opposite the attributes of bounty, but aspiration has no counterpart among the attributes of justice, implying that it is at a stage beyond duality.

As one progresses on the path, the lights of bounty rise over the attributes pertaining to justice and obliterate them. In testifying to unity (*tawḥīd*), the light of *tawḥīd* rises over the part pertaining to bounty, then through the part pertaining to bounty casts a light on the part pertaining to justice that obliterates its darkness and transforms it until it ceases to be a place of darkness and fire. The attributes of bounty appear to correspond to the seven oceans of light to which an-Nūrī is said to have referred in the *Majālis*, with the attributes of justice referring to the seven oceans of fire. The *himmah*, or aspiration, that lies beyond the duality of these oppositions would then correspond to the fish that swallows all who have ventured to that level, meaning that human aspiration has been consumed by Divine aspiration, such that one is in complete submission to God's will.

It is from the light of this *himmah* that light shines first on the secret core and then on the following attributes of bounty. As it passes from one attribute to the next it wipes out the darkness of the corresponding attribute of justice. These attributes of justice are then like the first part of the *shahādah*, "No god," the negation that only finds its purpose in the second part of the *shahādah*, "but God," the affirmation.

Thus the light of affirmation obliterates the darkness of negation. As the light of the *shahādah* comes to prevail, it shines through the seven attributes pertaining to bounty upon the seven attributes pertaining to justice,[37] then

> When the darkness of the negation vanishes by the light of affirmation, it illuminates the world of your being pertaining to justice with that light and its parts pertaining to justice are transformed into parts pertaining to bounty. Thus the blameworthy sense perception becomes a praiseworthy sense perception, caprice becomes intellect, murkiness of soul becomes an outer heart, humanness becomes spirit, nature becomes a secret core, and satan becomes a king. This is alluded to in the saying of the Prophet "My satan has submitted."[38]

The process whereby the attributes of bounty come to predominate over those of justice comprises three way stations that correspond to three worlds. In his presentation of these way stations, al-Ghazālī employs a standard Sufi division of the inner regions of the human being into three fundamental levels—heart (*qalb*), spirit (*rūḥ*), and secret core (*sirr*)—with the heart representing the outermost or lowest level and the secret core representing the most interior or highest level of the human being. As the Shaykh writes,

> The heart, the spirit, and the secret core are analogous to a pearl in a shell that is within a box, or a bird in a cage that is within a house. The box and the house are analogous to the heart, the cage and the shell are analogous to the spirit, and the bird and the pearl are analogous to the secret core. Whenever you do not reach the house, you do not reach the cage, and whenever you do not reach the cage, you will not reach Me. Likewise, whenever you do not reach the heart, you do not reach the spirit, and whenever you do not reach the spirit, you do not reach the secret core.[39]

In other words, "there is no reaching the world of spirits except after traversing the world of hearts, and there is no reaching the world of secret cores except after traversing the world of spirits."[40] This, however, is only an approximation to help one understand the process of traveling the path. In reality, "the world of spirits is bigger than the world of hearts and the world of secret cores is bigger than the world of spirits."[41] The world of secret cores is then the province of the recognizers, the world of spirits is the province of the lovers, and the world of hearts is the province of the penitent. Aḥmad al-Ghazālī also sees levels below these three: the soul is the province of the defiers, humanness is the province of the disbelievers, and base nature is the province of the hypocrites. The lowest realms are "the abysses and the lowest levels of the world of justice."[42] Those who are in these lowest realms, those of nature and humanness, "their eyes are blinded from desiring the highest, their desire is attached to the lowest, and their aspirations cling to the shares of this world, which is the still corpse in the animals' stable."[43] Those at the beginning of the spiritual path strive to separate themselves from these worlds through spiritual exercises, but something of these worlds remains so long as their religious outlook remains defined by hope for Paradise and fear of Hell. Though they may aspire to that which is higher, it distracts them from that which is Highest.[44] Rather than seeking reward, they must worship *desiring the Face of God* (6:52). But as this text is written for those who already incline to the spiritual path, its focus is on the process of interiorizing the *dhikr* until, when one is in the realm of the secret core, "[He] does not hear except from the unseen and does not see except from the unseen."[45]

So long as the wayfarer's attributes of justice have not submitted, he remains in the first way station, the world of annihilation (*ʿālam al-fanāʾ*), since it is here that his blameworthy attributes are erased. The one at this level must practice the invocation of the *shahādah*, "No god but God," since it negates the darkness of justice with the light of bounty. He is still in the early stages of wayfaring, in which the soul (*nafs*) and its blameworthy attributes predominate. He is therefore in need of that which will negate and erase such attributes, and this is the negation (*nafy*) of the *shahādah*, "No god." The affirmation (*ithbāt*) of the *shahādah*, "but God," is then the provision of hearts (*rizq al-qulūb*), and when the *shahādah*'s fullness is realized, it is the unveiler of hearts (*kāshif al-qulūb*).

When all of the attributes of justice have been erased or illuminated, the wayfarer moves to the second way station, the world of attraction (*ʿālam al-jadhabiyyah*), where he is no longer attracted to the darkness of the attributes of justice, but only to the Divine Kingdom. At this stage, blameworthy attributes have subsided, and the praiseworthy attributes predominate. One is therefore able to use the name *Allāh* in his *dhikr*, since it strengthens the praiseworthy attributes and increases one in the affirmation of God's incomparability (*tanzīh*).[46] In the name *Allāh* there lies the provision of spirits (*rizq al-arwāḥ*), and when its fullness is realized, it is the unveiler of spirits (*kāshif al-arwāḥ*).

The third way station is the world of possession (*ʿālam al-qabḍ*), wherein one persists in saying, "*Huwa Huwa*" ("He is He" or "Him, Him"). Here the turbidity of one's blameworthy attributes has vanished completely, the lights of the praiseworthy attributes have risen, and one is connected to the Real with no intermediary.[47] In this way station, "You become non-existent in relation to yourself and existent in relation to Him, annihilated in relation to yourself and subsisting in relation to Him. So make your remembrance *Huwa, Huwa,* for the existent is *Huwa* and the subsisting is *Huwa.*"[48] *Huwa* is then the provision of the secret cores (*rizq al-asrār*), and when its fullness is realized it is the unveiler of secret cores (*kāshif al-asrār*). In the world of possession, the wayfarer is fully possessed by the Real such that he has complete self-disposal (*taṣarruf*) through God, with no intermediary. This is the point in which the Divine will is said to have swallowed human aspiration (*himmah*).

The son of fourteen to which al-Ghazālī refers in the *Majālis* is the son of the fourteen stages of justice and bounty who has passed beyond them into the self-disposal of the world of Divine possession.[49] He has traveled through the way stations of the three worlds, and his invocation has reached the point where the invoker and the invocation have been completely absorbed in the Invoked. As Maybudī puts it in his commentary on Quran 2:121,

> The Pīr of the Path said, "The servant reaches a place in remembrance where the tongue reaches the heart, the heart reaches the spirit, the spirit reaches the secret core, and the secret core reaches the Light. The heart says to the tongue, "Silence!" The spirit says to the heart, "Silence!" The secret core says to the spirit, "Silence!" God says to the wayfarer, "My servant, for some time you have been speaking. Now I will speak, and you will listen."[50]

Remembrance of Death

For many Muslims, the remembrance of God is closely tied to remembering death, for whoever remembers his Lord knows that he will meet Him when he dies and is at all times on guard to die in a state of reverence for God, in *taqwā*. The remembrance of death has, therefore, always been an intrinsic dimension of Muslim religious life. As T.J. Winter observes, "From the first days of the Muslim experience the remembrance of death and the chastening facts of eschatology provided a characteristic underpinning to the devotional life."[51] Indeed, reminders of death permeate the entire Quran: *No soul knows in what land it shall die* (31:34); *Every soul tastes death* (3:185, 21:35, 29:57); *Say, "Fleeing will not benefit you if you flee from death or killing"* (33:17). The verb "to die," *mātᵃ/yamūtᵘ*, and its derivatives occur no less than 173 times in the Quran and is often combined with the mention of the reckoning that is to come: *Say, "The death from which you shrink will surely meet you, and afterward you will be returned unto the Knower of the invisible and the visible, and He will tell what you were doing"* (42:8).

Both the revelation and the teachings of its Messenger urge Muslims to work not for this life, but for the Hereafter: *Say, "The goods of the world are few and the hereafter is better for those who fear [God]"* (4:77); *Whosoever desires the harvest of the Hereafter, We shall give him increase in his tillage; and who desires the tillage of this world, We shall give him of it, but in the world to come he will have no share"* (42:20). As if commenting on such Quranic verses, the Prophet taught his followers, "Whosoever abhors meeting with God, God abhors meeting with him."[52] And he counted the remembrance of death as the mark of a person's intelligence: "The intelligent person is one who judges himself and acts for what follows death."[53]

Following upon such teachings, Sufis have long seen the remembrance of death as a central component of spiritual wayfaring—so much so that a motto of those who advocate a Sufi way has long been "Die before you die."[54] Aḥmad al-Ghazālī is thus in good company when in a sermon he enjoins his audience:

> Grab the hair upon your face, beat your head on the wall and say, "Death, death!" You will wake up. When your soul assents to death say, "Death is a path, where is the increase?" . . . Whoever dies in remembrance of God is taken up as one who is pious and resurrected as one well-sated.[55]

Like his brother Abū Ḥāmid, the fortieth and longest book of whose *Iḥyāʾ* is entitled "The Remembrance of Death and the Afterlife,"[56] Aḥmad al-Ghazālī saw the remembrance of death as a necessary condition of spiritual wayfaring. This is most evident in his letters and sessions. Like the Quran itself, his sermons sometimes read as a constant reminder of death and the judgment to follow. In the very first session he tells his audience, "You have wasted many years and you make excuses for the rest and perhaps this is your last day and your last night."[57] Remembrance of death is of the utmost importance because the spiritual path is long and the hour is not known to any:

> Say to your soul, "You have two affairs before you. If you are to be saved from this steep path, then the efforts of the remainder of your life are little in relation to this grave matter (*khaṭr*). If you are not saved, then the misery of endlessness (*abad*) will have the efforts of ten days joined to it." This is the wisdom of one who is conscious of it.[58]

The relentlessness with which Aḥmad al-Ghazālī continually preaches the remembrance of death is seen in his response to a member of the audience who pleads, "Be gentle with us." To this he responds, "O depraved ones, you are sleeping and the time is passing by you to your recompense and your death. How can I be gentle with you when the path is long?"[59] In another instance, when asked about the truth of astrologers' predictions, he replies:

> Whether the attainment of astrological conjunctions (*qirānāt*) is true or not, whether the astrologers lie or tell the truth—death, there is no doubt about it, and no one escapes from it. The attainment of them [the conjunctions] is death. If you are heedless of death, your conjunction occurs and if you are heedless of God, your conjunction occurs, a conjunction with Satan: *And he who is blind to the remembrance of the Merciful, We appoint for him a Satan, so he is a companion (qarīn) unto him* (43:37).[60]

The manner in which Shaykh Aḥmad addresses death throughout the sessions is evident in more compact form in the *ʿAyniyyah,* throughout the first half of which he enjoins ʿAyn al-Quḍāt to remember death: "Being aware of the attack of death by night is a condition and remembering the grave is part of the Shariah." As in the *Majālis,* he then weaves together several Quranic verses to remind his disciple of the reckoning that death must entail:

> *Before a day comes* (2:254, 14:31, 31:43, 42:47) on which they say, *"Oh that we had followed God and followed a messenger"* (33:44). *Before a day comes* wherein it does not profit to say, "I wish I had observed the Command of God and the messenger."[61] Before the coming of the angel of death

> and there is the request, *"If only you would delay me until a near moment"* (63:10), and His answer, *"Now! Yet you have disobeyed and were among the corrupt"* (10:91); and the threat, *"But did you not swear before that there would be no abandoning?"* (14:44); and the call, *"A barrier between them and what they desire"* (34:54).[62]

He then turns from the Quran to verses of poetry, sayings attributed to ʿAlī b. Abī Ṭālib, and Arabic proverbs to drive the point home:

> How many a mountain have men exalted in eminence,
> Then they pass, and the mountain remains a mountain?
>
> "Increase the remembrance of the Destroyer of pleasures" is a command,[63] and "Death suffices as an answer" is a cure.[64] "Today in the round, tomorrow in the ground."
>
> What will you say when you are called and do not answer?
> When you are asked and are in the throes of death?
>
> What will you say when you have no proof?
> When the spoiler of pleasures comes upon you?
>
> *Do not affairs return to God?* (42:53)
>
> Since your guide is an evil-teaching soul,
> Do not imagine that your affair will be triumphant.
>
> In the darkness of heedlessness and in the sleep of pride,
> I fear that when you awake, it will be the Day.[65]

This combination of poetry, proverbs, Quran, and Hadith, woven with Shaykh al-Ghazālī's Persian prose produces an immediacy that echoes the urgency of remembering death. This same tone is found in his sessions and letters and forms an essential component of the message he delivered to his disciples and most likely of his own spiritual practice.

Although most who attended Aḥmad's public sessions would most likely have understood his discussions of death as a reference to physical death, he was alluding to spiritual death, or what Maybudī refers to as "inner death" (*marg-i bāṭin*) as opposed to "outer death" (*marg-i ẓāhir*). This inner spiritual death would also have been the subject of Aḥmad's private letters. He does not elaborate on this point, but in various passages of the *Tamhīdāt,* his disciple ʿAyn al-Quḍāt provides details regarding the nature of spiritual death, which as he puts it is real death:[66] "According to us death is this, that one die from anything except the Beloved so that he finds all living through the Beloved and comes to live through the Beloved. Then you realize within yourself what death is."[67] From this perspective, real death is the inner death wherein the self is annihilated before God before being reborn such that one may then subsist in and through God. As ʿAyn al-Quḍāt puts it, "when you are you and you are caught up with yourself, you are not. And when you are not you, you will be entirely yourself." Phrasing this principle with more clarity, Maybudī states, "Inner death is that one dies in himself from himself without himself and comes to life from the Real in the Real with the Real."[68]

Regarding the relationship between inner spiritual death and outer corporeal death, ʿAyn al-Quḍāt writes, "Oh friend! In that world all is life within life. And in this world all is death within death. Until you transcend death, you will not attain life: *And surely the Abode of the Hereafter is life indeed, if they but knew* (29:64)."[69] To attain to "life within life," "the wayfarer must be born two times." The first is from his mother into this world, the second is "to be born from oneself" in order to see the world of subsistence.[70] The practice of remembering death is thus for one to "Know that there is a death beyond the death of this physical mold and realize that there is another life besides that of this physical mold."[71] Thus by embracing death, one moves toward that life within love to which true lovers aspire. In this vein Maybudī writes, "Until you die in yourself, you will not come to life through the Real. Die, O friend, if you want to live!"[72]

Night Vigil

As seen in his calls to remember death, Aḥmad al-Ghazālī warned his audience to be wary of sleep and advised ʿAyn al-Quḍāt that night is the time for remembrance. Night vigil (*tahajjud*) is intrinsic to the spiritual discipline he enjoins. This follows upon the injunction of the Quran: *Stay up in vigil at night, for there is benefit in that for you* (17:79), and the custom of the Prophet Muḥammad, who was known to stand in prayer at night until his feet were swollen. Regarding the efficacy of night prayers, the Prophet is reported to have said, "Every night our Lord descends to the lowest heaven when the last third of the night remains, saying, 'Who calls upon Me, I answer him. Who asks of Me, I give to him, and who asks forgiveness of Me, I forgive him.'"[73]

In the first session recorded in the *Majālis*, al-Ghazālī advises his listeners to spend the night in prayer. If they are too tired to stand, he advises them to continue praying while sitting, and if sleep overcomes them, he advises them to "sleep while the heart is remembering."[74] From his perspective, night vigil is more than a devotional activity—it is a practice wherein one's true nature is sought. Aḥmad al-Ghazālī and others have referred to this true nature as one's "moment" (*waqt*): "Devote your night to prostration and seek your moment in it. Devote your night to cycles of prayer (*rukū*ʿ) and the witness of your moment in it."[75] This "moment" is referred to in several other sessions with reference to the *ḥadīth*: "I have a moment with God which no angel brought nigh, nor prophet sent out beholds (*yaṭṭaliʿu*)."[76] In another session, he elevates the source of this sentiment, citing it as a *ḥadīth qudsī*: "The secret between Me and My servant which no angel brought nigh nor prophet sent out beholds."[77] To know one's moment is to be fully present to one's true self, what Aḥmad al-Ghazālī refers to as the secret (*sirr*) in *at-Tajrīd*. It is to have conquered the crispations and colorations (*talwīn*) of temporality to achieve the station of spiritual fixity (*tamkīn*) in which one is no longer the slave of passing moments, but their master. As al-Ghazālī writes of the station of fixity in the *Sawāniḥ*, "Here he is the master of the moment. When he descends to the sky of the world he will be over the moment, time will not be over him, and he will be free from the moment."[78] To find one's moment in night vigil can thus be seen as an essential practice for mastering one's moment in the state of spiritual fixity that is beyond all duality.

For al-Ghazālī, "'He who prays at night, his face is beautiful during the day, and it comes to hearts that you are a righteous (*ṣāliḥ*) man."[79] When questioned about the meaning of the saying that is transmitted in the manner of a *ḥadīth qudsī*—"He lies who claims love for Me then sleeps from Me when the night comes upon him,"[80]—he gives a commentary which also provides instructions as to how one should perform vigil:

> That is—ignores Me, and all of you have slept from Him, though you proceed along the paths. If you sleep in remembrance of Him and perform the ablution after the vigil fatigues you, then you have slept to Him or with Him, not from Him. Strive in your striving and perform night vigil. When the vigil fatigues you and sleep and tiredness overcome you, *Then God is watchful over you* (4:2).[81]

In a letter to a disciple, he provides specific instructions and identifies Friday as the best night for vigil:

> Depriving yourself of sleep on Friday night is a prudent act; the hard cash (*naqd*) of manhood appears therein.[82] In the beginning of the night pray, praise, and perform the ablution forty times. Being clean and performing the major ablution before dawn on Friday night is beautiful. Awaiting the return of good fortune (*dawlat*) without separation (*tamyīz*) on Friday night, on condition that the invocation is constant, will undoubtedly produce a result. If it does not produce a result in one night, there is no reason for anguish, for it is expected that grocers put a rock in the scales.[83] If one asks for honesty and sincerity from someone and spends many nights apologizing, that would not be so incredible. "I could spend a thousand years hoping for You" is the glorification from those whose souls are burning. One must persist in remembrance, and in this watchfulness; sleeping for the blink of an eye on Friday night would break the ablution. Preparing for it on Thursday and eating no food on Friday night would be helpful in attaining this objective.[84]

Khalwah and ʿUzlah

Though it is not discussed extensively in his writings, it is evident from the biographical dictionaries that Aḥmad al-Ghazālī, like Muslim devotees before and after him, is known to have practiced spiritual seclusion (*khalwah*) and isolation (*ʿuzlah*). That he was a proponent of this practice is supported by a passage in the sessions: "Blessed is he who has a cell for seclusion in his house."[85] But since he does not speak of seclusion in detail in his writings or sessions, one must look to other authors in order to examine this practice, with the caveat that whatever one can say regarding the practice of *khalwah* may be less representative of Aḥmad al-Ghazālī's practice than the other elements examined in this chapter. It should also be noted that Shams ad-Dīn Tabrīzī writes of Shaykh Aḥmad, "He did not sit in any of these forty-day seclusions, for that is an innovation in the religion of Muhammad. Muhammad never sat in a forty-day seclusion. That is in the story of Moses. Read, *And behold We appointed for Moses forty nights* (2:51)."[86] It may, nonetheless, be the case that Aḥmad engaged in shorter seclusions, as did many Sufi practitioners.

Unlike the practice of *dhikr* and the practice of night vigil (*tahajjud*), the Quranic foundations for the practices of *khalwah* and *ʿuzlah* are more allusive, and *khalwah* in particular is not discussed in the *ḥadīth*. Some have taken as justification for these practices two Quranic verses in which the word *iʿtizāl*, deriving from the same root as *ʿuzlah*, occurs. In the first instance, God tells the Companions of the Cave, *So when you have withdrawn from them (iʿtazaltumūhum) and what they serve, excepting God, take refuge in the cave. Your Lord will unfold to you from His mercy, and will furnish you with a gentle issue in your affair* (18:16). The second refers to Abraham, who for many Sufis represents the archetype of spiritual withdrawal, as when he said to his tribe:

> *"Now I will withdraw from you and that which you call upon apart from God; I call upon my Lord, and haply I shall not be, in calling upon my Lord, wretched." So when he withdrew from them and that which they were serving, apart from God, We gave him Isaac and Jacob, and each we made a Prophet: and We gave them of Our mercy, and We ordained for them a sublime, faithful, renown.* (19:48–49)

But as Aḥmad's brother Abū Ḥāmid al-Ghazālī observes in the *Kitāb Ādāb al-ʿuzlah* (Proper Conduct in Retreat) of the *Iḥyāʾ*, these verses are a weak support for the Sufi practice. In both of these Quranic stories, believers are retreating from companionship with nonbelievers and the injustices of their societies, whereas the Sufi retreat is a withdrawal from the society of "believers."[87] As such, the best support for this practice is to be found in the *ḥadīth* or the *sunnah* (prophetic practice), though there is no direct support for what was to become the standard practice of the spiritual retreat.

Some Sūfīs refer to God's appointing to Moses forty nights of seclusion as another prophetic prototype for the practice of seclusion.[88] Nonetheless, the classic example of seclusion to which many in the Sufi tradition refer is the Prophet Muḥammad's retreat on Mount Ḥirāʾ where he first received the revelation. As his wife ʿĀʾishah bint Abī Bakr (d. 58/678) is reported to have said, "Seclusion was made beloved to him, and he would seclude [himself] in the cave of Ḥirāʾ."[89] But after the revelation came and he was commanded to preach to the people of Mecca, he seems to have ceased this practice. The closest practice to it during the period of prophethood is that of *iʿtikāf*, literally "clinging." In this practice, the Prophet and some of his companions would remain in the Mosque for several days devoted solely to worship (*ʿibādah*), leaving only for personal necessities or calls of nature. This practice was associated mostly with the month of Ramaḍān, especially the last ten days,[90] though it was practiced at other times as well. Fasting was a requirement for *iʿtīkāf*, and the practitioner was to designate the number of days intended before beginning.

With such minimal requirements, the practice of *iʿtizāl* is a far cry from the practice of seclusion that was to develop among the Sufis. Just where and how this practice began is difficult to say. It appears that some early Muslims such as Sufyān ath-Thawrī (d. 161/777–78) took *ḥadīth* such as, "There will come trials (*fitan*) at the beginning of which are those who call to the fire. For you to die while clinging to the trunk of a tree would be better than for you to follow any of them" as a call to withdraw with their religion in tact, lest it be corrupted by society at large.[91] The earlier texts seem to indicate that *khalwah* and *ʿuzlah* were interchangeable terms referring not to a specific form of secluded remembrance, but to retreating in order to be alone with God. In the *Risālah* of al-Qushayrī, the section entitled *al-khalwah wa'l-ʿuzlah* occurs among the stations of the path and is treated more as an attribute of the seeker than as a spiritual practice. As al-Qushayrī writes, "It is said, 'Who is the recognizer?' They say, 'One who is present-absent (*kāʾin bāʾin*): present with mankind, separated from them in his inmost secret.'"[92] Affirming this same idea, he transmits that Abū Muḥammad al-Jurayrī (d. 312/924) was asked about *ʿuzlah* and replied, "It is entering among the crowd while your secret core refrains from mixing with them, the withdrawing of your soul from sins and your secret being connected to the Real."[93] Nonetheless, there is still some notion of the devotion to *dhikr* in *khalwah* that came to be an integral part of Sufi practice. Abū ʿUthmān al-Maghribī is recorded as saying, "Whoever chooses seclusion over companionship must be free of all remembrances save the remembrance of his Lord, and free from all desires, save the contentment of his Lord."[94]

The *Kitāb Ādāb al-ʿuzlah* of the *Iḥyāʾ* is probably the best place to look for attitudes towards *khalwah* and *ʿuzlah* that were prevalent at the time of Aḥmad al-Ghazālī, especially as we know that this is a work with which he was familiar. Here the words *ʿuzlah* and *khalwah* are treated as synonyms. In mentioning both the benefits and dangers of this practice, Abū Ḥāmid appears to be treading a cautious course between the perceived need to separate the heart from the distractions of the world and the need to observe the communal obligations of Muslim society. On the one hand, he transmits sayings like, "The joy of the believer and his delight is in the seclusion of intimate discourse with his Lord."[95] While on the other hand, he exerts much effort in reminding the reader of what can be gained through the fellowship of good companions, such as knowledge, etiquette, and humility. Indeed, Abū Ḥāmid joins the manners of *ʿuzlah* to those of companionship, noting that a precondition for the spiritual retreat is the desire that the evil of one's own soul be held back from others. Thus, in the *Iḥyāʾ*, spiritual seclusion and retreat are one and the same and serve both a communal function and an individual function, though ultimately it is not for everybody:

> No one is capable of seclusion except by holding firm to the Book of God. Those who hold firm to the Book of God are the ones who retreat from the world through the remembrance of God. The rememberers of God through God live by the remembrance of God, die by the remembrance of God, and meet God through the remembrance of God. There is no doubt that social intercourse prevents them from contemplation and remembrance, so retreat is more appropriate for them. Therefore, at the beginning of his affair, the Prophet would retire to Mount Ḥirāʾ and seek refuge in it until the light of prophethood became strong in him, such that mankind did not veil him from God and he was with them in his body while turning to God in his heart.[96]

Abū Ḥāmid's treatment of *khalwah* and *ʿuzlah* demonstrates that at this time they would most likely have been identical and gives some indication of an attitude towards this practice with which Aḥmad al-Ghazālī was familiar. Nonetheless, it does not examine the specific practice of those who sought to follow the spiritual path. No texts from al-Ghazālī's time or before indicate the precise nature of the practice among Sufis. It appears that the textual recording of rules for *khalwah,* and perhaps the rules themselves, was coincident with the rise of the Sufi orders in the sixth and seventh centuries. To get some idea of the practice in which Aḥmad, Abū Ḥāmid, and others of their generation might have engaged, one can thus look to some early spiritual descendants of Aḥmad al-Ghazālī, the aforementioned Abū Ḥafṣ ʿUmar as-Suhrawardī and Najm ad-Dīn Rāzī (d. 654/1256), both of whom wrote handbooks on Sufism that remain in use to this day.[97] It is likely that the practice of *khalwah* and *ʿuzlah* ascribed to Aḥmad al-Ghazālī in the biographical dictionaries is in some way similar to what is detailed by these later Sufi masters.

Both as-Suhrawardī's *ʿAwārif al-maʿārif* and Rāzī's *Mirṣād al-ʿibād* prescribe forty days of seclusion. This was to become the norm throughout the Islamic world, though adherence to this practice has weakened over time. As support for this practice, they cite a saying attributed to the Prophet: "Whoever worships God sincerely for forty mornings, the springs of wisdom shall well up from his heart to his tongue."[98] Both believe that this practice is prefigured in the practice of all prophets and cite the story of Moses in the Quran wherein God commanded that he observe forty nights of seclusion after being delivered from Egypt.[99]

As-Suhrawardī is adamant in maintaining that the *khalwah* is not for seeking mystical experiences and visions, though the adept might experience supernatural phenomena (*khawāriq al-ʿādāt*) that can advance him in knowledge and certainty. He writes that seeking such experiences is "pretension itself and sheer folly. People only choose seclusion and isolation (*waḥdah*) for the soundness of religion, inspecting the states of the soul and sincerity of action towards God."[100] This is fundamentally important for understanding the function of seclusion in Islamic thought. The purpose is to cultivate complete detachment from all that is other than God in the hopes that this transient state of detachment will become an enduring station. According to Rāzī, "The foundation of wayfaring and attaining the stations of certainty is seclusion, withdraw, and being cut off from people."[101]

Both authors address the correct inward attitude and the proper outward conduct. Regarding the former, as-Suhrawardī writes:

> Whoever chooses seclusion over companionship must be free of all thoughts, save the remembrance of his Lord, free of all desires, save the desire of his Lord, and free from the soul's seeking all intermediary causes (*asbāb*). For if he does not have this attribute, then his seclusion will land him in trial and tribulation.[102]

Regarding the latter, both as-Suhrawardī and Rāzī list several conditions that are necessary for the one who chooses seclusion. One must perform the ablution and retreat to an empty room, which Rāzī says he should "imagine to be his [funeral] shroud."[103] As-Suhrawardī states that one should begin with two cycles of the ritual prayer, "and repent to God for all his misdeeds, with crying and humility."[104] Both stress that there should be constant fasting for the entire forty days and that when breaking the fast the food should be minimal.

As-Suhrawardī advocates a sparse diet, consisting of only bread and water, though Rāzī is not as strict. Both advocate that one who is engaged in spiritual retreat leave the room only for communal prayer and calls of nature, always renewing the ablution. As-Suhrawardī stresses the need for communal prayers, writing:

> We have seen those whose intellect has become deranged in retreat. Perhaps that is from the calamity of his persistence in abandoning communal prayer even though it is necessary that he leave his seclusion for communal prayer while he is remembering [God], not subsiding in remembrance.[105]

Unlike Aḥmad al-Ghazālī, who prescribed *lā ilāha illā Llāh, Allāh Allāh,* and *huwa huwa* as formulas of remembrance or invocation, both as-Suhrawardī and Rāzī prescribe only the first formula. As-Suhrawardī specifies that the days chosen by most for ritual seclusion are the month of Dhu'l-Qaʿdah and the first ten days of Dhu'l-Ḥijjah, thus assuring that one will come out from the *khalwah* on the *ʿīd al-aḍḥā*. While both as-Suhrawardī and Rāzī recognize that one must undergo seclusion through the guidance of a shaykh, Rāzī maintains that, "the seeker must constantly join his heart to that of the shaykh."[106] This would seem to be a later development in keeping with the greater attachment to the shaykh that came about with the rise of the Sufi orders. It is believed that by employing the *khalwah* with sincerity one will experience the springs of wisdom referred to in the *ḥadīth* above, thus increasing the seekers in certainty until "they are in all moments as is their bearing during the forty days retreat."[107]

Samāʿ

Perhaps the most debated of those practices that Aḥmad al-Ghazālī is likely to have incorporated into his spiritual discipline is the music and ritual dancing known as *samāʿ*. Whereas other aspects of his spiritual practice can be shown to have roots in the Quran and *ḥadīth* tradition, there is no immediate Quranic support for *samāʿ*, and little can be found in the *ḥadīth*. The paucity of textual support for this practice is demonstrated by the widespread use of one *ḥadīth* to support the use of music:

> ʿĀʾisha said, "The Messenger of God entered during the festival of *tashrīq* and I had two slave girls of ʿAbd Allāh ibn Salām who were playing two drums and singing.[108]

> When the Messenger of God entered I said 'Stop!' and the Messenger of God retired to bed in the house, laid down, and wrapped his garments around himself. So I said, 'The day of singing is over' [or 'has been forbidden']." She said, "So I told them to go.
>
> "They left and by God I will never forget Abū Bakr entering—and he was a man of quick reason (*muṭṭār*), who was of keen mind (*ḥadīd*)—and he said, 'Are the songs of Satan in the house of the Messenger of God?' The Messenger of God uncovered his head and said, 'Abū Bakr, for all people there is a day of celebration; this is the day of our celebration.'"[109]

Proponents of *samāʿ* were well aware of the weakness of their position, and thus argued effectively that there is no basis for prohibiting music, rather than arguing that this practice had origins in the prophetic *sunnah*.

Though there was a grave lack of textual support for listening to music in a ritualized manner, and even less so for dancing, many Sufis pursued and defended this practice. Aḥmad al-Ghazālī has long been recognized as one of the foremost among them, but as mentioned in Chapter 1, this derives from the attribution to him of the *Bawāriq al-ilmāʿ fī'r-radd ʿalā man yuḥarrimu's-samāʿ bi'l-ijmāʿ*, a work that is clearly not of his pen. Nonetheless, several sources have recorded that Aḥmad al-Ghazālī incorporated *samāʿ* as part of his spiritual practice. One account in the *Tamhīdāt* of ʿAyn al-Quḍāt Hamadānī indicates that both attended Sufi sessions of *samāʿ*: "One night, my father, myself, and a group of leaders [*imāms*] from our city were present at the house of a Sufi leader [*muqaddam*]. Then we were dancing and Abū Saʿīd Tirmidhī said, my father looked, then said: 'I saw Khwājah Imām Aḥmad Ghazālī dancing with us."[110] As this is an account of a spiritual vision, it does not attest that al-Ghazālī participated in sessions himself, but the aforecited account from Ibn Ḥajar al-ʿAsqalānī's *Lisān al-mizān* does. Here al-Ghazālī is said to have spun on his head in a Sufi gathering "until he had no feet or hands upon the ground."[111] Though not historically verifiable, these stories demonstrate that Aḥmad al-Ghazālī was viewed by his contemporaries and by posterity as a practitioner and proponent of this oft-debated practice. The practice of *samāʿ* was so widespread among the Sufis of this period as to make it very unlikely that it was not a part of his practice.

Since *samāʿ* is not mentioned in Aḥmad al-Ghazālī's writings or sermons, as with the practice of spiritual retreat, one must look to other authors of the Sufi tradition to obtain some understanding of this practice. One of the earliest recorded instances of Sufi dance is a story of al-Junayd found in several Sufi texts. The most salient of these accounts is that in Najm ad-Dīn Kubrā's *Fawā'iḥ al-jamāl wa-fawātiḥ al-jalāl*:

> One day he was in a session of *samāʿ* with some of the brothers. The moment (*waqt*) became beneficent for them and they stood to dance and Junayd sat without moving. They thus thought that in his opinion dancing was forbidden, so they asked him about it. He replied, "*You see the mountains and consider them solid*" (Quran: 27:88).[112]

Here al-Junayd is referring to the fact that he was experiencing the state (*ḥāl*) of *samāʿ* within, though not participating physically.

That *samāʿ* was a practice of central importance to the Sufis is demonstrated by the extensive treatment of it in the handbooks of al-Hujwīrī, as-Sarrāj, and as-Suhrawardī, and a book of the *Iḥyā'* entitled *Kitāb Ādāb as-samāʿ wa'l-wajd* (Proper Conduct in Samāʿ and Ecstasy). Without trying to cover all of the various elements of these writings, one can identify four basic issues that dominate these discussions of *samāʿ*: (1) that it is permissible; (2) that it is dangerous for the unqualified; (3) that there is a hierarchy of those qualified for it; and (4) that it is a communal activity. The discussion of its permissibility predominates in most texts, indicating that it was a point of great contention. Some proponents of *samāʿ*, such as al-Hujwīrī, believed that dancing is forbidden while audition is permitted.[113] Aḥmad al-Ghazālī was most likely of the same opinion as his brother that both were permissible.[114] Despite the arguments for permissibility, most proponents acknowledge that *samāʿ* is not for all, as music can stir both noble, ascending passions and base, descending passions. As Abū Bakr ash-Shiblī (d. 394/945) is reported to have said, "Its outward is a trial and its inward is an admonition (*ʿibrah*). Whoever recognizes allusion (*al-ishārah*), is permitted to listen to the admonition. If not, he invites trial and is subjected to tribulations."[115] For this reason, the levels of qualification are often discussed. Most proponents agree that novices are not fit to attend sessions of *samāʿ*. Regarding this opinion, al-Hujwīrī relates a saying from al-Junayd to a young disciple: "If you wish to keep your religion safe and to maintain your penitence, do not indulge, while you are young, in the audition which the Sufis practice."[116] As Shaykh Abū Madyan (d. 594/1198) of the Moroccan Sufi tradition writes, "The beginner should not be present at ecstatic sessions until he has mortified his carnal soul with fasting, performing the fast of intimate union, and standing [in prayer]. Only then is it allowable for him to be present and [participation] is permissible for him."[117] Both Abū Ḥāmid al-Ghazālī and as-Sarrāj expand on the discussion of suitability by devoting several pages to the levels of audition and its auditors. That *samāʿ* is a communal activity is evident from the fact that all accounts of the practice presuppose a gathering. Furthermore, as al-Junayd is reported to have said, "Audition requires three things without which it is not heard . . . the time, the place, and the brothers [i.e., the Sufis; *as-zamān wa'l-makān wa'l-ikhwān*]."[118] In this last respect, *samāʿ* can be seen as the expansive outward complement of the inward and contracting retreat, both of which are aspects of *dhikr*.[119]

A detailed analysis of the various practices described in the many texts on *samāʿ* would take this study too far afield.[120] I will simply conclude by citing the rules laid down by al-Hujwīrī, rules likely quite close to those observed by Aḥmad al-Ghazālī, his master, his companions, and his disciples:

> The rules of audition prescribe that it should not be practiced until it comes (of its own accord), and that you must not make a habit of it, but practice it seldom, in order that you not cease to revere it. It is necessary that a spiritual director be present during the performance, that the place be cleared of common people, that the singer be a respectable person, that the heart be emptied of worldly thoughts, that the disposition not be inclined to amusement, and that every artificial effort (*takalluf*) be put aside. You must not exceed the proper bounds until audition manifests its power and when it has become powerful, you must not repel it, but must follow it as it requires: if it agitates, you must be agitated, and if it calms, you must be calm; and you must be able to distinguish a strong natural impulse from the ardor of ecstasy (*wajd*). The auditor must have enough perception to be capable of receiving the divine influence and doing justice to it. When its might is manifest in his heart, he must not endeavor to repel it, and when its force is broken, he must not endeavor to attract it . . . And if he has no part in the audition which is being enjoyed by others, it is not proper that he should look soberly on their intoxication, but he must keep quiet in accord with his own moment (*waqt*) and establish its dominion, that the blessing thereof may come to him.[121]

Shāhid-bāzī

The most controversial of the spiritual practices attributed to Aḥmad al-Ghazālī is *shāhid-bāzī* or "witness play," the practice of gazing upon beardless young men.[122] As seen in Chapter 1, Shaykh Aḥmad's engagement with this practice is portrayed in a positive light by Shams ad-Dīn Tabrīzī and ʿAbd ar-Raḥmān Jāmī and in a negative light by Sibṭ Ibn al-Jawzī. Unlike the practices discussed above, in none of his extant writings does Shaykh Aḥmad enjoin *shāhid-bāzī*. Nonetheless, there is evidence that it may have been a practice in which he engaged. This can be ascertained from allusions to gazing on the beauty of the human form, be it male or female, in the *Sawāniḥ*, the attribution of this practice to him in some Sufi and biographical works, and the metaphysical and theological explanation of the practice provided by his most famous disciple, ʿAyn al-Quḍāt Hamadānī.

The details of Aḥmad al-Ghazālī's understanding of the relationship between the lover and the beloved will be studied in Chapter 5. Here it should be noted that the distinction between love for God and love for humans is often difficult to discern in the *Sawāniḥ*. This may be intentional, as later advocates of the practice of *shāhid-bāzī* understand the contemplation of beauty in the human beloved to be the contemplation of the manifestation or self-disclosure of Divine beauty in the human form. Shams ad-Dīn Tabrīzī alludes to this when he writes of Aḥmad al-Ghazālī, "He did not incline to these beautiful forms out of appetite. He saw something that no one else saw." As ʿAyn al-Quḍāt explains in his *Tamhīdāt*, these beautiful forms are all manners in which God displays His own form:

> Alas! "I saw my Lord on the Night of the Ascent in the most beautiful form." This "most beautiful of forms" is the assumption of representational forms (*tamaththul*). If not, then what is it? "Truly God created Adam and his children upon the form of the Merciful" is another type of *tamaththul*. Oh! For His Names! One of them is *muṣawwir*, which is The Form Giver. But I say that He is *muṣawwar*, that is, The Form Displayer. Do you know in which bazaar these forms are displayed and sold? In the bazaar of the elite. Hear it from Muṣṭafā, blessings be upon him, when he said, "In Paradise there is a bazaar in which forms are sold." "In the most beautiful form" is this.[123]

That is to say that the forms one witnesses in this world are not only made by God, they also display God. The most beautiful form is that which was given to Adam, since as another *ḥadīth* states, "God created Adam upon His form."[124] In this vein, Rūzbihān Baqlī states that God made human beings "the niche of His splendor's light, the resplendence of His attributes, and the loci for the manifestation of the projection of His self-disclosure."[125] Human beauty is differentiated from other forms of created beauty because the human being displays the full radiance of the Divine Essence, whereas other created forms only display God's attributes.[126] The self-disclosure of Divine beauty in the human forms is thus the most immediate manner in which to contemplate Divine beauty. For most wayfarers on the path of love it is in fact necessary to contemplate the self-disclosure of Divine beauty in the human form because very few can obtain direct access to God's Supreme Beauty. As Rūzbihān Baqlī writes, "The beginning of all lovers (*ʿāshiqān*) proceeds from the path of those who witness (*shawāhid*), except for some of the elite among the People of recognizing Oneness, for whom witnessing the universal occurs in their spirit (*jān*) without witnessing transient existents. This is among the rare occurrences from the Unseen."[127] Thus for spiritual attainment on the path of love, most aspirants need to witness beauty as manifest in the form of individual existents in order to witness Divine beauty. As ʿAyn al-Quḍāt put it, engaging in *shāhid-bāzī* is necessary for attaining to the higher levels of the spiritual path wherein one lives through God and dies through God:

> If you want to know more about life and real death (*mawt-i maʿnawī*) hear what Muṣṭafā said in his supplication, "O God! I live through You and I die through You."[128] Do you not have any knowledge of what dying through Him is and of what and living through Him is?
>
> Alas! This is a state that is known by those who are witness players (*shāhid-bāzān*) and who know what it is to be alive with the witness and what death is without the witness. The witness and the witnessed reveal life and death to the true witness players.[129]

Summary of Practice

This brief sketch provides some idea of the spiritual practices Aḥmad al-Ghazālī employed for most of his adult life. Among these, he recognizes remembrance as the *sine qua non* for wayfaring upon the Sufi path. All of the other practices can be understood as supports for it. Some of these practices, such as night vigil and the remembrance of death, are employed by many Muslims independently of Sufi Islam and without the guidance of a spiritual master. But Sufis maintain that the use of spiritual retreat, audition, and progressive formulas of invocation require a guide. It is in this vein that in one of his sessions, Shaykh Aḥmad al-Ghazālī implores his audience, "The initiatic pact (*al-bayʿah*) is incumbent upon you."[130] Though in his time the relationship with the spiritual master was not as formalized as it would become thereafter,[131] his emphasis on initiation and the nature of the specific guidance that he offers in his letters indicate that it was central to his understanding of spiritual wayfaring.

Throughout Aḥmad al-Ghazālī's instructions to his pupils in both the letters and the sermons, two elements are emphasized consistently. First, the path must be traveled immediately with no questions asked:

> Do not be preoccupied with excuses! Take to the path and travel it! For there is no escape from Him but to Him. There is a steep path before you; if you do not scale it, you will be scaled. If you travel upon it, you will be at peace, and if you are made to travel, you will be destroyed. There is no doubt about that.[132]

The second aspect is that the path must be traveled with complete sincerity: "For every deed in which there is no sincerity (*ikhlāṣ*), its non-existence is better than its existence. For if you do not prolong supererogatory prayer perhaps you will say to yourself, 'O worthless one.'"[133] So although it is incumbent upon the serious seeker to devote himself at once, if it is not done with purity and sincerity, it can be more of a hindrance than a support. The performance of pious deeds without a sound heart will function as yet another veil.

Chapter 4

The Roots of Aḥmad al-Ghazālī's Teachings

Many aspects of Aḥmad al-Ghazālī's thought have clear precedents in the early Sufi tradition, particularly his emphasis on *dhikr*, which was examined in the previous chapter. But *dhikr* is of such central significance to all followers of Sufism that it is difficult to establish any definite direct influences. Spiritual principles such as scrupulousness (*war*ʿ), repentance (*tawbah*), reverence (*taqwā*), fear (*khawf*), hope (*rajā*ʿ), certainty (*yaqīn*), and many others are also discussed by al-Ghazālī, but not with such frequency as to constitute central themes. Although the use of such terms illustrates his direct relationship with the previous Sufi tradition, it does not tie him to any specific individuals or contingents within the early Sufi community, or serve to define his teachings. The two dimensions of his thought that differentiate them from those of other Sufi masters are his teachings on sympathy for Satan and on the centrality of love (*ʿishq*). The latter proves to be the defining element of his thought, one that establishes his distinct contribution to the development of Sufism and Persian Sufi literature.

Satanology

A sympathetic understanding of Satan can be seen as a logical outcome of Aḥmad al-Ghazālī's teachings on love. He believes that all of creation must necessarily have a face of beauty that is turned toward the divine beloved—otherwise it would not exist. From this perspective, the ugliness of Satan as he turns toward creation is because Satan knows that God alone possesses true beauty. His refusal to bow before Adam, which is attested in several Quranic passages (2:30–36;

7:11–25; 17:61–65; 20:115–124; 15:25–43; 38:71, 85), is thus an expression of sincere monotheism and sheer love for God. Nonetheless, as seen in Chapter 1, al-Ghazālī takes his teachings regarding Satan to an extreme that caused several biographers, beginning with Ibn al-Jawzī, to question his orthodoxy.

In several instances, al-Ghazālī evokes the standard Islamic teaching in which Satan is presented as a disobedient jinn who had risen to the level of the angels but was then obstinate when ordered to prostrate before Adam, claiming, "*I am better than him. Thou hast created me from fire, but Thou hast created him from clay*" (38:76). Having been cursed by God, he then became the enemy of both man and God, who is to be punished for his intransigence. But in his sessions and in several excerpts preserved in the biographical tradition, he portrays Satan as the greatest lover and the foremost of God's servants in testifying to unity (*tawḥīd*).[1] Here, Aḥmad al-Ghazālī's teachings reflect the discussion of Satan found in sixth *Tasīn* of Manṣūr al-Ḥallāj's *Kitāb al-Ṭāwasīn*, entitled, "Beinglessness and Ambiguity":

> 6. Among the inhabitants of heaven, there is none who affirms unity like Iblīs.
>
> 7. When Iblīs was veiled by the real essence (*ʿayn*), and he fled the glances and gazed into the secret, and worshipped the Worshipped stripped of all else.
>
> 8. Only to be cursed when he attained individuation and given demands when he demanded more.
>
> 9. He was told "Prostrate!" He said, "No other!" He was asked, "Even if My curse is upon you?" He replied, "No other! There is no way for me to one who is not You. I am an abject lover."[2]

Al-Ḥallāj continues his defense of Iblīs by allowing him to speak for himself during an encounter with Moses,

> 13. Moses encountered Iblīs on Mount Sinai and said to him, "O Iblīs, what prevented you from prostrating?" He replied, "The proclamation of one thing worshipped prevented me. Had I prostrated to him [Adam], I would have been like you, for you were called one time, '*Look to the*

> *mountain'* (7:139) and then looked. I was called to prostrate a thousand times, but did not prostrate; proclamations are in accord with meanings."
>
> 14. Moses said to him, "You abandoned the command."
>
> He replied, "That was a trial, not a command."
>
> Iblīs continued, "O Moses this and that are a dressing. The state cannot be relied upon, for it changes. But recognition (*ma'rifah*) is truly as it is and does not change even though the figure has changed."[3]

The version of this story attributed to Aḥmad al-Ghazālī reflects the influence of al-Ḥallāj, but is somewhat different:

> Moses encountered Iblīs on the road of Mount Sinai and said, "O Iblīs, why did you not prostrate to Adam?"
>
> Iblīs replied, "Never, God forbid! The Worshipped is one. For seven hundred thousand years I have been saying, 'Praise and Holy,' how could I blacken the face of my servitude with two?"
>
> Moses said, "O Iblīs, why did you abandon the command?"
>
> He replied, "That was the command of a trial, had it been the command of a wish, then, O Moses, would I have proclaimed the testification to unity."[4]

There is enough variation in their respective accounts to indicate that al-Ghazālī could have received these teachings through an oral tradition, rather than through direct access to the text.[5] Both accounts portray Iblīs as a sincere worshipper of the one God. But whereas al-Ḥallāj has him criticize Moses, al-Ghazālī uses Moses as an interlocutor. Al-Ḥallāj has Iblīs deliver a lesson regarding the nature of recognition, but in al-Ghazālī's account Iblīs explains only the nature of his particular relationship with God. This may demonstrate that al-Ghazālī, or those from whom he received this account, agreed with al-Ḥallāj regarding the nature of Iblīs' trial but did not agree that Moses was to be criticized for the nature of his worship.

In the biographical literature, al-Ghazālī is portrayed as representing Iblīs not only as a sincere worshipper, but also as a true lover. The ultimate significance of Satan is found in an account related by Ibn al-Jawzī in which al-Ghazālī says, "Whoever has not learned *tawḥīd* from Iblīs is a dualist (*zindīq*)."[6] For al-Ghazālī, as for al-Ḥallāj before him and ʿAyn al-Quḍāt and ʿAṭṭār after him, Iblīs is perfect in testifying to unity. His refusal to bow to Adam results not from hubris but from the purest and most sincere love of God. He is, therefore, a model for those who follow the path of love. As ʿAyn al-Quḍat has Iblīs say: "Whoever would be a lover of gentleness or a lover of severity is a lover of himself, not a lover of the Beloved,"[7] which is to say that whoever wants other than God in and of Himself is not yet a true lover.

Love

Shaykh Aḥmad al-Ghazālī's teachings on love are the most defining feature and most distinctive contribution of his writings. Like Aḥmad al-Ghazālī, previous Sufis, such as Shaqīq Balkhī (d. 194/810), Abu'l-Ḥasan ad-Daylamī (d. late 4th/10th century), Abū Ṭālib al-Makkī (d. 386/996), and others, had envisaged the spiritual path as degrees of love. But in his *Sawāniḥ*, Aḥmad al-Ghazālī makes a revolutionary move in Sufi thought by placing love at the center of metaphysics. He is not alone in this move, as many elements of this perspective can also be found in the works of his predecessor ʿAbdallāh Anṣārī of Herat (d. 481/1089), as well as those of al-Ghazālī's younger contemporaries, Samʿānī, Maybudī, and ʿAyn al-Quḍāt Hamadānī. Together, this cluster of authors marks the advent of a new expression regarding the nature of love. Among them the *Sawāniḥ* stands out as the most emphatic sustained discourse on the nature of love, in which all elements of creation and the Sufi path are defined in relation to love.

The poetry of such famous Sufi figures as Rābiʿah al-ʿAdawiyyah (d. 185/801–2) and Dhu'n-Nūn al-Miṣrī (d. 243/857 or 245/859) may appear to indicate a centrality of love similar to that expressed by Aḥmad al-Ghazālī, but authors from the early Sufi tradition emphasize a human love for God that is absolute, not a love that is the Absolute Itself—and this is the crux of the matter. Rābiʿah al-ʿAdawiyyah is often recognized as the first to speak of love as being due to God alone.[8] She expressed this realization in short poems such as these oft-cited verses:

O Beloved of hearts, I have none like unto Thee,
Therefore have pity this day on the sinner
    Who comes to Thee.

O my Hope and my Rest and my Delight,
The heart can love none other than Thee.[9]

And,

Two loves I give Thee, love that yearns,
And love because Thy due is love.

My yearning my remembrance turns
To Thee, nor lets it from Thee rove.[10]

The sentiment that God alone is worthy of love is echoed throughout the literature of early Sufism. Figures such as the famous Abū Bakr ash-Shiblī (d. 334/945), who was known for his teachings on love,[11] spoke of love (*maḥabbah*) as "a fire in the heart, consuming all save the will of the Beloved,"[12] or as that which "erases all that is other than God from the heart,"[13] and thus considered mystical love as an intense desire centering one's aspiration (*himmah*) on God alone and cutting one off from all that is other than the Divine. In contrast, Aḥmad al-Ghazālī makes *ʿishq* the center of an emphatic discourse on the nature of reality and the stages of the Sufi path, discussing all aspects of creation and of spiritual wayfaring in terms of *ʿishq*. Whereas previous Sufis, such as the famous al-Ḥallāj, recognized love as a Divine Attribute and, in turn, one of the highest human attributes, or like Abū Naṣr as-Sarrāj (d. 378/988), author of *Kitāb al-Lumaʿ* (The Book of Illumination), one of the most important early Sufi handbooks, as a particular state or station on the path of spiritual wayfaring, Aḥmad al-Ghazālī saw love as the Divine Essence Itself. Though previous accounts express the need for unconditional love for God alone and can be interpreted to present the path of spiritual wayfaring as degrees of love, they do not express the subtle metaphysics of love found in the *Sawāniḥ* and later writings of the Persianate Sufi tradition. The Sufis involved in this discussion would not always have employed terms such as "essence" and "attribute" in a technical manner. Nonetheless, the general understanding of the distinction between the Divine Essence and the Divine Attributes prevalent in Islamic thought undergirds their discussion. The "essence" (*dhāt*) refers to a thing in and of itself, while the "attributes" (*ṣiffāt*) and "names" (*asmā ʾ*) refer to the qualities and descriptions of that same thing. The Divine Essence in Itself is beyond human comprehension, but the names and attributes can be comprehended in some measure. To view "love" as the Divine Essence is thus to understand it as the very nature of God beyond the names and attributes by which one can know something of the Divine Nature. To claim that one can have some realization of that Divine Essence in Itself through love would then be seen by many as a radical claim that challenges the boundaries of orthodoxy.

The ideas regarding love and the Divine Essence most similar to those of Aḥmad al-Ghazālī are found in accounts of al-Ḥallāj's teachings on love transmitted by Abu'l-Ḥasan ad-Daylamī in his *ʿAṭf al-alif al-ma ʾlūf ʿala'l-lām al-ma ʿṭūf* (The Inclination of the Intimate Alif to the Lām Towards which it Inclines) and are alluded to in other early Sufi texts. It would also appear that an understanding of love similar to that expressed in the *Sawāniḥ* underlies the works of ʿAbdallāh Anṣārī, though it is not expressed as directly in Anṣārī's works. Before addressing the various discussions of love that preceded Aḥmad al-Ghazālī, I must briefly survey his teachings on love. These can be divided into two aspects: the ontological and the soteriological relationship with God, or the path of descent and the path of ascent. The ontological relationship is summed up by the well-known *ḥadīth qudsī* that is cited in Aḥmad al-Ghazālī's *at-Tajrīd fī kalimat at-tawḥīd* and which has been inserted at the beginning of some later manuscripts of the *Sawāniḥ*: "I was a hidden treasure and I loved to be known, therefore I created creation in order that I would be known."[14] Aḥmad al-Ghazālī sees love as the essence of God and the substance from which all else is woven. From this perspective, every existent thing is a self-disclosure (*tajallī*) of the Divine; everything is what he refers to in the *Sawāniḥ* as "a glance from loveliness (*kirishmeh-yi ḥusn*)." As he writes:

> The secret face of everything is the point of its connection, and a sign hidden in creation (*ṣan ʿ*), and beauty is the brand of creation. The secret of the face is that face that faces love. So long as one does not see the secret of the face, he will never see the sign of creation and beauty. The face is the beauty of *and the face of your Lord remains* (55:27). Other that it, there is no face, for *all that is upon it fades* (55:26).[15]

This ontological relationship is not, however, the focus of the *Sawāniḥ*, nor of any of Aḥmad al-Ghazālī's writings or sermons. He does not write as a theologian, theosopher, philosopher or Sufi theoretician. Rather, he is first and foremost a spiritual guide. From his perspective, it is not so important where and how things have come into being; what is important to know is that for the spiritual wayfarer "his being and attributes are themselves the provision of the (spiritual) path."[16] As such, Aḥmad al-Ghazālī always focuses on the path of wayfaring by which the lover—the spiritual adept or seeker—ascends through the beloved—the God of beliefs—to be annihilated in the ocean of Love—the Divine Essence.

The soteriological relationship is expressed in the Quranic verse *He loves them and they love Him* (5:54), which became the central verse for the discussion of love in the Persian tradition, and with which Aḥmad begins his *Sawāniḥ*. As love is the true essence of all creation, the realization of love is neither an emotion nor a sentiment but the natural response of one's being to God, and its locus is the heart: "The function of the heart is being a lover. So long as there is no love, it has no function. When it becomes a lover its affair will also become ready. Therefore, it is certain that the heart has been created for love and being a lover and knows nothing else."[17] In the *Sawāniḥ*, he presents the spiritual path as a subtle interplay of love in which the spiritual seeker is a lover who comes to realize his true identity as a locus for the beloved's love of himself. Here the Sufi path is envisaged as degrees of love wherein one ultimately transcends the duality of lover and beloved to arrive at the pure essence of Love Itself. The beloved is not the Absolute, as in the poetry and prose of the previous Sufis; rather, the beloved is here considered to be the God of beliefs that serves as a locus of spiritual aspiration for one traveling the path, but must be transcended in order to advance to the Divine Essence from which both the lover and the beloved are derived. As Aḥmad writes: "the derivation of the lover and the beloved is from Love. When the accidentalities of derivations arise, the affair is again dissolved in the oneness of its reality."[18]

In the beginning of the spiritual path, the wayfarer must be severed from all of creation such that he becomes a true lover, desiring none but the beloved and having intimacy with him alone. According to al-Ghazālī, the desire for just one hair of creation will prevent him from fully realizing his identity as lover. At the culmination of this stage, the lover comes to see the loveliness of the beloved in all things, for he realizes the inner face of beauty that is turned toward the beloved, rather than the outer face of ugliness turned toward creation. When the lover's love is pure, the beloved needs the lover, for the reflection of the beloved's loveliness (*ḥusn*) in the gaze of the lover is the only means by which the beloved can take nourishment from his own beauty. Through the full reflection of the beloved's beauty, the lover becomes more the beloved than the beloved himself and a connection (*wiṣāl*) is established between them. The lover thus becomes the beloved and all of the lover's need (*nayāz*) is transformed into *nāz*—the coquetry of one who feigns disdain for the lover. Here the duality of lover and beloved has been bridged, and the covetousness of being a lover is abandoned such that the spiritual wayfarer is immersed in the essence of Love and no longer deluded by love for an object. As Fakhr ad-Dīn 'Irāqī (d. 688/1289) writes in his *Lamaʿāt* (Flashes), "Love is a fire which when it falls in the heart burns all that it finds therein, to the extent that the form of the beloved is also wiped from the heart."[19] This is the stage which al-Ghazālī refers to as complete detachment (*tajrīd*) in the singularity (*tafrīd*) of Love. But from the point of view of Love Itself, "the lover and the beloved are both other, just like strangers,"[20] and have always been so, for they are necessarily marked by the stain of duality.

Love in Sufi Literature Before the 6th/12th Century

As with many developments in intellectual history, all the steps that may have preceded the expressions of love found in the *Sawāniḥ* and the later Sufi tradition cannot be traced. Within the Islamic tradition, love is addressed in all fields of knowledge, from belletristic literature to philosophy, theology, and even law. The Sufi teachings examined here are just one dimension of an extensive intellectual tradition. Sayings regarding love are attributed to almost all the early figures associated with the Sufi tradition. Among those figures who are said to have taught about love in later generations, such as Jaʿfar aṣ-Ṣādiq and Abū Sa'īd b. Abi'l-Khayr (d. 440/1021), the manuscript tradition calls into question the veracity of many of the sayings attributed to them. To some extent this can also be said for sayings attributed to earlier Sufis by Abū Naṣr as-Sarrāj, ʿAbd ar-Raḥmān as-Sulamī (d. 412/1021), ʿAbd al-Karīm al-Qushayrī (d. 465/1072), and others. But these sayings were attributed and recorded before the time of Aḥmad al-Ghazālī, whereas those sayings attributed to Abū Saʿīd were recorded after the *Sawāniḥ*. The sayings found in the works of as-Sarrāj, as-Sulamī, al-Qushayrī, and others are thus part of the textual tradition preceding the *Sawāniḥ* and illuminate the discussion of love that preceded Aḥmad al-Ghazālī.

The *Asrār-i tawḥīd*, which records the life and sayings of Abū Saʿīd, was compiled by his grandson Muḥammad Ibn al-Munawwar

(d. 598–9/1202) many years after Abū Saʿīd's death.[21] Given the complications in authenticating many of his statements, I will not incorporate the teachings on *maḥabbah* or *ʿishq* attributed to Abū Saʿīd in this study. The reports about his teachings may indicate that there was an extensive oral Sufi tradition regarding *ʿishq* prior to the *Sawāniḥ*, but the later compilation dates of the manuscripts that contain his teachings make it difficult to draw any historical conclusions from them. As will be demonstrated in the following analysis, many allusions in the written tradition before al-Ghazālī also indicate an extensive oral tradition, the full extent of which is difficult to measure.

Shaqīq Balkhī.[22]

Among the earliest extended discussions of love in Sufi texts is a treatise attributed to Shaqīq Balkhī entitled *Adab al-ʿibādāt* (The Comportment of Worshippers).[23] Balkhī lists four way stations (*manāzil*), which he presents in ascending order: *zuhd* (asceticism), *khawf* (fear), *shawq* (longing), and *maḥabbah* (love). In the way station of *zuhd* the adept has limited his food to two meals a day in which only a third of his stomach is filled, leaving the other two thirds for breath [of the Merciful], glorification, and reading the Quran. One accomplished in *zuhd* no longer seeks the world and has no need for anything from it, save the exigencies of life: "This is a beautiful, good and virtuous way-station."[24] *Khawf* is then connected to *zuhd* just as the spirit is connected to the body and "the light of fear is the light of *zuhd*."[25] "The principle of fear is to remember death until one is softened, until one fears God as if one sees Him."[26] The one who has practiced this for forty days has the light of fear upon his face, he does not stray and is not negligent, and "he is perpetually crying, supplicating much and sleeping little."[27] He never wearies of invoking or thanking God. This for Balkhī is the way station that is deemed great by the common people, as they do not know other than it. The third way station is desire (*shawq*) for entry into paradise, the principle of which is contemplating the blessing of heaven. When one has persisted in this for forty days, "the light of desire dominates his heart and makes him forget the fear which was in his heart."[28] He has intense love and is perpetually doing what is good.

For Shaqīq Balkhī, the highest and noblest way station is that of love, which is for those whose hearts God has strengthened with sincere certainty, who are purified of sins and free from flaws. The light of love overcomes the heart without being separated from the light of *zuhd, khawf,* and *shawq*. The heart forgets the desire and fear that was in it and is filled with love and desire for God. The principle of this way station is that "the heart loves what God loves and hates what God hates, until nothing is more beloved to him than God and those who please Him."[29] When one has purified his intention, he is then the beloved, the munificent (*karīm*), the one brought near and refined. He listens only to what God loves, and because of God's love for him, whosoever hears him or sees him loves him; for "the light of love for God is the strongest and highest of the lights of servitude."[30] In Balkhī's own summary he says of those who love: "Their hearts are attached to their Lord, enjoying intimate discourse with Him when they are alone with Him, submitting their hearts to what they hope from His mercy and kindness—and He is the one who conquers their hearts."[31]

Though Shaqīq Balkhī makes love the supreme spiritual way station, this treatise shows little of the all-encompassing view of love presented by Aḥmad al-Ghazālī and his contemporaries. The ontological element is not present, as it is not a treatise that touches on cosmogony or ontology, but only on spiritual wayfaring. In this respect it also falls well short of the total emphasis on love in the works of Aḥmad al-Ghazālī and the later Persian tradition, for even in the highest stages of love, the *duality* between lover and Beloved is firmly maintained. Thus he does not take love to the level wherein the substance of all that exists is a love from which both the Lord (the Beloved) and the servant (the lover) are derived.

Ad-Daylamī—ʿAṭf al-alif

The most important text for understanding the many theories of love in the early medieval period is Abu'l-Ḥasan ad-Daylamī's aforementioned *ʿAṭf al-alif al-maʾlūf ʿalaʾl-lām al-maʿṭūf*. Ad-Daylamī transmits many important theories of love from Sufis, philosophers, theologians, and *adībs*, ranging from the concept that love is an attribute pertaining to the Divine Essence to the belief that it is a malady of the heart akin to intoxication or stupefication. Among the most important contributions of this work is that it provides exposure to the controversies regarding the understanding of love in this period. As ad-Daylamī writes in the introduction:

> We have found love to be the most renowned and highest state among both the commoners and the elite, the ignorant and the knowledgeable, the noble and the lowly, the esteemed and the abased. For this reason its obscurity has

> increased, its falsification has been magnified, and corruption of it has appeared among its people through the adulteration of those who adulterate, the excess of those who enter into it, and the falsification of those who lay claim to it. So its truth has been hidden in its falsity, its beauty in its ugliness, and its reality in its metaphor [*majāz*], until the one cannot be distinguished from the other.[32]

He also reveals an underlying controversy regarding the term most central to the Persian Sufi love tradition, *ʿishq*. This is directly exposed when ad-Daylamī discusses the theologians (*mutakallimūn*) who, by his account, have almost nothing positive to say about love and are given to considering *ʿishq* as an affliction of the soul and a malady of the heart that is to be avoided.[33] For many generations the term *ʿishq* was a source of great debate among the belletrists (*udabāʾ*), the *fuqahāʾ*, and the *ʿulamāʾ*.[34] Though no strict definitions were agreed upon, it was regarded by many as a state of passionate love, or as a raw physical lust to be tamed and avoided at all costs. Many had serious misgivings about the use of this term, and the second half of Ibn al-Jawzī's *Dhamm al-hawā* (The Condemnation of Lust) is entirely about the evils of *ʿishq* and the fate of those who succumb to it. But for all those who opposed the use of the word "*ʿishq*" to designate love between God and human beings, there were also scholars such as Muḥammad b. Dāʾūd al-Iṣfahānī (d. 297/910) who admonished them for failing to understand the tender nature of those susceptible to the storms of true love.[35]

The effect the condemnation of the use of this term had is evident when ad-Daylamī feels the need to cite an accepted authority before employing the term himself:

> We begin by mentioning the permissibility of [claiming] *ʿishq* for God and from God and the difference of our shaykhs regarding that, so that one who hears this word from us will not condemn [it] and reject it when he comes upon it in its appropriate context, due to its unfamiliarity, because our shaykhs do not employ it in their discourse, save rarely or in isolated incidents.[36]

He then alludes to a division among the shaykhs regarding love and mentions those who have agreed that it is permissible to employ the term *ʿishq*:

> Among those who permit [the use of it] are Abū Yazīd al-Bistāmī, Abu'l-Qāsim al-Junayd, Ḥusayn b. Manṣūr al-Ḥallāj and others. As for our Shaykh, Abū ʿAbdallāh b. al-Khafīf, he rejected this for some time until he came upon a treatise by Abu'l-Qāsim al-Junayd concerning *ʿishq,* in which the meaning of *ʿishq,* its derivation and its quiddity (*māhiyyah*) were mentioned. He then retreated from his rejection, professed it, permitted it, and wrote a treatise about it.[37]

By citing al-Bistāmī, al-Junayd, and al-Ḥallāj as proponents of the term *ʿishq,* ad-Daylamī is making a strong case for its legitimacy, as these are three of the most renowned figures of early Sufism. Through the process of canonization, al-Junayd came to be respected as "the Peacock of the Sufis" and the Shaykh of Shaykhs.[38] Little information is provided that would let us know exactly what the treatise attributed to him by ad-Daylamī may have contained, save one saying: "Al-Junayd said '*ʿIshq* is taken from the verb "he loved" (*ʿashiqa*) and it is the top of the mountain and its peak. Because of this, it must be said that so and so loved (*ʿashiqa*) when love increases, is aroused and rises until it attains to its peak and reaches its reality.'[39] In presenting *ʿishq* as what is attained when love reaches its highest degree, this citation foreshadows a position that will be encountered again when discussing the treatment of love in Abū Ḥāmid al-Ghazālī's *Revival of the Religious Sciences*.

Ad-Daylamī's View of Love

While ad-Daylamī's text offers many avenues for studying teachings on love, two are of central concern for identifying precedents to the teachings of Shaykh Aḥmad al-Ghazālī and the later Persian tradition, those of al-Ḥallāj, who is the most prominent figure of the text, and those of ad-Daylamī himself. In ad-Daylamī's most extensive presentation of his own views, he presents an eleven-step path of love that culminates in *ʿishq.* In the beginning of the discussion he writes:

> Love has names derived from its levels and degrees that vary in expression, while the reality is one. Through its steady increase, its names differ. They are altogether ten stations and in the eleventh they culminate in *ʿishq,* which is the very limit. So when one reaches it, the name *maḥabbah* falls away from it and it is called by other names.[40]

The ten stations before ʿ*ishq* are concord (*ulfah*), intimacy (*uns*), affection (*wadd* or *mawaddah*), love (*maḥabbah*), comity (*khillah*), ardor (*sha'af*), zeal (*shaghaf*), devotion (*istihtār*), infatuation (*walah*), and rapture (*haymān*).[41] Like al-Junayd and perhaps his own Shaykh Ibn al-Khafīf (d. 371/982), ad-Daylamī sees ʿ*ishq* as the highest degree of love. As ad-Daylamī expresses it: "It is the boiling of love (*ḥubb*) until it pours over its outer and inner extremities. . . . As for its reality (*maʿnā*), it is that one's share (*ḥaẓẓ*) departs from everything except his beloved (*maʿshūq*) until he forgets his love (ʿ*ishq*) because of his beloved."[42] This means that one has surrendered all that one has—his share—and all that one is to the beloved.

The full attainment of love is described by ad-Daylamī later in the twenty-first chapter, "Regarding the Limit of the Perfection of Love," wherein love at its highest level is considered to be one and the same as recognition (*maʿrifah*):

> Know that love is an attribute belonging to the lover, so long as it remains valid to attribute it to him. When it is no longer valid to attribute it to him, he is transported from it to something other than it. Then when he is transported from it, a name is derived for him from that to which he is transported, and a quality [is derived] from the state engendered for him. The past state is subsumed in the future state. Then he is called drunk, overwhelmed, uprooted or subsumed. Such is the case when he is transposed form love to love—meaning when he attains to the limit of annihilation through it, for it and in it.
>
> When upon attainment he is transported to the locus of recognition, he is not overcome by it, nor uprooted or intoxicated by it, rather the attribution of love is subsumed in the attribution of recognition, so he is a recognizing lover. His locus will rise from this level until what has passed is pulverized in what he what he [now] sees. He tastes a type of it unlike this [previous] type. He is among those upon whom love descends after recognition, and love becomes for him a station after it was a state. This is a very noble station according to the people of recognition, and to this the people (i.e., the Sufis) allude.[43]

Ad-Daylamī refers only to Sumnūn al-Muḥibb—the lover[44] (d. 298/910)—as one who has reached this station. He is cautious to note that the transformation of intellect that occurs is not one of bewilderment (*dahshah*), but one of realization in witnessing:

> Know that the lovers among the people of nature (*ṭabiʿah*) attain to the loss of reason, bewilderment and estrangement (*tawahhush*). This leads from and through these [states] to destruction and death. But the state of the divine among them is not like that. The state of their attainment is either to unification (*ittiḥād*) with the Beloved, which is perpetual life, or the station of unity (*tawḥīd*), which is arriving at the Beloved and witnessing [divine] visions (*shawāhid*) through the Beloved Witness until it is as if He is the reality of everything, everything is of Him, through Him, for Him and from Him, and He is in everything, encompassing everything, for everything, through everything, and from everything. And it is as if he is through nothing, for nothing, from nothing, of nothing, in nothing, and no thing. So understand all that if you desire recognition of the states of those who love Him, so that you will not err in witnessing and will not bear witness to repudiation (*juḥūd*), lest you be counted among those who lie and make false claims.[45]

al-Ḥusayn b. Manṣūr al-Ḥallāj

Although in the previous discussions love was presented as the highest degree of spiritual attainment, it was considered only in relation to the states and stations of the spiritual wayfarer. But when discussing the teachings of al-Ḥallāj, ad-Daylamī enters into a discussion of love's ontological status and cosmogonic function. He introduces al-Ḥallāj when discussing the views of Empedocles and Heraclitus, whom he says maintain that "the love of this world is from the effects of this principial love (*al-maḥabbah al-aṣliyyah*) which was the first thing produced from the Real, from which issued all that is in the worlds—the lower and the upper, the Divine and the natural."[46] He then notes that none of the Sufi Shaykhs claim this except al-Ḥallāj, who says:

> In what does not cease, the Real is one in Itself through Itself without "anything mentioned,"[47] until It manifests figures, forms, spirits, knowledge and recognition. Then the address[48] came to comprise rule, ruler and ruled (*al-mulk wa'l-mālik wa'l-mamlūk*) and determined the act, the agent and what is acted upon. So the Real was contemplating

> Itself through Itself in Its beginninglessness in totality and not manifest.
>
> All that is known/determined from knowledge, power, love (*maḥabbah*), *ʿishq*, wisdom, greatness, beauty, magnificence and the rest of what It described Itself by—compassion, mercy, holiness, spirits and the rest of the attributes—were a form in Its Essence that are Its Essence. Then the Real turned from perfection toward what was in It from the attribute of *ʿishq*; and this attribute was a form in Its Essence that *was Its Essence*.[49] [Emphasis added].

Al-Ḥallāj then describes the manner in which the Real interacted with the attribute of *ʿishq* in beginninglessness, addressing it through all the other attributes, and then proceeded to do the same with each of the other attributes. This, however, is an extremely allusive discussion from which few definite philosophical or metaphysical positions can be derived. The most important aspect of the discussion is what is revealed in the passage above, that *ʿishq* is for al-Ḥallāj an attribute that pertains to God's Essence. As such, "In its essence *ʿishq* has attributes that comprise many realities (*maʿānī*)."[50] Like all the other qualities and attributes of the Essence it has an important cosmogonic function in that it is through addressing the attributes pertaining to the Essence that the Real begins to engender the created order. Nonetheless, al-Ḥallāj attributes a centrality to *ʿishq* that is far beyond that of any other attribute:

> *ʿIshq* is a fire, the light of a first fire.[51] In beginninglessness it was colored by every color and appearing in every attribute. Its essence flamed through its [own] essence, and its attributes sparkled through its [own] attributes. It is [fully] verified, crossing not but from beginninglessness to endlessness. Its source is He-ness, and it is completely beyond I-ness. The non-manifest of what is manifest from its essence is the reality of existence; and the manifest of what is not manifest from its attributes is the form that is complete through concealment that proclaims universality through completion.[52]

As ad-Daylamī observes, "The difference between him and the claim of the first philosophers is that the first philosophers make love a thing produced (*mubdaʾ*), and he makes it something pertaining to the [Divine] Essence."[53] This move is of great importance for identifying sources from which Aḥmad al-Ghazālī and the later Sufi tradition may have drawn, or figures by whom he may have been influenced. There is nothing that resembles this position in Sufi literature until the treatment of love in writings attributed to ʿAbdallāh Anṣārī, and no definite record of such teachings regarding *ʿishq* until the composition of the *Sawāniḥ* two centuries after the death of al-Ḥallāj. Indeed, ad-Daylamī claims that al-Ḥallāj is unique among Sufi shaykhs in maintaining this position:

> Al-Ḥusayn b. Manṣūr [al-Ḥallāj] is separate from the rest of the Shaykhs in this claim. He is separate in that *he indicated that love is an attribute among the attributes of the Essence in all respects and wherever it is manifest.* As for Shaykhs other than him, they have indicated the unification (*ittiḥād*) of the lover and the Beloved in a state where love attains to the annihilation of the whole of the lover in the Beloved, without claiming that the Divine nature (*lāhūt*) [is incarnated in] the human nature (*nāsūt*) [Emphasis added].[54]

Other than al-Ḥallāj, ad-Daylamī does not provide enough information to transmit the teachings on love from any individual except himself. We can, however, infer that his own position is quite close to that of his spiritual master Ibn al-Khafīf. Ad-Daylamī's own position is that love (*maḥabbah*) is a Divine Attribute that pertains to Unity (*aḥadiyyah*)—a term that usually designates a transcendent unity that excludes multiplicity and is considered by some to represent a level of Divinity that is directly below the Divine Essence (*adh-dhāt al-ilāhiyyah*). Ad-Daylamī writes,

> As for the root of *maḥabbah,* it is that God does not cease to be qualified by love, and it is an attribute abiding with Him. In what does not cease, He is looking at Himself to Himself through Himself, just as He is finding Himself for Himself through Himself. Likewise, He loved Himself through Himself for Himself. Here, the lover, the Beloved and love are one thing with no division in it, because it is the reality of Unity (*ʿayn al-aḥadiyyah*) and there is not a thing and a thing in Unity (i.e., there is no duality).[55]

From ad-Daylamī's perspective, God manifests the attributes that make up creation from His own Attributes, and love is the first of these attributes. For ad-Daylamī, love is an attribute pertaining to the Essence (*adh-dhāt*), but it is also manifest in God's actions. According to him the attributes pertaining to the Divine Essence and the Divine Names cannot be known in and of themselves, but they can be known insofar as they are manifest by and in the Divine Acts.[56] He maintains that insofar as love is the first of the Divine Attributes to issue from beginninglessness into temporality (*ḥadath*), "it was divided into three: lover, beloved and love, and they are from a single source," and "they are manifest in every intelligible, imagined and sensed thing."[57] From this perspective, love is an attribute that can be said to pertain to the Divine Essence and be manifest in Divine Actions and in all of the relationships between created things. For both al-Ḥallāj and ad-Daylamī, love is an attribute pertaining to the Divine Essence, and the manifestations of love are connected to their root in this Essence though distinct from it. Their fundamental position is the same, but ad-Daylamī appears to be somewhat more cautious in drawing a distinction between love as it pertains to the Divine Essence without division and the manifestations of love in creation. For al-Ḥallāj, *ʿishq* pertains directly to the Essence "wherever it (*ʿishq*) is manifest." Indeed, many famous verses of al-Ḥallāj's poetry can be read as allusions to this same position:

> I am the one who yearns, and the one who yearns is I.
> We are two spirits in one body.
>
> Since the time we made the pact of yearning,
> Examples have been struck for people through us.
>
> So if you see me . . . you see Him,
> And if you see Him, you see us.[58]

And,

> I saw my Lord with the eye of my heart.
> I said who are you, He said you.
>
> My inmost being points to You, until
> I cease to be and You remain.
>
> You are my life and the depth of my heart;
> Wherever I am, there you are.[59]

Other Sufis of the Early Middle Period

To further examine teachings on love, sayings from many Sufis, such as Abu'l-Ḥusayn an-Nūrī (d. 295/908), Rābiʿah al-ʿAdawiyyah, Dhu'n-Nūn al-Miṣrī, Abū Yazīd al-Bistāmī (d. 261/875), and Abū Bakr ash-Shiblī could be cited, for as demonstrated by ad-Daylamī, love was a central theme of early Sufi discourse. But as these sayings have been transmitted through a select group of texts that were readily available to Aḥmad al-Ghazālī and his peers, my main focus will be upon the presentation of love in the central texts of early Sufism. Texts such as al-Qushayrī's *Risālah,* as-Sarrāj's *Kitāb al-Lumaʿ*, al-Kalābādhī's (d. 380/990 or 385/395) *Kitāb at-Taʿarruf,* and ʿAbd ar-Raḥmān as-Sulamī's many contributions can be seen as calculated arguments for the orthodoxy of Sufism and of certain mystical teachings. Proponents of Sufism were subject to many challenges from political and religious authorities.[60] Thus the rise of Sufi handbooks served to answer these challenges, allay the concerns of other scholars, and present an "orthodox" image of Sufism.

It is important to bear the opposition to some Sufi ideas in mind when examining theories of love, for as ad-Daylamī revealed, love was a topic of much debate. The censure of discussions on love to which ad-Daylamī alludes may have in some way curtailed discussions of love, especially when employing the term *ʿishq,* such that those who represented an attitude toward love like that of al-Ḥallāj were not sanctioned in the central textual tradition, though they may have persisted in an oral tradition and in texts that are no longer extant, such as the aforementioned treatises attributed to al-Junayd and Ibn al-Khafīf. The central texts of Sufism in the early middle period provide many allusions to teachings on *ʿishq* that are not well preserved. The evidence of a continuing oral tradition does not resurface in the extant textual tradition until the beginning of the sixth Islamic century, when it found form in the writings of Aḥmad al-Ghazālī and his younger contemporaries, Samʿānī and Maybudī. Identifying all of the individuals who may have been proponents of these nuanced teachings regarding *ʿishq* and the possible reasons for suppressing them is difficult. The following discussion is intended only to demonstrate that although the understanding of love in the textual tradition of early Sufism is quite different from that of the Persian Sufi love tradition, which began in the early 6th/12th century, it nonetheless alludes to the presence of ideas similar to those that arose in later centuries.

In three central handbooks of Sufism written in Arabic that precede al-Ghazālī—as-Sarrāj's *Kitāb al-Luma'*, al-Kalābādhī's *Kitāb at-Ta'arruf*, and al-Qushayrī's *Risālah*—there is no positive discussion of *'ishq*, only of *maḥabbah*. Each author devotes one chapter to *maḥabbah*, that of al-Qushayrī being the most extensive, while that of as-Sarrāj, in keeping with the character of the book, is the most systematic. The remainder of this chapter will examine these texts and those of Abū Ṭālib al-Makkī (d. 386/996), 'Alī b. 'Uthmān al-Hujwīrī (d. 465/1073 or 469/1077), Abdallāh Anṣārī, and Abū Ḥāmid al-Ghazālī, in chronological order, as these are the texts prior to Aḥmad al-Ghazālī that most shaped the Sufi tradition for generations to come.

As-Sarrāj—Kitāb al-Luma'

As-Sarrāj places *maḥabbah* as the third state (*ḥāl*) among eleven. Within this state he recognizes three levels of *maḥabbah*: the first is that of the general public (*maḥabbat al-'awāmm*), wherein one loves the Beloved through praise. It is the "devotion of the hearts praising the Beloved, preferring to follow Him and to be in agreement with Him."[61] The second level is the love of "the truthful" (*aṣ-ṣādiqūn*) and "the verifiers" (*al-muḥaqqiqūn*). It is "born of considering God's richness, magnanimity, greatness, knowledge and power." As-Sarrāj says this is the stage characterized by an-Nūrī as "the rending of covers and the uncovering of secrets."[62] At this stage the desires, the attributes, and the needs of the lover are eradicated in the face of the Beloved. The third level of love is that of "the sincere" (*aṣ-ṣiddīqūn*) and the recognizers (*al-'ārifūn*). It is "born from considering their recognition of the eternity (*qadīm*) of the love of God without causes. Likewise, nothing causes Him to love them."[63] That is to say that they recognize that God's love is eternal and does not arise because of an intermediary cause such as one's good deeds. Regarding this state, as-Sarrāj quotes Dhu'n-Nūn al-Miṣrī: "The pure love (*ḥubb*) of God, in which there is no turbidity is when love (*maḥabbah*) falls from the heart and the limbs until there is no *maḥabbah* and all things are through God and to God—that is the one who loves God."[64] At this level, one ceases to be a lover through oneself; for, as al-Junayd is reported to have said:

> [It is] when the qualities of the Beloved come as a replacement for the qualities of the lover. This is in accord with the meaning of His saying, ". . . until I love him; for when

> I love him, I am his eye with which he sees, his hearing with which he hears, and his hand with which he strikes."[65]

These statements from Dhu'n-Nūn and al-Junayd could be seen as allusions to the final station of love, already discussed by ad-Daylamī, which is beyond annihilation and wherein recognition is attained. But in his discussion of love, as-Sarrāj does not draw out any such implications in the words of those whom he cites. In fact, no teachings from any single figure are cited extensively enough to develop a full theory of love.

To understand the place of love among other states and stations, one must view it in the full context of as-Sarrāj's treatment. For as-Sarrāj, a state is vaguely defined as "the station of a servant before God, regarding what is fixed in him by way of acts of worship, acts of [spiritual] endeavor, [spiritual] exercises and devotion to God."[66] The seven stations he lists are repentance, scrupulousness, asceticism, poverty, patience, trust in God, and contentment, each of which is a necessary condition for the following station. Unlike stations, states do not come through struggle and devotion; rather, "The state is an occurrence (*nāzilah*) that descends into the hearts, yet does not remain."[67] Nonetheless, for as-Sarrāj, states can be above stations, for "contentment is the last station after which follow the states of those who have hearts, perusing those things unseen, refining the secrets for the purity of remembrances and the realities of states."[68] As with stations, each state must be followed by the subsequent state. The states treated by as-Sarrāj are watchfulness, nearness, love, fear, hope, desire, intimacy, serenity, witnessing, and certainty. Love is thus the state that follows nearness and must be followed by fear. As the remainder of *Kitāb al-Luma'* deals with other issues, not returning to an ascending scheme, it appears that as-Sarrāj presents a seventeen-step path beginning with repentance and ending with certainty, in which love is the tenth degree. The place of love is thus one among other degrees of spiritual wayfaring. It is nowhere near the expression of love found in al-Ḥallāj and ad-Daylamī, nor the *Sawāniḥ*, where love is the alpha and omega of existence and of wayfaring. Nonetheless, the sayings attributed to Dhu'n-Nūn al-Miṣrī and al-Junayd in which all things are "through God and to God" allude to teachings on love in which love encompasses all things.

Abū Ṭālib al-Makkī

Another important text for early Sufi teachings is the famous *Qūt al-qulūb fī mu'āmalāt al-maḥbūb wa-waṣf ṭarīq al-murīd ilā maqām at-tawḥīd* (The Nourishment of Hearts Regarding Acts towards the Beloved and the Description of the Path of the Seeker to the Station of Unity) by an erstwhile student of al-Junayd and follower of the Sālimiyyah Sufi tradition, Abū Ṭālib Muḥammad b. ʿAlī al-Makkī.[69] Like Abū Ḥāmid al-Ghazālī's *Revival of the Religious Sciences*, some parts of which are modeled upon it,[70] *Qūt al-qulūb* employs extensive citations from Quran and Hadith to establish the orthodoxy of its content. As A.J. Arberry observes, "The pattern of the Qūt al-qulūb is a little reminiscent of the standard manuals of religious jurisprudence, with its minute discussion of the ritual practices of Islam which are, however, treated from the mystical standpoint."[71] Compared to the texts of al-Balkhī, as-Sarrāj, and especially ad-Daylamī, it is the jurisprudential nature of this treatise that prevails, it being focused more on the practical (*ʿamalī*) aspects of the spiritual path than on the intellectual (*ʿaqlī*) ones.[72]

The intellectual discussions include al-Makkī's treatment of love. In the thirty-second book, he presents love as the ninth and last station (*maqām*) among the stations of certainty. The stations, in ascending order, are *tawbah* (repentance), *ṣabr* (patience), *shukr* (thankfulness), *rajāʾ* (hope), *khawf* (fear), *zuhd* (asceticism), *tawakkul* (trust), *riḍā* (contentment), and *maḥabbah* (love). But despite the exalted position attributed to love, there is no aspect of al-Makkī's discussion that approaches the depth of those treatments provided by al-Ḥallāj and ad-Daylamī, let alone those of Aḥmad al-Ghazālī and the later Sufi tradition.

Al-Makkī takes a position regarding love alluded to in some parts of ad-Daylamī's *ʿAṭf al-alif*, equating the state of loving God with that of having faith in God: "Everyone who has faith in God loves God. But his love is according to his faith, the unveiling of witnessing Him and the self-disclosure of the Beloved,"[73] for as God says, *Those who have faith are more intense in love for God* (Quran 2:165). Here love corresponds to the faculty of the heart (*qalb*), which according to al-Makkī has both an inner cavity and an outer cavity. The outer cavity is the locus of Islam, which corresponds to the term *fuʾād*. The inner cavity is the source of the outer cavity, the heart itself (*al-qalb*), which is the locus of faith. Al-Makkī maintains that many love God with part of the heart, while others love Him with the entire heart. When one loves with the entire heart, faith has entered the inner region of the heart (*bāṭin al-qalb*): "He prefers God to all his caprices (*ahwāʾ*), and the one who loves Him predominates over the caprice of the servant until the love of God becomes what the servant loves in everything. Then he is a true lover of God."[74] At its highest level, this love is the completion of *tawḥīd*: "When *tawḥīd* is complete, love is complete."[75]

Although al-Makkī sees love as the highest of all stations and sees pure love as the fullness of faith and the completion of *tawḥīd,* his treatment of love is still far removed from that of Aḥmad al-Ghazālī and the later Sufi love tradition. In terms of al-Ghazālī's presentation, al-Makkī's remains on the level of the lover (*ʿāshiq*) who yearns for the beloved (*maʿshūq*), for in every phase of al-Makkī's description there remains a *duality* between the lover and the beloved. Such a difference is enough to make it apparent that this concept of love most likely had no influence on Aḥmad al-Ghazālī. While Aḥmad al-Ghazālī presents the whole path as degrees of love, like ad-Daylamī, and the whole of creation as degrees of love, like al-Ḥallāj, al-Makkī presents the path as degrees and stations of certainty (*yaqīn*), love being the foremost among these stages.

al-Kalābādhī—Kitāb at-Taʿarruf

Like al-Makkī's *Qūt al-qulūb*, Abū Bakr b. Muḥammad al-Kalābādhī's *Kitāb at-Taʿarruf li madhhab ahl at-taṣawwuf* (The Knowledge of the Sufis) is designed to defend the orthodoxy of Sufism. As A.J. Arberry observes, al-Kalābādhī intended "to bridge the chasm between orthodox theology and Sufism which the execution of al-Ḥallāj had greatly widened; and this explains why, in his chapters treating doctrinal beliefs of the Sufis, he quotes verbally from the creed *al-fiqh al-akbar II,* falsely ascribed to Abū Ḥanīfa."[76] In doing so he gives the impression that most major Sufi figures were of the same intellectual disposition as Abū Ḥanīfah and of Ashʿarī *kalām* in general.[77] As Alexander Knysh observes, this sets al-Kalābādhī apart from as-Sulamī and al-Qushayrī, who were staunch adherents of a Shāfiʿī/Ashʿarī theological position.[78] This may result from the fact that al-Kalābādhī was centered in Bukhārah, further east than any of the other authors examined here. Despite being far from what came to be the main line of Sufi traditions in Baghdad and Khurāsān, he demonstrates extensive knowledge of both traditions and draws most of his citations from them.[79] He thus falls within the same tradition as as-Sarrāj and al-Qushayrī, though his treatise is more reliant on al-Ḥallāj who, however, remains anonymous throughout. Despite this emphasis on the sayings attributed to al-Ḥallāj, there is nothing even remotely akin to the teachings on *ʿishq* attributed to him by ad-Daylamī.

Al-Kalābādhī's treatment of *maḥabbah* is the least extensive and most ambiguous of those examined here; only nine sayings and three short poems are cited. Unlike as-Sarrāj, he does not make a clear distinction between states and stations. The spiritual qualities listed by al-Kalābādhī are not given a particular hierarchical relation as they are in the *Kitāb al-Luma'*. The chapter on love comes after "Union" (*wiṣāl*) and before "Disengaging and Isolation" but does not seem to have any particular relation to either. It is thus difficult to define the relationship between love and the other spiritual degrees of which al-Kalābādhī writes. He discusses states and stations in the thirty-first chapter, "The Sciences of the Sufis, the Sciences of States." In a gloss on the saying of another Sufi, he writes that the Sufi is one who "expresses his station and articulates the knowledge of his state."[80] From this statement it appears that the state and station are not viewed by al-Kalābādhī as separate stages or categories. The most that he says of them is that "for every station there is a science and for every state there is an allusion."[81] It would thus appear that for al-Kalābādhī love is both a state and a station to which corresponds a certain knowledge and about which certain allusions can be given. Among the few citations on love that al-Kalābādhī transmits there are allusions to views of love as a delight and as an inclination; al-Junayd states, "love is the inclination of the heart," and Sa'īd b. Yazīd Abū 'Abdallāh an-Nibajī[82] states, "Love is a delight in the created and a being consumed in the Creator." Al-Kalābādhī explains, "The meaning of consumption is that no share remains for you, there is no cause for your love, and you do not abide through a cause."[83] Delight and inclination later become central to the teachings of love provided by Abū Ḥāmid al-Ghazālī in the *Revival of the Religious Sciences.* Nonetheless, al-Kalābādhī's treatment of love has had little influence on the later Sufi tradition. It is, however, significant to note that even though he cites many sayings of al-Ḥallāj without providing attribution, he does not provide sayings that concur with the discussion of love that ad-Daylamī attributes to al-Ḥallāj.

Al-Mustamlī—Sharḥ-i Ta'arruf

The first Persian treatise on Sufism is a lengthy commentary on al-Kalābādhī's *Kitāb at-Ta'arruf, Sharḥ-i Ta'arruf li madhhab-i taṣawwuf* (Commentary on the Knowledge of the Sufis) by Ismā'īl b. Muḥammad al-Mustamlī (d. 434/1042–3). Whereas al-Kalābādhī's text is a mere 150 pages and offers little commentary, al-Mustamlī's comes to 1,800 pages in the modern printed edition and offers extensive discussions regarding various aspects of Sufism. For al-Kalābādhī's chapter on love, al-Mustamlī provides a lengthy introduction that offers key distinctions between how love is understood by the theologians—or "People of Principles," as al-Mustamlī calls them—and the Sufis, or "People of Recognition (*ʿirfān*)." After discussing the degrees that some ascribe to love between humans, with *ʿishq* as the highest degree of love, he returns to a discussion of "love between the Real and the servant." Here he states, "The People of Principles maintain that the love of the Real for the servant is a desire for the good, and that the love of the servant for the Real is obedience."[84] He then presents them as juxtaposing Divine enmity with Divine love, the former being the means by which people receive bad for what they have done and latter being the means by which they receive good. In contrast, for the People of Recognition, "it is permissible for the servant to be empty of obedience, yet at the same time not be empty of love, for being empty of love is unbelief. Thus obedience is not love, but obedience is the influence of love."

Like al-Kalābādhī's discussion, al-Mustamlī's discussion of love had little discernible influence after him. Nonetheless, he offers an important discussion that may indicate why certain aspects of the discussion of love remain elusive in the textual tradition:

> No one who has described love has reported about love itself. Rather, they talk about its attributes, its influences, and the lover's acts. This is because the one who describes is one of two: either he is a lover or he is not. If he is not a lover, how will he describe something he has not seen? And if he is a lover, he will be so preoccupied with love's burning that he will not have an opportunity to describe it. And if he does, though those who hear have no trace of this burning, his description will not be understood. There is no use in describing it. This is why all tongues have been silent regarding love [itself]. They spoke of its influences, attributes, and acts. Someone who is not aware of love does not know what [those who describe it] are talking about, and someone who is under its influence [already] sees what the description describes.[85]

al-Qushayrī's Risālah

In the works of al-Makkī, as-Sarrāj, and al-Kalābādhī, the only word used for love is *maḥabbah*, but with al-Qushayrī's *Risālah* and al-Hujwīrī's *Kashf al-Mahjūb* the word *ʿishq* is re-introduced into the discussion of love, albeit in a negative fashion. The most extensive treatment of love among the three classical Arabic Sufi handbooks is that provided by al-Qushayrī, who makes a clear distinction between states and stations akin to that of as-Sarrāj yet does not list states as degrees after stations. Rather, he provides a list of forty-nine states and stations, beginning with repentance (*tawbah*) and ending with audition (*samāʿ*). Among these, love is the forty-sixth subject treated, immediately preceded by "recognition of God" and followed only by longing (*shawq*), preserving the hearts of Shaykhs, and *samāʿ*, though this does not appear to be a hierarchical arrangement.

Al-Qushayrī is most inclined to the perspective that sees love as an expression of God's desire to draw His servant near to Him. But it is man's love for God that dominates this chapter. It is described as both inclination to God and destruction (*istihlāk*) in God, but for al-Qushayrī, "It is better to describe the lover as being destroyed in the Beloved than as inclining [to Him]."[86] As with most sections of the *Risālah*, the bulk of what is said about love has no specific orientation. Al-Qushayrī indicates that all the statements herein transmitted are provisional, for "love is not described through a description. It is not defined by anything more clearly [than love], nor by anything closer to understanding than love."[87] In some citations, love is described as a state that obliterates all that is other. Al-Junayd states, "It is the entering of the attributes of the Beloved in place of the attributes of the lover, and completely forgetting the attributes of oneself and sensing through them." By this, explains al-Qushayrī, "he alluded to the overpowering of the remembrance of the Beloved until nothing predominates over the heart of the lover other than the remembrance of the attributes of the Beloved."[88] This theme is also taken up by Muḥammad b. Saʿīd Abū ʿAbdillāh al-Qurashī: "The reality of love is that you give all of yourself to whom you love, so that nothing from you remains for you."[89] And Abū Bakr ash-Shiblī states, "Love is called love because it erases (*yamhu*) what is other than the Beloved."[90]

Other sayings express a less extreme degree of love. Muḥammad b. ʿAlī al-Kattānī (d. 322/934)[91] is quoted as saying, "Love is preference for the Beloved."[92] Abu Yaʿqūb Yūsuf b. Hamadhān as-Sūsī[93] is reported to have said, "The reality of love is that the servant forgets his share from God and forgets what he needs from Him."[94] Muḥammad b. Faḍl (d. 319/931) says, "Love is the falling away of all love from the heart, save the love of the Beloved (*al-ḥabīb*)."[95] In a saying that is echoed by many Sufis: "It is said, 'Love is a fire in the heart that burns all that is other than what the Beloved desires (*murād al-maḥbūb*).'"[96] Love is also presented as the counterbalance of fear, a position in which one most often finds hope (*rajāʾ*) in Sufi literature: "Whoever is given something of love and is not given something of fear like it is mistaken."[97] Perhaps the closest any of these sayings comes to expressing the teachings of love attributed to al-Ḥallāj and found in the later Sufi tradition is from a figure in Aḥmad al-Ghazālī's spiritual heritage, Sarī as-Saqaṭī (d. 253/867), the uncle and erstwhile teacher of al-Junayd: "Love between two is not pure until one says to the other 'O I'" (*yā ana*).[98]

Al-Qushayrī relates a story in which a group of shaykhs are discussing love in Mecca and al-Junayd was asked to speak:

> His eyes wept then he said, "A servant going from his self attached to the remembrance of his Lord, undertaking to observe His rights, looking at Him with his heart—the fires of His He-ness (*huwiyyatihi*) burn his heart, and the purity of his drink is from the cup of His affection, and the Magnificent (*al-Jabbār*) is unveiled for him from the curtains of His unseen realities. So if he talks it is through God, if he pronounces it is from God, if he moves it is through the command of God, and if he rests it is with God. So he is through God, to God, and with God.[99]

Though these citations offer many different perspectives on love, and sayings such as those attributed to Sarī as-Saqaṭī and al-Junayd may be taken as allusion to the fullness of love expressed by al-Ḥallāj and later in the Persian Sufi tradition, all of this offers little guidance in finding a possible source for Aḥmad al-Ghazālī's teachings on love. Such sayings appear to confirm ad-Daylamī's claim that al-Ḥallāj is unique among Sufi Shaykhs in his view of *ʿishq* as an attribute of the Divine Essence. Nonetheless, *ar-Risālah al-Qushayriyyah* is of central importance for examining the history of the term *ʿishq*. Al-Qushayrī writes that he heard his Shaykh Abū ʿAlī ad-Daqqāq say:

> *ʿIshq* is exceeding the limit in love (*maḥabbah*), and the Real is not described as transgressing the limit, so He is not described by *ʿishq*. If all the loves of mankind were joined together in one person, that would not reach the measure [of love] due to God. So let it not be said that a servant has transgressed the limit in the love of God. The Real is not described as if He loves (*yaʿshaqu*), nor the servant in relation to God [as if he loves]. So *ʿishq* is negated and there is no way to describe the Real by it—neither from the Real toward the servant, nor from the servant toward the Real.[100]

This passage demonstrates that although few sayings regarding *ʿishq* are preserved from the early Sufi communities, there were most likely some who held that *ʿishq* is distinct from *maḥabbah* and that it is permissible to say that human beings can have *ʿishq* for God and that God has *ʿishq* for human beings. Otherwise there would be no reason for Abū ʿAlī ad-Daqqāq to refute such positions. Together, the three positions ad-Daqqāq refutes provide three of the main ingredients for the teachings on *ʿishq* expressed by al-Ḥallāj and, in a slightly different form, in the later love tradition: God, the Real, can be described by *ʿishq;* humans have *ʿishq* for God; God has *ʿishq* for humans. Though it is difficult, if not impossible, to know who, other than al-Ḥallāj, may have advocated such a position, this short refutation of the term *ʿishq* indicates the presence of an oral tradition that has not been fully preserved.

al-Hujwīrī's Kashf al-Maḥjūb

ʿAlī b. ʿUthmān al-Hujwīrī's (d. 465/1073 or 469/1077)[101] *Kashf al-Maḥjūb* (The Unveiling of the Veiled) is the first Sufi handbook written in Persian.[102] Unlike al-Qushayrī, al-Kalābādhī, and as-Sarrāj, al-Hujwīrī tends to be more open about expressing his own positions. His treatment of love is no exception. For al-Hujwīrī, love (*maḥabbah*) is of two kinds: (1) the love of the like for the like, as between a man and a woman, and (2) "the love of one who is unlike the object of his love and who seeks to become intimately attached to an attribute of that object; for example, hearing without speech or seeing without eye,"[103] the latter being the love of God. Those who love God are further divided into two kinds: (1) those who love the Benefactor due to His beneficence, and (2) "those who are so enraptured by love that they reckon all favors as a veil." For al-Hujwīrī, "The latter way is the more exalted of the two."[104]

Though al-Hujwīrī's own opinion regarding love falls short of the all-encompassing nature of love found in the later Persian tradition, he mentions Shaykh Sumnūn al-Muḥibb, whom ad-Daylamī had regarded as one of the few to have reached the fullness of love as a "recognizing lover." In a passage that is important for understanding the veiled nature of Sufi language, Hujwīrī reports of Sumnūn:

> He asserts that love is the foundation and principle of the way to God, that all states and stations are stages of love, and that every stage and abode in which the seeker may be admits of destruction, except the abode of love, which is not destructible under any circumstances so long as the way itself remains in existence. All the other shaykhs agree with him in this matter, but since the term "love"

> (*maḥabbah*) is current and well known, and they wish the doctrine of Divine love to remain hidden, instead of calling it love they gave it the name "purity" (*ṣafwat*),[105] and the lover they call "Sufi"; or they use "poverty" (*faqr*) to denote the renunciation of the lover's personal will in his affirmation of the Beloved's will, and they called the lover "poor" (*faqīr*).[106]

Whereas in *Qūt al-qulūb* al-Makkī expressed the view that love is the highest station (*maqām*), here for the first time we find an account that concurs with ad-Daylamī's belief that love comprises all the states and stations of the spiritual path. But there is still no expression of the supreme all-encompassing love alluded to by al-Ḥallāj and ad-Daylamī and found in the later Persian tradition. Nonetheless, as with the passage from ad-Daqqāq in the *Risālah* of al-Qushayrī, this alludes to another of the key ingredients in Aḥmad al-Ghazālī's view of love. It is significant that al-Hujwīrī tells us that the Shaykhs "wish the doctrine of Divine Love to remain hidden." This indicates that none of the texts of early Sufism have fully expressed the understanding of love as it existed among certain components of the early Sufi community, thus alluding, as did ad-Daqqāq, to an oral tradition that has not been fully preserved in the written tradition.

Something similar to the view attributed to Sumnūn al-Muḥibb is expressed in al-Hujwīrī's analysis of a passage attributed to al-Qushayrī:

> Master Abu'l-Qāsim Qushayrī says, "Love is the effacement of the lover as regards his attributes and the affirmation of the Beloved as regards His Essence. Love is that the lover negate all of his attributes in the reality of seeking the Beloved in the affirmation of the Essence of the Real." That is, since the Beloved is subsistent (*bāqi*) and the lover is annihilated (*fāni*), the jealousy of love requires that the lover should make the subsistence of the Beloved absolute by negating himself, and he cannot negate his own attributes, except by affirming the essence of the Beloved. No lover can stand by his own attributes, for in that case he would not need the Beloved's beauty; but when he knows that his life depends on the Beloved's beauty, he necessarily seeks to annihilate his own attributes, which veil him from the Beloved.[107]

Like al-Qushayrī, al-Hujwīrī provides an extensive debate regarding the use of the term *ʿishq*. Here al-Hujwīrī makes explicit the controversy that was implicit with Abū ʿAlī ad-Daqqāq in al-Qushayrī's *Risālah*:

> Concerning *ʿishq* the Shaykhs say many things. A contingent among this group holds that *ʿishq* for the Real is permissible, but that it is not permissible to hold that there is *ʿishq* from the Real. They say that *ʿishq* is the attribute of one debarred from his beloved, man is debarred from God, but God is not debarred from man. It is therefore permissible to say that man has *ʿishq* for Him, but from Him to man it is not permissible.[108]

But he also mentions the view expressed by ad-Daqqāq: that since *ʿishq* implies a passing beyond limits, it cannot apply to man's love of God, either. A later group maintains that *ʿishq* refers to love of the Divine Essence, but that since the Essence cannot be realized, *ʿishq* is not an appropriate term: "They also say that *ʿishq* only arises through observing form and that *maḥabbah* may arise through hearing, so that vision of the Real cannot arise since nobody can see Him in the world."[109] So according to this group no one may have *ʿishq* for God, since it pertains to the Essence, whereas *maḥabbah* pertains to the attributes and actions that can be perceived in this world.

This debate regarding the use of the two terms reveals that there must have been other groups or individuals maintaining both that man has *ʿishq* for God not only in his attributes but also in His Essence and that God has *ʿishq* for man. Otherwise, al-Hujwīrī would not feel the need to refute these positions. What is important here is not so much the difference in technical terminology but the debate that appears to underlie the use of these terms. This is not simply a philological debate. It is a philosophical and epistemological debate regarding the human being's ability to witness the Divine and know the Divine Essence. Shades of this debate were seen in ad-Daylamī's presentation of al-Ḥallāj's position that *ʿishq* is an attribute pertaining to the Divine Essence. As will be seen, Shaykh Aḥmad al-Ghazālī, Imām Abū Ḥāmid al-Ghazālī, and many others in the later Persian Sufi tradition clearly believe that one can realize the Divine Essence, but that such knowledge in no way pertains to the senses or to the mental faculties; rather, it is achieved through *baṣīrah*, insight, and is realized within the secret core, beyond the heart and the spirit. As

Aḥmad al-Ghazālī writes at the end of the *Sawāniḥ*, "The eyes of the intellect have been blocked from perceiving the quiddity and reality of the spirit, and the spirit is the shell of love. So since knowledge has no way to the shell, how can it have a path to the jewel concealed within the shell?"[110] In his sessions such insight is referred to as recognition (*maʿrifah*). He believes the ability to grasp this "jewel" with the human mind was beyond even the Prophet Muḥammad: "Whenever the Messenger of God was carried to the ocean of knowledge it would flow forth, but when he was cast into the ocean of recognition he said, 'I do not know; I only worship (*lā adrī innamā aʿbudu*).'"[111]

Unlike the texts of al-Makkī, as-Sarrāj, al-Kalābādhī, and al-Qushayrī, with al-Hujwīrī's treatment of love, the reader is cast into the center of an intense debate, not just about the use of particular technical terms, but about the nature of man's knowledge of God, the extent to which the spiritual aspirant can travel, and how much of these teachings should be revealed. Aḥmad al-Ghazālī and others in the Persian school of love firmly maintain that one can "perceive"—or to put it in their terms, "taste"—the Divine Essence, which for them is *ʿishq* itself, and that the spiritual aspirant can travel completely beyond the duality of lover and Beloved. As such, his *Sawāniḥ* marks an important juncture in the Sufi tradition where many of these teachings on the metaphysics of love are for the first time fully expressed. The allusions to such positions by al-Qushayrī and al-Hujwīrī indicate that the *Sawāniḥ* marks a point where particular oral teachings become a part of the written tradition, though in a form largely inaccessible to one who is not steeped in the language of Sufism. That such teachings existed but were not fully recorded is further illustrated by the fact that many of Aḥmad al-Ghazālī's teachings on love are alluded to but not fully stated in his brother's treatment of love in the *Revival*.

ʿAbdullāh Anṣārī

Among the Sufis discussed here, the teachings of Anṣārī are perhaps the most difficult to address. Many of the sayings attributed to him are difficult to authenticate, especially those preserved in Maybudī's *Kashf al-asrār*, where Anṣārī is frequently cited as *Pīr-i Ṭarīqat*, "The Master of the Paths," and those in his *Munājāt*, or "Intimate Discourses," which appear to have been collected by his disciples at a later time.[112] In addition, his *Ṭabaqāt as-Ṣūfiyyah* (Generations of the Sufis) was compiled posthumously from the notes of many students.[113] Anṣārī did, however, compose, or oversee the composition of, several works in Arabic and Persian. Among these is his *Treatise on Love* (Maḥabbat Nāmah), an allusive and aphoristic text that appears to be the first Persian treatise to be written on love. The place of love is also addressed in various ways in his four texts on the Sufi path: *The Hundred Fields* (Sad Madyān), *The Way Stations of the Travelers* (Manāzil al-sāʾirīn), *The Flaws of the Stages* (ʿIlal al-maqāmāt), and *Sayings and Advice* (Maqūlāt-o andarzhā). In *The Way Stations of the Travelers,* love is presented as the 61st way station:

> Love is the mark of the Tribe, the title of the path (*ṭarīqah*), and the seat of the relationship [with God]. It has three degrees: The first degree is a love that cuts of disquieting thoughts, makes service enjoyable, and offers solace in affliction. This love grows up from examining favors, becomes fixed by following the Sunnah, and grows into responding with poverty. The second degree is a love that incites preferring the Real to all else, induces *dhikr* on the tongue, and attaches the heart to witnessing Him. This is a love that becomes manifest from examining the attributes [of God], gazing upon the signs [of God], and undergoing the discipline of the stations. The third degree is a dazzling love that cuts off expression, makes allusions subtle, and does not attain description. Such love is the axis of this affair, and all loves beneath it are called by tongues, claimed by creatures, and declared obligatory by rational faculties.[114]

When viewed in relation to the other way stations, it appears that love occupies one of the way stations along the spiritual path, but not the highest. Regarding the final fields or stations of the path, Anṣārī states, "Togetherness is the final end of the stations of the wayfarers, the shore of *tawḥīd*'s ocean."[115] But in his *Treatise on Love,* he maintains that love is the mark of togetherness: "The reality of togetherness is the mark of unification, and unification is the mark of love."[116] In the final paragraph of *The Hundred Fields,* Anṣārī also states, "These hundred fields are all drowned in the field of love. The one hundred first field is love: *He loves them, and they love Him* (5:54). *Say, If you love God* (3:31). Love is three stations: the first is truthfulness; the middle is drunkenness, and the last is nonbeing."[117] Anṣārī also alludes to love itself being beyond the duality of lover and beloved when he states, "How then can the lover and the beloved be one? When created nature departs, the Real is suited for oneness."[118] From these passages, it would appear that Anṣārī shares the vision of love presented in the *Sawāniḥ*, wherein the whole of the Sufi path is viewed as different degrees and shades of love, although it is not stated as directly and emphatically.

Although Aḥmad al-Ghazālī employs the terms *ḥubb/maḥabbah* and *ʿishq* interchangeably, Anṣārī, like Abū Ḥāmid al-Ghazālī in the *Revival*, distinguishes between the two and places *ʿishq* above or beyond *ḥubb/maḥabbah*:

> *ʿIshq* is a burning fire and an ocean without shore. It is the spirit and the spirit of the spirit. It is story without end and pain without remedy. The intellect is bewildered in its perception, the heart unable to grasp it. It makes the hidden apparent and the apparent hidden. It is the ease of the spirit and the outset of openings. Although the spirit is the life of bodies, *ʿishq* is the life of the heart. When man is silent, *ʿIshq* tears his heart to pieces and purifies it of everything but itself. When he shouts out, it turns him upside down and gives news of his story to city and lane.
>
> *ʿIshq* is both fire and water, both darkness and sun. It is not pain, but a bringer of pain, not affliction but a bringer of affliction. Just as it causes life, so too it causes death. Just as it is the substance of ease, so too it is the means of blights. Love (*maḥabbah*) burns the lover, but not the beloved. *ʿIshq* burns both seeker and sought.[119]

In *The Hundred Fields* and his *Treatise on Love*, Anṣārī presents love as a reality in which the lover becomes entirely immersed, going beyond the duality of lover and beloved. In this respect, his understanding of the Sufi path can be seen as the most important precursor to the vision of love expressed in the *Sawāniḥ* and likely had some influence on Aḥmad al-Ghazālī. He is not, however, as clear in the expression of an understanding of love as the origin and reality of all things, though this understanding of love does appear to undergird his view of reality.

Abū Ḥāmid al-Ghazālī

The *Kitāb al-Maḥabbah wa'sh-shawq wa'l-uns wa'r-riḍā* (The Book of Love, Longing, and Contentment) of the *Revival* brings elements of several previous texts together into one coherent treatment of love. For Abū Ḥāmid al-Ghazālī:

> Love for God is the ultimate aim among the stations and the highest summit among the degrees, for there is no station beyond the perception (*idrāk*) of love except that it is a fruit from among its fruits and a consequence of its effects, such as longing (*shawq*), intimacy (*uns*), contentment (*riḍā*) and their sisters. And there is no station before love, except that it is a prelude to it, such as repentance (*tawbah*), forbearance (*ṣabr*), asceticism (*zuhd*) and the like.[120]

As with al-Hujwīrī and al-Qushayrī, there is an allusion to an ongoing debate regarding the nature of love, but here the debate centers on the term *maḥabbah*. Al-Ghazālī states that some scholars claim love is impossible except between the like and the like, and comments, "When they deny love, they deny intimacy, desire, the delight of intimate discourse [with God] (*munājāt*), and all the other effects and consequences of love. The veil must be lifted from this matter."[121] He then divides his treatment into seventeen clarifications (*bayyināt*), most of which center on the nature of man's love for God, and some of which treat God's love for man, which is in truth the source of man's love for God. Here I will first examine the discussion of man's love for God that Imām Abū Ḥāmid divides into five types. This study will begin by examining the nature of *ʿishq* that he, like Anṣārī, places beyond *maḥabbah* and conclude by examining his treatment of God's love for human beings.

MAN'S LOVE FOR GOD

While Abū Ḥāmid al-Ghazālī begins this book with the treatment of the foundation of love in the Quran and the *Ḥadīth*, it is clear that his discussion of love, as with that of the Sufi tradition preceding him, is not derived directly from these sources. The discussions of love in these sources always emphasize worship (*ʿibādah*), but the attitude of the proponent of love is, as expressed by Yaḥyā b. Muʿādh ar-Rāzī (d. 258/872), "[That] the weight of a single grain of love is more beloved to me than worshipping seventy years without love."[122]

In the first clarification, Abū Ḥāmid sets the tone for a discussion that focuses little on worship and much on realizing a direct relationship with God: "Know that what is sought from this section is not unveiled except through recognition (*maʿrifah*) of love itself, then recognition of its conditions and causes (*asbāb*), then after that examination (*naẓar*) of the verification of its reality (*maʿnā*) in the truth of God."[123] For Abū Ḥāmid al-Ghazālī, love must necessarily follow upon knowledge and perception because only that which is known and perceived can be loved, and "everything in which there is delight and ease in the perception of it is beloved unto the perceiver." "Thus love is an expression of the inclination or disposition to a thing in which there is delight."[124] This definition is very close to that attributed to al-Junayd in al-Kalābādhī's *Kitāb at-Taʿarruf*: "Love (*maḥabbah*) is the inclination of the heart."[125] But having defined love in this way, al-Ghazālī then makes a move like that attributed to al-Junayd by ad-Daylamī, stating that "if that inclination is firm and strong, it is called *ʿishq*."[126] This sets the stage for an emphatically positive treatment of the term *ʿishq* that places it above *maḥabbah* and equates it with the highest level of realization.[127]

As Imām Abū Ḥāmid al-Ghazālī writes throughout the *Revival* and in several other works, perception (*idrāk*) is divided into two major categories: outward (*ẓāhirī*) and inward (*bāṭinī*). The outward pertains to the five senses, whereas the inward is a sixth sense, known as the intellect (*ʿaql*), light, or the heart, and is far stronger:

> Inner vision is stronger than outward sight, and the heart is more intense in perceiving than the eye. The beauty of meanings perceived through the intellect is greater than the beauty of forms manifest to eyesight, and there is no doubt that the delight of the heart with what it perceives among the noble divine affairs that are too sublime to be perceived by the senses is more complete and more profound. So the inclination of the sound nature and the healthy intellect to it is stronger, and there is no meaning to love except the inclination to that in the perception of which there is delight. . . . So no one denies the love of God save he for whom being held back in the degree of beasts has disabled him, for he will not surpass the perception of the senses at all.[128]

Here Abū Ḥāmid al-Ghazālī combines and builds on ideas previously stated, that love is inclination and delight. But he is more emphatic, arguing, "There is no meaning to love except the inclination to that in the perception of which there is delight." He then lists five kinds of love that he believes comprise all modes of human love: (1) the love of man for himself, his perfection (*kamāl*), and his subsistence; (2) his love for whoever does what is beautiful (*al-muḥsin*) to him because it supports his own completion and subsistence; (3) his love for one who does good out of appreciation for the good he does; (4) his love for all that is beautiful in its essence (*fī dhātihi*); and (5) his love for one with whom he has a hidden inner relationship. But for Abū Ḥāmid al-Ghazālī, the only one who is truly worthy of any form of love is God: "Whoever loves what is other than God, not because of its relationship to Him, that is due to his ignorance and his lack of knowledge of God."[129] He thus argues that "according to the People of Insight, there is in reality no beloved except God and none worthy of love but Him."[130] So each of the five types of love is in fact love for God and is only complete in so far as it is realized as such. As for the love of self:

> This requires the utmost love for God. Whoever knows himself and knows his Lord knows for certain that he has no existence from his own essence and that the existence of his essence and the persistence of and perfection of his existence is only from God, for God and through God; for He is the Originator who gives him existence, the One who makes him subsist and the One who perfects his existence by creating the attributes of perfection, creating the effects which lead to it, and creating the guidance in the application of the effects. Otherwise, there would be no existence for the servant from his essence as concerns his essence; rather, he would be shear obliteration and pure non-existence if not for the grace of God upon him through existentiation. . . . In sum, there is nothing in existence for Him abiding though itself, except the Abiding, the Living, Who is abiding in His Essence. All that is other than Him is abiding through Him. So if the recognizer (*ʿārif*) loves his [own] essence and the existence of his essence pours forth from other than him, he must necessarily love the One who pours forth his existence, who makes him persist. If he knows Him to be a Creator, an Existentiator, an Originator, a Subsister and an Abider through Himself, then he does not love Him, that is due to his ignorance of himself and his Lord, for love is a fruit of knowledge.[131]

This passage goes a step beyond the discussion of love in al-Hujwīrī toward the fullness of love in which lover and Beloved emanate—or "derive," as Aḥmad al-Ghazālī expresses it—from Love Itself. Logically the four other types of love flow from this first love, for in understanding that one must love God because one's existence flows from Him and all that exists subsists through Him, one will necessarily realize that what is loved is loved for that in it that subsists through God.

As regards the love of one who does what is beautiful (*al-muḥsin*) for one's self because it completes one's perfection and subsistence, Imām al-Ghazālī follows his argument that God is the only perfecter and the only one who makes things subsist to its logical conclusion, saying, "The only one who does what is beautiful is God," and that "doing what is beautiful is only conceived for man metaphorically."[132] Thus loving another for the good he does for one's self "requires in its essence that one love none but God; for if he recognizes with the truth of recognition, then he knows that the one who does what is beautiful to him is God alone."[133] The love for the one who does what is beautiful simply for the beauty he performs follows this same argument:

> And this too requires the love of God; rather, it requires that one love no one other than Him at all except in so far as he is attached to Him through a cause. For God is the One who does what is beautiful to all, the One who blesses all types of creatures.[134]

This benevolence comes through bringing them into existence, perfecting them, comforting and blessing them, and beautifying them with those things that are beyond their needs.[135] For both the love of one who does what is good for oneself and the love of one who does what is beautiful in itself, it must be remembered that:

> He is the Creator of beauty, the Creator of the one who does what is beautiful, the Creator of doing what is beautiful, and the Creator of the causes (*asbāb*) of doing what is beautiful. For this reason, love for what is other than Him is also sheer ignorance. Whoever knows that will for this reason love none other than God.[136]

The fourth kind of love discussed by Imām Abū Ḥāmid—love for something beautiful for the beauty it possesses in itself—is love for God because "the beauty of everything is in the perfection that befits it,"[137] "perfection belongs to God alone, and nothing other than Him has perfection except by virtue of what God has given it."[138] As was made clear in the discussion of the love of one's self, God is the only one who is perfect and the only one who makes perfect. Thus all beauty is in fact God Himself; for as the Prophet Muḥammad has said, "God is beautiful and He loves beauty,"[139] and the Absolute Beauty is the only beauty that has no partner unto it in beauty, all beauty emanating from or being derived from it. So all love of beauty is love of the Absolute Beauty. This love is stronger than love for one who does what is beautiful, for doing what is beautiful (*iḥsān*) increases and decreases,[140] whereas what is beautiful pertains directly to God in His Absolute Perfection.

The fifth kind of love—for one with whom one has a hidden inner relationship—is the most exalted and elusive. Imām al-Ghazālī states that it is an inner reality and does not provide a full account, declaring, "It is permitted to record some of it in books and some of it is not permitted to be recorded, but is left under the cover of dust until the wayfarers on the path stumble upon it."[141] That about which one can write is the servant's "taking on the lordly character traits," comprised in the Divine attributes, by drawing close to his Lord. That which should be "left under the cover of dust" is alluded to in the Quranic verses 17:75, *They ask thee about the Spirit. Say, 'The Spirit is from the command of my Lord,'* and 15:29 and 38:72, *So when I established him and breathed into him from My Spirit.* It is not to be spoken of because it is in regard to this that the errors of "incarnationists" have arisen.[142] But when devoid of exaggeration, this appears to be the type of love wherein *ḥubb* or *maḥabbah* is transformed into *ʿishq*.

For Imām Abū Ḥāmid, it is of the utmost importance that one realize love of God in all of these modes because true salvation lies in love for God:

> Know that the happiest of mankind in the Hereafter are those who are strongest in love for God; for the meaning of the Hereafter is reaching God and realizing the happiness of meeting Him. What is greater for the lover than the blessing when he reaches his Beloved after prolonged desire? He attains to witnessing for eternity with no arouser or obfuscator, no overseer or competitor, with no fear or cutting off, except that this blessing is in accord with the strength of his love. So whenever the love increases the delight increases.[143]

ATTAINING TO ʿISHQ

In discussing the five phases of love, Imām Abū Ḥāmid uses the words *ḥubb* and *maḥabbah*. But for him, the highest level of delight, and thus love, is *ʿishq,* although few are able to attain this level: "As for the strength of love and its overpowering until it attains to the infatuation called *ʿishq,* most are separated from that."[144] This infatuation is reached by two means:

> The first of them is cutting off the attachments of this world and expelling the love of what is other than God from the heart. For the heart is like a container, it cannot hold vinegar, for example, so long as water is not expelled from it: *God did not make for man two hearts in his breast* (33:4). The perfection of love is in loving God with all of one's heart.[145]

When discussing the second means, Imām Abū Ḥāmid identifies love with recognition. This is a move first seen in ad-Daylamī but which was not repeated by anyone after him and was even opposed by some. As al-Qushayrī writes:

> Sumnūn [al-Muḥibb] gave precedence to love (*maḥabbah*) over recognition, but most give precedence to recognition over love. According to the verifiers, love is destruction in delight and recognition is witnessing in bewilderment (*dahshah*) and annihilation in awe (*haybah*).[146]

But for Abū Ḥāmid al-Ghazālī, recognition and love are one and the same:

> The second effect for the strength of love is the strength of recognition of God and its expanding and overpowering the heart, and that is after purifying the heart of all its preoccupations with the world and its attachments. . . . Then from this seed is born the tree of recognition and love. That is the good word of which God has struck an example when He says, *God strikes the example of a good word, like a good tree whose root is firm and whose branches are in the sky* (13:24).[147]

Abū Ḥāmid goes on to say, "Whenever this recognition is attained, love follows it necessarily."[148]

Considering the issues raised in al-Hujwīrī's refutation of certain positions regarding *ʿishq* that are not available in the textual tradition, it appears that Imām Abū Ḥāmid is also taking a stance on issues that were actively debated in the oral tradition. That discussions of love that are not recorded took place was suggested when he declared that the fifth form of love is "left under the cover of dust until the wayfarers stumble upon it."[149] That which is not recorded is according to Abū Ḥāmid the knowledge of God in Himself, for that is a higher path, and "the higher path is witnessing the Real beyond all creation. It is concealed and discussion of it is beyond the understanding of most people, so there is no benefit in seeking it in books."[150] This is similar to the understanding al-Mustamlī conveyed when maintaining that "Someone who is not aware of love does not know what [those who describe it] are talking about, and someone who is under its influence [already] sees what the description describes."[151]

Regarding these debates, it is clear that unlike al-Hujwīrī and Abū ʿAlī ad-Daqqāq, Abū Ḥāmid al-Ghazālī maintains that the human being can have *ʿishq* for God, that God has *ʿishq* for the human being, and that through *ʿishq* the human being can know God in His very Essence, not only through His attributes and actions. To know God in Himself is what he calls the higher path. He gives the reader some indication of what the higher path is in contrasting it to the lower path:

> Those who reach this level are divided into the strong whose first recognition is of God, then through Him they know His acts, and the weak whose first recognition is of the acts, then they ascend from that to the Agent. To the first there is an allusion through His word: *Does not your Lord suffice? Verily He is a witness over everything* (41:54), and through His word: *God bears witness that there is no god but Him* (3:18) . . . To the second there is allusion in His word: *We will show them Our signs on the horizons and within themselves until it becomes clear to them that He is the Real* (41:53) . . . This path is the lower according to most and it is more widespread among the wayfarers.[152]

Imām Abū Ḥāmid al-Ghazālī leaves the details of this higher path aside, but in the *Sawāniḥ* Shaykh Aḥmad al-Ghazālī goes directly for the higher path. Nonetheless, of all the teachings on love between the time of al-Ḥallāj and ad-Daylamī and the appearance of the *Sawāniḥ*, the *Revival* provides the clearest example of an attitude toward love similar to that expressed in the *Sawāniḥ* and later Persian writings. For the first time since the few passages attributed to al-Ḥallāj by ad-Daylamī over a century before, there appears a thoroughly positive treatment of *ʿishq* and an expression of the belief that in its highest degree it is tied to recognition (*ʿirfān*), not only of God's acts and attributes but of the Divine Essence in and of Itself.

GOD'S LOVE FOR MAN

In concluding this examination of Abū Ḥāmid al-Ghazālī's understanding of love, I must briefly discuss God's love for human beings. The Imām distinguishes the love of the servant for the Creator from that of the Creator for the servant. The love of the servant is for that from which it derives greater perfection: "And this is impossible for God, for every perfection, beauty, wonder and magnificence is possible in the truth of the Divinity."[153] The love of God for man is thus in fact God's inclination toward Himself. In one of the most important passages of this book of the *Revival*, he indicates that all love is ultimately God's love for Himself:

> None has a view of Him in so far as he is other than Him, rather, one's view is of His Essence and His acts only, and there is nothing in existence but His Essence and His acts. Therefore when the verse, *He loves them, and they love Him* (5:54) was read to him, Shaykh Abū Saʿīd al-Mihānī (d. 440/1048–9)[154] said, "He loves them truly, for there is nothing in love except Himself," meaning that He is the entirety and that there is nothing in existence except Him.[155]

Viewed in this light, every love, every inclination, and every delight is both for God and from God. The five stages of a human being's love for God are thus five ways in which God loves Himself through the love of His servants for Him.

Summary

There is little that can be done to determine all of the Sufi teachers who shared the understanding of love alluded to by ʿAbdallāh Anṣārī in multiple passages and by Abū Ḥāmid al-Ghazālī in the *Revival* and expressed in the *Sawāniḥ* and the later Persian Sufi tradition. In light of the extant texts, ad-Daylamī's claim that al-Ḥallāj was unique among the shaykhs in maintaining that *ʿishq* is an attribute pertaining to the Divine Essence and that every manifestation of it is directly connected to that Essence appears to be accurate. But it may be that he was unique in openly proclaiming teachings that others felt were best left unsaid, or that he was unique in using the word *ʿishq* where others felt the word *maḥabbah* was more appropriate. This is evident in the writings of al-Qushayrī, al-Hujwīrī, Anṣārī, and Abū

Ḥāmid al-Ghazālī. The first two allude to the pressures to criticize such teachings, but al-Hujwīrī also tells us that "the shaykhs wish the doctrine of Divine Love to remain hidden,"[156] thus alluding to the possibility that even those who agree with the teachings of al-Ḥallāj saw no benefit in exposing teachings to the uninitiated that might only befuddle their intellects. It is most likely in this vein that Imām Abū Ḥāmid tells us that the discussion of *ʿishq* is "left underneath the cover of dust until the wayfarers of the path stumble upon it,"[157] and that Anṣārī asks, "How can the tongue express something that does not come to the tongue? How can the spirit allude to something to which none can allude? How can a mark be given of something that has no mark?"[158] Such statements indicate that one must attain to a certain degree of spiritual maturity before one is able to properly understand the nature of love, and especially that of *ʿishq*. Read in this light, statements such as that of Abū ʿAlī ad-Daqqāq that criticize the use of the word *ʿishq* may in fact be meant to dissuade novices from speculating on teachings meant only for the advanced. Evidently Aḥmad al-Ghazālī felt differently about exposing such teachings. As he writes in the beginning of the *Sawāniḥ*:

> Sometimes an earthen vessel or a glass bead is put in the hand of a novice until he becomes a master artisan; but sometimes a precious, shining pearl that the master's hand of knowledge does not dare touch, let alone pierce, is put into his ignorant hand to pierce.[159]

This means that sometimes the most sublime truths can, and perhaps even should, be exposed to spiritual novices so that their treasures may be mined.

Given the paucity of textual evidence, efforts to uncover the reasons for limiting discussion of *ʿishq* would enter more into the realm of speculation than analysis. It is, however, clear that in the *Sawāniḥ* Aḥmad al-Ghazālī chose to put to paper that which others before him, with the exception of al-Ḥallāj and perhaps of ʿAbdallāh Anṣārī, had been reticent to make public. This choice was a watershed event in Sufi history, the impact of which has shaped Persian Sufi literature to this day.

Chapter 5

Aḥmad al-Ghazālī's Metaphysics of Love

To understand the content of Aḥmad al-Ghazālī's writings and sermons, one must also examine their form. In his attempts to transport his audience to the truth of which he is certain and to actualize the realization of it within them, Aḥmad al-Ghazālī is ever aware of the limitations inherent to words. My analysis of his teachings will therefore begin with an examination of his attitude toward language, since he often reminds the reader to be conscious of the relativity of the words with which he communicates. Having examined al-Ghazālī's reflections on the nature of language, I will then discuss his use of themes from the secular literary tradition, demonstrating how he transports them into a Sufi context. This will be followed by an examination of his attitude toward interpretation (*ta'wīl*) and of his allusive method of citing Quran, Hadith, and poetry.

The second half of the chapter provides a careful examination of the teachings in the *Sawāniḥ*, wherein all manifestations of love are said to derive from one eternal Love. Love begins before creation, descends into creation, and returns through the created order back to its uncreated origin. The beginning of love is God's love for the human being, who is privileged above all else to be God's beloved. But in creation the human being becomes the lover seeking to return through the beloved, which is the God of beliefs, to love itself, the God beyond all beliefs and all knowledge. Aḥmad al-Ghazālī's main concern is to assist the wayfarer on the path through the stages of love: loving what is other than the beloved; loving what is attached to the beloved; and loving the beloved until one goes beyond the beloved and is immersed in Love Itself.

Between Form and Meaning

Though Shaykh Aḥmad al-Ghazālī recognizes the need for words and expressions in order to convey his message, he often reminds his reader of the shortcomings that they cannot but entail. His is not a sustained apophatic discourse in which the premises he poses are repeatedly undone by what follows.[1] Rather, his often affirmative mode of expression indirectly and directly confirms the positive role of cataphatic religious discourse in both the exoteric and esoteric domains, as was seen in Chapter 3 in his attitude toward the Shariah. He does, however, maintain that there are fundamental limitations to cataphatic discourse and thus pushes the limits inherent to language. To his mind, the subject of spiritual discourse is by definition beyond the rational faculty. It is not grasped through thought, but through submission, tasting, burning, and immersion. As he writes in the *Sawāniḥ*:

> Love is hidden, none has seen it revealed.
> How long will these lovers boast in vain?
>
> Everyone boasts of what he imagines love to be;
> Love is free of imagination, and of this and that.[2]

In *at-Tajrīd fī kalimat at-tawḥīd* the insufficiencies of language are at times addressed. This theme is then somewhat more prevalent in the sessions. But in the *Sawāniḥ*, it becomes a central component of the text, such that many passages could be read as an apophatic discourse wherein what is attributed to the state of the lover is laid to waste before the beloved, and what is attributed to the beloved becomes naught in the Face of Love, whose reality is itself ineffable.

As discussed in Chapter 2, Aḥmad al-Ghazālī was well trained in Quran, Hadith, the religious sciences, and Arabic poetry. Like his brother Abū Ḥāmid, he displayed a marked mastery of the art of eloquence (*balāghah*) in Arabic and Persian, indicating both training and native ability. Despite such proficiency, he ascribes no value to language in and of itself; its words and expressions are at best allusions (*ishārāt*). They are tools by which one may convey a glimpse of a higher reality that then incites one to move toward that reality, but they must never be mistaken for that reality itself. His only intention in employing words is to move the reader or listener toward the ultimate reality to which no words can attain and from which no report can be given. In the first of his collected sessions, Aḥmad al-Ghazālī chides his audience, "You hear the verses but do not know their meaning."[3] Other such admonitions are found throughout the sessions. But his most penetrating discussion of the limitation of words is in the prologue of the *Sawāniḥ*: "Love cannot be expressed in words or contained in sentences, for the realities of love are like virgins, and the hand of grasping words cannot reach the skirts of their pudenda."[4] Here the virgins can be seen as allusions to the pure maidens promised to believers as a reward in the Hereafter, as in 55:56: *Therein are maidens of modest gaze, whom neither man or jinn has ever touched.*[5] For Aḥmad al-Ghazālī, the virgins do not represent mere sensual delights, but rather spiritual delights. The experience of inner spiritual realities is an experience of such heavenly realities. Words as we know them in the temporal world of form and contingency can never attain to the realities of this higher world, for words pertain to form (*ṣūrah*), and meanings or realities (*ma'ānī*) are by definition supra-formal. The task of one who uses words to provide guidance is thus a daunting one, "Though our task is to join the virgin realities to the men of words in the seclusions of discourse, the outward expressions (*'ibārāt*) in this discussion are allusions to various realities."[6] Here "men" translates *dhukūr*, which can also mean "penises," as rendered by William Chittick,[7] or have an implication of virility. Leili Anvar thus renders it "virile males."[8] These renderings indicate more emphatically that to "join virgin realities to the men" or penises "of words" is an impossible task, since the realities would then lose their virgin nature. Thus outward expressions are but allusions, for the men of words must be elevated beyond the realm of forms (*'ālam aṣ-ṣuwar*), which is the level of words and expressions, to the realm of meanings and realities (*'ālam al-ma'ānī*) in order to even glimpse the virgin realities. "In the seclusions of discourse" alludes to the heart, the organ through which realities are perceived. When one has arrived at the heart, one has in a sense already gone beyond the realm of form, since the heart can perceive and no longer needs reports. As Maybudī observes, "When a heart finds delight in His grasp and is inundated by face-to-face vision, what will it do with reports?"[9]

This link between seclusion and the heart is alluded to in one of Shaykh Aḥmad's sessions: "Where is this seclusion (*khalwah*)? Within the cavity of your heart."[10] Following this remark, Aḥmad quotes from a well-known saying often cited in Sufi texts wherein God addresses the Prophet David, saying, "David empty for Me a house that I may dwell in it. When you refine and empty your inner being, and your inner being becomes the heart of life, then in that will I dwell."[11] From this perspective, it is in the seclusion of a heart that has been emptied for God that spiritual realities are joined to the men of words, or penetrated by the penis of discourse. Only when one has attained to heart consciousness that is free of attachment to outer expressions is one able to perceive the realities to which the expressions allude. But until one reaches the seclusion of the heart where there is no longer any need for forms to convey meanings, the forms of language can serve to move one toward the heart by conveying some of its meanings and realities.

This conception of words is essential for understanding Aḥmad al-Ghazālī's writings and the intention behind his citations of Quran, Hadith, poetry, and Sufi sayings. As with Sufis before him, he sees a crucial divide between the forms (*ṣuwar*) of the words and their meanings or realities (*ma'ānī*). To explain this subtle relationship between words and realities, he speaks of "the allusion of an outward expression" (*ishārat-i 'ibārat*), wherein a seemingly straightforward citation actually alludes to many layers of inner meaning. He then flips these terms around to say that one must also be aware of "the outward expression of an allusion" (*'ibārat-i ishārat*), wherein a spiritual reality is given direct expression in simple terms, such as in the famous saying delivered in the form of a *ḥadīth qudsī*: "I am with those whose hearts are broken."[12] With "the allusion of an outward expression" the true meaning may be veiled by an apparent meaning. With "the outward expression of an allusion" the direct message may be obscured by overanalysis. As much as words, expressions, and allusions may be a support that moves the wayfarer toward the witnessing of higher realities, it is only by insight (*baṣīrah*) that such realities are perceived. As al-Ghazālī puts it, "In the hearts of words lie the edges of a sword that cannot be seen except by inner insight (*baṣīrat-i bāṭinī*),"[13] meaning only through insight can one pierce the forms and thus attain to the realities that they convey.

In discussing the secrets of realization through both the written and oral mediums, Aḥmad al-Ghazālī understood his function to be that of a guide whose tongue and pen had the power to evoke longing for the beloved and remembrance of the Divine. Regarding the tongue, he says in one of his sessions, "Whoever comes to me with ears pertaining to the spirit, I present to him the secrets of the kingdom."[14] Regarding the pen, he tells us that the *Sawāniḥ* was written so that the reader who experiences the pain of not attaining full union "can read the book to keep busy and employ its verses to take hold."[15] That is "to take hold" of the path of wayfaring in love. This intention predominates in all of his words. Aḥmad al-Ghazālī likens the nature of his writings to that of the Quran, which does not provide didactic explanation but rather *was sent down as guidance to mankind* (2:185). In this way he is more a guide and preacher than a formal instructor. His mode of discourse is like that of the Quran: terse, immediate, and allusive.[16] He does not explain his words or citations; rather, his intention is to create the spark of insight by which the fire of knowledge, or recognition, is ignited. He selects images not only for aesthetic value but to evoke an image of the Absolute that the wayfarer receives as a reflection of his beloved upon the screen of his own heart. This can be a wink, an eyebrow, a cheek, or the beloved's tress. In each case, "[it] is an indication of that searching of the spirit and the heart, and it is far from bodily deficiencies."[17]

In Aḥmad al-Ghazālī's frame of reference, the rational faculty corresponds to the level of knowledge (*ʿilm*), which is below the level of recognition (*ʿirfān*), according to the technical terminology employed in his sessions, or below the level of love, as expressed in this passage of the *Sawāniḥ*:

> The end of "knowledge" is the shore of love. If one is on the shore, some account from it will be his share, and if he steps forward, he will be drowned. Now how can he give any report? How can the one who is drowned have any knowledge?
>
> Your beauty is beyond my sight.
> Your secret is too deep for my knowledge.
>
> In loving You, my singleness is a crowd.
> In describing You, my ability is impotence.
>
> Nay, knowledge is the moth of love. Its knowledge is the outer aspect of the affair. In it the first thing that burns is knowledge. Now who can bring a report from that?[18]

The place of knowledge in relation to recognition is addressed in the sessions when Aḥmad al-Ghazālī is asked about the meaning of a famous saying of ʿAlī ibn Abī Ṭālib, regarded by some as a *ḥadīth*: "He who knows himself, knows his Lord."[19] To which he replies:

> Knowledge has become confused for you with recognition. Do you know what recognition is? [It is] the burning of moths in the flame of the candle. Do you see who informs you of the moth's state? *Moses said, "Perhaps I shall bring you a burning coal therefrom, or find guidance at the fire"* (20:10).

> Then someone said, "When it burns who comes?"
>
> He replied, "Fleeting thoughts pertain to the soul and have no path to the heart. Knowledge pertains to the heart and has no path to the spirit.[20] And recognition is in the spirit. The flame is from the spirit burning in the fires of longing. If the flame speaks, know that you have arrived."[21]

That which is described as the fire of love in the *Sawāniḥ* is thus described as the fire of recognition in the *Majālis*. Just as in the "Book of Love" of Abū Ḥāmid al-Ghazālī's *Revival*, for Aḥmad the stage of *ʿirfān* and the stage of *ʿishq* are one and the same and lie beyond the stages of knowledge. From this perspective, knowledge cannot penetrate the secrets of *ʿishq* and *ʿirfān*, for "this reality is a pearl in a shell, and the shell is in the depths of the ocean. Knowledge can only advance as far as the seashore, how could it reach the depths?"[22] In the final analysis, knowledge is what can be transmitted, while recognition and love must be experienced or tasted for oneself. As noted at the end of Chapter 4, for Aḥmad al-Ghazālī this limitation applies even to the Prophet Muḥammad: "Whenever the Messenger of God was carried to the ocean of knowledge it would flow forth, but when he was cast into the ocean of recognition he said, 'I do not know, I only worship' (*lā adrī innamā aʿbudu*)."[23]

As Shaykh Aḥmad's only concern is love or recognition (*ʿirfān*) and not knowledge in and of itself, the purpose of his words is to guide, not to transmit. From his perspective, recognition is not discursive; it is not a thing obtained and possessed at the level of the spirit; rather, it is an actualization of the spirit, the true essence of the human being that is breathed into him by God (Quran 15:29; 38:72). As al-Ghazālī's goal is never to offer didactic lessons regarding particular questions of doctrine or to establish a philosophical, theoretical, or metaphysical systematization, the Quranic verses, *aḥādīth*, and poetry cited in his works are not the objects of commentary, but loci that function as gateways to the contemplation of higher realities. It is often left to the reader or listener to make the connection between the citation and the point that the shaykh is discussing, as with the Quranic verse cited above (*Moses said, "Perhaps I shall bring you a burning coal therefrom, or find guidance at the fire"*: 20:10). Here the *burning coal* is seen as an allusion to partial knowledge brought as a report from the fire. It is far from the recognition alluded to in the words "find guidance." The allusion is made even more elusive when he does not finish the citation, but relies on one's previous knowledge of the context in which the verse occurs to make the full connection, as the verse comes just before Moses is told to remove his sandals and stand before God.

In this manner of citation, al-Ghazālī is following in the path of many Sufis before him, such as Sahl at-Tustarī (d. 283/869), Ibn ʿAṭāʾ (d. 309/922),[24] and the author of the commentary attributed to Jaʿfar b. Muḥammad aṣ-Ṣādiq (d. 148/765),[25] as well as many others whose commentaries are found in the *Ḥaqāʾiq at-tafsīr* (The Realities of Exegesis) of ʿAbd ar-Raḥmān as-Sulamī. As Gerhard Böwering observes, for the Sufis the verses and phrases of the Quran serve as keynotes that strike the Sufi's mind, signaling "the breakthrough to God, revealing Himself in His divine speech and opening a way to Himself through and beyond His divine word."[26] For Aḥmad al-Ghazālī, as for many others, Hadith and poetry can also open a way to God. When employed with such an intention, what appear to be commentaries are in fact allusions, often taken up in isolation from their particular textual context, such that the outward meaning of the text may seem to be at odds with the inner reality that the spiritual guide or aspirant may see within it.

Poetry

Many examples could be drawn from Aḥmad al-Ghazālī's extensive use of poetry, especially in the *Sessions*, where verses from famous poets such as Kuthayyir ʿAzzah (d. 105/723), Abū Nuwās (d. *ca.* 198/814), and al-Mutanabbī (d. 354/965) are cited side by side with verses from the Sufi tradition and anonymous verses, which may have been authored by Aḥmad al-Ghazālī himself. The Shaykh is particularly indebted to the traditions of wine poetry, or *khamriyyah*,[27] and longing love, or *ʿudhrī ghazāl*.[28] Like al-Qushayrī before him and ʿUmar Ibn al-Fāriḍ (d. 632/1235), Ibn al-ʿArabī, and Jalāl al-Dīn Rūmī over a century later, he weaves themes from the secular belletristic (*adab*) tradition into a thoroughly spiritual discourse. This provides a tapestry whose colors and texture would be familiar to any educated reader or listener, but whose aim and function are of a spiritual nature, such that the signified shifts from a secular, outward meaning to a spiritual, inward meaning.

While examples of verses from the *khamriyyah* tradition are scattered here and there, themes from the *ʿudhrī ghazal* tradition are prevalent throughout the *Sawāniḥ*. As Roger Allen writes of the *ʿudhrī ghazal*:

> The poet-lover places his beloved on a pedestal and worships her from afar. He is obsessed and tormented; he becomes debilitated, ill, and is doomed to a love-death. The beloved in turn becomes the personification of the ideal woman, a transcendental image of all that is beautiful and chaste. The cheek, the neck, the bosom, and, above all, the eyes—a mere glance—these are the cause of passion, longing, devastation and exhaustion.[29]

All of these elements are to be found in the *Sawāniḥ*, as well as Samʿānī's *Rawḥ al-arwāḥ*, Maybudī's *Kashf al-asrār*, ʿAyn al-Quḍāt's *Tamhīdāt*, and the Persian Sufi love tradition that was to follow. Within these texts the Divine becomes the supreme beloved for whom the wayfarer must give his very self, and "the glance of beauty" (*kirishmah-yi ḥusn*) from the beloved is the means by which the lover is drawn toward the beloved and beyond until being annihilated in love. Like many authors of the Arabic literary tradition and other Sufi writers, Shaykh Aḥmad al-Ghazālī employs the renowned Majnūn-Laylā legend. Like writers of the Persian tradition, he also takes the legendary love of Sultan Maḥmūd of Ghaznah (d. 421/1030) for his servant Ayāz b. Aymaq (d. 449/1059) as an example of the complete self-sacrificing love that a person of serious spiritual intent must have for God. In the example of Majnūn-Laylā, it is the love of a man for a woman; in the example of the Sultān, it is the love of a man for a man. What matters for Aḥmad al-Ghazālī is not the gender of the beloved but love itself, which is beyond the duality of gender. Unlike the authors of the secular literary tradition, wherein the love between two parties is celebrated or lamented, Aḥmad al-Ghazālī sees the relationship between the lover and the beloved as a transient phase on the spiritual path that must be surpassed in order for one to be immersed in the oneness of Divine Love. Whereas the secular literary tradition is filled with stories of those who were martyrs to love, Aḥmad al-Ghazālī, like Sufis before and after him, wrote not of the physical death that occurs because of love, but of spiritual annihilation (*fanāʾ*) in Love Itself.[30]

While the *ʿudhrī ghazal* tradition provided fertile soil for the central teachings of Aḥmad al-Ghazālī, in both his letters and the *Sawāniḥ*, the influence of the *khamriyyah* tradition is less profound. The best example of his extracting verses from their context in order to allude to Sufi teachings is found in the use of verses from Abū Nuwās in the following passage:

> But one cannot eat the nourishment of awareness from that which is the hard cash of his spirit, only in the reflection of the beauty of the beloved's face.
>
> Give me wine to drink and tell me it is wine.
> Do not give me drink in secret if it can be done openly.[31]
>
> The union with the beloved is eating the nourishment of awareness from the hard cash of one's own spirit, not finding.[32]

Abū Nuwās was known for leading a profligate life. Despite his at times penitent voice, there is little doubt that for him the meaning of these verses was literal. But for Aḥmad al-Ghazālī, as for al-Qushayrī and al-Hujwīrī before him and many after him, these verses allude to the wine of realization, of which al-Ghazālī writes:

> Of that wine which is not forbidden in our religion
> You'll not find our lips dry till we return to non-existence.[33]

The verses of Abū Nuwās are thus cited in this context as an allusion to the nourishment that the lover—the wayfarer—receives from his divine beloved on the spiritual path.

Interpretation

Aḥmad al-Ghazālī's allusive manner of employing other textual traditions, both religious and secular, is common to Sufi discourse and an intrinsic component of his writings and sermons. Many Sufis recognize such hermeneutics as allusions or inferences (*istinbāṭ*) drawn from one's relationship with the text, rather than exegesis (*tafsīr*) produced by reflection (*fikr*) on its meaning—the latter being the method of more exoteric exegetes.[34]

Aḥmad al-Ghazālī had contempt for the confining nature of most exegesis. This is exemplified in an invective he launches against interpretation (*ta'wīl*). In response to an inquiry as to who knows the interpretation of miracles, he responds:

> Whoever says that there are interpretations for the miracles which have occurred through the prophets is an unbeliever; there is no doubt regarding his unbelief and no doubt

> regarding the unbelief of one who doubts his unbelief. Do not doubt that the moon was cleaved by the Messenger of God—peace and blessings be upon him—*The hour has drawn nigh and the moon has been cleaved* (54:1). There is no magnanimity for the man of reason who interprets this. And Jesus—peace be upon him—brought the dead to life *by the leave of God* (3:49; cf. 5:110). There is no magnanimity for one who says: "He meant by it the revival of the heart." Likewise for one who shuts the door of Islam and roles up the carpet of the law and opposes some one hundred and twenty thousand prophets.[35] It is incumbent upon you; yes, it is incumbent upon you to watch over the guarded sanctuary in order that you do not fall into it.[36]

This last line is an allusion to a famous *ḥadīth* of the Prophet:

> The permissible (*ḥalāl*) is clear and the forbidden (*ḥarām*) is clear and between them are ambiguous issues which few people know. Whosoever is wary of ambiguities seeks to keep his religion and his honor pure, and whosoever falls into ambiguities falls into the forbidden, like the shepherd who pastures (his flock) around a guarded sanctuary verging on grazing therein. Verily for every king there is a guarded sanctuary. Verily God's guarded sanctuary is that which He forbids. And verily there is a lump of flesh in the body which, when it is sound, the entire body is sound, and, when it is corrupt, the entire body is corrupt. Indeed, it is the heart.[37]

This *ḥadīth* is known to many as one of the axiomatic *aḥādīth* of the Islamic tradition. Many in his audience would therefore be familiar with the allusion. Al-Ghazālī is thus drawing upon their knowledge of law to equate the proclivity for *ta'wīl* with the snares of Satan that pull one to the edge of that into which they should not venture. He goes on to say:

> Most of the diseases of human beings are of this kind. They see the beginnings (of the sciences [*ʿulūm*]) radiating and uncontested issues appear in the introductions of books. So they have a good opinion of the one who proclaims them and seek to acquiesce to what is behind them without any proof.[38]

Such is the path of the exoteric sciences and, in Aḥmad al-Ghazālī's vocabulary, the way of *ta'wīl*. But according to him, the way of truth and thus the way to recognition is to follow:

> It is incumbent upon you to follow the book of God and the *sunnah* of His Messenger, and to act according to one verse: *Whosoever believes in God, He guides his heart* (64:11). Whosoever seeks guidance from other than the door of faith, he is astray, leading astray.[39]

In other words, faith should not be mistaken for acquiescence to doctrinal expressions of particular creeds, nor for the acceptance of particular spiritual and metaphysical teachings and concepts. Rather, faith is accepting God's guidance without particular preconceptions of where that guidance must lead and how it must come about.

Given this approach, Aḥmad al-Ghazālī, like many Sufi authors who write in this same vein, rarely provides an introduction for citations of Quran and Hadith, poetry, love stories, and Sufi sayings. He introduces them in the middle of his discourse as if there were a seamless continuity between the message of his words and the cited passage(s). In the *Sawāniḥ,* only the reader steeped in early Persian poetry can distinguish between the author's poetry and that of his predecessors. In his writings and sermons, he rarely sets off citations with conventional expressions, such as "As God says . . . ," "As the Messenger of God says . . . ," or "As the poet says. . . ." Rather, they are so interwoven with his own words that they can elude even the most erudite and meticulous of scholars.[40] Nowhere is this organic fluidity more apparent than in his *ʿAyniyyeh,* where, in the Quranic style of rhyming prose (*sajʿ*), al-Ghazālī rhymes Persian prose with Arabic citations from Quran and Hadith and follows verses of Arabic poetry with verses of Persian poetry comprised of many of the same words and themes. Unfortunately, such rhetorical subtleties can almost never be captured in translation.[41]

Considering Aḥmad al-Ghazālī's conviction that language and interpretation have no access to higher realities, his teachings on love should not be read as an exposition of the phenomenon. Rather, love is the means by which he draws the reader to the deepest mysteries of the spiritual path. This immediacy is intended to pierce the reader's consciousness and penetrate the very soul so as to draw one toward the mysteries of love and recognition (*ʿirfān*). In both his writings and sermons, Aḥmad al-Ghazālī's one aim is that the reader join all his aspiration (*jamʿ al-himmah*) and focus his entire being with complete sincerity (*ikhlāṣ*) upon his only task: the remembrance of God. Joining together one's aspiration(s)—*jamʿ al-himmah* or *jamʿ al-ahimmah* is an important concept in Sufi texts. Regarding this, Aḥmad al-Ghazālī cites a saying that he attributes to Abū Bakr aṣ-Ṣiddīq: "One round of prayer from he who joins together his aspirations is weightier with God than one hundred horses fighting in the path of God."[42] With this as his goal, Shaykh Aḥmad does not present his words as commentary or interpretation but as signposts for wayfarers on the Sufi path who have the insight with which to pierce their forms and attain their meanings.

The Oneness of Love

As demonstrated in Chapter 4, there are fragmentary precedents for Aḥmad al-Ghazālī's understanding of love in the writings of previous Sufis, though for many early Sufis we do not have complete details of their teachings. In Aḥmad al-Ghazālī's teachings we find a more complete metaphysics of love. His is not a systematic account but a tapestry of allusions and openings woven for wayfarers who have already set out to travel the spiritual path, based on his position that "opening a door is sufficient for a discerning intelligence."[43] Much like the Quran, the *Sawāniḥ* may appear to the uninitiated as a disjointed collection of aphorisms pertaining to a particular set of themes. The underlying order is discerned only through close reading.

Here I will present Aḥmad al-Ghazālī's views on love in a more systematic manner, tracing the progressive stages and stations of love as they appear in many different sections of the *Sawāniḥ*. As the text is at times terse and elusive, I draw on other texts of this genre to flesh out its observations. These will be the *Kashf al-Asrār* of Maybudī, the *Rawḥ al-arwāḥ* of Samʿānī, the *Tamhīdāt* of ʿAyn al-Quḍāt, and the *Lamaʿāt* of Fakhr ad-Dīn ʿIrāqī. The *Tamhīdāt* is closer to the *Sawāniḥ*, and its technical vocabulary is similar. As he was al-Ghazālī's disciple, ʿAyn al-Quḍāt is concerned with many of the same issues, especially in Chapter 6, "The Reality and States of Love," and Chapter 7, "The Reality of the Spirit and the Heart." Fakhr al-Dīn ʿIrāqī describes his *Lamaʿāt* as "a few words explaining the levels of love in the tradition of the *Sawāniḥ*, in tune with the voice of each state as it passes."[44] Like al-Ghazālī, ʿIrāqī provides a subtle metaphysical discourse based on the idea that "the derivation of the lover and the beloved is from Love,"[45] and sees all of reality as an unfolding of Love wherein all is either lover or beloved and their duality is eventually subsumed in the reality of Love Itself. He explains metaphysical issues that pertain to both the school of Ibn al-ʿArabī and the teachings of Aḥmad al-Ghazālī in a manner that employs the technical vocabulary of both traditions, while retaining the dramatic tension of the *Sawāniḥ*. Nonetheless, in his overall metaphysics, ʿIrāqī is more a follower of his teacher Ṣadr ad-Dīn Qūnawī (d. 673/1274) and the school of Ibn al-ʿArabī than of Aḥmad al-Ghazālī. Ultimately, there can be no one-to-one correspondence between texts written at this level. As ʿIrāqī puts it:

> There is no doubt that every lover gives a different sign of the beloved, every recognizer provides a different explanation, and every verifier makes a different allusion. The declaration of each is:
>
> Our expressions are many and Your loveliness one,
> Each of us points to that single beauty.[46]

From this perspective, although the texts may diverge in their modes of expression, they complement one another because they each point to the beauty of God, which for these authors is the one beauty from which all other beauty derives.

Love's Two Beginnings

In the context of the *Sawāniḥ*, love could be said to have two beginnings: the first before creation, and the second within creation. The beginning within creation is the movement of the wayfarer toward love. That before creation begins with God's love for the human being, which is also the source of man's love for God. From the perspective of wayfaring, the human being is the beloved. This beginningless love is what distinguishes the human being from the rest of creation. As Aḥmad al-Ghazālī writes, "The special character of the human being is this: is it not enough that one is beloved before one is a lover? This is no small virtue."[47] Like many other Sufi authors, he maintains that this beginningless state of being beloved is what is referred to in the Quranic verse: *He loves them and they love Him* (5:57). Drawing upon this verse, he writes:

> The root of love grows from eternity. The dot under the letter *bāʾ* (b) in *He loves them* (*yuḥibbuhum*) was planted as

> a seed in the ground of *they love Him*. No, rather, that point was planted in *them* (*hum*), for *they love Him* to come forth.[48]

Aḥmad al-Ghazālī, like many before and after him, explains this love by referring to the Quranic story of the pre-temporal covenant with God made while all human beings were still in Adam's loins. As the Quran states:

> *And* [remember] *when thy Lord took from the Children of Adam, from their loins, their progeny, and made them bear witness concerning themselves, "Am I not your Lord?" They said, "Yea, surely, we bear witness"—lest you should say on the Day of Resurrection, "Truly, we were heedless of this"* (7:172).

This event is known in Islamic literature as "The Day of the Covenant" and in the Persian Sufi tradition as *rūz-i alast* (The Day of "Am I not [your Lord]?"). It is understood by Aḥmad al-Ghazālī and others as a covenant fashioned in love and through love. When God said to all human beings, *"Am I not your Lord,"* this was His love for them. When human beings responded by saying *"Yea"* (*balā*), this was their love for God. From this perspective, only through God's making them beloved did human beings become lovers, and all of human love and striving for God originates from God's pre-temporal love for man. As Aḥmad writes, *"He loves them* is before *they love Him*—no doubt. Bāyazīd [al-Basṭāmī] said, 'For a long time I imagined that I desired Him. He Himself had first desired me.'"[49]

From this perspective, the human being's love for God is the self-same love that God has for the human being. Although human love finds expression in the temporal order, like the human being himself, love's origin is beginninglessness and its goal is endlessness. Shaykh al-Ghazālī alludes to the fundamental unity of love in all of these phases through a metaphor, "When the jasmine of love came forth, the seed was the same color as the fruit, and the fruit was the same color as the seed."[50] The seed, the tree, and the fruit can each be spoken of as different entities, but they are in reality the same substance in different forms. The whole of the *Sawāniḥ* is about the derivation of all love's many branches and fruits from this one eternal seed of love and the inevitable return of all modes of love to Love in Love and through Love. As the Shaykh writes:

> Love is its own bird and its own nest, its own essence and its own attribute, its own wing and its own wind, its own

> arc and its own flight, its own hunter and its own game, its own direction and what is directed there, its own seeker and its own goal. It is its own beginning and its own end, its own sultan and its own subject, its own sword and its own sheath. It is garden as well as tree, branch as well as fruit, nest as well as bird.[51]

The entirety of this discussion thus regards the many faces that Absolute Love assumes as it unfolds Itself. In this sense, al-Ghazālī goes a step beyond the teachings on love attributed to al-Ḥallāj by ad-Daylamī. Whereas al-Ḥallāj is said to have spoken of *ʿishq* as an attribute pertaining to the Divine Essence and ad-Daylamī alludes to the same teaching while using the word *maḥabbah,* al-Ghazālī, like ʿAyn al-Quḍāt and ʿIrāqī after him, treats it as the Divine Essence Itself. Not only does God love man, God has fashioned everything through love. As ʿIrāqī writes, "Love flows in all existents . . . all is love."[52] So love is in fact the very essence of the lover. This same understanding may be implied in the teachings of al-Ḥallāj, ad-Daylamī, and Anṣārī, but none of them develops an extensive explanation. They do imply that all aspects of creation are manifestations of love, but they do not provide a detailed explanation wherein every phase of spiritual wayfaring is presented in relation to love.

The process by which the Divine Love-Essence unfolds Itself comprises two phases: the path of descent and the path of ascent. The former is the path from the Divine and the latter is the path of return to the Divine. The descent is the path from the love which begins before creation and the ascent is from the love which begins in creation. Most of the *Sawāniḥ* is concerned with the path of ascent because its many obstacles confront the lover and dilute his experience of love for that which is eternal with love for that which is contingent and temporal. Nonetheless, there is some discussion of the path of descent, since in order to fully understand his predicament the spiritual wayfarer must be aware that this affair began in beginninglessness (*abad*), attains to endlessness (*azal*), and cannot be fully realized in the temporal realm. As Aḥmad al-Ghazālī writes:

> O chivalrous one! The grace that eternity put in beginninglessness, how can contingency receive it all except in endlessness? No, rather contingency can only fully receive the grace that eternity placed in beginninglessness in endlessness.

> O chivalrous one! Beginninglessness has reached here [this world], but endlessness can never reach an end. The grace that descends will never reach complete exhaustion. If you gain insight into the secret core of your moment, know that the *two bows' length* (53:9) of beginninglessness and endlessness are your heart and your moment (*waqt*).[53]

The reference to "two bows' length" is taken from the Quranic account of the ascension (*miʿrāj*) of the Prophet Muhammad into the Divine Presence: *Then He drew nigh and came close, until he was within two bows' length or nearer. Then He revealed to His servant what He revealed. The heart lied not in what it saw* (53:8–11).[54] For Aḥmad al-Ghazālī, as for many Sufis, the two bows represent the arc of descent from beginninglessness and the arc of ascent to endlessness. Together they comprise the entire circle of existence. Beginninglessness is the point from which the arc of descent begins and endlessness is the point to which the arc of ascent returns. But in reality they are one and the same; the term employed is a question of perspective. As one descends into the corporeal world, various modes of manifestation are actualized. In order for these modes to be integrated and unified, one must return upon the path of ascent. To say that the path of descent from beginninglessness and the path of ascent to endlessness are the wayfarer's heart and moment is thus to say that one's true nature is determined by where one stands in the process of return. As will be explained below, the heart is the faculty of love whereby beauty and the beloved are perceived as many derivations of love, and this act of perception is the very process of spiritual reintegration. The moment is the state that alters in accord with the wayfarer's position as he moves through the phases of his or her journey. This moment will vacillate between pain and relief, sorrow and happiness, and expansion and contraction until the wayfarer is annihilated in Love Itself beyond its manifestations as lover and beloved.

The Descent of the Spirit

A crucial moment in the path of descent occurs when the spirit descends into the temporal order. For Aḥmad al-Ghazālī, as for Maybudī, Samʿāni, ʿAyn al-Quḍāt, and all representatives of the "School of Love," this spirit is what God refers to when He says, *Say, "The spirit is from the command of my Lord,"* (17:85) and *I breathed into him of My spirit* (15:29, 38:72). They take these verses to indicate that the spirit is the core of the human being, through which one is eternally connected to the command of God. As Samʿānī writes, "On the day He said, *'I breathed into him of My spirit'* [15:29], He set in place the human beings' qualification. In beginninglessness He had decreed that sheer servanthood would contract a marriage with complete lordhood: *"Am I not your Lord?"* [7:172].[55] As such, the spirit is not subject to the words *Be! And it is* (*kun fa-yakūn*; 2:117; 3:47; 6:73; 16:40; 19:35; 36:82; 40:69) by which God creates.[56] For ʿAyn al-Quḍāt, the spirit is in fact the command itself: "It is the commander, not the commanded. It is the actor, not the deed done; the conqueror, not the conquered."[57] According to al-Ghazālī, "When the spirit came from non-existence into existence, love was awaiting the spirit-mount on the frontier of existence."[58] The spirit was awaiting love because it is fashioned for love alone and is the only mount that is fit for love. As ʿAyn al-Quḍāt writes, the spirit "has the quality of beginninglessness."[59] Thus Shaykh al-Ghazālī writes, "love does not appear as a rider on anything except the mount of the spirit."[60] The spirit always maintains a position above the heart because the latter fluctuates between the dispersion of the soul and constancy of the spirit. As observed in Chapter 3, the heart, though more subtle and more exalted than the soul, nonetheless represents the outermost aspect of the wayfarer's inner being. The spirit and the secret core are more exalted and subtler dimensions of one's inner nature. As will be seen below, much of the journey is traveled within the heart as it moves closer to the spirit, but love can appear only in the spirit because only the spirit has the capacity to fully manifest love.

Since the wayfarer is veiled by many of the obfuscations that arise in the process of creation, the relation between love and the spirit upon which it is mounted can take on many forms. As al-Ghazālī writes:

> Sometimes the spirit is for love like the earth, such that the tree of love grows from it. Sometimes the spirit is like the essence, such that the attribute subsists through it. Sometimes it is like the partner in a house, such that love also has a turn in subsistence. Sometimes love is the essence and the spirit is the attribute, such that the spirit will subsist through it.[61]

These multiple relationships arise because "the spirit is the shell of love,"[62] so in seeking love the wayfarer must encounter the spirit before fully encountering love. Therefore, the spirit will sometimes appear to be riding on love, while love will appear to be subsisting through it, whereas in reality love is riding on the spirit and the spirit is subsisting through love. For most people, perception remains delimited by the contingencies of temporality, thus the relationship between love and the spirit appears distorted. Its reality is only perceived when one has entered what Shaykh al-Ghazālī refers to as "the world of the second affirmation" beyond effacement,[63] that is, when the individual existence of the lover is consumed and the lover abides in love alone.

The Heart

The faculty whereby the spiritual journey is undertaken is the heart, for the heart has been made to love alone, as mentioned previously:

> The function of the heart is being a lover. So long as love is not, it has no function. When it becomes a lover, its affair will also become ready. It is thus certain that the heart has been created for love and being a lover and knows nothing else.[64]

Aḥmad al-Ghazālī thus likens the heart to a nest for the beginningless bird of love:

> The secret of this—that Love never shows the whole of its face to anyone—is that it is the bird of beginninglessness. What has come here [in this world] is the traveler of endlessness. Here it does not show its face to the vision of contingent beings, for every house is not a nest for it, as it has hidden a nest from the magnificence of beginninglessness.[65]

In so far as one attempts to perceive love with the faculties of perception or to understand love with the mind, one will fail. As William Chittick observes, "Scholars and thinkers have no entrance into this realm unless they also become lovers."[66] To know love, or rather to taste love, one must know the heart and learn to see with it, for it alone can perceive manifestations of Love's attributes in the realm of contingent beings. In the temporal order, the wayfarer experiences the heart as the locus of the beloved's beauty, even when he is ignorant of this function. As Shaykh al-Ghazālī writes, "And it may be that the lover himself does not know this, but his heart itself is the locus of that beauty and seeks observation until it finds."[67] This is why he says that the lover "only drinks from the bowl of the heart."[68] For although his nourishment in love is from the beauty of the beloved, this beauty is only witnessed upon that screen by which love contemplates its own self-disclosures through the lover's witnessing of them, that is, the heart, since "the heart is the locus of [love's] attributes."[69]

Aḥmad al-Ghazālī's many allusions to the function of the heart are scattered throughout the *Sawāniḥ*. In his *Tamhīdāt*, ʿAyn al-Quḍāt provides a more lucid and concise discussion. Here he enjoins the reader to seek the heart, as it is in the heart that one's true nature is found:

> Seek the heart! And seize it! Do you know where the heart is? Seek the heart "between the two fingers of the Compassionate."[70] Alas! If the beauty of "the two fingers of the Compassionate" were to lift the veil of pride, every heart would find the remedy. The heart knows what it is and who it is. The heart is the object of God's gaze. And the heart itself is deserving of "Verily God does not look at your forms, nor at your deeds, but He looks at your hearts."[71] O friend, the heart is the locus of God's gaze. When the [bodily] frame (*qālib*) takes on the color of the heart and becomes the same color as the heart, the [bodily] frame is also the object of the gaze.[72]

In witnessing the traces and images of the beloved, the lover becomes the means by which God witnesses the attributes of His love, which are all composed of His beauty as it is reflected on the screen of the lover's heart. As the wayfarer progresses in love, the body itself takes on the color of the heart, for a subtle heart results in the Divine Love or Light penetrating into the Adamic clay.[73] Regarding the witnessing of the Divine within one's own heart, Aḥmad al-Ghazālī records these verses:

> You yourself, O beloved, are in the heart night and day.
> Whenever I want you, I look in the heart.[74]

The heart is, however, only the locus for the manifestation of love's attributes, not of Love Itself, since Love is the Divine Essence, and the Essence can never be fully manifest. This is why Aḥmad al-Ghazālī states, "love never shows the whole of its face to anyone." The various stages and degrees of the path can be understood as the various ways in which Love's attributes become manifest. But as Fakhr ad-Dīn ʿIrāqī observes, here the attributes also function as veils:

> His veils are His own names and attributes. As the author of *Qūt al-qulūb*[75] puts it, "Essence is veiled by attributes, attributes by acts." Ultimately, He Himself is His own veil, for He is hidden by the very intensity of His manifestation and covered by the very potency of His light.[76]

The veils are essential for manifestation. Without them, all that exists would be eradicated by God's immediate and overwhelming presence. In this sense, it is through God's own limitation of Himself that manifestation comes forth. Hence ʿIrāqī writes, "These names and attributes must not be raised, for if they were, the unity of the Essence would blaze forth from behind the screen of might, and all things would be totally annihilated."[77] The inability to perceive God may therefore not be due to distance, but rather proximity. As al-Ghazālī writes, "All that is unreachable is not so because of greatness and exaltedness. It is also from subtlety and excess of proximity."[78]

The spiritual wayfarer's first intuitions of love come through the perception of God's self-delimitations. By strengthening the inner faculties of perception and passing through the veils of the Divine attributes, the lover is gradually able to witness the Divine in a more direct manner. But this is a painful and arduous process, for not only must the outer veils be removed, so too, must the inner veils be removed. As Shaykh al-Ghazālī writes, "The inner worlds cannot be realized so easily. This is not so easy because there are screens, veils, treasures, and wonders there."[79] As such, he maintains that the spiritual path is characterized more by pain, affliction, and oppression than by ease, comfort, and consolation: "In reality, love is affliction, and intimacy and comfort in it are strange and are borrowed."[80] He goes on to say both that "Love is affliction" and that "affliction is the heart."[81] So to experience affliction in the heart is in the very nature of having a heart and part of its maturation. As Maybudī puts it, "When something is burnt, it loses value, but when a heart is burnt, it gains in value."[82] Affliction is a divine mercy that leads the spiritual wayfarer and helps one transcend many veils. Witnessing the beloved on the screen of the heart is the constant persecution of the lover by the beloved and is how the lover drinks nourishment from the cup of his heart. As al-Ghazālī writes, "Since love is affliction, its nourishment in knowledge is from the persecution which the beloved performs."[83]

Indeed, "the perpetuity of witnessing [the beloved] appears in the perpetuity of affliction."[84]

Beauty and Love

The central terms in Aḥmad al-Ghazālī's discussion of the relationship between the lover and the beloved are beauty (*ḥusn*) and love (*'ishq*). Without the latter there can be no lover, and without the former there is no beloved. Love is the seed of the lover's attributes, and beauty is the seed of the beloved's attributes. But as Nasrollah Pourjavady observes in his commentary on the *Sawāniḥ*:

> Seen from the point of view of the Absolute they are but one. The Ultimate Reality . . . has both these seeds in itself in perfect union. In fact it is one seed which will branch out in the forms of the beloved and the lover. The branch leading to the form of the beloved is *ḥusn* and the one leading to the form of the lover is love.[85]

To support this observation, Pourjavady cites a passage from *Ḥusn va-'ishq* by the Sufi master Nūr 'Alī Shāh Iṣfahānī (d. 1212/1798):

> People of mystical knowledge say that *ḥusn* is the final cause of creation and love constitutes *ḥusn*'s foundation. Moreover, it is obvious to everyone in possession of Intellect that *ḥusn* is nothing other than love. Though they have two names, they are one in essence.[86]

For Aḥmad al-Ghazālī, "the beginning of love is this, that the seed of beauty is planted in the ground of the heart's seclusion by the hand of witnessing."[87] Such is the beginning of the affair of love because that beauty is the means whereby the lover witnesses the manifestation of Absolute Love in the delimited form of the beloved. The beauty of each thing is called by al-Ghazālī "the brand of creation." This beauty is the secret face which faces Absolute Love and by virtue of which all things truly exist. For if they did not have a face turned toward the Absolute, there would be no way for them to derive their existence from it:

> The secret face of everything is the point of its connection, and a sign hidden in creation, and beauty is the brand of

creation. The secret face is that face which faces love. So long as one does not see that secret face, he will never see the sign of creation and beauty. That face is the beauty of *and there remains the Face of thy Lord* (55:27). Other than it there is no face, for *all that is upon it passes away* (55:26). And that face is nothing, as you know.[88]

In witnessing the beauty of the beloved, the lover-wayfarer is thus witnessing manifestations of the Divine. Addressing this same point, Fakhr ad-Dīn ʿIrāqī says that the face is the meaning or reality (*maʿnā*) of a thing that is "the self-disclosure of God" (*tajallī Allāh*).[89] He then addresses the reader:

> O friend, when you know that the meaning and reality of things is His Face, then you will say, "Show us things as they are"[90] until you see clearly that
>
> In everything there is a sign
> Indicating that He is one.[91]

But it is only the human being and, moreover, only the heart of the human being that is able to perceive the Divine countenance in beauty and thus able to read these signs. In this way, the beloved is entirely dependent on the lover for its beauty to be fully realized; otherwise, it would not be beloved:

> The eye of beauty looks away from its own beauty, for it cannot find the perfection of its own beauty except in the mirror of the love of the lover. In this way beauty must have a lover so that the beloved can eat nourishment from its own beauty in the mirror of love and the seeking of the lover. This is a great secret and the secret of many secrets.[92]

Bearing in mind the previous discussion of the heart, beauty assumes a form on the screen of the lover's heart by which a particular aspect or attribute of love is revealed as the beloved. From this perspective, only the lover is truly derived from love because the whole of the affair of love is the reflection of the beauty of the beloved on the screen of the lover's heart. Since the beloved is in fact reflections of beauty within the heart, it is from his own heart that the lover drinks the nourishment that is said to have been drunk from the beloved. Regarding the derivation of love from the lover and the derivation of love from the beloved, al-Ghazālī writes:

> The name of the beloved is borrowed in love and the name of the lover is the reality in love. The derivation of the beloved from love is a metaphor and is calumny. In reality derivation belongs to the lover, for he is the locus of the realm of love and its mount. But the beloved definitely has no derivation from love.[93]

In the early phases of love it appears that love derives from the beloved, but in reality all love is derived from the lover. The whole of the affair is an inward journey. The many phases of the relationship between the lover and the beloved can be understood as the manner in which Love is loving Itself through the manifestation and self-disclosure of Its own beauty within the heart of the lover.

Although beauty is the means whereby the lover witnesses the beloved, beauty in and of itself is beyond the beloved and does not turn toward creation. Considered in this light, witnessing the beloved is provisional and witnessing beauty itself is to see directly with the eye of the heart. Nonetheless, witnessing beauty through the intermediary of the beloved marks advancement on the spiritual path, though it is still only a stage of relativity and contingency. In alluding to this al-Ghazālī writes:

> The glance of beauty is one thing and the glance of belovedness is another. The glance of beauty has no face toward an other and has no connection with what is outside. But as for the glance of belovedness, amorous gestures, flirting, and coquetry, that is a reality which derives its support from the lover; without him they will find no way.[94]

As the glance of beauty "has no face toward an other and has no connection with what is outside," it cannot be witnessed by the lover while the duality of lover and beloved remains. So long as there is duality between the lover and the beloved, the lover must endure the trials of flirting and coquetry that come from the glance of belovedness, or rather from the divine manifestations of the attributes of Love on the screen of the lover's heart. For al-Ghazālī, the flirting and coquetry are what result in the many states of spiritual wayfaring, such as expansion (*basṭ*) and contraction (*qabḍ*), sorrow and happiness, and separation (*firāq*) and union (*wiṣāl*), all of which are defined in relation to an opposite. In enduring these colorations, the wayfarer is, nonetheless, moving closer to the perfection of love and beauty. Shaykh al-Ghazālī likens this process to cooking: "O chivalrous one! The glance of belovedness in beauty and the glance of beauty must be like salt in the pot, in order that the perfection of saltiness be connected to the perfection of beauty."[95] Only the fully cooked and seasoned heart—that is to say, the heart that is spiritually mature—is able to perceive the fullness of pure beauty beyond the interplay of lover and beloved.

The Stages of the Path

Once Love has descended into the world, it begins to seek itself through the love of the lover. The love realized within the lover pertains to the second beginning by which the path of ascent from the created temporal order to endlessness is traveled. For love to reach fulfillment along the path of ascent requires four stages: (1) that wherein one loves what is other than the beloved; (2) that wherein one loves what pertains to the beloved and is attached to it; (3) that wherein one loves only the beloved; and (4) that wherein one is immersed in the ocean of Love, beyond all duality. Though separable in theory, these stages are not always distinct from one another in practice. As the lover-wayfarer travels the path, he will fluctuate, sometimes residing completely in the witnessing of the beloved only to return again to love its shadows. Only when the lover has become completely immersed in the oneness of Love is he beyond ascending and descending—increase and decrease. The following section examines these stages in ascending order.

Love for What is Other

Even when one loves what is other than the beloved, his love is for the one single beloved, though he may not be aware of this. As ʿIrāqī writes, all forms of love are the same in substance:

> It is not fit to love anything other, rather it is impossible. Because whatever they love after essential love, whose necessary cause is not known—whether they love beauty or doing what is beautiful (*iḥsān*)—these two could not be other than it.[96]

But unlike ʿIrāqī and his brother Abū Ḥāmid, Aḥmad al-Ghazālī does not discuss this initial phase of love. Those who have already devoted themselves to spiritual wayfaring have done so because they are cognizant of the fact that there is only one beloved. This initial awareness is thus assumed to be the starting point, and the *Sawāniḥ* focuses upon the subtleties of the multifaceted relationship between the lover and the beloved, since the phases of this relationship are the phases of the spiritual path.

Contrast Between the Lover and the Beloved

So long as they exist, the lover and the beloved are bound to each other in a continuous interplay of union and separation. Both are derived from love, but each manifests different qualities. They are in fact polar opposites:

> The beloved is the beloved in every state, thus self-sufficiency is its attribute. And the lover is the lover in every state, thus poverty is its attribute. The lover always needs the beloved, thus poverty is always his attribute. And the beloved needs nothing, for it always has itself. Therefore, self-sufficiency is its attribute.[97]

Sometimes the lover and the beloved are drawn to one another; sometimes they are opposed to one another; and sometimes one opposes the other, while the other is drawn to it. But at all times they are dependent on one another. It is easy to imagine how the lover who is all poverty and need can be dependent on the beloved who is entirely self-sufficient, but it is more difficult to see how the beloved is dependent on the lover. Regarding this relationship, Aḥmad al-Ghazālī writes, "These attributes of the beloved do not become manifest except through the manifestation of their opposites in the lover—so long as the poverty of this is not, its self-sufficiency does not appear."[98] Ultimately, the lover and the beloved are two components of a complementary duality. It is through their interplay that love and beauty are perceived upon the screen of the heart, bringing it to seasoned perfection. Like different ingredients boiling in a pot, their positions are constantly changing. Eventually, their many modes evaporate and all that is left is what al-Ghazālī refers to as a roasted heart (*dilī biryān*), which resides in the oneness of pure love.

The Two Faces of Desire

So long as his heart is not fully "roasted," the lover-wayfarer must fully embrace the reality of his poverty in the face of the beloved so that he ceases to believe that he exists through his own self. As al-Ghazālī writes, "To be self through one's own self is one thing, and to be self through one's beloved is another. To be self through one's own self is the unripeness of the beginning of love."[99] While the lover is in this state of unripeness, he continues to love for himself, even though his love is directed toward the beloved: "The beginning of love is such that the lover wants the beloved for his own sake. This person is a lover of himself through the intermediary of the beloved, but he does not know that he wants to use her on the path of his own will."[100] Even his desire to find the beloved or to advance on the spiritual path can be a hindrance, since such desire can be a deleterious reaffirmation of self. Desire may in some way help to initiate this path, but in later stages, one must be free of all desire and allow the path to unfold. Seen from the end of the path, "Desire is entirely calumny. Calumny is entirely deficiency. Deficiency is entirely shame. And shame is entirely opposed to certainty and recognition and is the same as ignorance."[101] Nonetheless, "desire has two faces: one is its white face and one is its black face. That face which is turned toward generosity is white and that face which is turned toward claiming worthiness, or the calumny of claiming worthiness, is black."[102] In so far as the lover believes there is something within him which is other than the sheer poverty and blameworthiness which he has received from love, his desire is black, for he continues to believe he is a lover through himself. He can have desire for mercy from the beloved, but eventually even this must be eradicated through the pain of love.

The Pain of Love

When the lover-wayfarer remains in the unripeness of love where he seeks the lover for himself, he thinks that this relationship with the beloved is one of comfort and ease. But as mentioned in the discussion of the heart, this is not the reality of love. The more mature, or "cooked," lover-wayfarer becomes aware that pain and hardship are central to love, for "suffering is what is essential in love and comfort is borrowed."[103] The relationship between the lover and the beloved is one of pain and hardship because they are always two and duality necessarily implies opposition. As Aḥmad al-Ghazālī states:

> Know that the lover is an adversary, not a companion, and the beloved is also an adversary, not a companion, since companionship has been bound to wiping away their traces. So long as there is two-ness and each self is a self through itself, adversaries will be absolute. Companionship is in

> unification. Thus it will never happen that the lover and the beloved become companions of one another, for that they must not be. The suffering of love is entirely from this, for companionship will never be.[104]

From this perspective, ease and comfort are the desiderata of an unripened or uncooked self. So long as the lover seeks after them, he is at the mercy of his limitations, fluctuating between the realities of love and his illusory desires:

> Love comes and goes; it has increase, decrease, and perfection; and the lover has states in it. In the beginning he may deny it, then he may submit to it. Then he may be disgraced and again take to the path of denial. These states change according to the moment and the individual: sometimes love increases and the lover denies it; sometimes love decreases and the one who possesses it denies the decrease.[105]

Thus increase and decrease slowly break the illusions of independence and show the lover the relativity of his self, preparing him to accept the absoluteness of love; "For love must open the castle of the lover to have a house for itself within, so that the lover becomes tame and surrenders."[106] Through the trials of this path, love subdues the lover, bringing him from his illusory self to his true self. Alluding to this stage of the path, the Shaykh writes, "Affliction and oppression are castle-conquering, its mangonel is the baseness of your you-ness until you become it."[107]

Until love has subdued the lover through pain, affliction, and oppression, the lover remains the son of the moment, subject to whatever it decrees:

> Whatever edict the moment has he must follow the edict of the moment's color: the moment paints the lover according to its color and the edict will belong to the moment. In the path of annihilation from self, these edicts are wiped out and these opposites are removed, because they are a gathering of covetousness and defect.[108]

It is at this point between being a self through one's own self and being drawn to the beloved that the lover begins to obtain some knowledge (*ʿilm*). Such knowledge is from "observing a form which has been fixed within" the heart through the reflections of love's attributes in the form of the beloved. From the perspective of wayfaring, observing such forms upon the screen of one's heart is progress, but from the perspective of perfection, it is still a limitation. For the state of perfection is beyond the duality implied by knowledge; rather perfection can occur only when the lover is completely immersed in love. In juxtaposing knowledge and the perfection that lies beyond it, al-Ghazālī writes:

> So long as love has not taken hold completely, something from the lover remains, such that he brings a report about it back with the externality of knowledge so that he may be informed. But when it takes over the realm [of the wayfarer's heart] completely, nothing remains of the lover to give a report in order to derive nourishment from it.[109]

The lover who is not yet immersed in love continues to be enraptured by the images that flash upon the screen of his heart and to progress until he sees the beloved in all things. This is still what al-Ghazālī refers to as the beginning of love. It is, nonetheless, beyond the stage wherein the lover loves the beloved for the lover's self alone. In this second phase, "wherever he sees a likeness of this affair, he brings it back to the beloved,"[110] meaning that he relates all things back to the beloved rather than to himself. He now loves what is related to the beloved, seeking consolation from it. Then "the sword of the beloved's jealousy" falls, cutting him off from all that is other than the beloved.

Union between the Lover and the Beloved

The beloved, though superior to the lover in principle, is dependent on him for its own existence in the here and now. As the Shaykh expresses it:

> As regards the reality of the affair the beloved has no profit or loss from the lover. But as regards the wont (*sunnah*) of love's generosity, love binds the lover to the beloved. Through the connection of love, the lover becomes the locus of the beloved's gaze in every state.[111]

This occurs because "the love of the lover is real and the lover of the beloved is the reflection of the shining of the lover's love in [the beloved's] mirror."[112] When the lover witnesses the beloved, this can stir up the aforementioned "white face" of desire by which he advances on the path. Here "agitation arises within him, because his being is borrowed and has a face toward the *qiblah* of non-being. His existence becomes agitated in ecstasy, until he sits with the reality of the affair. Yet he is still not completely cooked."[113] That the lover is not yet cooked means that he has not yet matured in love. Such immaturity arises from the fact that one has not surrendered completely, and is thus a hypocrite in love:

> So long as he is still himself, he is not free of hypocrisy and he still fears blame. When he has become tame, he has no fear and has been saved from every kind of hypocrisy.
>
> The hypocrisy with the beloved is that the light of love shines within him and hides the outward, to the extent that for a while he hides love from the beloved, and while hiding from her, loves her. But when the defect withdraws and surrender comes, the light of love also shines upon his face, for his whole being has been lost in the beloved.[114]

When the lover has become lost in the beloved, he has arrived at "union." "This is that step where the lover knows the beloved is perfection and seeks unification, and whatever is outside of this will never be satiated."[115] Here the reality of love appears, and

> When the reality of love appears, the lover becomes food for the beloved. The beloved does not become food for the lover, because the lover can be contained in the craw of the beloved, but the beloved cannot be contained in the craw of the lover.[116]

Now that the lover has given himself completely to his beloved, he becomes the beloved:

> For one moment he becomes his own beloved, this is his perfection. All of his flying and circumambulating were for this one moment. When shall this be? Before this we have explained that the reality of union is this—one hour the attribute of "being fire" welcomes him and soon sends him out through the door of "being ash."[117]

From one perspective, the lover is contained within the beloved; from another perspective, he is even more the beloved than the beloved:

> Here, where the lover becomes more the beloved than the beloved the wonders of the attachments of connection are prepared, on condition of the non-attachment of the lover with himself. Love's connection will reach to the place where the lover claims that he himself is the beloved: "I am the Truth" and "Glory be to me" are this point.[118] And if he is in the midst of banishment, separation, and unwantedness, he imagines that he is indispensable and that he himself is the beloved.[119]

But as seen before, such proclamations are not considered by Aḥmad al-Ghazālī to be the full maturity of love; for they pertain to union between the lover and the beloved. But separation is more exalted than union in so far as there is a union beyond separation, meaning that after union the lover continues to bear the fullness of love through having realized union, but the lover no longer needs to be with the beloved in order to realize and manifest the fullness of love:

> Separation is beyond union by a degree because so long as there is no union there is no separation, for it is connected to it. In reality union is separation from self, just as in reality separation is union with self, except in defective love where the lover has still not been completely cooked.[120]

In fact, just as all of existence can be seen as a play of lover and beloved, so too, can it be seen as an intricate interplay of separation and union. The lover is the means of separation and the beloved is the instrument of union:

> Of all that the lover can have there is nothing that can become the means of union. The beloved can have the means of union. This is also a great secret, for union is the level of the beloved and her right. It is separation which is the level of the lover and his right. Thus the existence of the lover is the means of separation and the existence of the beloved is the means of union.[121]

While it is not directly evident in the text, separation is beyond union because union on the plane of duality is illusory. There is not even true familiarity:

> The beloved never becomes familiar with the lover, and at that moment that he considers himself to be closer to

> her and her to be closer to him, he is farther,[122] because the sultanate is hers, and "the sultan has no friend." The reality of familiarity is to be at the same level, and this is impossible between the lover and the beloved, because the lover is all the earth of baseness and the beloved is all the sky of exaltedness and grandeur.[123]

To realize the reality of separation is thus beyond union because it is to perceive the true nature of the relationship of the lover and the beloved.

Pain is essential for the path because it is the suffering of continuous separation from the beloved within one's own breast. As the pain of realizing separation from the many images of one's beloved increases, the lover is becoming closer to the reality of love: "Every moment the lover and the beloved become more alien to each other; although love is becoming more perfect, the alienation is becoming more."[124] Pain occurs because the lover is more familiar with love itself than with the beloved. The lover's existence is derived from love and in relation to the beloved he is always other: "Although the lover is familiar with love, he has no familiarity with the beloved."[125] Realizing the fullness of love is thus to go from the separation before union with the beloved, through union with the beloved, into the separation from the beloved that lies beyond union: "When on the path of ripening he does not belong to himself and arrives away from himself, then he has arrived beyond it [the beloved]. Then he arrives beyond himself with it [the beloved] and beyond it."[126]

At this stage pain does not decrease but rather becomes complete, because the end of the path and the perfection of love lie in the increase of affliction until there is no longer room for increase or decrease. Thus the Shaykh asks rhetorically, "But when he becomes completely and perfectly tame before love and the sultanate of love has taken over the realm completely, how will increase and decrease have a way there?"[127]

Complete Love

The full perfection of love is attained when nothing but love exists, such that all is perceived in its true nature as a modality of love. Here the lover has moved beyond the illusions that arise from the continuous play of lover and beloved. The lover-wayfarer is now immersed in the complete love that has nothing to do with the contingencies of separation and union. Of this stage Aḥmad al-Ghazālī writes, "Love Itself, in Its essence, is far from these attachments and defects, for Love has no attributes from union and separation. These are the attributes of the lover and the beloved."[128] The lover now realizes that union with the beloved is the same as separation from the beloved: "Union and separation are one for him, and he has passed beyond deficiencies and accidents."[129] He has transcended the coloration (*talwīn*) of moving from state to state in the lover-beloved duality and is now in the fixity (*tamkīn*) of love wherein nothing of his own being remains:

> Whatever leaves the lover in the coloration of love, he finds the substitute for that from the beloved in the fixity of love. But not everyone reaches this station, for this is quite a high station in love. The perfection of fixity is that nothing has remained of the lover's being.[130]

Aḥmad al-Ghazālī maintains that all the states the lover had previously experienced were modalities of complete love, bestowed upon him as substitutes until he was fit for "the robe of love" itself. From this perspective, all that he has ever received came to him "from the beloved as replacements for the robe of love."[131] Now that he is fit for that robe, he has no need for the beloved qua beloved.

The lover-wayfarer who has attained to this level does not cease to exist in the temporal world, but he is no longer subject to its illusory limitations. Rather than being veiled by love's names and attributes, he now sees them for the self-disclosures of love that they are, for he is beyond the delimitations of union and separation. As Shaykh al-Ghazālī writes of the one who has returned from immersion in the oneness of love:

> When He brings him from himself into Himself, his road to himself is from Him and by way of Him. Since his road to himself is from Him and by way of Him, these properties do not come over him. What would the properties of separation and union do here? When would receiving and rejecting entangle him? When would expansion and contraction and sorrow and happiness go around the court of His empire? As these verses say:
>
> We saw the structure of the universe and the source of
>   the world.
> And passed easily beyond cause and caused.
> And that black light which is beyond the point of *lā*,
> We also passed beyond this; neither this nor that remains.

> Here is the father of the moment (*abu'l-waqt*). When he descends to the sky of the world he will be over the moment. The moment will not be over him, and he will be free from the moment.[132]

The point of the *lā* referred to in the third verse is where the *lām* and *alif* are joined in the *lā* (no) of the first testimony of faith (*shahādah*)—*lā ilāha illa'Llāh*—No god, but God. Aḥmad al-Ghazālī sees this *lā* as the word of ultimate negation (*nafī*) in which attachment to everything save God is obliterated. The point of the *lā* is the very essence of negation, for were it not for that point, the *alif* and *lām* would not be joined. It is the archetype of annihilation (*fanā'*), beyond separation and union. The black light is then an allusion to the station of subsistence (*baqā'*) in which one abides with the Divine alone, beyond all dualities, all stations, and all states, what later Sufis refer to as "the station of no station."[133] Until one reaches the *lā*, one remains "a son of the moment" (*ibn al-waqt*), a slave to the edicts of separation and union, expansion and contraction, sorrow and happiness. But once in the black light of subsistence, the wayfarer is the "father of the moment," for the edicts of coloration cannot bear the effulgence of the black light. When the lights of all other colors are subsumed in the black light, there can be no more coloration as occurs when the wayfarer is subject to the vicissitudes of states and stations along the path. Regarding this stage no knowledge can be obtained, because it is beyond all distinctions and can be perceived or tasted only in the transpersonal depth of one's being, that is, in the heart when it has been brought into conformity with the spirit. But although everyone has a heart, not everyone reaches the point where they see with the heart and live in the heart. As Aḥmad al-Ghazālī writes:

> Not everyone reaches this place, for its beginnings are above all endings. How could its end be contained in the realm of knowledge, and how could it enter the wilderness of imagination? This reality is a pearl in a shell, and the shell is in the depths of the ocean. Knowledge can reach no more than the shore. How could it reach here?[134]

It is no coincidence that in writing of the black light that is beyond all else Aḥmad al-Ghazālī uses an expression similar to that which he uses to describe love. Love, he writes, "is free of this and of that," and the black light beyond the *lā* is where "neither this nor that remain." Both mark the end of the path where all is immersed in the beginningless and endless oneness of Love that transcends all dualities. It is the end beyond all ends and the beginning before all beginnings.

Conclusion

The end beyond all ends and the beginning before all beginnings is that which Shaykh Aḥmad al-Ghazālī strived to reach his entire life and to which he hoped to help others attain through his writings, sermons, and personal counsel. In the *Sawāniḥ* he accomplishes this task through an allusive discussion of love, beauty, the spirit, and the heart. In *at-Tajrīd fī kalimat at-tawḥīd* he focuses upon *dhikr* and its progressive penetration through the heart and the spirit to the inmost core. In his *Majālis* he enjoins *dhikr* but concentrates more on recognition (*ʿirfān*) as a means of spiritual attainment. These various ways of envisaging the Sufi path do not necessarily represent developments or changes in Aḥmad al-Ghazālī's perspective. Rather, they are different ways of expressing the same fundamental understanding of reality and the means of attaining it and of trying to convey some small taste of it to others in order to inspire them to wayfare upon the Sufi path. Like most Sufis of the medieval period, Aḥmad al-Ghazālī maintained that observance of Shariah was not complete without realization of *ḥaqīqah* (reality) and that realization of *ḥaqīqah* must be grounded in observance of Shariah. Unlike his more sober sibling, he left the definition of the particulars of Shariah to others, focusing instead on the *ḥaqīqah* and the *ṭarīqah* through which the *ḥaqīqah* can be attained. As such, the overall purpose of his extant writings is spiritual guidance.

For over nine hundred years, Aḥmad al-Ghazālī's words have been regarded by seekers in the Persianate world, especially Iran and India, as a summons to the spiritual path. In this small way, Aḥmad al-Ghazālī achieved at least one of his goals. The nature of his writings implies to many Sufi practitioners that he had also attained the other goal—immersion in the reality of Love that fully transcends the duality of lover and beloved. While he employs various modes of expressing Sufi teachings, his unique and lasting contribution lies in the discussion of love in the *Sawāniḥ*. Were it not for this text, Aḥmad al-Ghazālī's contributions to the Sufi tradition might not merit extensive investigation, and he would remain almost completely in the shadow of his older brother. His role as a Sufi Shaykh and his place within several Sufi *silsilah*s would remain of importance for the study of various Sufi orders. But in the absence of the *Sawāniḥ*, his place in Sufi *silsilah*s might also be diminished, since it was often through the teaching of this seminal text that he came to be revered by later generations in the Persianate world. When the *Sawāniḥ* is taken into consideration, Aḥmad al-Ghazālī emerges as a highly original thinker, whose teachings regarding love, though mostly condensed within a single brief text, altered the course of Persian Sufi literature.

As demonstrated in Chapter 4, the *Sawāniḥ* marks a new phase in discussions of love within the Sufi tradition. As a result of this new formulation, "Ahmad al-Ghazali is today generally regarded as the foremost metaphysician of love in the Sufi tradition."[1] The *Sawāniḥ* is one of several Persian texts that emerge in the first quarter of the sixth/twelfth century, the others being the *Rawḥ al-arwāḥ* of Samʿānī, Maybudī's *Kashf al-asrār*, and ʿAyn al-Quḍāt's *Tamhīdāt*. Love as the focus of Sufi discourse and the goal of spiritual attainment had existed in various forms expressed by many Sufis before these texts emerged. But the works of Aḥmad al-Ghazālī, Maybudī, Samʿānī, and ʿAyn al-Quḍāt present Love as the Ultimate Reality from which all else derives and outline the whole of the Sufi path as an intricate play between loverness and belovedness that is eventually subsumed in Love Itself. Several passages in Maybudī's *Kashf* make it clear that he was familiar with the *Sawāniḥ*, though as William Chittick has demonstrated, Maybudī was more directly influenced by ʿAbdallāh Anṣarī and Samʿānī.[2] Nonetheless, it is likely that Samʿānī was also familiar with the *Sawāniḥ* even if he does not quote directly from it. The question of the relationship between these texts merits further investigation. At this stage it is clear that together they mark a significant watershed in the development of the Persian Sufi literary tradition, a phase that gave rise to such luminaries as ʿAṭṭār, Rūmī, and Ḥāfiẓ.

Due to its brevity and the alluring nature of its allusive style, the *Sawāniḥ* appears to have had a more discernible influence over time than have *Rawḥ al-arwāḥ* and *Kashf al-asrār*. Regarding the significant impact of Aḥmad al-Ghazālī's literary style, Leili Anvar observes,

> In a deeper sense Ghazālī . . . remedies the narrowness of language by transmitting verbal expression into visionary

> experience. Rather than letting us merely hear about what love is, he makes us behold its various aspects through visual imagery, providing descriptions that resemble what came to be known in later works by Persian poets as 'divine flashes' (*Lamaʿāt*). Ghazālī's insistence on this visionary aspect of love, in which the radiance of the Beloved's beauty is the source of inspiration, soon became the founding principle of the tradition of the Persian mystical *ghazal*, which reached the absolute perfection of its lyrical art with Ḥāfiẓ.[3]

Given the importance of Aḥmad al-Ghazālī's contributions to the history of Persian Sufi literature, a clearer understanding of his corpus has been required for some time. As demonstrated in the first chapter, most of the works attributed to him are most likely not of his pen. For many of these texts, the confusion arises from cataloguing errors resulting from the relative obscurity of Aḥmad b. Muḥammad aṭ-Ṭūsī and the similarity of his name and that of Aḥmad b. Muḥammad al-Ghazālī. For most texts, this matter is not significant because the texts remained unpublished and no scholars have analyzed them in discussions of Aḥmad al-Ghazālī. The misattribution of *Bawāriq al-ilmāʾ* that was perpetuated in Western scholarship by James Robson has, however, resulted in an unfortunate situation wherein the majority of scholarly discussions regarding Aḥmad al-Ghazālī have centered on the discussions regarding *samāʿ* contained in the *Bawāriq*. Removing this dimension from discussions of Aḥmad al-Ghazālī allows us to focus more squarely on his actual teachings.

A proper understanding of the parameters of Aḥmad al-Ghazālī's corpus and his unique contributions also provides a solid foundation for comparing many aspects of the Ghazālī brothers' teachings, especially those regarding love and *dhikr*. Some Muslim philosophers such as ʿAyn al-Quḍāt al-Hamadānī and Ibn Ṭufayl (d. 581/1185–6) maintained that Abū Ḥāmid al-Ghazālī had never revealed the full extent of his teachings.[4] As Ibn Tufayl writes, "I have no doubt that our teacher al-Ghazālī was among those who reached this sublime goal and enjoyed the ultimate bliss. Nonetheless, his esoteric books on mysticism have not reached us."[5] Such assertions are supported by Abū Ḥāmid's own writings, as he sometimes maintains that certain teachings should be "left under the cover of dust until the wayfarers stumble upon it"[6] and that when approaching such teachings in writing "the reins of the pen must be drawn in."[7] In contrast Aḥmad al-Ghazālī was far less reticent. Like Maybudī and Samʿānī, he allows that the most sublime truths can be discussed so that wayfarers on the Sufi path might benefit from them. This is apparent in the nature of Aḥmad's discourse and in statements such as this previously cited passage:

> Sometimes an earthen vessel or a glass bead is put in the hand of a novice until he becomes a master artisan; but sometimes a precious, shining pearl that the master's hand of knowledge does not dare touch, let alone pierce, is put into his ignorant hand to pierce.[8]

Writing with the intention of placing these teachings within the grasp of wayfarers at all stages along the path, Aḥmad al-Ghazālī rarely retreats into the calculated discourse of a theologian or a philosopher. Rather, as Eve Feuillebois-Pierunek observes, "Each poem"—one could even say each sentence—"is an expression of a spiritual 'moment,' or sentence carved out of realization of a mystical truth."[9] It is in this vein that Shaykh Aḥmad al-Ghazālī can say of his own writings, "In the hearts of words lie the edges of a sword which cannot be seen except by inner vision (*baṣīrat-i bāṭinī*)."[10]

Notes

Introduction

1. For a study of Abū Ḥāmid al-Ghazālī's place as a "reviver" of Islamic moral life and the importance of his *The Revival of the Religious Sciences*, see Kenneth Garden, *The First Islamic Reviver: Abū Ḥāmid al-Ghazālī and His Revival of the Religious Sciences* (Oxford/New York: Oxford University Press, 2014). The best overview of Abū Ḥāmid al-Ghazālī's teachings is found in Eric Ormsby, *Ghazali: The Revival of Islam* (Oxford: Oneworld, 2008). For an example of the manner in which the *Iḥyā'* is still seen as a model for reviving aspects of Islamic life and thought, see Hamid Algar, *Imam Abu Hamid Ghazali: An Exponent of Islam in Its Totality* (Oneonta, NY: Islamic Publications International, 2000). Particularly noteworthy is the manner in which Abū Ḥāmid al-Ghazālī's magnum opus, *The Revival of the Islamic Sciences*, continues to serve as the basis for Islamic spiritual life in parts of the Hadramawt in Yemen.

2. William C. Chittick, *Divine Love: Islamic Literature and the Path to God* (New Haven/London: Yale University Press, 2013), xii.

3. For the place of the *Sawāniḥ* in the Sufi love tradition, see Chapter 4 of this study and Joseph Lumbard, "From *Hubb* to *'Ishq*: The Development of Love in Early Sufism," *The Oxford Journal Of Islamic Studies*, vol. 18, no. 2, April 2008, 345–385. While ʿAbdallāh Anṣārī's *Maḥabbat Nāma* and *Munājāt* also speak extensively of the love of God, Anṣārī does not provide a complete metaphysics of love as do Ghazālī and Samʿānī.

4. Leonard Lewisohn, introduction to *Hafiz and the Religion of Love in Classical Persian Poetry*, ed. Leonard Lewisohn (London: I.B. Taurus, 2010), xxii.

5. Leili Anvar, "The Radiance of Epiphany: The Vision of Beauty and Love in Ḥāfiẓ's Poem of Pre-Eternity," in *Hafiz and the Religion of Love in Classical Persian Poetry*, 124

6. For a full exposition of this aspect of the *Sawāniḥ*, see Chapters 4 and 5 of this study.

7. Seyyed Hossein Nasr, in foreword to William C. Chittick, *Divine Love: Islamic Literature and the Path to God* (New Haven/London: Yale University

Press, 2013), viii. In a previous publication, Nasr wrote, "With the Sawāniḥ begins an extremely rich spiritual tradition, leading to that elusively subtle treatise by Rūzbihān, the Abhār al-ʿāshiqīn—The Lovers' Jasmine, and on down to Fakhr al-Dīn ʿIrāqī (d. 688/1289)"; Introduction to *The Rise and Development of Persian Sufism,* ed. Leonard Lewisohn (London/New York: Khaniqahi Nimatullahi Publications, 1993), 7.

8. For a view of the initiatic chains that are said to have come through both Aḥmad al-Ghazālī and Abū Najīb as-Suhrawardī, see J. Spencer Trimingham, *The Sufi Orders* (Oxford: Oxford University Press, 1971), insert between 30 & 31 and the diagram of Sufi orders in the back of Aḥmad Mujāhid's *Majmūʿah-yi āthār-i fārsī-yi Aḥmad Ghazālī* (Tehran: Tehran University Publications, 1979; reprint 1997).

9. Shihāb ad-Dīn Abū Ḥafṣ ʿUmar as-Suhrawardī, *ʿAwārif al-maʿārif* (Cairo: Maktabat al-Qāhirah, 1393/1973), 69. The relationship between Aḥmad al-Ghazālī and as-Suhrawardī is examined more fully in Chapter 1.

10. For a study of *ʿAwārif al-maʿārif* and the history of the Suhrawardiyyah, see Erik S. Ohlander, *Sufism in an Age of Transition: ʿUmar al-Suhrawardī and the Rise of the Islamic Mystical Brotherhoods* (Leiden: E. J. Brill, 2008).

11. Saiyid Athar Abbas Rizvi, *A History of Sufism in India,* vol. 1 (New Delhi: New Delhi: Munshiram Manoharlal Publishers, 2003 [originally published in 1978]).

12. "Suhrawardiyyah," in *The Encyclopaedia of Islam* (hereafter cited as EI), 9:784–786.

13. Muhammad Isa Waley, "Najm ad-Dīn Kubrā and the Central Asian School of Sufism (The Kubrawiyyah)," in *Islamic Spirituality II: Manifestations,* ed. S.H. Nasr (New York: Crossroad Publication Company, 1991), 81. ʿAbd ar-Raḥmān Jāmī lists all three as Kubrā's instructors in Sufism, but only lists Qaṣrī as the one who bestowed the Sufi mantle *(khirqah)* upon him; *Nafaḥāt al-uns,* 421–422. J. Spencer Trimingham writes that Kubrā received his first *khirqah* from Rūzbihān, but that his real training took place under Qaṣrī, who also gave him a *khirqah; Sufi Orders,* 55.

14. For a brief history of the orders that flowed from the Kubrāwiyyah, see *Sufi Orders,* 56–57. For a history of the Dhahabiyyah, see Richard Gramlich, *Die schiitschen Derwischorden Persiens, Erster Teil: Affiliationen* (Wiesbaden: Franz Steiner, 1965), chap. 1.

15. For the best account of this commentary and its various stages of development under different Kubrāwiyyah authors, see Jamal J. Elias, *The Throne Carrier of God: The Life and Thought of ʿAlāʾ ad-Dawla as-Simnānī* (Albany, NY: SUNY Press, 1995), 203–206.

16. This text has been translated into English with an excellent introduction by Hamid Algar, *The Path of God's Bondsmen from Origin to Return* (Delmar, NY: Caravan Press, 1982).

17. *Najm al-qurʾān* is also known as *Tafsīr najm al-qurʾān, at-Taʾwīlāt an-najmiyyah,* and *Tafsīr baṭn al-qurʾān (A Commentary on the Inner Meaning of the Quran).* Simnānī's introduction to the commentary is known by the name *Maṭlaʿ an-nuqat wa-majmaʿ al-luqat.*

18. Hermann Landolt, "Der Breifwechsel zwischen Kāšānī und Simnānī über Waḥdat al-Wuǧūd," in Landolt, *Recherches en Spiritualité Iranienne* (Tehran: Institut Fraçais de Recherche en Iran, 2005), 246–300; idem, "Simnānī on waḥdat-al-wujûd," *Collected Papers on Islamic Philosophy and Mysticism*, ed. M. Mohaghegh and H. Landolt (Tehran, 1971), 93ff.

19. See *The Throne Carrier of God*, 2, 162.

20. For a history of the Niʿmatallāhī *silsilah*, see Richard Gramlich, *Die schiitschen Derwischorden Persiens, Erster Teil: Die Affiliationen*, chap. 2; Javad Nurbaksh, "The Nimatullāhī," in *Islamic Spirituality II: Manifestations*, 144–161.

21. Shams ad-Dīn Aḥmad Aflākī, *Manāqib al-ʿārifīn*, ed. Taḥsīn Yazici (Tehran: Dunyā-yi Kitāb, 1362/1983); translated by John O'Kane as *The Feats of the Knowers of God* (Leiden: E. J. Brill, 2002), 700.

22. *Manāqib al-ʿārifīn*, 1:219; *Feats of the Knowers*, 152.

23. *Feats of the Knowers of God*, 154.

24. Ibid., 153.

25. Jan Rypka, *History of Iranian Literature* (Dordrecht: D. Reidel, 1968); Edward Granville Brown, *A Literary History of Persia: From Firdawsī to Saʿadī* (New York: Charles Scribner's & Sons, 1906).

26. Nasrollah Pourjavady, *Sulṭān-i ṭarīqāt* (Tehran: Intishārāt-i Agāh, 1358 HS/1979), 75.

27. Omid Safi, "The Sufi Path of Love in Iran and India," in *A Pearl in Wine* (New Lebanon, NY: Omega Publications, 2001), 224.

28. The full extent of commentaries on the *Sawāniḥ* is a subject that merits further investigation. Three of these commentaries—one from the ninth/fifteenth century by an unknown author, one by ʿIzz ad-Dīn Maḥmūd Kāshānī (d. 730/1330), and one by Ḥusayn Nāgūrī (d. 901/1496)—have been published in *Sharḥ-i Sawāniḥ: seh sharḥ bar Sawāniḥ al-ʿushshāq-i Aḥmad Ghazālī*, ed. Aḥmad Mujāhid (Tehran: Soroush Press, 1372 HS).

29. Aḥmad al-Ghazālī, *Makātibāt-i Khwājah Aḥmad Ghazālī bā ʿAyn al-Quḍāt Hamadānī*, ed. Nasrollah Pourjavady (Tehran: Khānqāh-i Niʿmat Allāhī, 1356/1978).

30. *ʿAyn al-Quḍāt Abu'l-Maʿālī ʿAbdallāh b. Muḥammad b. ʿAlī al-Mīyānagī Hamadānī, Tamhīdāt*, ed. ʿAfīf ʿUsayrān (Tehran: Tehran University Press, 1962), 96–141.

31. For an examination of the commentaries on the *Tamhīdāt* in India, see Firoozeh Papan-Matin, *Beyond Death: The Mytsical Teachings of ʿAyn al-Quḍāt al-Hamadhānī* (Leiden/Boston: E. J. Brill, 2010), 161–190.

32. Gerhard Böwering, "ʿAyn al-Qoẓāt Hamadānī," in *Encyclopaedia Iranica*, 2:140–143.

33. Fakhr ad-Dīn ʿIrāqī, *Lamaʿāt*, ed. Muḥammad Khwājavī (Tehran: Intishārāt-i Mūlā, 1413 AH), 45; translated by W.C. Chittick and Peter Lamborn Wilson as *Fakhr ad-Dīn ʿIrāqī: Divine Flashes* (New York: Paulist Press, 1982), 70. I have consulted the translation of Chittick and Wilson, but altered it slightly.

34. Lamaʿāt, 49; *Divine Flashes*, 73.

35. ʿAbd ar-Raḥmān Jāmī, *Ashiʿʿat al-Lamaʿāt* (Qum: Būstān-i Kitāb, 1383/2004).

36. Pourjavady, *Sulṭān-i ṭarīqāt,* 78.

37. Aḥmad Ghazālī, *Risālat at-ṭayr,* ed. Aḥmad Mujāhid; *Majmūʿah,* 213.

38. Seyyed Hossein Nasr, *Islamic Art and Spirituality* (Albany: SUNY Press, 1987), 100.

39. Nūr ad-Dīn ʿAbd ar-Raḥmān Jāmī, *Nafaḥāt al-uns min ḥaḍarāt al-quds,* ed. Maḥmūd ʿĀbidī (Tehran: Intishārāt-i Iṭṭilaʿāt, 1380 HS), 596.

40. This is according to the *silsilah* provided by J. Spencer Trimingham, in *Sufi Orders* (insert between 56–57).

41. For the relation between Bahāʾ ad-Dīn Zakariyyā and Fakhr ad-Dīn ʿIrāqī, see *Divine Flashes,* 37–46.

42. Safi, "Sufi Path of Love in Iran and India," 252–258.

43. ʿAbd al-ʿAzīz Wāʿiẓī, Ta'rīkh-i Ḥabībī, (Hyderabad: N.P., 1368 A.H.), 65; cited in Syed Shah Khusro Hussaini, *Sayyid Muḥammad al-Ḥusaynī-i Gīsūdirāz: On Sufism* (Delhi: Idarah-i Adabiyat-i Delli, 1983), 23.

44. S.A.A. Rizvi, *A History of Sufism in India,* 1:171.

45. Craig Davis, "The Yogic Exercises of the 17th Century Sufis," in *Theory and Practice of Yoga: Essays in Honour of Gerald James Larson,* ed. Knut A. Jacobsen (Delhi: Motilal Banarsidass, 2005), 315.

46. For ʿAyn al-Quḍāt Hamadānī's influence in India, see Papan Matin, "ʿAyn al-Quḍāt al-Hamadhānī, His Work and His Connection with the Early Chishtī Mystics," *Comparative Studies in South Asia, Africa and the Middle East,* 30:3 (2011), 341–355.

47. Hishmatallāh Riyāḍī, *Āyāt-i ḥusn va-ʿishq* (Tehran: Kitābkhānah-yi Ṣāliḥ, 1369 HS/1989).

48. *Tracts on Listening to Music: Being Dhamm al-malāhī,* by Ibn Abi'd-Dunyā and Bawāriq al-ilmāʿ, by Majd ad-Dīn aṭ-Ṭūsī al-Ghazālī, trans. and ed. James Robson (Hertford: Stephen Austin & Sons, 1938).

49. This information is from a discussion with Pourjavady in which he stated that he was unwilling to republish *Sulṭān-i ṭarīqāt* without substantially rewriting these sections. His many discussions of Aḥmad al-Ghazālī in subsequent articles provide a more refined analysis of Aḥmad al-Ghazālī's teachings.

50. E.g., Kenneth Avery, *A Pyschology of Early Sufi samāʿ: Listening and Altered States* (London/New York: Routledge, 2004). The *Bawāriq* is referenced on multiple occasions throughout Avery's study of *samāʿ*, and treated as a text by Majd ad-Dīn al-Ghazālī; also see Jean-Louis Michon, "Sacred Music and Dance in Islam," in *Islamic Spirituality II, Manifestations,* ed. S.H. Nasr (New York: Crossroad, 1991), 478–479; Syed Shah Khusro Hussaini's *Sayyid Muḥammad al-Ḥusaynī-i Gīsūdirāz* (721/1321–825/1422) on Sufism also provides an extended analysis of Gīsū Dirāz's teachings that draws extensively from *Bawāriq al-ilmāʿ* under the misunderstanding that it was a text of Aḥmad al-Ghazālī for whose *Sawāniḥ* Gīsū Dirāz had an expressed affinity; see 110–174; Firoozeh Papan-Matin also draws extensively on the *Bawāriq* in her analysis of *samāʿ* in *Beyond Death;* see 192–209.

51. Helmut Ritter, art., "al-Ghazālī, Aḥmad," EI2 2:1041.

52. Richard Gramlich, *Aḥmad Ghazzālī, Gedanken über die Liebe* (Wiesbaden: Franz Steiner, 1976).

53. Gisela Wendt, *Aḥmad Ghazzālī: Gedanken über die Liebe* (Amsterdam: Castrum Peregrini, 1978).

54. Nasrollah Pourjavady, *Sawāniḥ: Inspirations from the World of Pure Spirits; The Oldest Persian Sufi Treatise on Love* (London: Routledge & Kegan Paul, 1986).

55. Richard Gramlich, *Der reine Gottesglaube: das Wort des Einheitsbekenntnisses: Aḥmad Al-Ghazzalis Schrift At-Taǧrid fī kalimat at-tawḥīd* (Wiesbaden: Otto Harrasowitz, 1983); Muhammad ad-Dahbi, *La citadelle de Dieu* (Le dépouillement dans la parole de l'Unité) (Paris: Les Éditions Iqra, 1995).

Chapter 1: Sources for the Aḥmad al-Ghazālī Tradition

1. Shams ad-Dīn Aḥmad Aflākī, *Manāqib al-ʿārifīn*, 1:219; trans. John O'Kane, 152.

2. There are many printed editions of the *Sawāniḥ*. The four most reliable editions are *Sawāniḥ*, ed. Aḥmad Mujāhid, in *Majmūʿah-yi āthār-i fārsī-yi Aḥmad Ghazālī*, 89–173; *Sawāniḥ*, ed. Nasrollah Pourjavady (Tehran: Intishārāt-i Bunyā va Farsang-i Īrān, 1359 HS/1980); *Sawāniḥ*, in *Ganja-yi ʿirfān*, ed. Ḥāmid Rabbānī (Tehran: Ganjinah, 1973); *Sawāniḥ*, ed. Helmut Ritter (Tehran: Markaz-i Nashr-i Dānishgāhī, 1368 HS/1989). English translation, Nasrollah Pourjavady, *Sawāniḥ: Inspirations form the World of Pure Spirits, The Oldest Persian Sufi Treatise on Love* (London: Routledge & Kegan Paul, 1986).

The edition by Pourjavady is based on that of Ritter and supplemented by additional manuscripts that predate those on which Ritter relied. Though five editions were published between those of Ritter and Pourjavady, none surpassed Ritter's. The edition of Pourjavady can in some ways be seen as a supplement to Ritter's, since he builds on Ritter's extant apparatus. Mujāhid's edition has a critical apparatus adopted in part from other editions. Rabbānī's edition does not provide an apparatus, but in several instances Rabbānī provides readings that make more sense than those of Pourjavady or Ritter. For this study, I will therefore rely on the editions of Pourjavady, Ritter, and Rabbānī. They will be cited in this order, and the discrepancies in paragraph order will be noted by placing the paragraph number in parentheses after each citation. All translations are my own. In rendering the *Sawāniḥ*, I am indebted to Pourjavady's translation for guidance and have placed the page number for his translation after the backslash.

3. There are two critical editions of this text and one English translation: *Dastān-i murghān*, ed. Nasrollah Pourjavady (Tehran: Anjuman-i Shahanshāhi-yi Falsafā-yi Īrān,1355 HS/1976); ed. Muhjāhid, in *Majmūʿah*, 69–85; English translation by Peter Avery as an appendix to his translation of Farīd ad-Dīn ʿAṭṭār's *Speech of the Birds* (Cambridge: Islamic Texts Society, 1998), 551–560.

4. For the relationship between ʿAyn al-Quḍāt and both Ghazālī brothers, see Hamid Dabashi, *Truth and Narrative: The Untimely Thoughts of ʿAyn al-Quẓāt Hamadhānī* (London: Curzon, 1999), chap. 7. Though highly problematic, this study still provides a good discussion of ʿAyn al-Quḍāt's personal, intellectual, and spiritual relationship with the Ghazālī brothers.

5. There are four critical editions of the *Risālah-yi ʿAyniyyah*: (1) in *Armaghān*, 8:1 (1308 HS), 8–42; (2) under the title *Tāzīyāne sulūk*, ed. Nasrollah Taqawi (Tehran, 1319 HS); (3) under the title *Mawʿiẓe* (Exhortation), ed. Javad Nurbakhsh (Tehran, 1352 HS); (4) in *Majmūʿah*, ed. Mujāhid, 175–214.

6. There are two critical editions of the letters between Aḥmad and ʿAyn al-Quḍāt: *Makātibat-i Khwājah Aḥmad al-Ghazālī bā ʿAyn al-Quḍāt Hamadānī*, ed. Nasrollah Pourjavady (Tehran: Khānagāh-i Niʿmatallāhī, 1356 HS/1978); ed. Muhjāhid, in *Majmūʿah*, 461–509. In addition, two brief letters directed to spiritual aspirants have been edited: "Maktūbi az Aḥmad al-Ghazālī," ed. Nasrollah Pourjavady, in *Jāvādīn-i khurd*, 1 (AH 1354), 32–37; ed. Mujāhid in *Majmūʿah*, 248–260.

7. Carl Brockelmann, *Geschichte der arabischen Litteratur* (Leiden: E. J. Brill, 1937–49), 2:756.

8. No. 159/5 in E. Blochet, *Catalogue des manuscrits persans de la Biblioteque Nationale* (Paris, 1905), 1:123.

9. *Majmūʿah*, 1–68; *Baḥr al-ḥaqīqah*, ed. Nasrollah Pourjavady (Tehran: Imperial Iranian Academy of Philosophy, 1977).

10. Nasrollah Pourjavady, from English introduction to *Baḥr al-ḥaqīqah*, 3.

11. Aḥmad al-Ghazālī, *Majālis-i Aḥmad Ghazālī*, ed. with Persian translation by Aḥmad Mujāhid (Tehran: Tehran University Press, 1998), 22.

12. For the centrality of *dhikr* in Sufi practice, see G.C. Anawati et Louis Gardet, *Mystique Musulman* (Paris: Libraire Philosophique J. Vrin, 1968), 187–260; Gerhard Böwering, "Ḏekr," in *Encyclopaedia Iranica* 7:229–233; William Chittick, "Dhikr," in *Encyclopedia of Religion*, ed. Mircea Eliade, et al. (New York: Macmillan, 1987), 4:341–344; Chittick, *Sufism: A Short Introduction* (Oxford: Oneworld, 2000), 52–60; Louis Gardet, "Dhikr," in *EI*[2]; Martin Lings, *What is Sufism?* (London: Unwin Hyman, 1981), 74–91; Joseph Lumbard, "The Function of *Dhikrullāh* in Ṣūfī Psychology," in *Knowledge is Light: Essays in Honor of Seyyed Hossein Nasr*, ed. Zailan Moris (Chicago: ABC International Group, 1999), 251–274; Annemarie Schimmel, *Mystical Dimensions of Islam* (Chapel Hill: University of North Carolina Press, 1975), 167–178.

13. *Majālis*, 21.

14. *Majmūʿah*, 258.

15. There is one noncritical printing of *at-Tajrīd fī kalimat at-tawḥīd* (Cairo: Sharikat Maktaba wa-Maṭbaʿ Muṣṭafā al-Bābī al-Ḥalabī, 1386/1967). This treatise has also been translated into German by Richard Gramlich, *Das Wort des Einheitsbekenntnisses* (Wiesbaden: Franz Steiner, 1983), and into French by Muḥammad ad-Dahbī, *La citadelle de Dieu . . . (Le dépouillement dans la parole de l'Unité)* (Paris: Iqra, 1995).

16. Tāj ad-Dīn Abū Naṣr ʿAbd al-Wahhāb b. ʿAlī as-Subkī, *aṭ-Ṭabaqāt ash-shāfiʿiyyah al-kubrā* (Cairo: ʿĪsā'l-Bābī al-Ḥalabī, 1964–76), 6:60.

17. The manuscripts of this text are identified as a work of Aḥmad al-Ghazālī by Brokelmann (*GAL*, 1:422; *Suppl.* 1:748). This attribution derives from the biographical tradition, which attributes the treatise to Aḥmad al-Ghazālī from the seventh century forward. The manuscripts I have examined do not attribute the text to Aḥmad al-Ghazālī, but to Abū Ḥāmid al-Ghazālī: MS Berlin, Wetzstein 99 (Ahlwardt no. 1708), and MSS Princeton, Yahuda 838 and 3717 (Mach no. 2164). A shorter abridgement of the *Iḥyāʾ* catalogued under the title *Lubb al-Iḥyāʾ* (The Kernel of the Revival) provides no attribution to either Aḥmad al-Ghazālī or Abū Ḥāmid al-Ghazālī: MS Yale University, Beinecke Library, Salisbury 38, foll. 1–45 (1025/1616), and MS Berlin, Wetzstein II 1807, foll. 120–146b (Ahlwardt 1707).

18. There are two noncritical printed editions of this work: Bombay: n.p., 1894 and New Delhi: n.p., n.d., under the title *Aḥsan al-qiṣaṣ* (*The Best of Stories*). It is also known by the titles *Tafsīr sūrat Yūsuf al-musammā bi durrat al-bayḍāʾ*, *Baḥr al-ʿishq fī tafsīr sūrat Yūsuf*, and *Tafsīr sūrat Yūsuf*. There is a Persian translation by Mirza Abu'l-Ḥasan Faqīhī, *Kitāb-i asrār-i ʿishq ya daryā-i maḥabbat* (Tehran: n.p., AH 1325).

19. Rida 1473 (AH 929).

20. Khayr ad-Dīn az-Ziriklī, *al-Aʿlām: Qāmūs tarājim li-ashhar ar-rijāl wa'n-nisāʾ min al-ʿarab wa'l-mustaʿribīn wa'l-mustashriqīn* (Beirut: Dār al-ʿIlm li'l-Malāyīn, 1992), 1:215. It should also be noted that ʿUmar Riḍā Kaḥḥālah refers to Aḥmad al-Ghazālī by the honorific "Shihāb ad-Dīn." He is the only biographer to do so. The only apparent source for this is the erroneous attribution of the *Bawāriq* to him, though Kaḥḥālah does not list it among his writings: *Muʿjam al-muʿallifīn tarājim muṣannifi al-kutub al-ʿarabiyyah* (Damascus: al-Maktabah al-ʿArabiyyah bi'dimashq, 1957), 1:147.

21. Kenneth Avery, *A Pyschology of Early Sufi samāʿ: Listening and Altered States*, 175. For other studies that treat the *Bawāriq* as a work by Aḥmad al-Ghazālī, see note 50 in the introduction to this volume.

22. Cairo, *Dār al-Kutub al-Miṣriyyah* (*Taṣawwuf*, 377), 9 folios, 1138/1725–26; Paris, Bibliothèque Nationale (De Slane, 4580), 12 folios, seventeenth century.

23. Berlin, Staatsbibliothek (Ahlwardt, 5505, foll. 17a–36b), 750/1349.

24. Aḥmad Mujāhid, "Introduction," Aḥmad aṭ-Ṭūsī, *Samāʿ wa-futuwwah*, ed. Aḥmad Mujāhid (Tehran, 1360 HS), 17–18.

25. Robson, 97 (English translation); 155 (Arabic text).

26. Ibid., 97.

27. ʿAyn al-Quḍāt al-Hamadānī, *Tamhīdāt*, 251.

28. Ibn Ḥajar al-ʿAsqalānī, *Lisān al-mīzān* (Hyderabad: Maṭbaʿat Majlis Dāʾirāt al-Maʿārif an-Niẓāmiyyah, 1329/1911), 1:293.

29. See Avery, 177, 185.

30. Berlin Or. 1726; Fez, Qarawiyyīn 1467, from Brockelmann, *GAL*, 2:756.

31. Ibn al-Mustawfī Sharaf ad-Dīn al-Irbilī, *Ta'rīkh Irbil: Nabāhat al-balad al-khāmil bi-man waradahu min al-amāthil* (Baghdad: Dār ar-Rashīd li'n-Nashr; Wizārat Thaqāfa wa'l-A'lām al-Jumhūriyyah al-'Irāqiyyah, 1972), 1:37.

32. Brockelmann, *GAL*, 2:756.

33. Al-Irbilī, *Ta'rīkh Irbil*, 1:37.

34. Aḥmad b. Muḥammad aṭ-Ṭūsī, *Sirr al-asrār fī kashf al-anwār*, ed. 'Abd al-Ḥamīd Dālih Hamadān (Cairo: ad-Dār al-Miṣriyyah al-Lubnāniyyah,1408/1988).

35. Berlin Or., oct. 3707 (AH 1109).

36. Cairo I, 368 (AH 1257); Aleppo, Ḥalab Library (AH 997).

37. Berlin Or., 2832.

38. Vatican, Arabo 299, foll. 80v–113v; for a full list of works attributed to Aḥmad al-Ghazālī see Mujāhid, *Majmū'ah*, 263–266.

39. Were the use of the name Aḥmad aṭ-Ṭūsī the result of an effort to remove Aḥmad al-Ghazālī from the deep shadow cast by his brother, as some who are ignorant of the nature of the Islamic historiographical tradition have proposed, it would be more widely attested in both the manuscript tradition and the Sufi tradition. The name Aḥmad aṭ-Ṭūsī does not appear in any of the extant manuscripts of *at-Tajrīd fī kalimat at-tawḥīd* or of the *Sawāniḥ* that I have perused. While I have not seen all of these manuscripts, of the dozens I have examined, all that do state the name of the author in the beginning employ the name Aḥmad b. Muḥammad al-Ghazālī or a variation of it. Furthermore, Aḥmad al-Ghazālī is never referred to as Aḥmad aṭ-Ṭūsī by his greatest admirers, the Sufis.

40. *Ma'nā* is an important technical term of Sufi discourse, often juxtaposed to *sūrah* (form). While *ma'nā* can be understood to mean, "meaning," it also has the connotation of what we understand by the word "reality" in modern usage. Thus I sometimes render the term "meaning," sometimes "reality," and sometimes write "meaning or reality" in order to convey the broader range of *ma'nā*.

41. This saying is often attributed to the Prophet in Sufi texts but is most likely not an actual *ḥadīth* of the Prophet.

42. Aḥmad b. Muḥammad aṭ-Ṭūsī, *Sirr al-asrār fī kashf al-anwār*, 23–25.

43. Aṭ-Ṭūsī, *Manhaj al-albāb*, 47a–b.

44. While Abū Ḥāmid al-Ghazālī also has extensive discussions of *faqr* in book 34 of the *Iḥyā' 'ulūm al-dīn* and in book 34 of *Kimiyā as-sa'ādah*, there is nothing in Abū Ḥāmid's writings that is at all reminiscent of the discussion of poverty found in the works discussed here. As Anthony F. Shaker, the translator for book 34 of the *Iḥyā'*, "The Book of Poverty and Asceticism" (*Kitāb al-faqr wa'z-zuhd*), wrote when asked about any resemblances between the passage here cited from *Sirr al-asrār* and Abū Ḥāmid al-Ghazālī's "Book of Poverty and Asceticism" from the *Iḥyā'*, "Despite superficial resemblances, this text does not fit well at all with *K. al-faqr wa'l-zuhd*" (email correspondence, November, 18, 2013).

45. aṭ-Ṭūsī, *Sirr al-asrār*, 50–54.

46. Employing the presence of philosophical terminology as one of, but not the only, criteria for excluding works from Aḥmad al-Ghazālī's oeuvre is not the same as the use of this criterion to evaluate the authenticity of works attributed to Abū Ḥāmid al-Ghazālī. In the case of Abū Ḥāmid al-Ghazālī, we know from his biography that he studied philosophy and from his extant works that he employed philosophical terminology. In the case of Aḥmad, we have no authenticated works that employ philosophical terminology, and there is no discussion of his having studied philosophy. For an example of the over-application of philosophical terminology as a criteria for discounting the authenticity of the works of Abū Ḥāmid, see H. Lazarus-Yafeh, "Philosophical Terminology as a Criterion of Authenticity in the Writings of al-Ghazzālī," *Studia Islamica,* 25 (1966), 111–121, and W. Montgomery Watt, "A Forgery in al-Ghazālī's *Mishkāt*?," *Journal of the Royal Asiatic Society,* 81.1 (1949), 5–22

47. Mujāhid, introduction to *Samāʿ wa futuwwah,* 10–11, cited from *Risālah fī faḍl al-faqr wa'l-fuqarāʾ*.

48. Mujāhid, introduction to *Samāʿ wa futuwwah,* 7–12.

49. Mujāhid, *Majmūʿah,* 265; Pourjavady, *Sulṭān-i ṭarīqāt,* 277.

50. Mujāhid, *Majmūʿah,* 266.

51. ʿAzīz Allāh ʿAṭṭāridī Qūchānī, *Makhṭūṭāt-i Fārsī dar Madīnah Munawwarah,* 32, MS 305.

52. Mujāhid, *Majmūʿah,* 265.

53. Farīd ad-Dīn ʿAṭṭār, *Ilāhī Nāmeh,* ed. Helmut Ritter (Istanbul: Maṭbaʿa-yi Maʿārif, 1940), 359–360.

54. ʿAyn al-Quḍāt Abu'l-Maʿālī ʿAbdallāh b. Muḥammad b. ʿAlī al-Mīyānajī Hamadānī, *Zubdat al-ḥaqāʾiq,* ed. ʿAfīf ʿUsayrān (Tehran: Tehran University Press, 1961), 7.

55. Hamadānī, *Tamhīdāt,* 280; Hamadānī, *Nāmahā-yi ʿAyn al-Quḍāt Hamadānī,* ed. ʿAfīf ʿUsayrān and ʿAlīnaqī Munzavī (Tehran: Bunyād-i Farhang-i Īrān, 1961), 2:51.

56. Hamadānī, *Tamhīdāt,* 251.

57. Ibid., 281, 349.

58. Shihāb ad-Dīn Abū Ḥafṣ ʿUmar as-Suhrawardī, *ʿAwārif al-maʿārif* (Cairo: Maktabat al-Qāhirah, 1393/1973), 69.

59. Najm ad-Dīn Rāzī, *Mirṣād al-ʿibād min al-mabdaʾ ila'l-maʿād,* ed. Muḥammad Amīn Riyāḥī, 7th ed. (Tehran: Sharikat-i Intishārāt-i ʿIlmī va Farhangī, 2000), 297.

60. See *Mirṣād al-ʿibād,* 308, 427.

61. This story is attributed to Ṣadr ad-Dīn Qūnawī by Ḥāfiẓ Ḥusayn Karbalāʾī in *Rawḍāt al-jinān wa jannāt al-janān,* ed. Jaʿfar Sulṭān al-Qarāʾī (Tehran: Bungāh-i Tarjumah va Nashr-i Kitāb, 1344–49 HS/1965–70), 2:342. It is originally found in the treatise *Tabṣirat al-mubtadiʾ wa'tadhkirat al-muntahī* (*Clarifications for Beginners and Reminders for the Advanced*). But as William Chittick argues in the appendix to his translation of several texts attributed to Ṣadr ad-Dīn Qūnawī, this treatise is most likely by Nāṣir (or Naṣīr) ad-Dīn Qūnawī (or Juwaynī or Khūʾī) who lived around the same time as Ṣadr

ad-Dīn Qūnawī and may have known him; see Chittick, *Faith and Practice of Islam* (Albany: State University of New York Press, 1992), 255–259.

The quotation is from a famous *ḥadīth*: Aḥmad b. Ḥanbal, 2:285, 2:539; Muslim, *Kitāb al-Birr*, 33; Ibn Mājah, *Kitāb az-Zuhd*, 9 [Wensinck, 3:439b]: "Verily God does not look at your bodies, nor at your forms, but He looks at your hearts." Another variation—"God does not look at your forms, nor at your works, but He looks at your hearts and your states"—is cited by Aḥmad al-Ghazālī in *Majālis*, 4, 9. "Verily God does not look at your forms, He only looks at your hearts" is cited in *at-Tajrīd fī kalimat at-tawḥīd*, 5.

62. Shams ad-Dīn at-Tabrīzī, *Maqālāt-i Shams-i Tabrīz*, ed. Muḥammad ʿAlī Muwaḥḥid (Tehran: Intishārāt-i Khwārazmī, 1990), 320; trans., William Chittick, *Me and Rūmī* (Louisville, KY: Fons Vitae, 2004), 146.

63. *Maqālāt-i Shams-i Tabrīz*, 320.

64. Ibid., 321.

65. Ibid., 320, trans. Chittick, 146.

66. Ibid., 323.

67. For an analysis of the stories regarding the practice of *shāhid-bāzī* in the biographies of Aḥmad al-Ghazālī, see Nasrollah Pourjavady, "Stories of Aḥmad al-Ghazālī 'Playing the Witness'" in *Reason and Inspiration in Islam: Theology, Philosophy and Mysticism in Muslim Thought*, ed. Todd Lawson (London: I.B. Tauris, 2005), 200–220. For other sources, see the discussion regarding the metaphysical understanding of this practice in Chapter 3.

68. Julian Baldick demonstrates that the *ʿUshshāq Nāmah* was almost certainly written by a contemporary of Fakhr ad-Dīn ʿIraqī by the name of ʿAtā'ī. Among the most convincing arguments he presents is that a note in a ninth/fifteenth-century manuscript of ʿIrāqī's *Dīwān* attributes the *ʿUshshāq Nāmah* to ʿAtā'ī; evidence that the poem's dedication reflects different political leanings than those for which ʿIrāqī is known; and the inclusion of *ghazals* that are markedly inferior to those of ʿIrāqī. See Julian Baldick, "The Authenticity of ʿIrāqī's ʿUshshāq-nāma," *Studia Iranica*, 1973: 2, 67–78.

69. Chittick, 148–149.

70. Ibid., 151.

71. Nasrollah Pourjavady, "Stories of Aḥmad al-Ghazālī 'Playing the Witness,'" 205.

72. *Maqālāt-i Shams-i Tabrīz*, 618.

73. A reference to another section of the *Maqālāt* in which it is stated that Abū Ḥāmid al-Ghazālī sent Aḥmad al-Ghazālī a copy of *adh-Dhakhīrah fī ʿilm al-baṣīrah* and *Lubāb al-Iḥyā'* in order to help him refute those who objected that the was not familiar with the "outward sciences." *Maqālāt*, 320–321; Chittick, 146–147.

74. *Maqālāt*, 325–326; my translation is a slight modification of that provided by Chittick, *Me and Rumi*, 275–276.

75. This *silsilah* is found in an appendix to Aḥmad Mujāhid's *Majmūʿah*, but he does not cite a source.

76. Nūr ad-Dīn ʿAbd ar-Raḥmān Jāmī, *Nafaḥāt al-uns min ḥaḍarāt al-quds*, 379–80; Sirāj ad-Dīn Abū Ḥafṣ ʿUmar b. ʿAlī b. Aḥmad b. al-Mulaqqin al-Miṣrī, *Ṭabaqāt al-awliyā'* (Cairo: n.p., 1393/1973), 102–104.

77. Abu'l-Faraj ʿAbd ar-Raḥmān b. ʿAlī b. al-Jawzī, *al-Muntaẓam fi't-taʾrīkh al-mulūk wa'l-umam* (Beirut: Dār al-Kutub al-ʿIlmiyyah, 1413/1992), 17:136–38; *Kitāb al-quṣṣāṣ wa'l-mudhakkirīn*, ed. and trans. Merlin S. Swartz (Beirut: Dār al-Machreq, 1986), 104–106 (Arabic), 184–188 (English).

78. A famous *ḥadīth* scholar and biographer, sometimes cited by biographers as Abū Saʿīd instead of Abū Saʿd and sometimes as Ibn as-Samʿānī instead of as-Samʿānī. Perhaps a casualty of the Mongol invasion, as-Samʿānī's *Dhayl taʾrīkh Baghdād* has only been preserved in excerpts, the extent of which indicates the importance of this work. Nonetheless, his major works on *ḥadīth* scholars, *al-Ansāb* and *at-Taḥbīr fi'l-muʿjam al-kabīr*, have been fully preserved. See *EI*², 8:1024–1025.

79. Ibn al-Jawzī, *al-Muntaẓam fi't-taʾrīkh*, 9:178.

80. Ibn al-Jawzī, *al-Muntaẓam*, 17:238; *Kitāb al-quṣṣāṣ wa'l-mudhakkirīn*, 101–102 (Arabic), 187 (English).

81. ʿAbd ar-Raʾūf b. Tāj al-ʿĀrifīn al-Munāwī, *al-Kawākib ad-durriyyah fī tarājim as-sādah aṣ-ṣūfiyyah*, ed. ʿAbd al-Ḥāmid Ṣāliḥ Ḥimdān (Cairo: al-Maktabat al-Azhariyyah li't-turāth, 1994), 1:650.

82. *al-Muntaẓam*, 17:239.

83. ʿAbd al-Karīm b. Muḥammad ar-Rāfiʿī al-Qazwīnī, *at-Tadwīn fī akhbār Qazwīn*, ed. Shaykh ʿAzīz Allāh al-ʿAṭṭārī (Beirut: Dār al-Kutub al-ʿIlmiyyah, 1987), 2:251.

84. Ibid.

85. Jāmī, *Nafaḥāt al-uns*, 380.

86. Ibid.; Ghiyāth ad-Dīn b. Hamām ad-Dīn Khwāndamīr al-Ḥusaynī, *Taʾrīkh ḥabīb as-siyar fī akhbār afrād bashar* (Tehran: Kitābkhāneh-yi Khayyām, 1333 HS), 2:319.

87. Al-Ḥāfiẓ Muḥibb Allāh Abū ʿAbdallāh Muḥammad b. Maḥmūd Ibn an-Najjār al-Baghdādī, *al-Mustafād min dhayl taʾrīkh Baghdād* (Beirut: Dār al-Kutub al-ʿIlmiyyah, 1978), 80–81.

88. Ibn an-Najjār, 80; al-Mustawfī, 1:35, 38 (slight variation); adh-Dhahabī, *Taʾrīkh al-Islām wa-wafayāt al-mashāhīr wa'l-aʿlām*, Ed. ʿUmar ʿAbd as-Salām Tadmurī (Beirut: Dār al-Kitāb al-ʿArabī, 1415/1994), 35 (AH 501–520): 129 (in the biography of Abū Ḥāmid with no specific attribution); Ṣalāḥ ad-Dīn Khalīl b. Aybak aṣ-Ṣafadī, *al-Wāfī bi'l-wafayāt*, ed. Youssef Najm (Wiesbaden: Franz Steiner Verlag, 1391/1971), 8:117; Muḥammad b. Shākir al-Kutubī, *ʿUyūn at-tawārīkh*, ed. Fayṣal as-Sāmir (Baghdad: Wizārat al-Aʿlām, al-Jumhūriyyah al-ʿIrāqiyyah, 1397/1977), 12:177. The version in the printed edition of Ibn an-Najjār is somewhat problematic. This translation is taken from Ibn al-Mustawfī, who reports that it is transmitted from as-Samʿānī (1:38).

89. Brackets added; in every instance where the common expressions "*al-āyah*" after a Quranic verse, or "*al-ḥadīth*" or "*al-khabr*" after a *ḥadīth* are used to indicate that the entire verse or report is intended, I have entered the remainder of the citation in brackets in order to fully convey the author's intentions.

90. Ibn an-Najjār, 80; as-Subkī, 1:61; Ibn Khallikān, 1:86; ʿAbd ar-Raḥmān Jāmī, *Nafaḥāt al-uns*, 379; aṣ-Ṣafadī, 8:115; al-Kutubī, 12:175; al-Munāwī, 1:650;

Muḥammad Maʿṣūm Shīrāzī, *Ṭarāʾiq al-ḥaqāʾiq* (Tehran: Kitābkhānah-i Bārānī, 1980), 2:650. These verses are also found in *Majālis-i Aḥmad Ghazālī* (25), though not in the same context.

91. Al-Mustawfī goes on to say that he found three of the verses recited by al-Ghazālī in a *dīwān* of the Maghribī poet Abu'l-Qāsim Muḥammad b. Hānī al-Maghribī (d. 362/972–973) and in the book *Unmūdhaj shuʿarāʾ al-maghrib* by Ibn Sharaf al-Qayrawānī (d. 460/1067–68). But no extant works can be found to corroborate the attribution of these verses to Abu'l-Qāsim al-Maghribī; al-Mustawfī, 36.

92. ʿUmar Riḍā Kaḥḥālah, *Muʿjam al-muʾallifīn*, 1:147; Khayr ad-Dīn az-Ziriklī, *al-Aʿlām*, 1:214.

93. Taqī ad-Dīn Abū ʿAmr ʿUthmān b. ʿAbd ar-Raḥmān Ibn aṣ-Ṣalāḥ ash-Shahrazūrī, *Ṭabaqāt al-fuqahāʾ ash-shāfiʿiyyah* (Beirut/London: Dār al-Bashāʾir al-Islāmiyyah, 1413/1996), 1: 340–397.

94. Ibid., 1:397–398.

95. Ibid., 1:399–400.

96. Aḥmad al-Ghazālī, *at-Tajrīd fī kalimat at-tawḥīd*, 50. Although this saying is attributed to Aḥmad al-Ghazālī in the *ṭabaqāt* literature, it is most likely drawn from the earlier Sufi tradition. It is attributed to the Sufi Yaḥyā b. Muʿādh ar-Rāzī (d. 258/872) in Ibn al-ʿArabī's *Jadhwat al-iṣṭilāʾ wa ḥaqīqat al-ijtilāʾ* (The firebrand of excitation and the reality of contemplation; Landberg MS 64, Yale University, Beinecke Library, verso fourth folio). However, the saying is not recorded in any of the biographical entries for Yaḥyā b. Muʿādh. It is most likely that this saying was part of the Sufi tradition as a variation on the noncanonical *ḥadīth*, "In God there is a representative from every destruction (*talaf*)" or he said "from every one who vanishes," cited by Abū Ibrāhīm Ismāʿīl b. Muḥammad Mustamlī in his *Sharḥ-i Taʿarruf li madhhab ahl-i taṣawwuf*, 1:819.

97. Muḥammad b. Shākir al-Kutubī, *ʿUyūn at-tawārīkh*, ed. Fayṣal as-Sāmir (Baghdad: Wizārat al-Aʿlām, al-Jumhūriyyah al-ʿIrāqiyyah, 1397/1977), 12:176.

98. Ṣalāḥ ad-Dīn Khalīl b. Aybak aṣ-Ṣafadī, *al-Wāfī bi'l-wafayāt*, 8:116: "He whose destruction is in God, his vicegerency is upon me."

99. Tāj ad-Dīn as-Subkī, *aṭ-Ṭabaqāt ash-shāfiʿiyyah al-kubrā*, 6:61.

100. Aḥmad Ibn al-Mulaqqin al-Miṣrī, *Ṭabaqāt al-awliyāʾ*, 102.

101. Al-Munāwī, *al-Kawākib ad-durriyyah*, 1:649.

102. For an explanation of the *abdāl* and other spiritual ranks, see Michel Chodkiewicz, *Seal of the Saints: Prophethood and Sainthood in the Doctrine of Ibn al-ʿArabī*, trans. Liadain Sherrard (Cambridge: Islamic Texts Society, 1993), chap. 7.

103. Zakāriyyah b. Muḥammad al-Qazwīnī, *Āthār al-bilād wa-akhbār al-ʿibād*, ed. al-Imām al-ʿĀlim (Beirut: Dār aṣ-Ṣādir, 1960), 413.

104. Ibid.

105. Ibid.

106. Ibn Abi'l-Ḥadīd, *Sharḥ Nahj al-balāghah*, ed. ash-Shaykh Ḥasan Tamīm (Beirut: Dār Maktabat al-Ḥayāt, 1963), 1:101–102.

107. Ibid., 1:101.

108. Ibid.

109. Aḥmad al-Ghazālī, *Majālis-i Aḥmad Ghazālī*, 13. This aspect of Aḥmad al-Ghazālī's thought is examined more extensively in Chapter 4.

110. Ibn Abi'l-Ḥadīd, *Sharḥ Nahj al-balāghah*, 1:101.

111. Ibid., 1:102.

112. For an account of the Sufi position of *Ta'aṣṣub ash-Shayṭān* as expressed by al-Ḥallāj, Aḥmad al-Ghazālī, 'Ayn al-Quḍāt, and others, see Peter J. Awn, *Satan's Tragedy and Redemption: Iblīs in Sufi Psychology* (Leiden: E.J. Brill, 1983), chap. 3, "Iblīs: Model of the Mystic Man." This aspect of al-Ghazālī's thought is examined more extensively in Chapter 4.

113. Ibn Ḥajar Aḥmad b. 'Alī al-'Asqalānī, *Lisān al-mīzān* (Hyderabad: Maṭba'at Majlis Dā'irat al-Ma'ārif an-Niẓāmiyyah, 1329–31/1911–13), 1:293–294.

114. Ibid., 1:293.

115. Ibn Abi'l-Ḥadīd, *Sharḥ Nahj al-balāghah*, 1:102.

116. Ibn Khallikān, *Wafayāt al-a'yān*, 1:86–87.

117. Ibn Khallikān, 1:86; al-Kutubī, 12:175; aṣ-Ṣafadī, 8:115; M. Bāqir al-Mūsawī al-Iṣfahānī al-Khwānsārī, *Rawḍāt al-jannāt fī aḥwāl al-'ulamā' wa's-sādāt* (Beirut: 1411/1991), 1:285; Shīrāzī, 2:564; Ibn Kathīr, 1:196; al-Miṣrī, 102; Jamāl ad-Dīn 'Abd ar-Raḥmān b. al-Ḥasan al-Isnawī, *Ṭabaqāt ash-shāfi'iyyah* (Baghdad: n.p., 1391), 245.

118. Ibn Qāḍī Shuhbah, 1:280; 'Abd al-Ḥayy b. Aḥmad Ibn al-'Imād, *Shadharāt adh-dhahab fī akhbār man dhahab* (Beirut: n.p., 1931), 4:60.

119. Al-Kutubī, *'Uyūn at-tawārīkh*, 12:175–177; aṣ-Ṣafadī, *al-Wāfī bi'l-wafayāt*, 8:115–117.

120. Kuthayyir 'Azzah, *Sharḥ Dīwān Kuthayyir 'Azzah*, 1:50; Ibn Abi'l-Ḥadīd, 1:101; aṣ-Ṣafadī, 8:112; al-Kutubī, 12:176.

121. Ibn al-Jawzī, *al-Muntaẓam*, 17:239.

122. Aṣ-Ṣafadī, *al-Wāfī bi'l-wafayāt*, 8:115–116. The poem cited by al-Kutubī (12:176) differs slightly in that *fawqahu* replaces *furqatu* in the last hemistich, but this appears to be an error.

123. 'Afīf ad-Dīn 'Abdallāh b. Asad b. 'Alī al-Yāfi'ī, *Mir'āt al-janān wa-'ibrat al-yaqẓān fī ma'rifat mā yu'tabaru min ḥawādith az-zamān* (Hyderabad: Dā'irat al-Ma'ārif an-Niẓāmiyyah), 3:224–325.

124. As-Subkī, *Ṭabaqāt ash-shāfi'iyyah*, 6:60–62.

125. Ibid., 6:51; al-Kutubī, 12:176; aṣ-Ṣafadī, 8:116. The accounts in the latter two works differ from that translated only in that the account of Abraham precedes that of 'Alī.

126. As-Subkī, 6:60.

127. Ibid.

128. Ash-Shahrazūrī, 1:397.

129. As-Subkī, 6:62; al-Munāwī, 1:650; al-Ghazālī, *Majālis*, 20.

130. Ibn al-Mulaqqin al-Miṣrī, *Ṭabaqāt al-awliyā'*, 102–104.

131. This is a noncanonical *ḥadīth qudsī* often cited in Sufi literature. See Abu'l-Qāsim 'Abd al-Karīm al-Qushayrī, *ar-Risālah al-Qushayriyyah*

(Beirut: Dār al-Khayr, 1413/1993), 366; and Abu'l-Ḥasan ʿAlī b. Muḥammad ad-Daylamī, *Kitāb ʿaṭf al-alif al-maʾlūf ʿala'l-lām al-maʿṭūf*, ed. J. C. Vadet (Cairo: L'Institut Français d'Archéologie Orientale, 1962), 86.

132. Ibn al-Mulaqqin al-Miṣrī, *Ṭabaqāt al-awliyāʾ*, 102.

133. Al-Ghazālī, *Majālis*, 11.

134. Jāmī, *Nafaḥāt al-uns*, 419.

135. Ibid., 380.

136. Ḥāfiẓ Ḥusayn Karbalāʾī Tabrīzī, *Rawḍāt al-jinān wa-jannāt al-jinān*, 2:339–343; Ḥusayn b. Ḥasan Sabzawārī, *Jawāhir al-asrār* (Lucknow: n.p., 1893), 40–42.

137. The role of philosophy and Sufism and the relationship between the two in the works of Abū Ḥāmid al-Ghazālī is among the most contested discussions in the academic study of Islamic philosophy. Contrary to recent studies of Treiger and Gardner, I maintain that it is best to take Abū Hāmid al-Ghazālī at his word that he did indeed come to see Sufism as the preeminent means of obtaining knowledge, especially as this idea is reflected in many passages of the *Iḥyāʾ*. As he writes in the *Iḥyāʾ*, "Abū Yazīd and others used to say, 'The knower (*ʿālim*) is not one who memorizes something from a book, for if he forgets what he has memorized he becomes ignorant. Rather the knower is one who takes his knowledge from his Lord, whenever He wills, without memorization and without study.' This is Lordly knowledge to which there is allusion in His saying, transcendent is He, *We taught him knowledge from Our Presence* (18:65). Although all knowledge is from His Presence, yet some of it comes through the medium of instructing human beings (*taʿlīm*) and we do not call that 'Knowledge by Presence' (*ʿilm ladunī*), rather [knowledge by] Presence is that which is opened in the secret of the heart without an external customary secondary cause (*sabab maʾlūf min khārij*)": *Iḥyāʾ ʿulūm ad-Dīn*, n.e. (Beirut: Dār al-Kutub al-ʿIlmiyyah, 1419/1998), 3:23. For the most recent discussion of this issue, see Alexander Treiger, *Inspired Knowledge in Islamic Thought: al-Ghazālī's Theory of Mystical Cognition and its Avicennian Foundation* (London/New York: Routledge, 2012); Kenneth Garden, *The First Islamic Reviver.* For different treatments of Abū Ḥāmid al-Ghazālī's classification of the Islamic sciences, see Alexander Treiger, "Al-Ghazālī's Classification of the Sciences and Descriptions of the Highest Theoretical Science," *Dīvān* 30.1 (2011), 1–32, and Osman Bakar, *The Classification of Knowledge in Islam* (Cambridge: Islamic Texts Society, 1998), chaps. 7–9.

138. It appears from the context that Awḥad ad-Dīn Kirmānī (d. 635/1238) is who is meant here, especially since he was known for making *shāhid-bāzī* a central part of his spiritual practice.

139. *Nafaḥāt al-uns*, 591

140. Karbalāʾī Tabrīzī, *Rawḍāt al-jinān wa-jannāt al-jinān*, 2:339.

141. Ibid., 2:342.

142. Ibid., 2:340–41; al-Ghazālī, *ʿAyniyyah*, ed. Aḥmad Mujāhid in *Majmūʿah*, 203–204.

143. Al-Munāwī, *al-Kawākib ad-durriyyah,* 1:649–650.

144. Ibid., 1:649.

145. Ibid., 1:650.

146. Ibid., 1:649.

147. Sabzawārī, *Jawāhir al-asrār,* 42.

148. Muḥammad b. Muḥammad b. al-Ḥusayn al-Murtaḍā az-Zabīdī, *Itḥāf as-sādah* (Cairo: n.p., 1311), 1:8. In translating this passage I have drawn on the translation of J. Spencer Trimingham, *The Sufi Orders in Islam,* 33.

149. M. Bāqir al-Mūsawī al-Iṣfahānī al-Khwānsārī, *Rawḍāt al-jannāt fī aḥwāl al-ʿulamāʾ wa's-sādāt,* 1:285–288.

150. Ibid., 1:287.

151. Ibid., 1:288.

152. Khwāndamīr, 2:319; al-Khwānsārī, 1:288.

153. ʿUmar Riḍā Kaḥḥālah, *Muʿjam al-muʾallifīn tarājim muṣannifī'l-kutub al-ʿarabiyyah,* 1:147.

154. Shihāb ad-Dīn Abū ʿAbdallāh b. ʿAbdallāh Yāqūt, *Muʿjam al-buldān* (Beirut: Dār Beirut li'ṭ-ṭibāʿah wa'n-nashr, 1376/1957), 4:49–50.

155. Yūsuf b. Qīzoghlu Sibṭ Ibn al-Jawzī, *Mir'āt az-zamān (A.H. 495–654) by Shams ad-Dîn Abu 'l-Muzaffar Yûsuf ben Qizughlu ben ʿAbdallāh, commonly known by the surname of Sibṭ ibn al-Jauzī; a facsimile reproduction of manuscript no. 136 of the Landberg collection of Arabic manuscripts belonging to Yale university;* ed. James Richard Jewett (Chicago: University of Chicago Press, 1907), 73–74; Ḍiyāʾ ad-Dīn Naṣr Allāh b. Muḥammad Ibn al-Athīr, *al-Kāmil fī't-taʾrīkh* (Beirut: 1386/1966), 10:640.

156. Shams ad-Dīn Abū ʿAbdallāh M. b. Aḥmad adh-Dhahabī, *al-ʿIbar fī khabar man ghabar* (Beirut: n.p., 1985), 412–413; adh-Dhahabī, *Taʾrīkh al-Islām wa-wafayāt al-mashāhīr wa'l-aʿlām* (Beirut: n.p., 1415/1994), 35 (AH 501–20): 126–129; adh-Dhahabī, *Mīzān al-iʿtidāl fī naqd ar-rijāl,* ed. ʿAlī Muḥammad al-Bijāwī (Beirut: Dār Iḥyāʾ al-Kutub al-ʿArabī, 1372/1963), 1:150.

157. Sibṭ Ibn al-Jawzī, *Mirʾāt az-zamān,* 61.

158. Jamāl ad-Dīn al-Isnawī, *Ṭabaqāt ash-shāfiʿiyyah,* 2:234; Ibn aṣ-Ṣalāḥ, 1:397.

159. Ismāʿīl b. ʿUmar ad-Dimashqī Ibn Kathīr, *al-Bidāyah wa'n-nihāyah fī't-taʾrīkh* (Beirut: 1386/1966), 1:196.

160. ʿAbd al-Ḥayy Ibn al-ʿImād, *Shadharāt adh-dhahab fī akhbār man dhahab,* 4:60–61.

161. Muḥammad Maʿṣūm Shīrāzī, *Ṭarāʾiq al-ḥaqāʾiq* (Tehran: Kitābkhāneh-yi Bārānī, 1980), 2:564–568.

162. Ibn an-Najjār, 19:80.

163. Ibn al-Jawzī, *Kitāb al-quṣṣāṣ wa'l-mudhakkirīn,* 101 (Arabic), 187 (English).

164. For an account of the rise of "Jamāʿī Sufism" and its increasingly important political and intellectual role in Sunni Islam, see Marshall G.S. Hodgson, *The Venture of Islam* (Chicago: The University of Chicago Press, 1977), vol. 2, esp. 201–254.

Chapter 2: The Life and Times of Aḥmad al-Ghazālī

1. The significance of Daylamī influence in this period has been detailed by Vladimir Minorsky in *La domination des Daîlamites* (Paris: E. Leroux, 1932).

2. For a study of the various methods employed by the Saljuqs to legitimize their rule, see Omid Safi, *The Politics of Knowledge in Premodern Iran: Negotiating Ideology and Religious Inquiry* (Chapel Hill: University of North Carolina Press, 2006).

3. Ẓāhir ad-Dīn Nīshāpūrī, *Saljūq-nāmah* (Tehran: Kalāla Khāvar, 1953), 20; Muḥammad Rāwandī, *Rāḥat aṣ-ṣudūr*, ed. Muḥammad Iqbāl (London: Luzac & Co., 1921), 108; Khwāndamīr, *Tārīkh-i ḥabīb as-siyar*, 2:311.

4. C.E. Bosworth, "The Political and Dynastic History of the Iranian World (A. D. 1000–1217)," in *The Saljuq and Mongol Periods*, ed. J.A. Boyle, vol. 5 of *The Cambridge History of Iran* (Cambridge: Cambridge University Press, 1968), 45.

5. Francis Robinson, *A Historical Atlas of the Islamic World Since 1500* (New York: Facts on File, 1982), 26.

6. Ibn Kathīr, *al-Bidāyah wa'n-nihāyah fi't-ta'rīkh*, 12:139.

7. See Daphna Ephrat, "The Seljuqs and the Public Sphere in the Period of Sunni Revivalism: The View from Baghdad" in *The Seljuqs: Politics, Society and Culture*, ed. Christian Lange and Songul Mecit (Edinburgh: Edinburgh University Press, 2011), 139–156.

8. C.E. Bosworth, "Saldjukids," in *EI2*, s.v.

9. Ibn al-Athīr, *al-Kāmil fi't-ta'rīkh*, 10:33.

10. Regarding the establishment of fixed stipends, Ibn Khallikān credits Niẓām al-Mulk with this innovation: Ibn Khallikān, *Kitāb Wafayāt al-aʿyān, Ibn Khallikān's Biographical Dictionary*, trans. William Mac Guckin De Slane (Beirut: Librarie du Liban, 1970), 1:414.

11. As-Subkī, *aṭ-Ṭabaqāt ash-shāfiʿiyyah al-kubrā*, 4:314.

12. For a study of Abū Ḥāmid al-Ghazālī's role in the Saljuq support of Sunni Islam, see Massimo Campanini, "In Defence of the Sunnism: al-Ghazālī" in *The Seljuqs: Politics, Society and Culture*, 228–239. For a brief overview of Abū Ḥāmid al-Ghazālī's contributions to *uṣūl al-fiqh, kalām*, philosophy, and Sufism see Marshall Hodgson, *The Venture of Islam* (Chicago: University of Chicago Press, 1990; originally published 1975), 2:180–193.

13. Frank Griffel, *Al-Ghazālī's Philosophical Theology*. Oxford/New York: Oxford University Press, 2009, 24.

14. Pourjavady, *Sulṭān-i ṭarīqāt*, 10.

15. Mujāhid, *Majmūʿah*, 15.

16. Adh-Dhahabī, *Ta'rīkh al-Islām*, vol. AH 501–520 (no. 35): 126; al-Subkī, *Ṭabaqāt* vol. 6, 193. (6:193.10).

17. For a comprehensive account of the debate on the origin of this name and its proper spelling—"Ghazālī" or "Ghazzālī"—see Aḥmad Mujāhid, *Majmūʿah*, 8–14 and Frank Griffel, "Al-Ghazālī or al-Ghazzālī? On a Lively Debate Among Ayyūbid and Mamlūk Historians of Damascus," in *Islamic Thought in the Middle Ages. Studies in Transmission and Translation in Honour*

of Hans Daiber. Ed. Anna Ayşe Akasoy and Wim Raven. Leiden: Brill, 2008, 101–112.

18. As-Subkī, *aṭ-Ṭabaqāt ash-shāfiʿiyyah al-kubrā*, 3:417. For an analysis of this passage and its historical accuracy, see Frank Griffel, *Al-Ghazālī's Philosophical Theology* (Oxford/New York: Oxford University Press, 2009), 26–27.

19. Ibid., 6:61.

20. Adh-Dhahabī, *Ta'rīkh al-Islām*, vol. AH 501–520 (no. 35): 127.

21. Subkī, *Tabaqāt*, 5:204. This sentence reflects a quote that is cited by Abū Ḥāmid al-Ghazālī in both *Iḥyā' ʿulūm ad-Dīn* (1:71.24–25; 1:84.2–3) and *Mīzān al-ʿamal* (115; 343), where he attributes it to "one of the verifiers" (*baʿḍ al-muḥaqqiqīn*).

22. Griffel, *Al-Ghazālī's Philosophical Theology*, 26.

23. Some scholars have misread the primary sources as saying that Aḥmad ar-Radhakānī was the pious friend entrusted with the care of the Ghazālī brothers (e.g., Pourjavady, *Sulṭān-i ṭarīqāt*, 12). This, however, is not confirmed by the sources. Unfortunately, this has become a common belief, even among some historians. For a more comprehensive account of Abū Hāmid al-Ghazālī's education, see Griffel, *Al-Ghazālī's Philosophical Theology*, 27–31.

24. As-Subkī, *aṭ-Ṭabaqāt ash-shāfiʿiyyah al-kubrā*, 3:418.

25. Pourjavady, *Sulṭān-i ṭarīqāt*, 20.

26. Roy Mottahedeh, *Loyalty and Leadership in an Early Islamic Society* (Princeton: Princeton University Press, 1980; repr., London: I.B. Tauris, 2001), 140.

27. George Makdisi, "Muslim Institutions of Learning in Eleventh-Century Baghdad," in *Religion, Law, and Learning in Classical Islam* (Brookfield: Variorum, 1990), 10–12.

28. R. Brunschvig, "Perspectives," in *Unity and Variety in Muslim Civilization*, ed. G.E. von Grunebaum (Chicago: University of Chicago Press, 1955), 5.

29. John L. Esposito, *Women in Muslim Family Law* (Syracuse: Syracuse University Press, 1982), 12.

30. Marshall Hodgson, *Venture of Islam*, 2:153.

31. As-Subkī, *aṭ-Ṭabaqāt ash-shāfiʿiyyah al-kubrā*, 2:142.

32. Ibid., 2:334.

33. Wael B. Hallaq, "Was al-Shāfiʿī the Master Architect of Islamic Jurisprudence?," *International Journal of Middle Eastern Studies* 25 (1993): 595–597; see also, Ahmed El Shamsy, *The Canonization of Islamic Law: A Social and Intellectual History* (Cambridge: Cambridge University Press, 2013).

34. A famous story in Subkī's *aṭ-Ṭabaqāt ash-shāfiʿiyyah* (3:418) tells us that during his return to Ṭūs, Abū Ḥāmid al-Ghazālī was waylaid by bandits who stole all his possessions. When al-Ghazālī asked that the books be returned as they had his knowledge and would be of no value to the bandits, they ridiculed him, asking how it could be knowledge if it left him when his notes were gone. Stung by the truth of this rebuke, al-Ghazālī set out to

memorize all he had learned so that his knowledge would not leave him through exterior events. Regarding the historical accuracy of this account, see Griffel, *al-Ghazālī's Philosophical Theology*, 27.

35. For more on Imām al-Ḥaramayn al-Juwaynī, see Tilman Nagel, *Die Festung des Glaubens: Triumph und Scheitern des islamischen Rationalismus im 11. Jahrhundert* (München: C.H. Beck, 1988).

36. For an excellent translation and study of this work, see Aladdin M. Yaqub, *Al-Ghazālī's Moderation in Belief* (Chicago: University of Chicago Press, 2013).

37. Al-Ghazālī, *at-Tajrīd*, 34; Gramlich, *Der reine Gottesglaube*, 27.

38. ʿAbd al-Karīm al-Qazwīnī, *at-Tadwīn fī akhbār Qazwīn*, 2:251.

39. Imād ad-Dīn Muḥammad b. Muḥammad al-Kātib al-Iṣfahānī, *Kitāb Zubdat an-nuṣrah wa'nukhbat al-ʿuṣrah* (Leiden: E.J. Brill, 1889), 80.

40. C.E. Bosworth writes that Abu'l-Futūḥ al-Ghazālī taught at the Tājiyyah madrasah in Baghdad around 480–482. "The Political and Dynastic History of the Iranian World (A.D. 1000–1217)," in *The Cambridge History of Iran*, 74.

That Aḥmad al-Ghazālī taught in the Tājiyyah is confirmed by Ibn al-Jawzī (*al-Muntaẓam*, 17:237) and Ibn an-Najjār (19:80), though the exact dates are not mentioned.

41. In book 33 of the *Iḥyā'*, al-Ghazālī writes that al-Fārmadhi taught him obedience to the Shaykhs, though the precise nature of their relationship is not certain.

42. Jāmī, *Nafaḥāt al-uns*, 376.

43. Hamadānī, *Tamhīdāt*, 280–281.

44. Hamadānī, *Nāmehā-yi ʿAyn al-Quḍāt Hamadānī*, 2:51.

45. Jāmī, *Nafaḥāt al-uns*, 376, 379.

46. Louis Massignon, *The Passion of al-Ḥallāj*, trans. Herbert Mason (Princeton: Princeton University Press, 1982), 2:164.

47. Pourjavady, *Sulṭān-i ṭarīqāt*, 40.

48. Dabashi, *Truth and Narrative*, 120.

49. Hamid Dabashi, "Historical Conditions of Persian Sufism during the Seljuq Period," in *Classical Persian Sufism: From its Origins to Rumi*, ed. Leonard Lewisohn (London: Khaniqahi Nimatullahi Publications, 1993), 150.

50. Al-Ghazālī, *Majālis*, 63–64.

51. Shihāb ad-Dīn Aḥmad Samʿānī, *Rawḥ al-arwāḥ fī sharḥ asmā' al-malik al-fattāḥ*, ed. Najīb Māyil Hirawī (Tehran: Shirkat-i Intishārāt-i ʿIlmī va Farhangī, 1368/1989),168.

52. ʿAbdallāh Anṣārī, "Chihil u daw faṣl," in *Majmūʿah-yi rasā'il-i farsī*, ed. Muḥammad Sarwar Mawlā'ī (Tehran: Intishārāt-i Ṭūs), 22.

53. Hodgson, *Venture of Islam*, 1:393.

54. Abū ʿAbd ar-Raḥmān as-Sulamī, *Ṭabaqāt aṣ-ṣūfiyyah*, ed. Nūr ad-Dīn Sharība (Cairo: Maṭbaʿat al-Madanī, 1987), 440.

55. Ibid., 180; Abū Bakr Aḥmad b. ʿAlī al-Kātib al-Baghdādī, *Taʿrīkh Baghdād* (Beirut: Dār al-Kutub al-ʿArabī, 1966), 7:430–432.

56. Abū Nuʿaym al-Iṣfahānī, *Ḥilyat al-awliyā*ʾ, ed. Muṣṭafā ʿAbd al-Qādir ʿAṭāʾ (Beirut: Dār al-Kutub al-ʿIlmiyyah, 1997), 10:274.

57. Regarding the relationship between Saljuq Sultans and Sufi shaykhs, see D.G. Tor, "Sovereign and Pious: The Religious Life of the Great Seljuq Sultans," in *The Seljuqs: Politics, Society and Culture*, 39–62.

58. As-Subkī, *aṭ-Ṭabaqāt ash-shāfiʿiyyah al-kubrā*, 4:293–294, 3:369.

59. Jāmī, *Nafaḥāt al-uns*, 295.

60. Richard Bulliet, *The Patricians of Nishapur* (Cambridge, MA: Harvard University Press, 1972), 151.

61. Muḥammad Ibn Munawwar Mayhanī, *Asrār-i tawḥīd fī maqāmāt Shaykh Abī Saʿīd*, ed. Muḥammad Riḍā Shāfiʿī Kadkanī (Tehran: Muʾassisiyeh Intishārāt-i Āgāh, 1376 HS), 1:119; Jāmī, *Nafaḥāt al-uns*, 373–374.

62. Jāmī, *Nafaḥāt al-uns*, 376. For more on the relationship between these two aspects of Abū Ḥāmid al-Ghazālī's activities in his final years, see Griffel, *Al-Ghazālī's Philosophical Theology*, 49–58, and Garden, *The First Islamic Reviver*, 125–142.

63. As William Chittick writes of Sufism in the modern period: "Sufism became the scapegoat through which Islam's 'backwardness' could be explained. In this view Sufism is the religion of the common people and embodies superstition and un-Islamic elements adopted from local cultures; in order for Islam to retain its birthright, which includes modern science and technology, Sufism must be eradicated." William Chittick, "Sufism: Sufi Thought and Practice," *Oxford Encyclopedia of the Modern Islamic World*, ed. John L. Esposito et al. (New York: Oxford University Press, 1994), 107.

64. For a detailed analysis of the protestant roots of current notions of mysticism, see Bernard McGinn, *The Foundations of Mysticism: Origins to the Fifth Century*, vol. 1 of *The Presence of God: A History of Western Christian Mysticism* (New York: Crossroad, 1994), appendix 1.

65. In translating the terms *maʿrifah* and *ʿirfān*, I have chosen to follow William Chittick in employing the more literal rendering, "recognition," rather than the more widespread translations, "gnostic" and "gnosticism," especially in employing "recognition" for a more fluid translation of the verbal form *ʿarifa/yaʿrifu* as "to recognize."

66. For Abū Ḥāmid al-Ghazālī's own account of this crisis, see *The Faith and Practice of al-Ghazālī*, 58–63. For analysis of this account, see Garden, *The First Islamic Reviver*, 56–59.

67. Jāmī, *Nafaḥāt al-uns*, 379–380; Ḥusayn b. Ḥasan as-Sabzawārī, *Jawāhir al-asrār*, 42; M. Bāqir al-Khwānsārī, *Rawḍāt al-jannāt fī aḥwāl al-ʿulamāʾ wa-ṣ-ṣādāt*, 1:285–288; Muḥammad al-Murtaḍā az-Zabīdī, *Itḥāf as-sāda*, 1:8.

68. For various aspects of the relationship between the scholars and the Saljuq rulers and viziers, see George Makdisi, "The Sunni Revival" in *Islamic Civilizations 950–1150*, ed. D.S. Richards (Oxford, 1973), 155–168. Richard Bulliet, *Islam: the View from the Edge* (New York, 1994), 101, 126–127, 146–148, proposes that this process was less a "revival" and more a "recasting" that entailed a homogenization of Sunni religious life. Bulliet's interpretation

is elaborated by Jonathan P. Berkey in *The Formation of Islam: Religion and Society in the Near East 600–1800* (Cambridge, 2003), 189–202. For the more social dimension of these activities that demonstrates the broad support for this Sunni homogenization, see Daphna Ephrat, "The Seljuqs and the Public Sphere in the Period of Sunni Revivalism: The View from Baghdad" in *The Seljuqs: Politics, Society and Culture*, 139–156.

69. C.E. Bosworth, "The Iranian World (A.D. 1000–1217)," in *The Saljuq and Mongol Periods*, vol. 5 of *The Cambridge History of Iran*, 74.

70. Sibṭ Ibn al-Jawzī, *Mīrʿāt az-zamān*, 61.

71. Rāshid ad-Dīn Faḍl Allāh, *Jāmiʿ at-tawārīkh*, 2:259; Rāwandī, *Rāḥat aṣ-ṣudūr*, 133.

72. Al-Kātib al-Iṣfahānī, *Kitāb Zubdat an-nuṣrah wa'nukhbat al-ʿuṣrah*, 61.

73. Omid Safi, *The Politics of Knowledge in Premodern Iran*, 69–70.

74. Niẓām al-Mulk, *The Book of Government and Rules for Kings*, trans. Hubert Drake (London: Routledge & Kegan Paul, 1960), 163.

75. Bernard Lewis, *The Assassins* (New York: Basic Books, 1968), 47. Lewis bases his account on the later Mongol era histories of ʿAtā Mālik Juvaynī (1226–83), *Taʾrīkh-i Jahān-gushā*, and Rashīd ad-Dīn Faḍl Allāh (ca. 1247–1318), *Jāmiʿ at-tawārīkh*, who both had access to Ismāʿīlī sources. Lewis does not appear to have consulted most of the earlier accounts, and though he cites Marshall Hodgson, he seems to ignore his more nuanced understanding wherein he states, "most historians assumed that the Ismāʿīlīs were in collusion with Niẓām al-Mulk's enemies at court." Hodgson, *The Order of Assassins: The Struggle of the Early Nizārī Ismāʿīlīs Against the Islamic World* (The Hague: Mouton & Co., 1955), 75.

76. As-Subkī, *aṭ-Ṭabaqāt ash-shāfiʿiyyah al-kubrā*, 3:13.

77. Ibid., 3:14.

78. Ibn Khallikān, *Kitāb Wafayāt al-aʿyān, Ibn Khallikān's Biographical Dictionary*, 1:415.

79. Ibid.

80. Ibid.

81. Rāwandī, 135; Ẓāhir ad-Dīn Nīshāpūrī, *The History of the Seljuq Turks From The Jāmiʿ al-Tawārīkh: An Ilkhanid Adaptation of the Saljūq-nāma*, trans. Kenneth Allin Luther (London: Curzon, 2001), 62.

82. Nīshāpūrī, *History of the Seljuq Turks*, 61–62.

83. Niẓām al-Mulk, *Book of Government and Rules*, 194.

84. As-Subkī, *aṭ-Ṭabaqāt ash-shāfiʿiyyah al-kubrā*, 3:15.

85. Mustafa Mahmoud Abu-Sway, "al-Ghazālī's 'Spiritual Crisis' Reconsidered," *Al-Shajarah: Journal of the International Institute of Islamic Thought and Civilization* 1 (1980), 77–94.

86. Garden, *The First Islamic Reviver*, 29.

87. Pourjavady, *Sulṭān-i ṭarīqat*, 14.

88. Mujāhid, *Majmūʿah*, 21.

89. As-Subkī, *aṭ-Ṭabaqāt ash-shāfiʿiyyah al-kubrā*, 4:350.

90. Aḥmad al-Ghazālī, *Majālis-i Aḥmad Ghazālī*, 60.

91. Samʿānī, *Rawḥ al-arwāḥ*, 396.

92. Aḥmad al-Ghazālī [attributed], *Lubb al-iḥyā'*, MS Princeton University, Garret Collection 1079H, fol. 2.

93. As-Subkī, *aṭ-Ṭabaqāt ash-shāfi'iyyah al-kubrā*, 6:201.

94. Ibn al-Jawzī, *al-Muntaẓam fi't-ta'rīkh*, 9:178.

95. Mujāhid, *Majmū'ah*, 22; Pourjavady, *Sulṭān-i ṭarīqāt*, 15.

96. 'Ayn al-Quḍāt Hamadānī, *Zubdat al-ḥaqā'iq*, 7.

97. Pourjavady places this meeting in 513/1115 (*Sulṭān ṭarīqāt*, 16), while Aḥmad Mujāhid relates Raḥīm Farmanish's argument that this meeting occurred in 515/1117 (*Majmu'ah*, 22). Considering 'Ayn al-Quḍāt's belief that the spiritual path is not followed without the guidance of a shaykh (*Zubdat al-ḥaqā'iq*, 72), it appears that Pourjavady's position may be more accurate. The exact date of this encounter cannot, however, be pinpointed.

98. Ibn al-Jawzī, *al-Muntaẓam*, 17:237.

99. Ibid., 17:192.

100. Abū Ḥafṣ 'Umar as-Suhrawardī, *'Awārif al-ma'ārif*, 69.

101. Ibn Mustawfī al-Irbilī, *Ta'rīkh Irbil*, 24.

102. Ibid., 16.

103. Zakariyyā b. Muḥammad al-Qazwīnī, *Āthār al-bilād wa-akhbār al-'ibād*, 415.

104. For an account of Abū Hāmid al-Ghazālī's continued interactions with the Saljuq Sultans and their viziers and the political intrigue involved, see Griffel, *Al-Ghazālī's Philosophical Theology*, 31–59, and Garden, *The First Islamic Reviver*, chaps. 4 and 5.

105. The only discussion of Aḥmad al-Ghazālī's relationship with the Saljuq sultans is found in Mujāhid, *Majmū'ah*, 102–103.

106. 'Abd al-Karīm al-Qazwīnī, *at-Tadwīn fī akhbār Qazwīn*, 2:251.

107. Brockelmann and Massignon follow 'Abd ar-Raḥmān Jāmī in listing 517/1123: Brockelmann, *Geschichte der arabischen Litteratur*, 1:756; Massignon, *Passion of Ḥallāj*, 2:227.

108. Mīnū Dār, 672–673; cited by Mujāhid in the introduction to *Majmū'ah*, 112.

109. Joseph Lumbard, Field Notes, July 15, 2001.

Chapter 3: Aḥmad al-Ghazālī's Spiritual Practice

1. Leigh Eric Schmidt, "The Making of Modern 'Mysticism,'" *Journal of the American Academy of Religion* 71.2 (2003), 273.

2. For more extensive discussions of the state of Sufism and other traditions in this period, see Jacqueline Chabbi, "Reflexions sur le soufisme iranien primitif," *Journal Asiatique* 266, no. 1–2 (1978): 37–55; Chabbi, "Remarques sur le dévelopment historique des mouvements ascétiques et mystiques au Khurasan," *Studia Islamica* 46 (1977): 5–72; Alexander Knysh, *Islamic Mysticism: A Short Introduction* (Leiden: E. J. Brill, 2000), chaps. 4–5; Margaret Malamud, "Sufi Organizations and Structures of Authority in Medieval Nishapur," *International Journal of Middle East Studies* 26 (1994):

427–442; Bernd Radtke, "Taṣawwuf," *EI²*; Radtke, "Theologen und Mystiker in Ḫurāsān und Transoxanien," *Zeitschrift der Deutschen Morgenländischen Gesellschaft* 136 (1986): 537–569.

3. Nile Green, *Sufism: A Global History* (Oxford/Malden: Wiley-Blackwell, 2012), 8.

4. Al-Ghazālī, *at-Tajrīd*, 64–65.

5. This appears to be a variation of a saying attributed to ʿAlī b. Abī Ṭālib, "Encountering the people of recognition supports hearts and engenders wisdom." ʿAbd al-Wāḥid al-Āmadī al-Tamīmī, *Ghurar al-ḥikam wa durar al-kalim*, ed. As-Sayyid, Mahdī ar-Rijāʾī (Qum: *Dār al-kitāb al-islāmī*, 1410/1990), 572–573.

6. Al-Ghazālī, *ʿAyniyyah*, ed. Mujāhid, *Majmūʿah-yi āthār-i fārsī-yi Aḥmad Ghazālī*, 213.

7. Al-Ghazālī, *Majālis*, 37.

8. Ibid., 20.

9. Al-Ghazālī, *Letter*, ed. Mujāhid, *Majmūʿah-yi āthār-i fārsī-yi Aḥmad Ghazālī*, 253.

10. Ibid., 251.

11. Al-Ghazālī, *Majālis*, 63–64.

12. Sarrāj, *Lumaʿ*, 28.

13. Another version of a canonical *ḥadīth*: "Many a faster receives nothing from his fast but hunger and many a one who spends the night in prayer receives nothing from his prayer but sleeplessness." Ibn Mājah: *Kitāb aṣ-Ṣiyām*, 21; *at-Tajrīd*, 36.

14. Al-Ghazālī, *ʿAyniyyah*, ed. Mujāhid, *Majmūʿah-yi āthār-i fārsī-yi Aḥmad Ghazālī*, 200.

15. Al-Ghazālī, *Majālis*, 46–47.

16. ʿAbdallāh Anṣārī, *Sad Maydān*, 255–257.

17. Maybudī, *Kashf al-asrār*, 3:140.

18. This is a rendition of a *ḥadīth*: "The first thing which man is called to account for on the Day of Judgment is the ritual prayer." Tirmidhī, *Kitāb aṣ-Ṣalāt*, 188; Abū Dāʾūd, *Kitāb aṣ-Ṣalāt*, 145; Nisāʾī, *Ṣalāt*, 9; Ibn Mājah, *Kitāb al-Iqāmah*, 202.

19. Part of a famous *ḥadīth*: "Three things of your world have been made beloved to me: women, perfume, and the coolness of my eye is found in prayer." Nisāʾī, *Kitāb an-Nisāʾ*, 1.

20. Al-Ghazālī, *Majālis*, 35.

21. *Majālis*, 21.

22. Ibid., 9.

23. Ibid., 21. This is a saying that occurs in several forms in several Sufi texts. In some places it is attributed to the Prophet Muḥammad, in others to al-Junayd al-Baghdādī, and in others to anonymous Sufis: "Two rounds of prayer in the depths of the night are a treasure from the treasures of love," ʿAyn al-Quḍāt Hamadānī, *Nāmahā-yi ʿAyn al-Quḍāt*, 3:317.

24. Aḥmad b. Muḥammad Ibn ʿAṭāʾullāh as-Skandārī, *Miftāḥ al-falāḥ wa miṣbāḥ al-arwāḥ* (Cairo, 1381/1961), 3.

25. Al-Ghazālī, *Majālis*, 21.

26. Al-Ghazālī, *Letter*, ed. Mujāhid, *Majmū'ah-yi āthār-i fārsī-yi Aḥmad Ghazālī*, 258.

27. Abū Bakr Muḥammad b. Ibrāhīm al-Kalābādhī, *at-Ta'arruf li madhhab ahl at-taṣawwuf*, ed. Aḥmad Shams ad-Dīn (Beirut: Dār al-Kutub al-'Ilmiyyah, 1413/1993), 9; English translation, A.J. Arberry, *The Doctrine of the Sufis* (Cambridge: Cambridge University Press, 1935; reprint, Lahore: Ashraf Press, 1966), 76. I have checked my translation against that of Arberry, but to maintain consistency I have chosen to employ my own translations.

28. Rashīd ad-Dīn al-Maybudī, *Kashf al-asrār wa-'uddat al-abrār*, ed. 'Alī Aṣghar Ḥikmat (Tehran: Intishārāt-i Dānishgāhī, 1952–60), 3:794.

29. *Majālis*, 49–50.

30. *Tamhīdāt*, 288 (376).

31. Najm ad-Dīn Kubrā, *Fawā'iḥ al-jamāl wa-fawātiḥ al-jalāl*, ed. Fritz Meier (Wiesbaden: Franz Steiner, 1957), 24.

32. *Majālis*, 22.

33. An allusion to the statement the prophet Abraham is reported have made upon rejecting the idols worshipped by his tribe: "*O my people! Truly I am quit of the partners you ascribe. Truly I have turned my face toward Him Who created the heavens and the earth, as a ḥanīf, and I am not of the idolaters.*" (6:78–79)

34. Muslim, *Kitāb at-tawbah*.

35. *Tajrīd*, 6 (1).

36. Ibid., 9 (3).

37. Ibid., 41 (36).

38. Ibid., 43 (37). The words attributed to the Prophet at the end are part of a *ḥadīth*, the whole of which reads, "The Messenger of God said, 'There is none among you who does not have a satan.' They asked, 'And you, O Messenger of God?' he replied, 'And me, except that God has helped me overcome it, so my satan has submitted.'" (Muslim, *Kitāb ṣifāt al-qiyamah wa'l-jannah wa'n-nār: Bāb Tahrish ash-shayṭān*). Also cited by 'Ayn al-Quḍāt Hamadānī, *Tamhīdāt*, 196.

39. *Tajrīd*, 67 (40).

40. Ibid., 67 (40).

41. Ibid., 67 (40).

42. Ibid., 68–69 (42).

43. Ibid., 46 (33).

44. Ibid.

45. Ibid., 72 (47).

46. Ibid., 60.

47. *Tajrīd*, 61 (38).

48. *Tajrīd*, 61 (38).

49. *Majālis*, 26.

50. Maybudī, *Kashf al-asrār*, 1:344.

51. T.J. Winter, introduction to *The Remembrance of Death and the Afterlife: Kitāb Dhikr al-mawt wa-mā ba'dahu; Book XL of The Revival of the Religious Sciences* (Cambridge: Islamic Texts Society, 1989), xiii.

52. Bukhārī, *Kitāb ar-riqāq*, 41; Muslim, *Kitāb adh-dhikr*, 14.

53. Tirmidhī, *Kitāb al-qiyāmah*, 25; Ibn Mājah, *Kitāb az-zuhd*, 21.

54. This saying is often cited in Sufi texts as a *ḥadīth* but is regarded by *ḥadīth* scholars as a Sufi saying: Ajlūnī, Ismā'īl b. Muḥammad, *Kashf al-khafā' wa muzīl al-ilbās 'ammā ishtahara min al-aḥādīth 'alā alsinat an-nās* (Beirut: Dār at-Turāth al-'Arabī, 1932–33; reprint 1968), 2:384.

55. *Majālis*, 48.

56. See *The Remembrance of Death and the Afterlife: Book XL of the Revival of the Religious Sciences*, trans. T J. Winter.

57. *Majālis*, 1.

58. Ibid., 15.

59. Ibid., 18.

60. Ibid., 55.

61. Persian translation of the Quranic verse cited above.

62. Al-Ghazālī, *'Ayniyyah*, ed. Mujāhid, *Majmū'ah-yi āthār-i fārsī-yi Aḥmad Ghazālī*, 192.

63. Mujāhid cites this as a saying attributed to 'Alī b. Abī Ṭālib. It follows the style of sayings attributed to him in the *Ghurar al-ḥikam* but is not among the actual sayings.

64. Mujāhid cites this as a saying attributed to 'Alī b. Abī Ṭālib. I have not found it listed among his sayings.

65. Al-Ghazālī, *'Ayniyyah*, ed. Mujāhid, *Majmū'ah-yi āthār-i fārsī-yi Aḥmad Ghazālī*, 192–193.

66. For an analysis of 'Ayn al-Quḍāt's understanding of spiritual death, see Leonard Lewisohn, "In Quest of Annihilation: Imaginalization and Mystical Death in the *Tamhīdāt* of 'Ayn al-Quḍāt Hamadānī" in *Classical Persian Sufism from its Origins to Rumi*, ed. Leonard Lewisohn, 285–336.

67. *Tamhīdāt*, 288 (374)

68. *Kashf al-asrār*, 8:133–134

69. *Tamhīdāt*, 319 (418).

70. *Tamhīdāt*, 319–320 (418).

71. *Tamhīdāt*, 320 (418).

72. *Kashf al-asrār*, 4:12.

73. Bukhārī, *Kitāb at-Tahajjud*, 14.

74. *Majālis*, 1.

75. *Majālis*, 8.

76. *Majālis*, 37. This *ḥadīth* is often cited in Sufi texts but is not found in the standard *ḥadīth* collections. The version cited by Aḥmad al-Ghazālī differs from others in that the verb "beholds me" (*yaṭṭali'u 'alayya*) replaces "encompasses me" (*yasa'unī*). Ismā'īl b. Muḥammad Mustamlī (d. 434/1042–43), *Sharḥ-i ta'arruf li-madhhab-i taṣawwuf*, ed. Muḥammad Rawshan (Tehran: Intishārāt-i Asāṭīr, 1363 HS/1984), 2:613 and eight more places; Rashīd ad-Dīn Maybudī, *Kashf al-asrār wa 'uddat al-abrār*, 1:269 and six more places; Abu'l-Qāsim al-Qushayrī records it as "I have a moment in which none encompasses me save my Lord," *ar-Risālah al-Qushayriyyah fī 'ilm at-taṣawwuf*, 79; and Abū Naṣr as-Sarrāj records, "I have a moment with God in which nothing encompasses me with Him other than God," *Kitāb al-Luma'*, ed. 'Abd al-Ḥalīm

Maḥmūd and Taha ʿAbd az-Zāqī Surūr (Cairo: Dār al-Kutub al-Ḥadīthiyyah, 1970), 115.

77. *Majālis*, 29.

78. *Sawāniḥ*, ed. Pourjavady, 20 (trans., 39); ed. Ritter, 37; ed. Rabbānī, 170.

79. *Majālis*, 11.

80. This saying, which is stated as if it were a *ḥadīth qudsī*, is cited in many Sufi texts. Sufis were well aware that such sayings were not in fact canonical but related them as expressing an aspect of the Divine.

81. *Majālis*, 11.

82. The "hard cash of manhood" refers to the true state of the spiritual seeker. Aḥmad al-Ghazālī is likening the soul to coinage that can be of pure metal, mixed metal, or completely adulterated metal.

83. Meaning that the grocer will weigh what is being sold so that the proper price is to be paid. There is allusion here to the weighing of one's good and bad deeds on the Day of Judgment.

84. Al-Ghazālī, *Letter*, ed. Mujāhid, *Majmūʿah-yi āthār-i fārsī-yi Aḥmad Ghazālī*, 252.

85. *Majālis*, 60.

86. *Maqālāt-i Shamsī Tabrīzī*, 323; Chittick 147.

87. Abū Ḥāmid al-Ghazālī, *Ihyāʾ ʿulūm ad-dīn*, 2:203.

88. See e.g. *Mirṣād al-ʿibād*, 281.

89. Bukhārī, *Kitāb Badʾ al-waḥy*, 3. For an example of how those in Aḥmad al-Ghazālī's spiritual lineage employed this *ḥadīth* to enjoin the practice of spiritual seclusion, see Najm al-Dīn Daya Rāzī, *Mirṣād al-ʿibād*, 281.

90. It is reported from ʿAbd Allāh b. ʿUmar, "The Messenger of God used to practice complete devotion (*yaʿtakifu*) the last ten days of Ramaḍān." Bukhārī, *Kitāb al-Iʿtīkāf*, 1.

91. Ibn Mājah, *Kitāb al-Fitnah, bāb al-ʿuzlah*.

92. Al-Qushayrī, *ar-Risālah al-Qushayriyyah*, 102. Translated into English by Barbara Von Schlegell, *Principles of Sufism* (Berkeley: Mizan Press, 1990), 20. I have retranslated all the passages cited in this monograph in order to maintain consistency with other citations. All my translations are indebted to Professor Von Schlegell's translation.

93. Ibid., 103; Von Schlegell, 22.

94. Ibid., 102; Von Schlegell, 21.

95. Abū Ḥāmid al-Ghazālī, *Ihyāʾ*, 2:205, attributed to Dhu'n-Nūn al-Miṣrī.

96. Ibid., 2:205.

97. For a study of the continuing influence of these works, see Qamar ul Huda, *Striving for Divine Union: Spiritual Exercises for Suhrawardī Ṣūfīs* (London/New York: Routledge/Curzon, 2002) and Erik S. Ohlander, *Sufism in an Age of Transition*.

98. Shihāb ad-Dīn Abū Ḥafṣ ʿUmar as-Suhrawardī, *ʿAwārif al-maʿārif*, 190; Najm ad-Dīn Rāzī, *Mirṣād al-ʿibād min al-mabdaʾ ila'l-maʿād*, 281.

99. See Quran 2:51: *And [remember] when We appointed forty nights for Moses, and you took up the calf while he was away, while you were wrongdoers.*

100. As-Suhrawardī, *ʿAwārif al-maʿārif*, 196.

101. Rāzī, *Mirṣād al-ʿibād*, 281 (trans, 279).

102. *ʿAwārif al-maʿārif*, 196.

103. *Mirṣād al-ʿibād*, 282.

104. *ʿAwārif al-maʿārif*, 203.

105. Ibid.

106. *Mirṣād al-ʿibād*, 284.

107. *ʿAwārif al-maʿārif*, 190.

108. The three days following the day of Immolation (10th of Dhu'l-Ḥijjah) during the Ḥajj festival.

109. This is the version cited by ʿAbd ar-Raḥmān as-Sulamī in his *Kitāb al-ʿArbaʿīn fi't-taṣawwuf*, n.e. (Hyderabad, 1950); and Muḥammad ʿAbd ar-Raḥmān as-Sakhāwī, *Takhrīj al-Arbaʿīn as-Sulamiyyah fi't-taṣawwuf*, ed. ʿAlī Ḥasan ʿAlī ʿAbd al-Ḥamīd (Beirut: al-Maktab al-Islāmī, 1988). Another version is cited by Aḥmad aṭ-Ṭūsī in *Bawāriq al-ilmāʿ*, 79. Yet another is found in as-Sarrāj's *Kitāb al-Lumaʿ*, 345.

110. Hamadānī, *Tamhīdāt*, 251.

111. Ibn Ḥajar al-ʿAsqalānī, *Lisān al-mizān*, 1:293.

112. Najm ad-Dīn Kubrā, *Fawāʾiḥ*, 45. Another account of this story with some variations is found in as-Sarrāj's *Kitāb al-Lumaʿ*, 363.

113. ʿAlī b. ʿUthmān al-Jullābī al-Hujwīrī, *Kashf al-maḥjūb*, ed. Vālintīn Zhūkōfskī (Tehran: Kitābkhāneh-yi Ṭahūrī, 1383 HS), 541. Translated into English by R.A. Nicholson, *Kashf al-Maḥjūb of al-Hujwīrī: The Oldest Persian Treatise on Sufism* (London: Luzac & Co., 1911; reprint 1976), 416. In some citations I have followed Nicholson's translation closely; in others I have retranslated for the sake of consistency. Nonetheless, I am indebted to Nicholson for guidance in those passages that I chose to retranslate.

114. Abū Ḥāmid al-Ghazālī, *Iḥyāʾ*, 2:249.

115. As-Sarrāj, *Kitāb al-Lumaʿ*, 342.

116. Al-Hujwīrī, *Kashf al-maḥjūb*, 534; Nicholson, 412.

117. Vincent J. Cornell, ed. and trans., *The Way of Abū Madyan* (Cambridge: Islamic Texts Society, 1996), 82.

118. As-Sarrāj, *Kitāb al-Lumaʿ*, 342; Abū Ḥāmid al-Ghazālī, *Iḥyāʾ*, 2:269.

119. The place of *dhikr* in *samāʿ* may be best expressed by Jean During in his essay "What is Sufi Music" in *The Legacy of Medieval Persian Sufism*, ed. Leonard Lewisohn (London: Khaniqahi Nimatullahi Publications, 1992), 286:

> Many Sufi melodies . . . are marked by the form of *dhikr*. In some of them, the *dhikr* formula provides the basis for a distinct melody. In others, the melody runs independently, but the listener who is attuned may feel a call to recite the *dhikr* inwardly. In other cases, there remains only the 'taste' of the *dhikr*, a recollection and an awareness. How does this happen? It is because the musician himself mobilizes all of his psychic energy in an attitude of 'remembrance' (*dhikr*), uttering words and sounds of his song with the same total concentrated consciousness which he invests in his *dhikr*.

120. For a detailed study of *samāʿ*, see Kenneth S. Avery, *A Psychology of Early samāʿ: Listening and Altered States.*

121. Al-Hujwīrī, *Kashf al-maḥjūb*, 544–545; Nicholson, 418–419. My translation, with reference to Nicholson.

122. The most comprehensive examination of *shāhid-bāzī* can be found in Cyrus Ali Sargar, *Sufi Aesthetics: Beauty, Love, and the Human Form in the Writings of Ibn ʿArabi and ʿIraqi* (Columbia: University of South Carolina Press, 2011), especially chapter 5. Awḥad ad-Dīn Kirmānī's association with *shāhid-bāzī* is discussed in Lloyd Ridgeon, "The Controversy of Shaykh Awḥad al-Dīn Kirmānī and Handsome, Moon-Faces Youths: A Case Study of *Shāhid-Bāzī* in Medieval Sufism," *Journal of Sufi Studies* 1 (2012), 3–30. Leonard Lewisohn also touches on *shāhid-bāzī* in the works of Ḥāfiẓ in his essay "Ḥāfiẓ in the Socio-historical, Literary and Mystical Milieu of Medieval Persia," in *Ḥāfiẓ and the Religion of Love*, 3–73.

123. *Tamhīdāt*, 296 (388).

124. Muslim, *Kitāb al-birr*.

125. Rūzbihān Baqlī, *Le Jasmin des Fidèles d'amour, Kitāb-e ʿAbhar al-ʿāshiqīn*, ed. Henri Corbin and Muḥammad Muʿīn. Bibliotthèque Iranienne, 8 (Tehran: Intishārāt-i Manūchihrī, 1365/1981), 3 (4).

126. *ʿAbhar al-ʿāshiqīn*, 35 (79). Regarding Rūzbihān Baqlī's place in the Sufi tradition, see Carl W. Ernst, *Ruzbihan Baqli: Mysticism and the Rhetoric of Sainthood in Persian Sufism* (London: RoutledgeCurzon, 1996). For a study of his teachings regarding love, see Carl W. Ernst "The Stages of Love in Early Persian Sufism from Rābiʿa to Rūzbihān," in *Classical Persian Sufism from its Origins to Rumi*, ed. Leonard Lewisohn (London/New York: Khaniqahi Nimatullahi, 1993), 435–455. For a study of the relation of Rūzbihān Baqlī's teachings to those in ad-Daylamī's *ʿAṭf al-alif al-maʾlūf*, see Masataka Takeshita, "Continuity and Change in the Tradition of Shirazi Love Mysticism," *Orient* XXIII (1987), 113–131.

127. *ʿAbhār al-ʿāshiqīn*, 17 (35)

128. Persian translation of Arabic deleted.

129. *Tamhīdāt*, 320 (419–420).

130. *Majālis*, 24.

131. While there was emphasis on the dedication to the Sufi master in this period, it became a more formalized institution as the Sufi orders developed. See Ahmet T. Karamustafa, *Sufism: The Formative Period* (Berkeley/Los Angeles: University of California Press, 2007), 114–134.

132. *Majālis*, 3.

133. Ibid., 21.

Chapter 4: The Roots of Aḥmad al-Ghazālī's Teachings

1. The most vivid and developed treatment of this theme is found in the *Tamhīdāt* of ʿAyn al-Quḍāt. It is in fact one of the central themes of the

text; while it is discussed and alluded to throughout, the most extensive treatment is in *Tamhīdāt* #283–303, 221–233. For analysis of the Satanology of ʿAyn al-Quḍat, ʿAṭṭār and others, see Peter J. Awn, *Satan's Tragedy and Redemption: Iblīs in Ṣūfī Pyschology* (Leiden: E. J. Brill, 1997), esp. 122–183.

2. Abu'l-Mugīth al-Ḥusayn b. Manṣūr al-Ḥallāj, (Paris: P. Geuthner, 1913), 41–43. This translation draws on that of Michael Sells in *Early Islamic Mysticism: Sufi, Qur'an, Miʿraj, Poetic and Theological Writings* (NY: Paulist Press, 1996), 274.

3. Ibid. 45–47.

4. *Majālis,* 13.

5. Louis Masignon maintains that Aḥmad al-Ghazālī read portions from the *Ṭāwasīn* in his sermons at the Behruz Ribāṭ in Baghdad (*The Passion of Ḥallāj,* 2:162). This claim is not, however, substantiated by the sources.

6. Ibn al-Jawzī *al-Muntaẓam,* 17:239.

7. *Tamhīdāt,* 224.

8. Margaret Smith, *Rābiʿa the Mystic and Her Fellow Saints in Islam* (Cambridge: Cambridge University Press, 1928; reprint. Cambridge: Oneworld, 1994); Annemarrie Schimmel, *Mystical Dimensions of Islam,* 55.

9. *Rābiʿa the Mystic,* 55.

10. Martin Lings, *Sufi Poetry* (Cambridge: Islamic Texts Society, 2004), 4.

11. For a list of ash-Shiblī's many sayings on love, see Richard Gramlich, *Alte Vorbilder des Sufitums* (Wiesbaden: Harrasowitz Verlag, 1995), 1:654–665.

12. Abu l-Qāsim al-Qushayrī, *ar-Risālah al-Qushayriyyah fī 'ilm at-taṣawwuf* (Beirut: Dār al-Khayr, 1413/1993), 324. Translated into English by Barbara Von Schlegell, *Principles of Sufism* (Berkeley, CA: Mizan Press, 1990). I have retranslated all the passages cited in this paper in order to maintain consistency in the technical vocabulary translated throughout the article, but have followed Professor Von Schlegell's translation in many other respects.

13. Al-Qushayrī, *Risālah,* 321.

14. Aḥmad al-Ghazālī, *at-Tajrīd fī kalimat at-tawḥīd,* 41; trans. Gramlich, *Das Wort des Einheitsbekenntnisses,* 30. This is a famous *ḥadīth qudsī* that is often cited in Sufi texts but which does not appear in any of the canonical collections. It is also cited at the beginning of *Baḥr al-maḥabbah fī asrār al-muwaddah fī tafsīr Surat Yūsuf,* which is attributed to Aḥmad al-Ghazālī (Bombay: n. p., 1984), 2.

15. *Sawāniḥ,* ed. Pourjavady 15/33; ed. Rabbānī 166; ed. Ritter, 28.

16. Ibid., ed. Pourjavady, 32/54 (39); ed. Ritter, 60 (39); ed. Rabbānī, 181 (38).

17. Ibid., ed. Pourjavady, 45/62 (48); ed. Ritter, 73 (44); ed. Rabbānī, 189 (53).

18. Ibid., ed. Pourjavady, 10/27 (4); ed. Ritter, 18 (4); ed. Rabbānī, 161 (3).

19. Fakhr ad-Dīn 'Irāqī, *Lama'āt,* ed. Muḥammad Khāqavī (Tehran: Intishārāt-i Mullā, 1371 HS), 119; English translation by W.C. Chittick and Peter Lamborn Wilson, *Fakhr ad-Dīn 'Irāqī: Divine Flashes* (New York: Paulist Press, 1982), 117. (My translation).

20. Ibid., ed. Pourjavady, 10/26 (4); ed. Ritter, 17 (4); ed. Rabbānī, 161 (3).

21. Muḥammad Ibn al-Munawwar (d. 598–9/1202), *Asrār at-tawḥīd fī maqāmāt ash-shaykh Abī Saʿīd*, ed. Muḥammad Riḍā Shāfiʿī Kadakānī (Tehran: Intishārāt-i Āgāh, 1366 HS; reprint, 1376 HS); English translation by John O'Kane, *The Secrets of God's Mystical Oneness [Asrār at-Tawḥīd]* (Costa Mesa and New York: Mazda Press and Bibliotheca Persica, 1992).

Nasrollah Pourjavady argues that some of the statements in *Asrār at-tawḥīd* appear to be conscious of discussions that were not prevalent at the time of Abū Saʿīd, thus making this a very unreliable source for studying historical developments of ideas in the 5th/11th century. Pourjavady, *Ruʾyat-i māh dar asmān* (Tehran: Markaz-i Nashr-i Dānishgāhi, 1375 HS/1996), 238.

22. After repenting from a lavish life in his youth, Balkhī traveled widely for knowledge in Iran, Iraq, Arabia, Syria, and Egypt. He settled in the region of Khurāsān, where he had many students. He is recognized as one of the first to bring the practice of asceticism to this region, is known for his asceticism and his emphasis on *tawakkul* (trust) and is said to be among the first to discuss the spiritual states. Abū ʿAbd ar-Raḥmān as-Sulamī, *Ṭabaqāt aṣ-ṣūfiyyah*, ed. Nūr ad-Dīn Sharībah (Cairo: Maṭbaʿāt al-Madanī, 1987), 61–66; Shams ad-Dīn Abū ʿAbdallāh M. b. Aḥmad adh-Dhahabī, *Siyar ʿalām an-nubalāʾ*, ed. Shuʾayb Arnaut et al (Beirut: Muʾassasah ar-Risālah, 1996), 9:313–316; Nūr ad-Dīn ʿAbd ar-Raḥmān Jāmī, *Nafāḥāt al-uns min ḥaḍarāt al-quds*, ed. Maḥmūd ʿĀbidī (Tehran: Intishārāt-i Iṭṭilāʿāt, 1380 HS), 46–47; J. van Ess, *Theologie und Gesellschaft im 2. und 3. Jahrhundert Hidschra* (Berlin-New York: Walter de Gruyter, 1992), vol. 2, 545–549; Gramlich, *Alte Vorbilder des Sufitums*, vol. 2, 13–62.

23. Shaqīq Balkhī, *Adab al-ʿibādāt*, Edited by P. Nwyia in *Trois oeuvres inedités de mystiques muslumans* (Beirut: Dār al-Mashriq, 1982), 17–22.

24. Shaqīq Balkhī, *Adab al-ʿibādāt*, 18.

25. Ibid., 19.

26. Ibid., 19.

27. Ibid., 20.

28. Ibid., 20.

29. Ibid., 20.

30. Ibid., 21.

31. Ibid., 22.

32. Abu'l-Ḥasan ʿAlī b. Muḥammad ad-Daylamī, *ʿAṭf al-alif al-maʾlūf ʿala'l-lām al-maʿṭūf: Livre de l'inclinasion de l'alif uni sur le lām inlcliné*, ed. J.C. Vadet (Cairo: L'Institute Francais d'Archeologie Orentale, 1962), 2. English translation by Joseph Norment Bell and Hasan Mahmoud Abul Latif al Shafie, *A Treatise on Mystical Oneness* (Edinbugh: Edinburgh University Press, 2005). I have checked all translations against those of Bell and Al Shafie but have chosen to keep my own translations in order to maintain consistency in the translation of technical Sufi terms.

33. ad-Daylamī, *ʿAṭf al-alif*, 151.

34. Lois Anita Giffen, *Theory of Profane Love Among the Arabs: The Development of the Genre* (New York: New York University Press, 1972).

35. *Ibid.* 10. For the most comprehensive discussion of various positions regarding *ʿishq* available in Western academic literature, see section 3, chapter II. Also see Massignon, *The Passion of al-Ḥallāj*, 1:340–358.

36. *Aṭf al-alif*, 5.

37. Ibid., 5.

38. For more of the significance of Junayd, see Ahmet T. Karamustafa, *Sufism: the Formative Period* (Berkely, University of California Press, 2007), chap. 1; especially pp. 15–18.

39. *ʿAṭf al-alif*, 18.

40. Ibid., 20.

41. As demonstrated by Giffen, such outlines of the stages of love are common in the secular love tradition. But I have found no direct parallels with ad-Daylamī's stages of love.

42. *ʿAṭf al-alif*, 24.

43. Ibid., 111.

44. Abu'l-Ḥasan Sumnūn b. Ḥamza al-Muḥibb, a contemporary of al-Junayd in Baghdad who, like al-Junayd, was a disciple of both Sarī as-Saqaṭī and Muḥammad b. ʿAlī al-Qaṣṣāb al-Baghdādī. He is a famous example of the early "ecstatic school" of Sufism. He was known for extreme forms of devotion and for his public sermons on love which are said to have stirred not only humans, but all objects, be they living or inanimate. Sulamī, *Ṭabaqāt aṣ-ṣūfiyyah*, 196–198; Jāmī, *Nafaḥāt al-uns*, 100–101; Abū Nuʿaym Aḥmad b. ʿAbdallāh al-Iṣfahānī, *Ḥilyat al-awliyāʾ wa ṭabaqāt al-aṣfiyāʾ*, ed. Muṣṭafā ʿAbd al-Qādir ʿAtāʾ (Beirut: Dār al-Kutub al-ʿIlmiyyah, 1997), 10:329–330; Arberry, *The Doctrine of the Sufis*, 164–165; *Muslims Saints and Mystics* (London, 1996), 239–240.

45. *ʿAṭf al-alif*, 111–112.

46. Ibid., 25.

47. Allusion to Quran 76:1: *Has there come unto mankind a moment of time when there was not anything mentioned?*

48. This is an allusion to the belief that all things are created through the Divine Word. For an extended discussion of Islamic beliefs regarding creation through the Divine Word see Harry Wolfson, *The Philosophy of the Kalam* (Cambridge: Harvard University Press, 1976).

49. *ʿAṭf al-alif*, 26. This appears to be the first instance of this saying preserved in any Sufi text. According to Louis Massignon, this same passage is found in Ruzbihān Baqlī's *Manṭiq al-asrār*, ML ms., f. 56b, in which *ʿishq* is replaced by *maḥabbah;* Massignon, *The Passion of al-Ḥallāj*, 3:102.

50. *ʿAṭf al-alif*, 27.

51. This could also be read, "*ʿIshq* is the fire of the light of the first fire."

52. *Aṭf al-alif*, 44.

53. Ibid., 28.

54. Ibid., 44. *An-Nahūt* is the level of reality pertaining to the world of forms and gross bodies. *Al-Lāhūt* is the level where the Divine discloses Its perfect attributes to Itself within Itself. *Al-Lāhūt* is often considered to be the level of the first Divine determination after the undetermined Divine Essence.

55. Ibid., 36–37.

56. Ibid., 20.

57. Ibid., 37.

58. Al-Ḥusayn b. Manṣūr al-Ḥallāj, *Diwān al-Ḥallāj*, ed. Saʿdī Dannāwī (Beirut: Dār aṣ-Ṣādir, 1998), 65.

59. Ibid., 31.

60. For examinations of the opposition to Sufism in the early period, see Massignon, *The Passion of al-Ḥallāj*, vol. 1, ch. 5 & 6; and Frederick De Jong and Bernd Radtke ed., *Islamic Mysticism Contested: Thirteen Centuries of Controversies and Polemics* (Leiden: E. J. Brill, 1999).

61. Abū Naṣr as-Sarrāj aṭ-Ṭūsī, *Kitāb al-Lumaʿ*, ed. ʿAbd al-Ḥalīm Maḥmūd and Ṭāhā ʿAbd az-Zāqī Surūr (Cairo: Dār al-Kutub al-Ḥādithiyyah, 1970), 87.

62. Ibid., 87.

63. Ibid., 87.

64. Ibid., 88.

65. Ibid., 88; The last line is another version of a famous *ḥadīth qudṣī*, known as *Ḥadīth an-Nawāfil* (the *Ḥadīth* of supererogatory prayers): "God has said, 'Who shows enmity toward my friend, I am at war with him. My servant does not draw near to Me with anything more beloved to me than obligatory religious duties, and My servant ceases not to draw near unto Me with supererogatory devotions (*nawāfil*) until I love him; and when I love him, I am the hearing with which he hears, the sight with which he sees, the hand with which he grasps and the foot upon which he walks." Bukhārī, *Kitāb ar-Riqāq*, 38. The version quoted here is the end of the version cited by ʿAlī b. ʿUthmān al-Jullabī al-Hujwīrī, *Kashf al-maḥjūb*, ed. Valintin Zhukofski (Tehran: Kitābkhāneh-yi Tahurī, 1383 HS), 393.

66. *Kitāb al-Lumaʿ*, 65.

67. Ibid., 66.

68. Ibid., 81.

69. A native of the Persian province of Jibāl, al-Makkī first studied Sufism in Makka with Abū Saʿīd al-Aʾrabī (d. 341/952), who had been a companion of an-Nūrī, and with al-Junayd in Baghdad. Al-Makkī then traveled to Baghdad, where he may have studied with as-Sarrāj. From there he went to Baṣrah, where he joined the Sālimiyyah movement that developed around the teachings of Sahl at-Tustarī (d. 283/896) and was continued by Abu'l-Ḥasan Aḥmad b. Muḥammad b. Sālim (d. 356/967), the son of Sahl at-Tustarī's lifelong companion Muḥammad b. Sālim. (As-Sulamī, *Ṭabaqāt*, 427.) Scholars disagree as to whether or not al-Makkī had direct contact with the younger Ibn as-Sālim. For a discussion of the different views and their support in the primary sources, see Bowering, *The Mystical Vision of Existence in Classical Islam: The Qurʾānic Hermeneutics of the Sufi Sahl at-Tustarī (d. 283/896)* (Berlin/NY: Walter de Gruyter, 1980), 25–26. As has been observed by Louis Massignon, Bernd Radtke, and Gerhard Bowering, al-Makkī's *Qūt al-qulūb* represents the teachings of the Sālimiyyah movement. (Massignon—[B. Radtke], EI, 8: 993–994 [art. "Salimiyyah"]; Gerhard Bowering, *Mystical*

Vision, 26.) Al-Makkī often refers to Abu'l-Ḥasan as "our Shaykh" and to Sahl at-Tustarī as "our Imām." But as he cites Sufis of many predilections, his writings are not limited to the teachings of the Sālimiyyah.

70. For the influence of al-Makkī's *Qūt al-qulūb* on al-Ghazālī's *Iḥyā'*, see Saeko Yazaki, *Islamic Mysticism and Abu Ṭālib al-Makkī: The Role of the Heart* (London: Routledge, 2013); H. Lazarus-Yafeh, *Studies in al-Ghazzālī* (Jerusalem: The Magnes Press, 1975), 34–35; Kojiro Nakamura, "Makkī and Ghazālī on Mystical Practices," *Orient* (Tokyo), 20 (1984), 83–91; Mohamed Sherif, *Ghazali's Theory of Virtue* (Albany: State University of New York Press, 1975), 105–107.

71. A.J. Arberry, *Sufism: an account of the mystics of Islam* (London: George Allen & Unwin, 1950; reprint, 1969), 68.

72. If it is the practical aspect of Sufism that is the focus of the *Qūt al-qulūb,* the intellectual aspect is more prevalent in al-Makkī's later treatise, *'Ilm al-qulūb (Knowledge of the Hearts).* As Gerhard Bowering observes, "Large passages of this text are marked as a definitely esoteric, enthusiastic Sufism, and stand in obvious contrast to the sober disciplined Sufism described in the *Qūt al-qulūb*" (Bowering, *Mystical Vision,* 27). Despite an extensive chapter entitled "The Attribute of Sincerity and Degrees of the Sincere at Heart" and a shorter section entitled "Sayings Regarding Love," *'Ilm al-qulūb* provides little insight into Sufi teachings on love, being more focused, as the title suggests, on knowledge, recognition, and wisdom (*ḥikmah*).

73. Abū Ṭālib Muḥammad b. 'Alī b. 'Aṭiyyah al-Ḥārithī al-Makkī, *Qūt al-qulūb fī mu'āmalāt al-maḥbūb wa-waṣf ṭarīq al-murīd ilā maqām at-tawḥīd,* ed. Basil Uyun as-Sud (Beirut: Dār al-Kutub al-'Ilmiyyah, 1417/1997), 2:83.

74. Ibid., 85.

75. Ibid., 86.

76. Arberry, *SEI,* 210, art. "Kalābādhī."

77. Arberry, *Sufism,* 69.

78. Alexander Knysh, *Islamic Mysticism: A Short Introduction* (Leiden: E.J. Brill, 2000), 123.

79. For a discussion of al-Kalābādhī's place within the early Sufi tradition, see Ahmet T. Karamustafa, *Sufism: The Early Period,* 67–71.

80. al-Kalābādhī, *at-Ta'arruf li madhhab ahl at-taṣawwuf,* 106; A.J. Arberry, *The Doctrine of the Sufis,* 97. I have checked my translation against that of Arberry, but to maintain consistency I have chosen to employ my own translations.

81. Al-Kalābādhī, *at-Ta'arruf,* 101; Arberry, *Doctrine,* 85. (My Translation)

82. Abū 'Abdallāh Sa'īd b. Yurid an-Nibājī is a little known Sufi for whom no exact dates are recorded: adh-Dhahabī, *Siyar a'lām an-nubalā',* 9:586.

83. Kalābādhī, 128; Arberry, *Doctrine,* 85. This could also be read, "love does not abide through a cause." In rendering this citation as it appears in the body of the text, I am following the *Sharḥ-i Ta'arruf li madhhab-i taṣawwuf* of Ismā'īl b. Muḥammad Mustamlī, ed. Muḥammad Rawshan, (Tehran: Intishārāt-i Asātir, 1363 HS/ 1984), 1400.

84. Al-Mustamlī, *Sharḥ-i Ta'arruf,* 1389.

85. Ibid., 1391–1392. This translation draws from the translation of the same passage by William Chittick, *Divine Love*, 288.

86. *Risālah*, 319; Von Schlegell, *Principles of Sufism*, 328.

87. *Risālah*, 319; Von Schlegell, *Principles of Sufism*, 330. A similar saying is attributed to Sumnun al-Muḥibb by ad-Daylamī, *ʿAtf al-alif*, 13.

88. *Risālah* 321; Von Schlegell, 330.

89. Ibid., 321; Von Schlegell, 330.

90. Ibid., 321; Von Schlegell, 330.

91. Abū Bakr Muḥammad b. ʿAlī b. Jaʿfar al-Baghdādī al-Kattānī, a native of Baghdad and a companion of al-Junayd, an-Nūrī and Abū Saʿīd al-Kharrāz. He later traveled to Mecca where he died in 322/934. Jāmī, *Nafaḥāt al-Uns*, 181; Abū Nuʿaym al-Isfahānī, *Ḥilyah*, 10:365–366.

92. *Risālah*, 322; Von Schlegell, 332.

93. A native of Ubulluh, a small village four farsangs from Baṣrah, he was a teacher of Abū Yaʿqūb an-Nahrajūrī, who was later a companion of al-Junayd; he most likely lived in the second half of the third century *hijrī*; Jāmī, *Nafāḥāt al-Uns*, 131.

94. *Risālah*, 322; Von Schlegell, 332.

95. Ibid., 323; Von Schlegell, 333.

96. Ibid., 324; Von Schlegell, 334.

97. Ibid., 325; Von Schlegell, 336.

98. Ibid., 324; Von Schlegell, 334.

99. Ibid., 327; Von Schlegell, 339; the last line is an allusion to the famous *Ḥadīth an-Nawāfil*, Bukhari, *Kitāb ar-Riqāq*, 38. See note 64..

100. Ibid., 321–2; Von Schlegell, 330–331.

101. Al-Hujwīrī was a Persian Sufi from the area of Ghazna in present-day Afghanistan. He studied Sufism under Abu'l-Faḍl al-Khuttālī, through whom he is linked to the circle of ash-Shiblī and al-Junayd in Baghdad (Knysh, *Islamic Mysticism*, 133). He also traveled to Iraq, where he studied with many other Sufi shaykhs who are mentioned throughout the treatise.

102. *Kashf al-maḥjūb* is the earliest Sufi handbook in Persian. The earliest extant treatise on Sufism in Persian is the *Sharḥ-i Taʿarruf li madhhab-i taṣawwuf* by Abū Ibrahīm Ismāʿīl b, Muḥāmmad al-Mustamlī (d. 1042–1043).

103. Al-Hujwīrī, *Kashf al-maḥjūb*, 397; Translated into English by R.A. Nicholson, *Kashf al-Maḥjūb of al-Hujwīrī: The Oldest Persian Treatise on Sufism* (London: Luzac & Co., 1911; reprint 1976), 308. In some citations I have followed Nicholson's translation closely, others I have retranslated to maintain consistency in the rendering of technical terms.

104. *Kashf al-maḥjūb*, 398; Nicholson, 308.

105. *Ṣafwat* is from the same root as *Ṣūfī*, ṣ-f-y. This is one of the many origins proposed for the word *Ṣūfī*.

106. *Kashf al-maḥjūb*, 398; Nicholson, 308.

107. Ibid., 401–2; Nicholson, 311.

108. Ibid., 400; Nicholson, 310. (My translation).

109. Ibid., 401; Nicholson, 310. (My translation).

110. *Sawāniḥ,* ed. Pourjavady, 55/80; ed. Ritter, 75–76; ed. Rabbānī, 199.

111. Aḥmad al-Ghazālī, *Majālis.*

112. Some of the passages attributed to Anṣārī in Maybudī's *Kashf al-Asrār* are taken from works whose authenticity can be established, such as *Manāzil as-sā'irīn* and *Sad Madyān.* The authenticity of other passages is, however, difficult to verify. Shāfi'ī-Kadkanī goes so far as to claim that the commentary from which Maybudī drew was that of another Sufi teacher of Herat, Abū Aḥmad 'Umar b. 'Abdallāh b. Muḥammad al-Harawī (d. ca. 400/1009); see Shāfi'ī-Kadkanī, "Pīr-i Hirawī ghayr az Khwājah 'Abdallāh Anṣārī Ast," *Nāmah-yi Baharestan,* 10, 15, 2009, 175–192. If Shāfi'ī-Kadkanī's findings are correct, it would establish a more open discourse regarding the nature of love a full hundred years before the composition of the *Sawāniḥ.*

113. For details regarding the manner in which these texts were compiled, see Serge Beaurecueil, "Khwāja Abdullāh Ansāri (396–481H./1006–1089), Mystique Hanbalite," Recherches d'Institut de Lettres Orientales de Beyrouth, XXVI, Beirut, 1965; and A.G. Ravan Farhadi, *'Abdullāh Anṣārī of Herat* (1006–1089 C.E.): *An Early Sufi Master* (Richmond Surrey: Curzon, 1996); idem., "The Hundred Grounds of 'Abdullāh Anṣārī of Herat," *Classical Persian Sufism: From its Origins to Rūmī,* ed. Leonard Lewisohn, 381–399. As Farhadi observes, "Anṣārī is considered a great writer and yet he almost never wrote," *'Abdullāh Anṣārī of Herat,* 19.

114. 'Abdallāh Anṣārī, *Manāzil al-sā'irīn/Les etapes des itinerants vers Dieu.* Text and translation by S. de Laugier de Beaurecueil (Cairo: Imprimerie de l-Institut Français d'Archeologie Orientale, 1962), 71–72.

115. Ibid., 109.

116. 'Abdallāh Anṣārī, *Maḥabbat Nāmah,* in *Majmū'ah-yi rasā'il-i farsī-yi Khwājah 'Abd Allāh Anṣārī,* ed. Muḥammad Sarwar Mawlā'ī (Tehran: Intishārāt-i Ṭūs, 1377/1998), 367

117. 'Abdallāh Anṣārī, *Sad Maydān,* in *Majmū'ah-yi rasā'il-i farsī-yi Khwājah 'Abd Allāh Anṣārī,* 333.

118. *Maḥabbat Nāmah,* 367.

119. *Maḥabbat Nāmah,* 356–357.

120. Abū Ḥāmid al-Ghazālī, *Iḥyā' 'ulūm ad-dīn,* 4:257.

121. Ibid., 4:257.

122. Ibid., 4:259; al-Qushayrī, *Risālah,* 326; Von Schlegell, 337.

123. *Iḥyā',* 4:259.

124. Ibid., 4:259.

125. *Ta'arruf,* 128.

126. *Iḥyā',* 4:259.

127. Some parallels to this view of *'ishq* can be found in the secular love tradition. For example, in his *Risālah fi'l-'ishq* al-Jāhiẓ (d. 255/868–9) defines *'ishq* as that which exceeds *ḥubb* (Giffen, *Theory of Profane Love Among the Arabs,* 85). But the possible connections between the Sufi discussion of love and those of the secular love tradition are beyond the scope of this study.

128. *Iḥyā',* 4:260.

129. Ibid., 4:263.

130. Ibid., 4:263.
131. Ibid., 4:263.
132. Ibid., 4:264.
133. Ibid., 4:264.
134. Ibid., 4:265.
135. Ibid., 4:265.
136. Ibid., 4:265.
137. Ibid., 4:261.
138. Ibid., 4:266.
139. Muslim: *Kitāb al-īmān,* 147; Ibn Mājah: *Kitāb ad-du'ā'*; Aḥmad b. Ḥanbal: 4:133.
140. *Iḥyā',* 4:267.
141. Ibid., 4:267.
142. Ibid., 4:268.
143. Ibid., 4:275–276.
144. Ibid., 4:276.
145. Ibid., 4:276.
146. *Risālah,* 327; Von Schlegell, 338.
147. *Iḥyā',* 4:276.
148. Ibid., 4:277.
149. Ibid., 4:276.
150. Ibid., 4:277.
151. Al-Mustamlī, *Sharḥ-i Ta'arruf,* 1391–1392.
152. *Iḥyā',* 4:277.
153. Ibid., 4:286.
154. Abū Sa'īd Faḍl b. Abi'l-Khayr Muḥammad b. Aḥmad al-Mihānī aṣ-Ṣūfī—a Sufi Shaykh in Khurāsān known for asceticism, practicing seclusion, and performing miracles. He is said to have sat with as-Sulamī, and it is reported that Imām al-Ḥarāmayn al-Juwaynī transmitted reports from him. Adh-Dhahabī, *Siyar a'lām an-nubalā',*17:622; Tāj ad-Dīn Abū Naṣr 'Abd al-Wahhāb b. 'Alī as-Subkī, *aṭ-Ṭabaqāt ash-Shāfi'iyyah al-kubrā* (Cairo: 'Īsa'l-Bābī al-Halabī, 1964–76), 5:306.
155. *Iḥyā',* 4:286.
156. *Kashf,* 398; Nicholson, 308.
157. *Iḥyā',* 4:267
158. 'Abdallāh Anṣārī, *Chihil wa daw faṣl,* in *Majmū'ah-yi rasā'il-i farṣī-yi Khwājah 'Abd Allāh Anṣārī,* 111.
159. *Sawāniḥ,* ed. Pourjavady, 4/1 (18); ed. Ritter, 5 (1); ed. Rabbānī, 156 (intro.).

Chapter 5: Aḥmad al-Ghazālī's Metaphysics of Love

1. For a discussion of apophasis in mystical discourse, see Michael Sells, *Mystical Languages of Unsaying* (Chicago: University of Chicago Press, 1994).
2. *Sawāniḥ,* ed. Pourjavady, 6/21–22 (3), ed. Ritter, 10 (3), ed. Rabbānī, 158 (2).

3. *Majālis*, 2.

4. *Sawāniḥ*, ed. Pourjavady, 1/15; ed. Ritter, 2; ed. Rabbānī, 154.

5. Cf. 44:54; 52:20; 55:70–74; 56:22–23, 35–37.

6. *Sawāniḥ*, ed. Pourjavady, 1/15; ed. Ritter, 2; ed. Rabbānī, 154.

7. Chittick, *Divine Love*, 312.

8. Leili Anvar, "The Radiance of Epiphany: The Vision of Beuty and Love in Ḥāfiẓ's Poem of Pre-Eternity," in *Hafiz and the Religion of Love in Classical Persian Poetry*, 124.

9. *Kashf al-asrār*, 1: 52.

10. *Majālis*, 37.

11. This saying is also cited by Aḥmad al-Ghazālī in the *Majālis*, 37, and *at-Tajrīd*, 16.

12. Part of a noncanonical *ḥadīth qudsī*, the whole of which reads, "David said, 'My God! Where would I find You if I searched for You?' He said, 'With those whose hearts are broken.'" *Qūt al-qulūb*, 1:535; Abū Nuʿaym al-Iṣfahānī, *Ḥilyat al-awliyā*ʾ, 2:32; *Kashf al-maḥjūb*, 125 (attributed to Moses); *at-Tajrīd*, 20.

13. *Sawāniḥ*, ed. Pourjavady, 1/15; ed. Ritter, 2; ed. Rabbānī, 154.

14. *Majālis*, 37.

15. *Sawāniḥ*, ed. Pourjavady, 1/15; ed. Ritter, 2; ed. Rabbānī, 154.

16. As regards the *Sawāniḥ*, Bo Utas observes, "The Savāniḥ offers not only a difficult but also quite compressed and partly enigmatic text." For his analysis of the ambiguities created by this use of language, see Bo Utas, "'Ambiguity' in the Savāniḥ of Aḥmad Ghazālī," *Proceedings of the Second European Conference of Iranian Studies*, ed. Bert G. Fragner, Christa Fragner, Gherardo Gnoli, Roxane Haag-Higuchi, Mauro Maggi and Paola Orsatti (Rome: Instituto Italiano per Il Medio ed Estremo Oriente, 1995), 701–710.

17. Ibid., ed. Pourjavady, 45/53 (38); ed. Ritter, 58 (38); ed. Rabbānī, 180 (37).

18. Ibid., ed. Pourjavady, 7/22 (3); ed. Ritter, 11 (3); ed. Rabbānī, 158–159 (2).

19. This famous saying, usually quoted as a *ḥadīth*, is not accepted as canonical by the specialists (see *Muʿjam*, 1261). It is frequently cited in Sufi texts.

20. In this passage, Aḥmad al-Ghazālī is using the terms heart and spirit in a different manner than in the *Sawāniḥ*. While the heart is the ultimate faculty of true perception in the *Sawāniḥ*, here it is a level below that function and thus more limited.

21. *Majālis*, 60–61.

22. *Sawāniḥ*, ed. Pourjavady, 8–9/24 (4); ed. Ritter, 14 (4); ed. Rabbānī, 160 (3).

23. *Majālis*, 61. It is not clear whether al-Ghazālī is citing this last line as a *ḥadīth*. I can find no record of it in any sources.

24. Ed. Paul Nwyia, *Trois oeuvres inédites de mystiques musulmans* (Beirut: Dār al-Mashriq, 1972), 23–182. Ibn ʿAṭā's commentary has also been translated into German by Richard Gramlich, *Abū l-ʿAbbās b. ʿAṭāʾ: Ṣūfī und Koranausleger* (Stuttgart: Deutsche Morgenlandische Gesellschaft, 1995).

25. Ed. Paul Nwyia, "Le Tafsir mystique attribue à Jaʿfar Ṣādiq," *Mélanges de L'Université Saint Joseph,* Beirut, 43 (1968): 181–230. Translated by Farhana Mayer, *Spiritual Gems: The Mystical Qur'an Commentary Ascribed by the Sufis to Imam Jaʿfar al-Ṣādiq (d. 148/765)* (Louisville, KY: Fons Vitae, 2011).

26. Gerhard Böwering, "The Quran Commentary of as-Sulamī," in *Islamic Studies Presented to Charles J. Adams,* ed. Wael B. Hallaq and Donald P. Little (Leiden: E. J. Brill, 1991), 46.

27. For a study of the *khamriyyah* tradition, see F. Harb, "Wine Poetry (*khamriyyāt*)," in *ʿAbbāsid belles-lettres, The Cambridge History of Arabic Literature,* vol. 2, ed. Julia Ashtiyani et al. (Cambridge: Cambridge University Press, 1990), 219–234; and Philip Kennedy, *The Wine Song in Classical Arabic Poetry: Abū Nuwās and the Literary Tradition* (Oxford: Clarendon Press, 1997). Kennedy's study is particularly important for the connection between love and wine in the classical tradition, one that Aḥmad al-Ghazālī appears to play upon.

28. For a brief history of the development of the *ʿUdhrī ghazal* see Andras Hamori, "Love Poetry (*Ghazal*)," in *ʿAbbāsid belles-lettres,* 202–217.

29. Roger Allen, *An Introduction to Arabic Literature* (Cambridge: Cambridge University Press, 2000), 105.

30. For an examination of the theme of death in love see Lois Anita Giffen, *Theory of Profane Love Among the Arabs: The Development of a Genre* (New York: New York University Press, 1971), pt. 3, chap. 1, "The Martyrs of Love."

31. This verse is cited both in the *Sawāniḥ* (cited below) and the *Majālis,* 47.

32. *Sawāniḥ,* ed. Pourjavady, 48–49/65 (65); ed. Ritter, 93 (63); ed. Rabbānī, 193–194 (61). Ritter's version also contains two lines of poetry not found in the other editions.

33. Ibid., ed. Pourjavady, 3/17 (1); Ritter, 4 (1); ed. Rabbānī, 155 (intro.).

34. For an examination of the Sufi approach to the Quran, see Kristin Sands, *Sufi Commentaries on the Quran in Classical Islam* (London/New York: Routledge), 2006.

35. This is an allusion to a famous *ḥadīth* wherein it is said that God has sent 315 messengers and 124,000 prophets: *Al-Musnad li'l-Imām Aḥmad bin Ḥanbal,* ed. Muḥammad Jamīl al-ʿAṭṭār (Beirut, Dār al-Fikr, 1414/1994) (5, 265); viii, 302.

36. *Majālis,* 62.

37. Bukhārī, *Kitāb al-Īmān,* 39, *Kitāb al-Buyūʿ,* 2; Muslim, *Kitāb al-Musāfāt,* 20; Abū Dā'ūd, 3330; Tirmidhī, *Kitāb al-Buyūʿ,* 1; Nasā'ī, *Kitāb al-Buyūʿ,* 2, *Kitāb al-Ashribah,* 50; Ibn Mājah, *Kitāb al-Fitan,* 14.

38. *Majālis,* 62–63.

39. Ibid., 63.

40. An example of this is found in Richard Gramlich's translation of *at-Tajrīd fī kalimat at-tawḥīd.* Though Gramlich is among the most meticulous of modern scholars of Sufism, there are at least three citations that he did not detect: *Das Wort des Einheitsbekenntnisses,*13 (Ar., 8), "Ins Elend gerät der Anbeter des Dīnār, ins Elend gerät der Anbeter des Dirham, ins Elend gerät

der Anbeter des Kleides": This is a noncanonical prophetic *ḥadīth*, though often cited. It is also found in Ismā'īl b. Muḥammad Mustamlī's *Sharḥ-i ta'ārruf*, 1071. Another version that adds, "The slave of hunger and garments (*qaṭīfah*) is wretched" is cited by 'Alī b. 'Uthmān al-Hujwīrī, in *Kashf al-maḥjūb*, 68; 14 (Ar., 8); "Wer Gottes ist, dessen ist Gott": This is a noncanonical *ḥadīth* that is also cited by Aḥmad al-Ghazālī in his *Majālis*, 29, 42; and 28 (Ar., 26); "Wie mancher Faster hat von seinem Fasten nichts als den Hunger und der Durst! Wien mancher Beter hat von seinem Gebet nicht als die Mühe und die Anstregung!": A well-known and oft-cited *ḥadīth*: Bukhārī, *Kitāb al-īmān*, 17; Muslim, *Kitāb al-īmān*, 32; Abū Dā'ūd, *Kitāb al-jihād*, 95; Tirmidhī, *Kitāb tafsīr sūrah*, 88; Nasā'ī, *Kitāb az-zakāt*, 3; Ibn Māja, *Kitāb al-fitan*, 1.

41. A good example of this style is the passage cited in Chapter 3, Aḥmad al-Ghazālī, *'Ayniyyah*, in Mujāhid, *Majmū'ah*, 196.

42. *Majālis*, 20, 22. Regarding the centrality of sincerity and remembrance, Aḥmad al-Ghazālī says, "Every deed which does not comprise sincerity, its non-existence is better than its existence. Because if you do not spend many hours in supererogatory prayers, perhaps you will say to yourself, 'O worthless one' . . . There is no occupation save the remembrance of God." *Majālis*, 21.

43. *Sawāniḥ*, ed. Pourjavady, 39/62 (46); ed. Ritter, 80 (54); ed. Rabbānī, 189 (52).

44. *Lama'āt*, 45; Chittick and Wilson, 70.

45. *Lama'āt*, 49; Chittick and Wilson, 73.

46. *Lama'āt*, 63; Chittick and Wilson, 81. According to Chittick and Wilson these verses are attributed to an-Nūrī, but they do not provide any citation. (I have drawn more heavily on Chittick and Wilson in this citation than in others).

47. *Sawāniḥ*, ed. Pourjavady, 13/29 (8); ed. Ritter, 21 (8); ed. Rabbānī, 163 (7). Although al-Ghazālī does not mention this, the Quran speaks often of God's love, but in all cases the objects of His love are human beings. This would appear to confirm his assertion that love is "the special character of man."

48. Ibid., ed. Pourjavady, 44/68 (58); ed. Ritter, 83 (58); ed. Rabbānī, 190 (56).

49. Ibid., ed. Pourjavady, 21–22/42 (21); ed. Ritter, 41 (21); ed. Rabbānī, 171 (20).

50. Ibid., Pourjavady, 44/68–69 (58); ed. Ritter, 83 (58); ed. Rabbānī, 190 (56).

51. Ibid., ed. Pourjavady, 13/31 (10); ed. Ritter, 24 (10); ed. Rabbānī, 164 (9).

52. *Lama'āt*, 68 (7); Chittick and Wilson, 84–85.

53. *Sawāniḥ*, ed. Pourjavady, 12/29 (8); ed. Ritter, 22 (8); Rabbānī, 163 (7).

54. While for practitioners of Sufism and other Muslims, this passage is taken as a reference to the Prophet ascending to the Divine Throne, others take it as a reference to the Prophet Muḥammad's vision of the angel Gabriel during the same journey, in which case *He drew nigh* would be rendered as

"he drew nigh"; see Muḥammad b. Jarīr al-Ṭabarī, *Jāmiʿ al-bayān ʿan taʾwīl āy al-Qurʾān*, ed. Maḥmūd Shākir al-Hirstanī (Beirut: Dār iḥyāʾ al-turāth al-ʿarabī, 1421/2001), 27:55–56; Abū ʿAbdallāh Muḥammad b. Aḥmad al-Qurṭubī, *al-Jāmiʿ li aḥkām al-Qurʾān*, ed. Muḥammad Ibrahīm al-Ḥafnāwī (Cairo: Dār al-Ḥadīth, 1323/2002), 9:78–80. Here it has been rendered to better match the interpretive context to which al-Ghazālī alludes. For a study of the place of the *miʿrāj* in Sufism, see *Early Islamic Mysticism: Sufi, Qur'an, Miraj, Poetic and Theological Writings*, trans. Michael Sells (NY: Paulist Press, 1995).

55. *Rawḥ al-arwāḥ*, 512.

56. *Tamhīdāt*, 150 (203).

57. Ibid., 150 (203).

58. *Sawāniḥ*, ed. Pourjavady, 3/17 (1); ed. Ritter, 4 (1); ed. Rabbānī, 155 (intro.).

59. *Tamhīdāt*, 150 (203).

60. *Sawāniḥ*, ed. Pourjavady, 31/52 (37); ed. Ritter, 57 (37); ed. Rabbānī, 179 (36).

61. Ibid., ed. Pourjavady, 5/20 (3); ed. Ritter, 8 (3); ed. Rabbānī, 157 (2).

62. Ibid., ed. Pourjavady, 43/66 (53), 55/81 (77); ed. Ritter, 49 (49), 105 (75); ed. Rabbānī, 187 (47), 199 (73).

63. Ibid., ed. Pourjavady, 5/20 (3); ed. Ritter, 8 (3); ed. Rabbānī, 157 (2).

64. Ibid., ed. Pourjavady, 45/63 (48); ed. Ritter, 73 (45); ed. Rabbānī, 175 (43).

65. Ibid., ed. Pourjavady, 12/30 (9); ed. Ritter, 22–23 (9); ed. Rabbānī, 163 (8).

66. *Divine Love*, 317.

67. *Sawāniḥ*, ed. Pourjavady, 43/67 (55); ed. Ritter, 78 (51); ed. Rabbānī, 188 (49).

68. Ibid., ed. Pourjavady, 52/78 (71); ed. Ritter, 100 (69); ed. Rabbānī, 196 (67).

69. Ibid., ed. Pourjavady, 31/52 (37); ed. Ritter, 57 (37); ed. Rabbānī, 179 (36).

70. This saying is part of a prophetic *ḥadīth*, the whole of which reads: "The hearts of all the children of Adam are like a single heart between two fingers of the Compassionate. He turns it where He desires. O God, O Turner of hearts, turn our hearts towards obeying You" (Muslim, *Kitāb al-Qadar*, 17; Tirmidhī, *Kitāb al-Qadar*, 7, *Kitāb ad-Daʿwāt*, 89; Ibn Mājah, *Muqaddimah*, 13; Aḥmad b. Ḥanbal, 2:168, 173; 6:182, 251, 302, 315). Several *aḥādīth* refer to God as "the Turner of hearts" (*muṣarrif al-qulūb*) and as "The Revolver of hearts" (*muqallib al-qulūb*); see Wensinck, *Concordance*, 5:459.

71. This is a famous prophetic *ḥadīth* often cited in Ṣūfī texts: "Verily God does not look at your bodies and your forms, but He looks at your hearts" (Aḥmad b. Ḥanbal, 2:285, 539; Muslim, *Kitāb al-birr*, 33; Ibn Mājah, *Kitāb az-zuhd*, 9). Another variation—"Verily God does not look at your forms, He only looks at your hearts"—is cited by Aḥmad al-Ghazālī in *at-Tajrīd*, 5: "God does not look at your forms and your works, but He looks at your hearts and your states" is cited by Aḥmad al-Ghazālī in the *Majālis*, 4, 9.

72. *Tamhīdāt*, 146 (198).

73. I owe this observation to William Chittick's invaluable comments on an earlier version of the manuscript.

74. *Sawāniḥ*, ed. Pourjavady, 45/64 (49); ed. Ritter, 74 (46); ed. Rabbānī, 176 (44).

75. That is, Abū Ṭālib al-Makkī, see Chapter 4.

76. *Lamaʿāt*, 88; Chittick and Wilson, 97.

77. *Lamaʿāt*, 87; Chittick and Wilson, 96.

78. *Sawāniḥ*, ed. Pourjavady, 7/22 (3); ed. Ritter, 11 (3); ed. Rabbānī, 158 (2).

79. Ibid., ed. Pourjavady, 27/48 (30); ed. Ritter, 51 (30); ed. Rabbānī, 176 (29).

80. Ibid., ed. Pourjavady, 17/36 (16); ed. Ritter, 32 (16); ed. Rabbānī, 168 (15).

81. Ibid., ed. Pourjavady, 17/36 (16); ed. Ritter, 33 (15); ed. Rabbānī, 168 (15).

82. *Kashf al-asrār*, 4:36.

83. *Sawāniḥ*, ed. Pourjavady, 18/36 (17); ed. Ritter, 33 (17); ed. Rabbānī, 168 (16).

84. Ibid., ed. Pourjavady, 45/69 (59); ed. Ritter, 84 (59); ed. Rabbānī, 190 (57).

85. Pourjavady, commentary on *Sawāniḥ* translation, 94.

86. Pourjavady, commentary on *Sawāniḥ* translation, 95; *Majmūʿah-yi āthār-i Nūr ʿAlī Shāh Iṣfahānī*, ed. Javad Nurbakhsh (Tehran: Firdawsī, 1971), 2.

87. *Sawāniḥ*, ed. Pourjavady, 21/41 (21); ed. Ritter, 39 (21); ed. Rabbānī, 171 (20).

88. Ibid., ed. Pourjavady, 15/33 (12); ed. Ritter, 28 (12); ed. Rabbānī, 166 (11). In the editions of Ritter, Pourjavady, and Rabbānī, the text reads "ugly" (*qubḥ*), rather than "nothing" (*hīch*). In this case the translation would read, "And that face is ugliness—when you know it." In this instance, I have chosen to follow the text edited by Mehdi Bayānī ([Tehran, 1322/1943], 12). In his critical apparatus, Ritter also notes that this alternative appears in at least one manuscript. Both readings are viable, but given the nature of the discussion, in which all other faces are said to pass away before the face of God and *there remains the Face of thy Lord* (55:27), "nothing" (*hīch*) appears to be a better interpretation.

89. *Lamaʿāt*, 133; Chittick and Wilson, 126.

90. This is an allusion to an oft-cited supplication, that although at times attributed to the Prophet, was most likely first said by either ʿUmar ibn al-Khaṭṭāb or Abū Bakr aṣ-Ṣiddīq: "O God show me things as they are in themselves. Show me truth as truth and give me the strength to follow it. Show me falsehood as falsehood and give me the strength to avoid it."

91. *Lamaʿāt*, 134; Chittick and Wilson, 126. Another version of this verse is cited by Aḥmad al-Ghazālī in *at-Tajrīd*, 18: "And in everything there is a sign / indicating that He is the One." This is a verse of poetry often cited

by Ṣūfīs from the ascetic poet Abu'l-ʿAṭāhiyyah (d. 210/825 or 211/826). The full poem is:

Oh we are all perishing!
Which of the sons of Adam is immortal?
Their beginning is from their Lord,
And all are unto Him returning.
What a wonder that one opposes the Divine
or that the denier denies Him.
In every movement and in every resting
There belongs to God a witness.
And in everything there is a sign
indicating that He is the One.

Abu'l-ʿAṭāhiyyah, Ismāʿīl b. al-Qāsim, *Dīwān Abi'l-ʿAṭāhiyyah* (Beirut: Dār aṣ-Ṣadr, 1964), 122. Another version of the last *bayt* is cited by Abū Naṣr as-Sarrāj in his *Kitāb al-Lumaʿ*: "And in everything there is a witness, indicating that He is one," 53.

92. *Sawāniḥ*, ed. Pourjavady, 15/33–34 (13); ed. Ritter, 29 (13); ed. Rabbānī, 166 (12).

93. Ibid., ed. Pourjavady, 48/73 (63); ed. Ritter, 92 (62); ed. Rabbānī, 193 (60).

94. Ibid., ed. Pourjavady, 13–14/31 (11); ed. Ritter, 25 (11); ed. Rabbānī, 164–165 (10).

95. Ibid., ed. Pourjavady, 14/32 (11); ed. Ritter, 27 (11); ed. Rabbānī, 165 (10).

96. *Lamaʿāt*, 69; Chittick and Wilson, 85.

97. *Sawāniḥ*, ed. Pourjavady, 36/59 (43); ed. Ritter, 70 (44); ed. Rabbānī, 184–185 (42).

98. Ibid., ed. Pourjavady, 36/58 (41); ed. Ritter, 69 (42); ed. Rabbānī, 184 (41).

99. Ibid., ed. Pourjavady, 18/37 (18); ed. Ritter, 34 (18); ed. Rabbānī, 169 (17).

100. Ibid., ed. Pourjavady, 29/50–51 (34); ed. Ritter, 54 (34); ed. Rabbānī, 177–178 (33).

101. Ibid., ed. Pourjavady, 49–50/75 (67); ed. Ritter, 95 (65); ed. Rabbānī, 194 (63).

102. Ibid., ed. Pourjavady, 50/75 (67); ed. Ritter, 95 (65); ed. Rabbānī, 194–195 (63).

103. Ibid., ed. Pourjavady, 39/62 (47); ed. Ritter, 81 (55); ed. Rabbānī, 189 (53).

104. Ibid.

105. Ibid., ed. Pourjavady, 11/28 (7); ed. Ritter, 20 (7); ed. Rabbānī, 162 (6).

106. Ibid., ed. Pourjavady, 11/28 (7); ed. Ritter, 20–21 (7); ed. Rabbānī, 162 (6).

107. Ibid., ed. Pourjavady, 20/40 (20); ed. Ritter, 38 (20); ed. Rabbānī, 179 (19).

108. Ibid., ed. Pourjavady, 19/38 (19); ed. Ritter, 36 (19); ed. Rabbānī, 169 (18).

109. Ibid., ed. Pourjavady, 26/47 (29); ed. Ritter, 49–50 (29); ed. Rabbānī, 175 (28).

110. Ibid., ed. Pourjavady, 22/43 (23); ed. Ritter, 43 (23); ed. Rabbānī, 172 (22).

111. Ibid., ed. Pourjavady, 35/57 (40); ed. Ritter, 66–67 (40); ed. Rabbānī, 183 (39).

112. Ibid., ed. Pourjavady, 21/40 (21); ed. Ritter, 40 (21); ed. Rabbānī, 171 (20).

113. Ibid., ed. Pourjavady, 24/44 (25); ed. Ritter, 44–45 (25); ed. Rabbānī, 173 (24).

114. Ibid., ed. Pourjavady, 28/49 (32); ed. Ritter, 52–53 (32); ed. Rabbānī, 177 (31).

115. Ibid., ed. Pourjavady, 23/42–43 (23); ed. Ritter, 43 (23); ed. Rabbānī, 172 (22).

116. Ibid., ed. Pourjavady, 32/54 (39); ed. Ritter, 60 (39); ed. Rabbānī, 180 (38).

117. Ibid., ed. Pourjavady, 32/54 (39); ed. Ritter, 60 (39); ed. Rabbānī, 180–181 (38).

118. "I am the Truth" and "Glory be to me" are two much debated ecstatic utterances that are often cited in Sufi texts. The former is attributed to al-Ḥallāj, the latter to Bisṭāmī. Many Sufis criticize both figures for having gone too far in having expressed such utterances. Others maintain that they reveal a high degree of spiritual attainment. See Carl Ernst, *Words of Ecstasy in Sufism* (Albany, NY: SUNY Press, 1984).

119. *Sawāniḥ*, ed. Pourjavady, 16/34 (13); ed. Ritter, 30 (13); ed. Rabbānī, 166–167 (12).

120. Ibid., ed. Pourjavady, 25–26/47 (28); ed. Ritter, 48 (28); ed. Rabbānī, 175 (27).

121. Ibid., ed. Pourjavady, 32–33/54–55 (39); ed. Ritter, 60–61 (39); ed. Rabbānī, 181 (38).

122. Given the ambiguity of Persian, this phrase could also be read "she is farther," meaning that the beloved is farther from the lover.

123. *Sawāniḥ*, ed. Pourjavady, 30/51 (36); ed. Ritter, 56 (36); ed. Rabbānī, 178 (35).

124. Ibid., ed. Pourjavady, 45–46/70 (60); ed. Ritter, 86 (61); ed. Rabbānī, 191 (59).

125. Ibid., ed. Pourjavady, 47/72 (61); ed. Ritter, 90 (61); ed. Rabbānī 192 (59).

126. Ibid., ed. Pourjavady, 18/37 (18); ed. Ritter, 34–35 (18); ed. Rabbānī, 169 (17).

127. Ibid., ed. Pourjavady, 38/61 (45); ed. Ritter, 80 (53); ed. Rabbānī, 188 (51).

128. Ibid., ed. Pourjavady, 43/55 (39); ed. Ritter, 61 (39); ed. Rabbānī, 181 (38).

129. Ibid., ed. Pourjavady 52/78 (72); ed. Ritter, 100 (70); ed. Rabbānī, 197 (68).

130. Ibid., ed. Pourjavady, 52/78 (72); ed. Ritter, 100 (70); ed. Rabbānī, 197 (68).

131. Ibid.

132. Ibid., ed. Pourjavady, 19–20/39 (19); ed. Ritter, 36–37 (19); ed. Rabbānī, 169–170 (3).

133. For an explanation of "the station of no station," see William Chittick, *The Sufi Path of Knowledge: Ibn al-ʿArabī's Metaphysics of Imagination* (Albany, NY: SUNY Press, 1989), 355–356.

134. *Sawāniḥ*, ed. Pourjavady, 8–9/24 (4); ed. Ritter, 14 (4); ed. Rabbānī, 160 (3).

Conclusion

1. Leonard Lewisohn, "Sawanih" in *Encyclopedia of Love in World Religions*, ed. Yudit Kornberg Greenberg (New York: Macmillan Reference & Thomson Gale, 2007), 2:538.

2. *Divine Love*, xviii–xix.

3. Leili Anvar, "The Radiance of Epiphany: The Vision of Beauty and Love in Ḥāfiẓ's Poem of Pre-Eternity" in *Hafiz and the Religion of Love in Classical Persian Poetry*, ed. Leonard Lewisohn (London: I.B. Taurus, 2010), 124.

4. In one of his letters, ʿAyn al-Quḍāt laments that due to fear of social strife (*fitnah*) Abū Ḥāmid al-Ghazālī had never discussed the level of the Quran that pertains to the intellectual elite in any of his works (*Nāmeh-hā*, 1:79).

5. *Ibn Tufayl's Hayy ibn Yaqẓān*, trans. Lenn Evan Goodman (Los Angeles: Gee Tee Bee, 1991), 102.

6. *Iḥyāʾ*, 4:276.

7. *Iḥyāʾ*, 4:268.

8. *Sawāniḥ*, ed. Pourjavady, 4 (1) (trans. 18), ed. Ritter, 5 (1), ed. Rabbānī, 156 (intro.).

9. Eve Feuillebois-Pierunek, "Mystical Quest and Oneness in the Mukhtār-nāma Attributed to Farīd al-Dīn ʿAṭṭār" in *Attar and the Persian Sufi Tradition*, ed. Leonard Lewisohn and Christopher Shackle (London: I.B. Tauris, 2006), 309.

10. *Sawāniḥ*, ed. Pourjavady, 1/15; ed. Ritter, 2; ed. Rabbānī, 154.

Bibliography

Works by Aḥmad al-Ghazālī

al-Ghazālī, Aḥmad. *Dāstān-i murghān*. Edited by Nasrollah Pourjavady. Tehran: Anjuman-i Shāhānshāhī-yi Falsafa-yi Īrān, 1976. English translation by Peter Avery as an appendix to his translation of Farīd ad-Dīn ʿAṭṭār's *Speech of the Birds*. Cambridge: Islamic Texts Society, 1998, 551–560.

———. *Dāstān-i murghān*. Edited by Aḥmad Mujāhid in *Majmūʿah-yi āthār-i fārsī-yi Aḥmad Ghazālī*, 69–85.

———. *Majālis-i Aḥmad Ghazālī*. Edited with Persian translation by Aḥmad Mujāhid, Tehran: Tehran University Press, 1966.

———. *Majmūʿah-yi āthār-i fārsī-yi Aḥmad Ghazālī*. Edited by Aḥmad Mujāhid. Tehran: Muʾassasah-yi Intishārāt va Chāp-i Dānishgāh-i Tehrān, 1358/1979.

———. *Mukātabāt-i Khwājah Aḥmad Ghazālī bā ʿAyn al-Quḍāt Hamadānī*. Edited by Nasrollah Pourjavady. Tehran: Intishārāt-i Khānaqāh-i Niʿmat Allāhī, 1356/1978.

———. *Mukātabāt-i Khwājah Aḥmad Ghazālī bā ʿAyn al-Quḍāt Hamadānī*. Edited by Aḥmad Mujāhid, *Majmūʿah-yi āthār-i fārsī-yi Aḥmad Ghazālī*, 461–509.

———. "*Maktūbī* az Aḥmad al-Ghazālī." Edited by Nasrollah Pourjavady. In *Jāwīdān-i khirād*, 1 (1975), 32–37. Edited by Mujāhid in *Majmūʿah-yi āthār-i fārsī-yi Aḥmad Ghazālī*, 248–260.

———. *Risālah-yi ʿAyniyyah*. Edited by Aḥmad Mujāhid in *Majmūʿah-yi āthār-i fārsī-yi Aḥmad Ghazālī*, 175–214.

———. *Risālah-yi ʿAyniyyah,* In *Armaghān,* 8:1 (1929): 8–42.

———. *Risālah-yi ʿAyniyyah*. Edited by Nasrollah Taqawi under the title *Tāzīyāne sulūk*. Tehran, 1940.

———. *Risālah-yi ʿAyniyyah*. Edited by Javad Nurbakhsh under the title *Mawʿiẓe* (Exhortation). Tehran, 1973.

———. *Sawāniḥ*. Edited by Aḥmad Mujāhid, in *Majmūʿah-yi āthār-i fārsī-yi Aḥmad Ghazālī*, 89–173.

———. *Sawāniḥ*. Edited by Nasrollah Pourjavady. Tehran: Intishārāt-i Bunyād-i Farhang-i Īrān, 1980. English translation by Nasrollah Pourjavady as *Sawāniḥ: Inspirations form the World of Pure Spirits, The Oldest Persian Sufi Treatise on Love*. London: Routledge & Kegan Paul, 1986.

———. *Sawāniḥ*. Edited by Ḥāmid Rabbānī in *Ganjah-yi ʿirfān*. Tehran: Ganjīnah, 1973.

———. *Sawāniḥ*. Edited by Helmut Ritter. Tehran: Markaz-i Nashr-i Dānishgāhī, 1989.

———. *Sawāniḥ*. Edited by Mehdī Bayānī. Tehran: 1943.

———. *at-Tajrīd fī kalimat at-tawḥīd*. Cairo: Sharikat Maktabah wa Maṭbaʿ Muṣṭafā al-Bābī al-Halabī, 1386/1967.

———. *at-Tajrīd fī kalimat at-tawḥīd*. MS Paris, Bibliothèque Nationale, Arabe 1248, fols. 219v–229.

———. *at-Tajrīd fī kalimat at-tawḥīd*. MS Paris, Bibliothèque Nationale, Arabe 5546, fols. 64v–85.

———. *at-Tajrīd fī kalimat at-tawḥīd*. MS Paris, Bibliothèque Nationale, Arabe 5657, fols. 126v–151.

———. *at-Tajrīd fī kalimat at-tawḥīd*. MS Paris, Bibliothèque Nationale, Arabe 5796, fols. 40–59.

———. *at-Tajrīd fī kalimat at-tawḥīd*. MS Vatican, Arabo 1253, fols. 1b–24b.

Works Attributed to Aḥmad al-Ghazālī

Baḥr al-ḥaqīqah. Edited by Nasrollah Pourjavaday. Tehran: Imperial Iranian Academy of Philosophy, 1977. Persian translation by Mirza Abu'l-Ḥasan Faqīhī, *Kitāb-i asrār-i ʿishq ya daryā-i maḥabbah* (Tehran: n.p., AH 1325).

adh-Dhakhīrah li ahl al-baṣīrah. MS Berlin, Peterman I 597, fols. 1–49a (Ahlwardt 1726).

Ghazālī, Abū Ḥāmid. (?), *Lubb al-Iḥyā'*. MS Yale University, Beinecke Library, Salisbury 38, fols. 1–45 (1025/1616).

———. (?) *Lubāb al-Iḥyāʿ*. MS Berlin, Wetzstein 99 (Ahlwardt 1708); MS Princeton, Yahuda 838 and 3717 (Mach 2164).

———. (?) *Lubb al-Iḥyā'*. MS Berlin, Wetzstein II 1807, fols. 120–146b (Ahlwardt 1707).

Ṭūṣī, Aḥmad b. Muḥammad al-. *Laṭā'if al-fikr wa jawāmiʿ ad-durar*. MS Berlin, Oct. 3707 (AH 1109).

———. *Manhaj al-albāb*. MS Berlin, Wetzstein 1812 (Ahlwardt 2832), fols. 37b–48.

———. *Mukhtaṣar as-salwah fi'l-khalwah*. MS Vatican, Arabo 299, fols. 80v–113v.

———. *Risālah fī faḍl al-faqr wa'l-fuqarā'*. Edited with Persian translation by Aḥmad Mujāhid under the title *Samāʿ wa futuwwah*. Tehran: Kitābkhānah-i Manūchhirī, 1981.

———. *Sirr al-asrār fī kashf al-anwār*. Edited by ʿAbd al-Ḥamīd Dālih Hamadān. Cairo: ad-Dār al-Miṣriyyah al-Lubnāniyyah, 1408/1988.

Ṭūsī, Majd ad-Dīn al-. *Bawāriq al-ilmāʿ fī radd ʿalā man yuḥarrimu as-samāʿ bi'l-ijmāʿ*. Translated and edited by James Robson. Hertford: Stephen Austin & Sons, 1938.

———. *Bawāriq al-ilmāʿ fī radd ʿalā man yuḥarrimu as-samāʿ bi'l-ijmāʿ*. MS Paris, Bibliothèque Nationale, Arabe 4580, fols. 1–12.

Selected Bibliography

Abbadi, Mansur ibn Ardashir. *al-Taṣfiyah fī aḥwāl aṣ-ṣūfiyyah*. Edited by Ghulam Husayn Yusufi. Tehran: Bunyād-i Farhang-i Iran, 1347/1968.

'Abdul Haq, Muhammad. "'Ayn al-Quḍāt Hamdānī's Concept of Time and Space in the Perspective of Sūfism." *Islamic Quarterly* 31, no. 1 (1987): 5–37.

Abrahamov, Binyamin. *Divine Love in Islamic Mysticism: The Teachings of Al-Ghazali and Al-Dabbagh*. London: Routledge, 2003.

———. "Ibn al-ʿArabī on Divine Love." In *Tribute to Michael: Studies in Jewish and Muslim Thought Presented to Professor Michael Schwarz*. Edited by Sarah Klein-Braslavy, Binyamin Abrahamov, and Joseph Sadan, 7–36. Tel Aviv: Tel Aviv University Press, 2009.

Abu-Sway, Mustafa Mahmoud. "Al-Ghazālī's 'Spiritual Crisis' Reconsidered." *Al-Shajarah: Journal of the International Institute of Islamic Thought and Civilization* 1 (1996): 77–94.

Addas, Claude. "The Experience and Doctrine of Love in Ibn 'Arabi." *Journal of the Muhyiddin ibn 'Arabi Society* 32 (2002): 25–44.

Aflākī, Shams ad-Dīn Aḥmad. *Manāqib al-ʿārifīn*. Edited by Tahsin Yazici. Tehran: Dunyā-yi Kitāb, 1362/1983. Translated by John O'Kane as *The Feats of the Knowers of God*. Leiden: E.J. Brill, 2002.

Afrāsiyābī, Ghulām Riḍāʾ. *Sulṭān-i ʿushshāq*. Shiraz: Dānishgāh-i Shīrāz, 1993.

———. "Zindānī-yi Baghdād: ḥaqāʾiqī az zindagī wa falsafa-yi ʿAyn al-Quḍāt Hamadānī." *Guwhar* 23–24 (1974): 1074–1079; *Guwhar* 26 (1975): 141–145.

Allen, Roger. *An Introduction to Arabic Literature*. Cambridge: Cambridge University Press, 2000.

Anawati, G. C., and Louis Gardet, *Mystique Musulman*. Paris: J. Vrin, 1968.

Anṣārī, ʿAbdallāh. *Majmūʿah-yi rasāʾil-i farsī*. Edited by Muhammad Sarwar Mawlāʾī. Tehran: Intishārāt-i Ṭūs, 1377/1998.

———. *Manāzil as-sāʾirīn/Les étapes des itinérants vers Dieu*. Translated by S. de Laugier de Beaurecueil as *Les étapes des itinérants vers Dieu*. Cairo: Imprimerie de l'Institut Français d'Archéologie Orientale, 1962.

———. *Ṭabaqāt aṣ-ṣūfiyyah*. Edited by Muhammad Sarwar Mawlāʾī.Tehran: Intishārāt-i Ṭūs, 1386/2007.

Anvar, Leili. "The Radiance of Epiphany: The Vision of Beauty and Love in Ḥāfiẓ's Poem of Pre-Eternity," In *Hafiz and the Religion of Love in Classical Persian Poetry*. Edited by Leonard Lewisohn, 123–139. London: I.B. Taurus, 2010.

Anwar, Etin. "Ibn Sīna's Philosophical Theology of Love: A Study of Risālah fī al-ʿishq." *Islamic Studies*, 42, no. 2 (2003): 331–345.

Anwār, Sayyid ʿAbd-i Ilah. "*Nāmahā*-yi ʿAyn al-Quḍāt Hamadānī: jild-i siwwum wa-muqadimma-yi āqā-yi duktur Munzawī bar īn nāmahā." *Chista* 171 (2000): 119–122.

Arberry, A.J. *The Doctrine of the Sufis*. Cambridge: Cambridge University Press, 1935.

———. *Sufism: An Account of the Mystics of Islam*. London: George Allen & Unwin, 1950.

Asad Allāhī, Khudābakhsh. "Andīshahā-yi ʿirfānī-yi ʿAyn al-Quḍāt dar mawḍūʿ-i ʿishq." *Pazhūhish-hā-yi Zabān wa-Adabiyyāt-i Fārsī* 1 (2009): 33–44.

———. "Andīshahā-yi ʿirfānī-yi ʿAyn al-Quḍāt dar bāb-i Iblīs." *Zabān wa-Adabiyyāt-i Fārsī* 14 (2009): 9–26.

ʿAsqalānī, Ibn Ḥajar. *Lisān al-mīzān*. Hyderabad: Maṭbaʿat Majlis Dāʾirāt al-Maʿārif an-Niẓāmiyyah, 1329/1911.

ʿAṭṭār, Farīd al-Dīn. *Farid al-Din ʿAttar's Memorial of God's Friends*. Partial translation by Paul Losensky. Mahwah, N.J.: Paulist Press, 2009.

———. *Ilāhī-nāmah*. Edited by Helmut Ritter. Istanbul: Maṭbaʿah-yi Maʿārif, 1940.

———. *Manṭiq aṭ-ṭayr*. Edited by Muhammad-Rida Shafii Kadkani. Tehran: Intishārāt-i Sukhan, 1384/2005. Translated by Peter Avery as *The Speech of the Birds*. Cambridge: Islamic Texts Society, 1998.

———. *Tadhkirat al-awliyāʾ*. Edited by Muhammad Istiʿlāmī. Tehran: Zuwwār, 1346/1967.

Avery, Kenneth. *A Psychology of Early Sufi samāʿ: Listening and Altered States*. New York: Routledge Curzon, 2004.

Avicenna (Ibn Sīnā). *al-Ilahiyyat min al-shifāʾ/The Metaphysics of The Healing*. Translated by Michael E. Marmura. Provo, Utah: Brigham Young University Press, 2005.

———. *al-Ishārāt wa't-tanbīhāt*. Edited by Sulaymān Dunyā. Cairo: Muṣṭafā al-Bābī al-Ḥalabī, 1947.

———. *Risālah fi'l-ʿishq*. Edited by Ḥusayn aṣ-Ṣiddīq and Rawiyya Jamus. Damascus: Dār al-Fikr, 2005.

———. *A Treatise on Love by Ibn Sina*. Translated by Emil L. Fackenheim. *Medieval Studies* 7, 1945, 208–228.

Bakar, Osman. *The Classification of Knowledge in Islam*. Cambridge: Islamic Texts Society, 1998.

Balkhī, Shaqīq. "Adab al-ʿibādāt." In *Trois oeuvres inedités de mystiques muslumans*. Edited by Paul Nwyia, 17–22. Beirut: Dār al-Mashriq, 1982.

Baltaci, Halil. "Saf Aşkın Üstadı: Ahmed Ghazzalī ve Tasavvuf Analyışı." *Tasavvuf* 14 (2013): 1–41.

Baqlī, Rūzbihān. *Le Jasmin des Fidèles d'amour, Kitāb-e ʿAbhar al-ʿāshiqīn*. Edited by Henri Corbin and Muḥammad Muʿīn. Tehran: Intishārāt-i Manūchihrī, 1365/1981.

———. *ʿArāʾis al-bayān fi ḥaqāʾiq al-Qurʾān*. Edited by Aḥmad Farīd al-Mizyādī. 3 vols. Beirut: Dār al-Kutub al-ʿIlmiyyah, 2008.

Bashir, Shahzad. *Sufi Bodies: Religion and Society in Medieval Islam*. New York: Columbia University Press, 2011.

Bell, Joseph Norment. *Love Theory in Later Hanbalite Islam*. Albany: State University of New York Press, 1979.

Beneito, Pablo. "On the Divine Love of Beauty." *Journal of the Muhyiddin ibn 'Arabi Society* 18 (1995), 4–17.

———. "The Servant of the Loving One: On the Adoption of the Character Traits of al-Wadud." *Journal of the Muhyiddin ibn 'Arabi Society* 32 (2002).

Blochet, E. "Number 159/5." *Catalogue des manuscrits persans de la Bibliothèque Nationale*. Paris, 1905.

Bosworth, C.E. "The Political and Dynastic History of the Iranian World (A.D. 1000 1217)." In *The Saljuq and Mongol Periods (Vol. 5 of The Cambridge History of Iran)*. Edited by J.A. Boyle, 1–202. Cambridge: Cambridge University Press, 1968.

Böwering, Gerhard. "ʿAyn al-Qożāt Hamadānī," *Encyclopaedia Iranica*, 3:140–143; http://www.iranicaonline.org/articles/ayn-al-qozat-hamadani-abul-maali-abdallah-b

———. "Ḏekr," in *Encyclopaedia Iranica* 7:229–233; http://www.iranicaonline.org/articles/dekr

———. "'Erfān." *Encyclopaedia Iranica* 8:551–554. http://www.iranicaonline.org/articles/erfan-1.

———. *The Mystical Vision of Existence in Classical Islam: The Quranic Hermeneutics of the Ṣūfī Sahl at-Tustarī (d. 283/896)*. New York: de Gruyter, 1980.

———. "The Quran Commentary of al-Sulamī." In *Islamic Studies Presented to Charles J. Adams*. Edited by Wael B. Hallaq and Donald P. Little, 41–56. Leiden: E.J. Brill, 1991.

Brockelmann, Carl. *Geschichte der arabischen Litteratur*. 6 vols. Leiden: E.J. Brill, 1937–49.

Brown, Edward Granville. *A Literary History of Persia: From Firdawsī to Saʿdī*. New York: Charles Scribner's & Sons, 1906.

Bruijn, J.T.P. de. *Of Piety and Poetry: The Interaction of Religion and Literature in the Life and Works of Ḥakīm Sanāʾī of Ghazna*. Leiden: E.J. Brill, 1983.

———. *Persian Sufi Poetry: An Introduction to the Mystical Use of Classical Poems*. Surrey, U.K.: Curzon, 1997.

Brunschvig, R. Perspectives." In *Unity and Variety in Muslim Civilization*. Edited by G.E. von Grunebaum. Chicago: University of Chicago Press, 1955.

Bukhārī, Abū Ibrāhīm Ismāʿīl ibn Muḥammad Mustamlī. *Sharḥ-i taʿarruf li madhhab at-taṣawwuf*. Edited by Muhammad Rawshan. 4 vols. Tehran, 1363/1984.

Bulliet, Richard. *The Patricians of Nishapur*. Cambridge: Harvard University Press, 1972.

Campanini, Massimo. "In Defence of Sunnism: al-Ghazālī and the Seljuqs." In *The Seljuqs: Politics Society and Culture*. Edited by Christian Lange and Songül Mecit, 228–239. Edinburgh: Edinburgh University Press, 2011.

Chabbi, Jaqueline. "Remarques sur le development historique des mouvements ascètiques et mystiques au Khurasan." *Studia Islamica* 46 (1977): 5–72.

Chittick, William C. "The Aesthetics of Islamic Ethics." In *Sharing Poetic Expressions: Beauty, Sublime, Mysticism in Islamic and Occidental Culture*. Edited by A.T. Tymieniecka, 3–14. Dordrecht: Springer, 2011.

———. "The Anthropology of Compassion." *Journal of the Muhyiddin ibn 'Arabi Society* 48 (2010): 1–15.

———. "Divine and Human Love in Islam." In *Divine Love: Perspectives from the World's Religious Traditions*. Edited by Jeff Levin and Stephen G. Post, 163–200. West Conshohocken, Pa.: Templeton Press, 2010.

———. *Divine Love: Islamic Literature and the Path to God*. New Haven/London: Yale University Press, 2013.

———. *Faith and Practice of Islam*. Albany: State University of New York Press, 1992.

———. *Ibn 'Arabi: Heir to the Prophets*. Oxford: Oneworld, 2005.

———. *Imaginal Worlds: Ibn al-ʿArabī and the Problem of Religious Diversity*. Albany: State University of New York Press, 1994.

———. *In Search of the Lost Heart: Explorations in Islamic Thought*. Edited by Mohammed Rustom, Atif Khalil, and Kazuyo Murata. Albany: State University of New York Press, 2012.

———. "Love as the Way to Truth." *Sacred Web* 15 (2005): 15–27.

———. *Me & Rumi: The Autobiography of Shams-i Tabrizi*. Louisville, Ky.: Fons Vitae, 2004.

———. *The Sufi Path of Knowledge: Ibn al-ʿArabī's Metaphysics of Imagination*. Albany: State University of New York Press, 1989.

———. *The Sufi Path of Love: The Spiritual Teachings of Rumi*. Albany: State University of New York Press, 1983.

———. *Sufism: A Beginner's Guide*. Oxford: Oneworld, 2008.

———. "The Sword of *Lā* and the Fire of Love." *Mawlana Rumi Review* 2 (2011): 10–27.

Corbin, Henry. *Spiritual Body and Celestial Earth*. Translated by Nancy Pearson. Princeton, NJ: Princeton University Press, 1977.

———. *The Man of Light in Iranian Sufism*. Translated by Nancy Pearson. Boulder, Colo.: Shambhala, 1978.

Cornell, Vincent. *The Way of Abū Madyān*. Cambridge: Islamic Texts Society, 1996.

Dabashi, Hamid. "'Ayn al-Quḍāt Hamadānī and the Intellectual Climate of His Times." *History of Islamic Philosophy*. Edited by Seyyed Hossein Nasr and Oliver Leaman, 2:374–433. New York: Routledge, 1996.

———. 'Ayn al-Quḍāt Hamadānī va *Risālah-yi Shakwā al-gharīb*-i ū." *Irān-Nāma* 41 (1992): 57–74.

———. "Historical Conditions of Persian Sufism during the Seljuq Period." In *Classical Persian Sufism: From its Origins to Rumi*. Edited by Leonard Lewisohn, 137–174. London: Khaniqahi Nimatullahi Publications, 1993.

———. *Truth and Narrative: The Untimely Thoughts of ʿAyn al-Quḍāt al-Hamadhānī.* Richmond, Surrey: Curzon, 1999.

Dahbi, Muhammad. *La citadelle de Dieu (Le dépouillement dans la parole de l'Unité).* Paris: Les Editions Iqra, 1995.

Dakake, Maria M. "Guest of the Inmost Heart: Conceptions of the Divine Beloved among Early Sufi Women." *Comparative Islamic Studies* (2008): 72–97.

Davis, Craig. "The Yogic Exercises of the 17th Century Sufis," in *Theory and Practice of Yoga: Essays in Honour of Gerald James Larson.* Edited by Knut A. Jacobsen, 303–316. Delhi: Motilal Banarsidass, 2005.

Daylamī, Abu'l-Ḥasan. *ʿAṭf al-alif al-maʾlūf ʿala'l-lām al-maʿṭūf: Livre de l' inclinasion de l'alif uni sur le lām inlcliné.* Edited by J. C. Vadet. Cairo: L'Institute Francais d'Archeologie Orientale, 1962; *A Treatise on Mystical Love.* Translated by Joseph Norment Bell and Hasan Mahmood Abdul Latif Al Shafie. Edinburgh: Edinburgh University Press, 2006.

Derin, Suleyman. *Love in Sufism: From Rabia to Ibn al-Farid.* Istanbul: Insan Publications, 2008.

Deweese, Devin. "Review of Omid Safi's *The Politics of Knowledge in Premodern Islam.*" *Journal of the American Academy of Religion* 76, no. 1 (2008): 177–183.

Dhahabī, Shams ad-Dīn Abū ʿAbd Allāh M. b. Aḥmad-al. *Mīzān al-iʿtidāl fī naqd ar-rijāl.* Edited by ʿAlī Muḥammad al-Bijāwī. Beirut: Dār Iḥyāʾ al-Kutub al-ʿArabiyyah, 1372/1963.

———. *Siyar aʿlām an-nubalāʾ.* Edited by Shuʿayb al-Arnaʾūṭ. 28 vols. Beirut: Muʾassassat ar-Risālah, 1996.

———. *Taʾrīkh al-Islām wa wafayāt al-mashāhīr wa'l-aʿlām.* Edited by ʿUmar ʿAbd as-Salām Tadmurī. Beirut: Dār al-Kitāb al-ʿArabī, 1415/1994.

Dunyā, Ibn Abī. *Tracts on Listening to Music: Being Dhamm al-malāhī.* Translated and edited by James Robson. Hertford: Stephen Austin & Sons, 1938.

Elias, Jamal J. *The Throne Carrier of God: The Life and Thought of ʿAlāʾ ad-Dawla as-Simnānī.* Albany: State University of New York Press, 1995.

Ephrat, Daphna. "The Seljuqs and the Public Sphere in the Period of Sunni Revivalism: The View from Baghdad" in *The Seljuqs: Politics Society and Culture.* Edited by Christian Lange and Songül Mecit, 139–156. Edinburgh: Edinburgh University Press, 2011.

Ernst, Carl. *Ruzbihan Baqli: Mysticism and the Rhetoric of Sainthood in Persian Sufism.* London: RoutledgeCurzon, 1996.

———. "Rūzbihān Baqlī on Love as 'Essential Desire.'" In *God is Beautiful and He loves Beauty: Festschrift in honour of Annemarie Schimmel.* Edited by A. Geise and J.C. Bürgel. Berlin: Peter Lang, 1994, 181–189.

———. "The Stages of Love in Early Persian Sufism, from Rabiʿa to Ruzbihan." In *The Heritage of Sufism. Vol. 1, Classical Persian Sufism from its Origins to Rumi* (700–1300). Edited by Leonard Lewisohn, 435–436. Oxford: Oneworld, 1999.

———. *Words of Ecstasy in Sufism*. Albany: State University of New York Press, 1984.

Esposito, John L. *Women in Muslim Family Law*. Syracuse, NY: Syracuse University Press, 1982.

Farmanish, Raḥīm. *Aḥwāl wa athār-i ʿAyn-i Quḍāt*. Tehran: Chāp-i Āftāb, 1959.

Feuillebois-Pierunek, Eve. "Mystical Quest and Oneness in the Mukhtār-nāma Attributed to Farīd al-Dīn ʿAṭṭār." In *Aṭṭār and the Persian Sufi Tradition*. Edited by Leonard Lewisohn and Christopher Shackle, 309–329. London: I.B. Tauris, 2006.

Garden, Kenneth. *The First Islamic Reviver*. London/New York: Oxford University Press, 2014.

Ghazālī, Abū Ḥāmid al-. *The Alchemy of Happiness*. Translated by Jay R. Crook. Chicago: Kazi Publications, 2002.

———. *Ihyā' ʿulūm al-dīn*. 4 vols. Beirut: Dār al-Hādi, 1993.

———. *Kimiyā-yi saʿādat*. Edited by Aḥmad Ārām. Tehran: Kitābfurūshī-i Markazī, 1365/1966.

———. *Love, Longing, Intimacy, and Contentment*. Translated by Eric Ormsby Cambridge: Islamic Texts Society, 2011.

———. *The Marvels of the Heart*. Translated by Walter James Skellie. Louisville, Ky.: Fons Vitae, 2010.

Ghazi bin Muhammad. *Love in the Holy Quran*. Chicago: Kazi Publications, 2011.

Ghomshei, Husayn Ilahi-. "The Principles of the Religion of Love in Classical Persian Poetry." In *Hafiz and the Religion of Love in Classical Persian Poetry*. Edited by L. Lewisohn, 77–106. London: I.B. Tauris, 2010.

Giffen, Lois Anita. *Theory of Profane Love Among the Arabs: The Development of the Genre*. New York: New York University Press, 1971.

Gramlich, Richard. *Aḥmad Ghazzālī, Gedanken über die Liebe*. Wiesbaden: Franz Steiner, 1976.

———. *Alte Vorbilder des Sufitums 1 Scheiche des Westens*. Wiesbaden: Otto Harrasowitz, 1995.

———. *Alte Vorbilder des Sufitums 2 Scheiche des Ostens*. Wiesbaden: Otto Harrasowitz, 1996.

———. *Der reine Gottesglaube: das Wort des Einheitsbekenntnisses: Aḥmad Al-Ghazzālis Schrift At-Tağrid fī kalimat at-tawḥīd*. Wiesbaden: Otto Harrasowitz, 1983.

———. *Die schiitschen Derwischorden Persiens: Affiliationen*. Wiesbaden: Franz Steiner, 1965.

Green, Nile. *Sufism: A Global History*. Oxford/Malden: Wiley-Blackwell, 2012.

Griffel, Frank. *Al-Ghazālī's Philosophical Theology*. Oxford/New York: Oxford University Press, 2009.

Ḥadīd, Ibn Abī -al. *Sharḥ Nahj al-balāghah*. Edited by Ḥasan Tamīm. Beirut: Dār Maktabat al-Ḥayāt, 1963.

Ḥallāj, al-Ḥusayn b. Manṣūr al-. *Kitāb aṭ-Ṭawasīn*. Edited by Louis Massignon. Paris: P. Geuthner, 1913. Reprint: Paris: Dar Albouraq, 1970.

———. *Diwān al-Ḥallāj*. Edited by Saʿdī Dannāwī. Beirut: Dār aṣ-Ṣādir, 1998.

Hallaq, Wael B. "Was al-Shāfiʿī the Master Architect of Islamic Jurisprudence?" *International Journal of Middle Eastern Studies* 25 (1993): 595–597.

Hamadānī, ʿAyn al-Quḍāt Abu'l-Maʿālī ʿAbdallāh b. Muḥammad b. ʿAlī al-Mīyānajī. *Nāmahā*. Edited by ʿAlī Naqī Munzawī (vols. 1–3) and ʿAfīf ʿUsayrān (vols. 1–2). Tehran: Intishārāt-i Āsāṭīr, 1998.

———. Extracted English translations by Omid Safi as *The Letters* in *An Anthology of Philosophy in Persia*. Edited by Seyyed Hossein Nasr and Mehdi Aminrazavi, 4:401–412. London: I.B. Tauris in association with The Institute of Ismaili Studies, 2015.

———. *Tamhīdāt*. Edited by ʿAfīf ʿUsayrān. Tehran: Tehran University Press, 1962; English translation by Omid Safi as *The Tamhidat of ʿAyn al-Qudat Hamadani*. Mahwah, NJ: Paulist Press, forthcoming.

———. *Shakwā al-gharīb*. In ʿAyn al-Quḍāt Hamadānī, *Zubdat al-ḥaqāʾiq*. Edited by ʿAfīf ʿUsayrān. Tehran: Intishārāt-i Dānishgāh-i Tehrān, 1962. English translation by A.J. Arberry as *A Sufi Martyr*. London: Keagan and Paul, 1969.

———. *Zubdat al-ḥaqāʾiq*. Edited by ʿAfīf ʿUsayrān. Tehran: Intishārāt-i Dānishgāh-i Tehrān, 1961. English translation by Omar Jah as *The Zubdat al-Ḥaqāʾiq of ʿAyn al-Quḍāh al-Hamadānī*. Kuala Lumpur: ISTAC, 2000.

Ḥamawī, Shihāb ald-Dīn Yāqūt al-. *Muʿjam al-buldān*. Beirut: Dār Beirut li'ṭ-Ṭibāʿah wa'n-Nashr, 1376/1957.

Heath, Peter. *Allegory and Philosophy in Avicenna (Ibn Sīnā), with a Translation of the Book of the Prophet Muhammad's Ascent to Heaven*. Philadelphia: University of Pennsylvania Press, 1992.

Hodgson, Marshall. *The Venture of Islam*. Chicago: University of Chicago Press, 1975.

Homerin, Th. Emil. *The Wine of Love and Life: Ibn al-Fāriḍ's al-Khamrīyah and al-Qayṣarī's Quest for Meaning*. Chicago: Middle East Documentation Center, 2005.

Hujwīrī, ʿAlī ibn ʿUthmān. *Kashf al-maḥjūb*. Edited by Maḥmūd ʿĀbidī. Tehran: Surūsh, 2004. English translation by R. A. Nicholson as *The Kashf al-Mahjūb: The Oldest Persian Treatise on Sufism*. Leiden: E.J. Brill/London: Luzac, 1911.

Hussaini, Syed Shah Khusro. *Sayyid Muḥammad al-Ḥusaynī-i Gīsūdirāz: On Sufism*. Delhi: Idarah-i Adabiyat-i Delli, 1983.

Ibn al-ʿArabī, Muḥyi'd-Dīn. *al-Futuḥāt al-makkiyyah*. 4 vols. Beirut: Dār Ṣādir, n.d.

———. *Traité de l'amour*. Translated by Maurice Gloton. Paris: Albin Michel, 1986.

Ibn al-Athīr. *The Annals of the Saljuq Turks: Selections from al-Kāmil fī'l-Taʾrīkh of ʿIzz al-Dīn Ibn al-Athīr*. Translated by D.S. Richards, London: Routledge, 2002.

Ibn Dabbāgh. *Kitāb Mashāriq anwār al-qulūb wa mafātiḥ asrār al-ghuyūb*. Edited by Hellmut Ritter. Beirut: Dār Ṣadir, 1959.

Ibn al-Fāriḍ, ʿUmar. *Dīwān*. Translated by Emil Homerin as *ʿUmar Ibn al-Fāriḍ: Sufi Verse, Saintly Life*. Mahwah, N.J.: Paulist Press, 2001.

Ibn al-Jawzī, Abu'l-Faraj ʿAbd ar-Raḥmān b. ʿAlī. *al-Muntaẓam fi't-ta'rīkh al-mulūk wa'l-umam*. Beirut: Dār al-Kutub al-ʿIlmiyyah, 1413/1992.

———. *Kitāb al-quṣṣāṣ wa'l-mudhakkirīn*. Edited and translated by Merlin S. Swartz. Beirut: Dār al-Machreq, 1986.

Ibn Kathīr, Ismāʿīl b. ʿUmar ad-Dimashqī, *al-Bidāyah wa'n-nihāyah fi't-ta'rīkh*. Beirut: Darussalam, 2000.

Ibn al-Munawwar, Muḥammad. *Asrār at-tawḥīd fī maqāmāt as-shaykh Abī Saʿīd*. Edited by Muḥammad Riḍā Shāfiʿī Kadakānī. Tehran: Intishārāt-i Āgāh, 1987. Translated by John O'Kane as *The Secrets of God's Mystical Oneness [Asrār at-Tawḥīd]*. Costa Mesa and New York: Mazda Press and Bibliotheca Persica, 1992.

Ibn an-Najjār, al-Ḥāfiẓ. *al-Mustafād min dhayl ta'rīkh Baghdād*. Beirut: Dār al-Kutub al-ʿIlmiyyah, 1978.

Ibn Qayyim al-Jawziyyah. *Rawḍat al-muḥibbīn wa-nuzhat al-mushtāqīn*. Aleppo: Dār al-Waʿī, 1397/1977.

Ibn Tufayl, Abu Bakr. *Hayy ibn Yaqẓān*. Translated by Lenn Evan Goodman. Los Angeles: Gee Tee Bee, 1991.

Ikhwān aṣ-Ṣafā'. *Rasā'il Ikhwān aṣ-Ṣafā'*. 4 vols. Beirut: Dār Ṣāḍir, 1957.

ʿImād, ʿAbd al-Ḥayy b. Aḥmad Ibn -al. *Shadharāt adh-dhahab fī akhbār man dhahab*. Beirut: n.p., 1931.

Irāqī, Fakhr ad-Dīn -al. *Lamaʿāt*. Edited by Muḥammad Khwājawī. Tehran: Intishārāt-i Mawlā, 1413 AH, 45; Edited by Javad Nurbakhsh. Tehran: Intisharat-i Khānaqah-i Niʿmatullāhī, 1353/1974. English translation by W.C. Chittick and Peter Lamborn Wilson as *Fakhr ad-Dīn ʿIrāqī: Divine Flashes*. New York: Paulist Press, 1982.

Irbilī, Ibn al-Muṣtawfī Sharaf ad-Dīn al-. *Ta'rīkh Irbil: Nabāhat al-balad al-khāmil bi man waradahu min al-amāthil*. Baghdad: Dār ar-Rashīd li'n-Nashr; Wizārat Thaqāfa wa'l-Aʿlām al-Jumhūriyyah al-ʿIrāqiyyah, 1972.

Iṣfahānī, Abū Nuʿaym Aḥmad b. ʿAbd Allāh al-. *Ḥilyat al-awliyā'*. Edited by Muṣṭafā ʿAbd al-Qādir ʿAṭā'. Beirut: Dār al-Kutub al-ʿIlmiyyah, 1997.

Iṣfahānī, Imād ad-Dīn al-. *Kitāb Zubdat an-nuṣrah wa-nukhbat al-ʿuṣrah*. Leiden: E.J. Brill,1889.

Iskandārī, Aḥmad b. Muḥammad Ibn ʿAṭā'ullāh al-. *Miftāḥ al-falāḥ wa- miṣbāḥ al-arwāḥ*. Cairo: Muṣṭafā al-Bābī al-Ḥalabī, 1381/1961.

Isnawī, Jamāl ad-Dīn ʿAbd ar-Raḥmān b. al-Ḥasan. *Ṭabaqāt ash-shāfiʿiyyah*, Baghdad: n.p., 1391.

Izutsu, Toshihiko. "Mysticism and the Linguistic Problem of Equivocation in the Thought of 'Ayn al-Qudat Hamadani." *Studia Islamica* 30 (1976): 153–170. Reprinted in Izutsu, *Creation and the Timeless Order of Things: Essays in Islamic Mystical Philosophy*, 98–118. Ashland, Ore.: White Cloud Press, 1994.

———. "Creation and the Timeless Order of Things: A Study in the Mystical Philosophy of 'Ayn al-Qudat Hamadani." *Philosophical Forum* 4, no. 1 (1972): 124–140. Reprinted in Izutsu, *Creation and the Timeless Order of Things: Essays in Islamic Mystical Philosophy*, 119–140. Ashland, Ore: White Cloud Press, 1994.

Jahanbakhsh, Forugh. "The Pīr-Murīd Relationship in the Thought of 'Ayn al-Quḍāt Hamadānī." In *Consciousness and Reality: Studies in Memory of Toshihiko Izutsu*. Edited by S.J. Āshtiyānī et al., 129–147. Leiden: E.J. Brill, 1998.

Jalāl al-Dīn Rūmī. *Diwān-i Shams-i Tabrīzī*. Edited by Badiuzzaman Furuzanfar. Tehran: Amīr Kabīr.

———. *Mathnawī-yi ma'nawī*. Edited and translated by R.A. Nicholson as *The Mathnawí of Jalál'uddín Rúmí*. London: Luzac, 1925–1940.

Jāmī, 'Abd ar-Raḥmān. *Ashi''at al-Lama'āt*. Qum: Būstān-i Kitāb-Qum, 1383/2004.

———. *Nafaḥāt al-uns min ḥaḍarāt al-quds*. Edited by Maḥmūd 'Ābidī. Tehran: Intishārāt-i Iṭṭila'āt, 1380 HS.

Kaḥḥālah, Umar Riḍā. *Mu'jam al-mu'allifīn tarājim muṣannifi'l-kutub al-'arabiyyah*. Beirut: Mu'assasat al-Risālah, 1986.

Kalābādhī, Abū Bakr al-. *The Doctrine of the Sufis*. Translated by A. J. Arberry. Lahore: Sh. Muhammad Ashraf, 1966.

———. *at-Ta'arruf li-madhhab ahl at-taṣawwuf*. Edited by 'Abd al-Ḥalīm Maḥmūd and Tāhā 'Abd al-Bāqi Surūr. Cairo, 1960.

Karamustafa, Ahmet T. *Sufism: The Formative Period*. Edinburgh: Edinburgh University Press, 2007.

Keeler, Annabel. *Sufi Hermeneutics: The Qur'an Commentary of Rashīd al-Dīn Maybudī*. Oxford: Oxford University Press, 2006.

Khalil, Atif. "Abū Ṭālib al-Makkī and the *Nourishment of Hearts* (*Qūt al-Qulūb*) in the Context of Early Sufism." *Muslim World* 102, no. 2 (2012): 335–356.

———. "*Tawba* in the Sufi Psychology of Abū Ṭālib al-Makkī (d. 996)." *Oxford Journal of Islamic Studies* 23, no. 3 (2012): 294–324.

Khwāndamīr, Ghiyāth ad-Dīn b. Hamām ad-Dīn. *Ta'rīkh ḥabīb as-siyar fī akhbār afrād bashar*. Tehran: Kitābkhāne-yi Khayyām, 1333.

Khwānsārī, Bāqir al-Mūsawī al-Iṣfahānī. *Rawḍāt al-jannāt fī aḥwāl al-'ulamā' wa's-sādāt*. Tehran: Dār al-Kutub al-Islāmiyyah, 1962.

Kīmīyā'ī, Mas'ūd. *'Ayn al-Quḍāt*. Tehran: Farhang-i Kāwush, 1997.

Knysh, Alexander. *Islamic Mysticism: A Short History*. Leiden: E.J. Brill, 2000.

Kubrā, Najm ad-Dīn. "*Fawā'iḥ al-ǧamāl wa fawātiḥ al-ǧalāl*. Edited by Fritz Meier. Wiesbaden: Franz Steiner, 1957.

Kutubī, Muḥammad b. Shākir. *'Uyūn at-tawārīkh*. Edited by Fayṣal as-Sāmir. Baghdad: Wizārat al-A'lām, al-Jumhūriyyah al-'Irāqiyyah, 1397/1977.

Landolt, Hermann. "Der Breifwechsel zwischen Kāšānī und Simnānī über Waḥdat al-Wuǧūd. In Landolt, *Recherches en Spiritualité Iranienne*, 245–300. Tehran: Institut Fraçais de Recherche en Iran, 2005.

———. "Simnānī on waḥdat-al-wujûd." In *Collected Papers on Islamic Philosophy and Mysticism*. Edited M. Mohaghegh and H. Landolt. Tehran: Dānishgāh-i Makgīl, 1971.

———. "Walaya." *Encyclopedia of Religion*. New York: MacMillan, 1987.

Laugier de Beaurecueil, *Serge de. Khwadja 'Abdullah Ansari (396–481H./1006–1089): Mystique hanbalite*. Beirut: Institut de Lettres orientales, 1965.

Lange, Christian. *Justice, Punishment and the Medieval Muslim Imagination.* Cambridge: Cambridge University Press, 2008.

Lange, Christian and Mecit, Songül (eds.), *The Seljuqs: Politics, Society and Culture.* Edinburgh: Edinburgh University Press, 2011.

Lawrence, Bruce. "The *Lawa'ih* of Qazi Hamid Ud-Din *Naguri.*" *Indo-Iranica* 28, no. 1 (1975): 34–53.

Lewis, Bernard. *The Assassins.* New York: Basic Books, 1968.

Lewis, Franklin. *Rumi: Past and Present, East and West.* Oxford: Oneworld, 2000.

Lewisohn, Leonard. (ed.). *ʿAṭṭār and the Persian Sufi Tradition: The Art of Spiritual Flight.* London: Tauris, 2006.

———. *Beyond Faith and Infidelity: The Sufi Poetry and Teachings of Mahmud Shabistari*: Richmond: Curzon: 1995.

———. "Divine Love in Islam." In *Encyclopaedia of Love in World Religions.* Edited by Yudit Greenberg, 1:163–165. New York: Macmillan Reference & Thomson Gale, 2007.

———. (ed.). *Hafiz and the Religion of Love in Classical Persian Poetry.* London: I.B. Tauris, 2010.

———. (ed.). *The Heritage of Sufism: Classical Persian Sufism from its Origins to Rumi (700–1300).* Oxford: Oneworld, 1999.

———. "In Quest of Annihilation: Imaginalization and Mystical Death in the *Tamhīdāt* of ʿAyn al-Quḍāt Hamadhānī." In *The Heritage of Sufism,* Edited by Leonard Lewisohn (vols. 1–3) and David Morgan, 1:285–336 (vol. 3). Oxford: Oneworld, 1999.

———. "Sufism's Religion of Love, from Rābiʿa to Ibn al-ʿArabī." In *The Cambridge Companion to Sufism.* Edited by Lloyd Ridgeon,150–180. Cambridge: Cambridge University Press, 2015.

———. "Sawanih" in *Encyclopedia of Love in World Religions.* Edited by Yudit Kornberg Greenberg, 2:535–538. New York: Macmillan Reference & Thomson Gale, 2007.

———. *The Wisdom of Sufism.* Oxford: Oneworld, 2001.

Lings, Martin. *Sufi Poetry: A Medieval Anthology.* Cambridge, Islamic Texts Society, 2004.

Lumbard, Joseph Edward Barbour. "From Ḥubb to ʿIshq: The Development of Love in Early Sufism." *Journal of Islamic Studies* 18 (2007): 345–385.

———. Field Notes, January 2001. Ms. in possession of author.

———. "The Function of Dhikru Llāh in Sufi Psychology." In *Knowledge is Light: Essays in Honor of Seyyed Hossein Nasr.* Edited by Zailan Moris, 251–274. Chicago: Kazi Publications, 1999.

———. "Review of Hamid Dabashi, *Truth and Narrative: The Untimely Thoughts of ʿAyn al-Quḍāt Hamadhānī.*" *Muslim World* 96 (2006): 532–534.

———. Selections from Aḥmad al-Ghazālī's *Sawāniḥ* in *An Anthology of Philosophy in Persia.* Edited by Seyyed Hossein Nasr with Mehdi Aminrazavi, 4:375–397. London: I.B. Tauris, in association with The Institute of Ismaili Studies, 2008–2015.

Makdisi, George. "Muslim Institutions of Learning in Eleventh-Century Baghdad." In *Religion, Law, and Learning in Classical Islam*. Brookfield: Variorum, 1990.

Makkī, Abū Ṭālib. *Qūt al-qulūb fī mu'āmalāt al-maḥbūb wa-waṣf ṭarīq al-murīd ilā maqām at-tawḥīd*. Edited by Sa'īd Nasīb Makārim. Beirut: Dār Ṣādir, 1995.

Massignon, Louis. *The Passion of al-Ḥallāj*. Translated by Herbert Mason. Princeton, NJ: Princeton University Press, 1982.

Maybudī, Rashīd ad-Dīn. *Kashf al-asrār wa-'uddat al-abrār*. Edited by 'Alī Asghar Ḥikmat. 10 vols. Tehran: Danishgāh, 1331–1339/1952–1960.

Mayhanī, Muḥammad Ibn Munawwar. *Asrār-i tawḥīd fī maqāmāt Shaykh Abī Sa'īd*. Edited by Muḥammad Riḍā Shāfi'ī Kadkanī. Tehran: Mu'assasah-yi Intishārāt-i Āgāh, 1376.

Meisami, Julie Scott. *Medieval Persian Court Poetry*. Princeton, NJ: Princeton University Press, 1987.

Michon, Jean-Louis. "Sacred Music and Dance in Islam." In *Islamic Spirituality: Manifestations*. Edited by S.H. Nasr, 2:469–505. New York: Crossroad, 1994.

Mojaddedi, Jawid. *Beyond Dogma: Rumi's Teachings on Friendship with God and Early Sufi Theories*. New York: Oxford University Press, 2012.

Morris, James. "Ibn 'Arabi's 'Short Course' on Love." *Journal of the Muhyiddin ibn 'Arabi Society* 50. (2011): 1–22.

Mottahedeh, Roy. *Loyalty and Leadership in an Early Islamic Society*. Princeton, NJ: Princeton University Press, 1980.

Mujāhid, Aḥmad. Introduction to *Samā' wa futuwwah* by Aḥmad aṭ-Ṭūsī, 17–18. Tehran: Kitābkhānah-yi Manūchihrī, 1981.

———. *Majmū'ah-yi āthār-i fārsi-yi Aḥmad Ghazālī*. Tehran: Mu'assasah-yi Intishārāt wa Chāp-i Dānishgāh-i Tehrān, 1358/1979.

———. (ed.) *Sharḥ-i Sawāniḥ: seh sharḥ bar Sawāniḥ al-'ushshāq-i Aḥmad Ghazālī*. Tehran: Surūsh Press, 1372 HS.

Mulk, Niẓām ad-Dīn. *The Book of Government and Rules for Kings*. Translated by Hubert Drake. London: Routledge & Kegan Paul, 1960.

Munāwī, 'Abd ar-Ra'ūf b. Tāj al-'Ārifīn -al. *al-Kawākib ad-durriyyah fī tarājim as-sāda aṣ-ṣūfiyyah*. Edited by 'Abd al-Ḥāmid Ṣāliḥ Ḥimdān. Cairo: al-Maktabat al-Azhariyyah li't-turāth, 1994.

Murata, Sachiko, William Chittick, and Tu Weiming. *The Sage Learning of Liu Zhi: Islamic Thought in Confucian Terms*. Cambridge: Harvard University Press, 2009.

———. *The Tao of Islam: A Sourcebook on Gender Relationships in Islamic Thought*. Albany: State University of New York Press, 1992.

Nasr, Seyyed Hossein. "Foreword." In William C. Chittick, *Divine Love: Islamic Literature and the Path to God*, vii–x. New Haven: Yale University Press, 2013.

———. *The Heart of Islam*. San Francisco: HarperOne, 2004.

———. Introduction to *The Rise and Development of Persian Sufism*. Edited by Leonard Lewisohn. London/New York: Khaniqahi Nimatullahi Publications, 1993, 1–18.

———. *Islamic Art and Spirituality*. Albany: State University of New York Press, 1987.

———. (ed.). *Islamic Spirituality I: Foundations*. New York: Crossroad Publication Company, 1991.

———. (ed.). *Islamic Spirituality II: Manifestations*. New York: Crossroad Publication Company, 1994.

———. "Mystical Philosophy in Islam." *The Routledge Encyclopedia of Philosophy*. Edited by Edward Craig, 6:616–620. London: Routledge, 1998.

Nīshāpūrī, Ẓāhir ad-Dīn. *The History of the Seljuq Turks From The Jāmiʿ al-Tawārīkh: An Ilkhanid Adaptation of the Saljūq-nāma*. Translated by Kenneth Allin Luther. London: Curzon, 2001.

———. *Saljūq-nāmah*. Tehran: Kalāla Khāvar, 1953.

Nwiya, Paul. "Le Tafsir mystique attribue à Jaʿfar Ṣādiq." *Mélanges de L'Université Saint Joseph* 43 (1968): 181–230.

———. *Trois oeuvres inédites de mystiques musulmans*. Beirut: Dār al-Mashriq, 1972

Nurbaksh, Javad, "The Nimatullāhī." In *Islamic Spirituality II: Manifestations*. Edited by S.H. Nasr, 144–161. New York: Crossroad Publication Company, 1987–1991.

Ohlander, Erik, S. *Sufism in an Age of Transition: ʿUmar al-Suhrawardī and the Rise of the Islamic Mystical Brotherhoods*. Leiden: E.J. Brill, 2008.

Papan-Matin, Firoozeh. "'Ayn al-Qudat al-Hamadhani, His Work, and His Connection with the Early Chishti Mystics." *Comparative Studies of South Asia, Africa and the Middle East* 30, no. 3 (2010): 341–355.

———. *Beyond Death: Mystical Teachings of ʿAyn al-Quḍāt Hamadhānī*. Leiden: E.J. Brill, 2010.

———. "Gisudaraz, an Early Chishti Leader of the Deccan, and His Relationship with Twelfth-Century Mystics of Iran." *The Journal for Deccan Studies* (special issue on "Sufism in the Deccan." Edited by Scott Kugle and M. Suleman Siddiqi) 7, no. 2 (2009): 112–132.

Peacock, A.C.S. *Early Seljūq History: A New Interpretation*. London: Routledge, 2010.

Picken, Gavin. *Spiritual Purification in Islam: The Life and Works of al-Muḥāsibī*. New York: Routledge, 2012.

Pourjavady, Nasrollah. "Ahmed et Mohammad al-Ghazali: influence reciproque." In *Ghazali: la raison et le miracle*, 163–168. Table ronde UNESCO 9-10, Paris, 1987.

———. "ʿĀlam-i khayyāl az naẓr-i Aḥmad Ghazālī." *Maʿāref* 3, no. 2 (1986): 3–54.

———. *ʿAyn al-Quḍāt wa ustādān-i ū*. Tehran: Intishārāt-i Aṣāṭīr, 1995.

———. "Metaphysik der Liebe: Der Sufismus des Ahmad al-Gazzali." *Spektrum Iran* 3, no. 1 (1990): 45–72.

———. "Mūnis al-ʿushshāq-i Suhrawardī wa taʾthīr-i ān dar adabiyyāt-i fārsī," *Nashr-i Dānish*, 18, no. 2 (1380/2001), 7.

———. "Selfhood and Time in the Sufism of Ahmad Ghazzali." *Sophia Perennis* 4, no. 2 (1981): 32–37.

———. Stories of Aḥmad al-Ghazālī 'Playing the Witness' in Tabrīz (Shams-i Tabrīzī's Interest in *shāhid bāzī*). Translated by Scott Kugle in *Reason and Inspiration in Islam: Theology, Philosophy, and Mysticism in Muslim Thought*. Edited by Todd Lawson, 200–220. London: I.B. Tauris in association with The Institute of Ismaili Studies, 2005.

———. *Sulṭān-i ṭarīqāt*. Tehran: Intishārāt-i Agāh, 1979.

———. *Zabān-i ḥāl dar 'irfān wa adabiyyāt-i Pārsī*. Tehran: Intishārāt-i Ḥirmis, 2006.

Qazwīnī, 'Abd al-Karīm b. Muḥammad ar-Rāfi'ī. *at-Tadwīn fī akhbār Qazwīn*. Edited by 'Azīz Allāh al-'Aṭṭārī. Beirut: Dār al-Kutub al-'Ilmiyyah, 1987.

———. *Āthār al-bilād wa akhbār al-'ibād*. Edited by al-Imām al-'Ālim. Beirut: Dār Ṣādir, 1960.

Qushayrī, Abu'l-Qāsim -al. *Laṭā'if al-ishārāt*. Edited by Ibrahim Basyuni. 6 vols. Cairo: Dār al-Kātib li't-Tibā'ah wa'n-Nashr, 1971. "*Laṭā'if al-ishārāt*"

———. *Al-Qushayri's Epistle on Sufism*. Translated by Alexander D. Knysh. Reading, U.K.: Garnet, 2007.

———. *Al-Risālah*. Edited by 'Abd al-Halīm Maḥmūd and Maḥmūd ibn ash-Sharīf. Cairo: Dār al-Kutub al-Ḥadīthah, 1972–1974.

———. *ar-Risālah al-Qushayriyyah*. Translated by Barbara Von Schlegell. Berkeley: Mizan Press, 1990.

Radtke, Bernd. "Review of Firoozeh Papan-Matin's *Beyond Death: The Mystical Teachings of 'Ayn al-Quḍāt al-Hamadhānī*." *Oriens* 41, no. 1–2 (2013): 194–205.

Rawan Farhadi, A. G. *Abdullah Ansari of Herat (1006–1089 CE): An Early Sufi Master*. Richmond, U.K.: Curzon Press, 1996.

Ridgeon, Lloyd. "The Controversy of Shaykh Awḥad al-Dīn Kirmānī and Handsome, Moon-Faced Youths: A Case Study of *Shāhid-Bāzī* in Medieval Sufism." *Journal of Sufi Studies* 1, no. 1 (2012): 3–30.

———. *Javanmardi: A Sufi Code of Honour*. Edinburgh: Edinburgh University Press, 2011.

———. *Morals and Mysticism in Persian Sufism: A History of Sufi*-Futuwwat *in Iran*. Abingdon: Routledge, 2010.

———. *Persian Metaphysics and Mysticism: Selected Treatises of 'Azīz Nasafī*. Richmond: Curzon, 2002.

Rāwandī, Muḥammad. *Rāḥat aṣ-ṣudūr*. Edited by Muḥammad Iqbāl. London: Luzac & Co., 1921.

Rāzī, Najm ad-Dīn. *Mirṣād al-'ibād min al-mabda' ila'l-ma'ād*. Edited by Muḥammad Amīn Riyāḥī. Tehran: Sharīkat-i Intishārāt-i 'Ilmī wa-Farhangī, 2000.

Ritter, Hellmut. *The Ocean of the Soul: Man, the World, and God in the Stories of Farid al-Din 'Attar*. Translated by John O'Kane and Bernt Radtke. Leiden: E.J. Brill, 2003.

———. "al-Ghazālī, Aḥmad." *Encyclopaedia of Islam, Second Edition*. Edited by P. Bearman, Th. Bianquis, C.E. Bosworth, E. van Donzel, W.P. Heinrichs. Brill Online, 2014.

Riyāḍī, Hashmatallāh. *Āyāt-i ḥusn wa-'ishq*. Tehran: Kitābkhānah-yi Ṣāliḥ, 1369/1989.

Rizvi, Saiyid Athar Abbas. *A History of Sufism in India*. New Delhi: New Delhi: Munshiram Manoharlal Publishers, 2003 (reprint).

Robinson, Francis. *A Historical Atlas of the Islamic World Since 1500*. New York: Facts on File, 1982.

Rusek, Renata. The Defence of Eblis by 'Eyno-l-Qozāt-e-Hamadāni (1096/98–1131)." *Folia Orientalia* 40 (2004): 259–266.

Rustom, Mohammed. "Review of Firoozeh Papan-Matin's *Beyond Death: The Mystical Teachings of ʿAyn al-Quḍāt al-Hamadhānī*." *Journal of Sufi Studies* 2, no. 2 (2013): 213–216.

———. "Philosophical Sufism." In *The Routledge Companion to Islamic Philosophy*. Edited by Richard Taylor and Luis Xavier López-Farjeat, 399–411. New York: Routledge, 2015.

Rypka, Jan. *History of Iranian Literature*. Dordrecht: D. Reidel, 1968.

Sabzawārī, Ḥusayn b. Ḥasan. *Jawāhir al-asrār*. Lucknow: n.p., 1893.

Ṣādiq, Jaʿfar al-. *Spiritual Gems: The Mystical Qur'an Commentary Ascribed by the Sufis to Imam Jaʿfar al-Ṣādiq (d. 148/765)*. Translated by Farhana Mayer. Louisville, Ky.: Fons Vitae, 2011.

Ṣafadī, Ṣalāḥ ad-Dīn Khalīl b. Aybak al-, *al-Wāfī bi'l-wafayāt*. Edited by Youssef Najm. Wiesbaden: Franz Steiner Verlag, 1391/1971.

Safi, Omid. *The Politics of Knowledge in Premodern Islam*. Chapel Hill: University of North Carolina Press, 2006.

———. "The Sufi Path of Love in Iran and India." In *A Pearl in Wine: Essays on the Life, Music and Sufism of Hazrat Inayat Khan*. Edited by Pirzade Zia Inayat Khan, 221–266. New Lebanon: Omega Publications, 2001.

Sākit, Salmān. "ʿIshq az dīdgāh-i ʿAyn al-Quḍāt Hamadānī." *Nāma-yi Anjuman* 12 (2003): 92–112.

Samʿānī, Aḥmad. *Rawh al-arwāḥ fī sharḥ asmā' al-malik al-fattāḥ*. Edited by Najīb Māyil Hīrawi. Tehran: Shirkāt-i Intishārāt-i 'Ilmī wa Farhangī, 1368/1989.

Sanā'ī, Abu'l-Majd. *Dīwān*. Edited by Mudarris Raḍawī. Tehran: Ibn Sīnā, 1341/1962.

———. *Ḥadīqat al-ḥaqīqah wa sharīʿat at-ṭarīqah*. Edited by Maryam Ḥuṣaynī. Tehran: Markaz-i Nashr-i Dānishgāhī, 1382/2004.

Sattārī, Jalāl. *ʿIshq-i ṣūfiyyah*. Tehran: Nashr-i Markaz, 1374 AH/1995.

Schimmel, Annemarie. *And Muhammad Is His Messenger: The Veneration of the Prophet in Islamic Piety*. Chapel Hill: University of North Carolina Press, 1985.

———. *A Two-Colored Brocade: The Imagery of Persian Poetry*. Chapel Hill: University of North Carolina Press, 1992.

———. *Mystical Dimensions of Islam*. Chapel Hill: University of North Carolina Press, 1975.

Schmidt, Leigh Eric. "The Making of Modern 'Mysticism.'" *Journal of the American Academy of Religion* 71, no. 2 (2003): 273–302.

Sells, Michael. *Early Islamic Mysticism: Sufi, Qur'an, Miʿraj, Poetic and Theological Writings*. NY: Paulist Press, 1996.

Shafī'ī-Kadkānī, Muhammad-Riḍā. "Pīr-i Hirawī ghayr az Khwāja 'Abdallāh Anṣārī Ast." *Nāmah-yi Bahāristān* 10, 15 (2009): 175–192.

Shahrazūrī, Ibn aṣ-Ṣalāḥ al-. *Ṭabaqāt al-fuqahā' ash-shāfi'iyyah*. Beirut/London: Dār al-Bashā'ir al-Islāmiyyah, 1413/1996.

Shīrāzī, Muḥammad Ma'ṣūm 'Alī Shāh. *Ṭarā'iq al-ḥaqā'iq*. Tehran: Kitābkhānah-yi Bārānī, 1980.

Smith, Margaret. *Rābi'a the Mystic and Her Fellow Saints in Islam*. Cambridge: Cambridge University Press, 1928.

Smith, Wilfred Cantwell. *The Meaning and End of Religion*. Minneapolis: Fortress Press, 1990.

Subkī, Tāj ad-Dīn al-. *aṭ-Ṭabaqāt ash-shāfi'iyyah al-kubrā*. Cairo: 'Īsa'l-Bābī al-Ḥalabī, 1964–1976.

Suhrawardī, Shihāb ad-Dīn al-. "Fī ḥaqīqat al-'ishq/On the Reality of Love." In *The Philosophical Allegories and Mystical Treatises*. Translated by Wheeler Thackston. Costa Mesa, California: Mazda, 1999.

Suhrawardī, 'Umar ibn Muḥammad al-. *'Awārif al-ma'ārif*. Cairo: Maktabat al-Qāhirah, 1393/1973.

Sulamī, Abū 'Abd ar-Raḥmān -al. *aṭ-Ṭabaqāt aṣ-ṣūfiyyah*. Edited by Nūr ad-Dīn Sharība. Cairo: Maṭba'at al-Madanī, 1987.

Tabrīzī, Shams ad-Dīn. *Maqālāt-i Shams-i Tabrīz*. Edited by Muḥammad 'Alī Muwaḥḥid. Tehran: Intishārāt-i Khwārazmī, 1990.

Tabrīzī, Ḥāfiẓ Ḥusayn Karbalā'ī. *Rawḍāt al-jinān wa jannāt al-jinān*. Tehran, Bungāh-i Tarjumah va Nashr-i Kitāb, 1965–1970.

Takeshita, Masataka. "Continuity and Change in the Tradition of Shirazi Love Mysticism: A Comparison between Daylami's 'Atf al-Alif and Ruzbihan Baqli's Abhar al-Ashiqin." *Orient* 23 (1987).

Tor, D.G. "Sovereign and Pious: The Religious Life of the Great Seljuq Sultans." In *The Seljuqs: Politics Society and Culture*. Edited by Christian Lange and Songül Mecit, 39–62. Edinburgh: Edinburgh University Press, 2011.

Treiger, Alexander. "Al-Ghazālī's Classification of the Sciences and Descriptions of the Highest Theoretical Science." *Dīvān* 30.1 (2011): 1–32.

———. *Inspired Knowledge in Islamic Thought: al-Ghazālī's Theory of Mystical Cognition and its Avicennian Foundation*: London/New York: Routledge, 2012.

Trimingham, J. Spencer. *The Sufi Orders*. Oxford: Oxford University Press, 1971.

Ṭūsī, Abū Naṣr as-Sarrāj -al. *Kitāb al-Luma'*. Edited by 'Abd al-Ḥalīm Maḥmūd and Ṭāhā 'Abd az-Zāqī Surār. Cairo: Dār al-Kutub al-Ḥadīthah, 1970.

ul-Huda, Qamar. *Striving for Divine Union: Spiritual Exercises for Suhrawardī Ṣūfīs*. London/New York: RoutledgeCurzon, 2002.

Utas, Bo. "'Ambiguity' in the *Savanih* of Ahmad Ghazali." *Proceedings of the Second European Conference of Iranian Studies*. Edited by Bert G Fragner, 701–710. Rome: Istituto Italiano per il Medio ed Estremo Oriente, 1995.

Vansina, Jan. *Oral Tradition as History.* Madison: University of Wisconsin Press, 1985.

Waley, Muhammad Isa. "Najm ad-Dīn Kubrā and the Central Asian School of Sufism (The Kubrawiyyah)." In *Islamic Spirituality.* Edited by S.H. Nasr, 2:80–104. New York: Crossroad Publication Company, 1991.

Watt, Montgomery. "A Forgery in al-Ghazālī's *Mishkāt*?" *Journal of the Royal Asiatic Society,* 81, no. 1 (1949): 5–22.

Wendt, Gisela. *Aḥmad Ghazzālī: Gedanken über die Liebe.* Amsterdam: Castrum Peregrini, 1978.

Wensinck, A.J. *Concordance et Indices de la Tradition Musulmane.* 8 Vols. Leiden: E.J. Brill, 1992.

Winter, T.J. "Introduction." In *The Remembrance of Death and the Afterlife: Kitāb Dhikr al-mawt wa-mā baʿdahu; Book XL of The Revival of the Religious Sciences,* xii–xxx. Translated by T. J. Winter. Cambridge: Islamic Texts Society, 1989.

Yāfiʿī, ʿAfīf ad-Dīn ʿAbdallāh b. Asad b. ʿAlī -al. *Mirʾāt al-janān wa-ʿibrat al-yaqẓān fī maʿrifat mā yuʿtabaru min ḥawādith az-zamān.* Hyderabad: Dāʾirat al-Maʿārif al-Niẓāmiyyah. n.d.

Yāqūt, Shihāb ad-Dīn Abū ʿAbdallāh b. ʿAbdallāh. *Muʿjam al-buldān.* Beirut: Dār Beirut li'ṭ-ṭibāʿah wa'n-nashr, 1376/1957.

Zabīdī, Muḥammad b. Muḥammad b. al-Ḥusayn al-Murtaḍā. *Itḥāf as-sādah al-muttaqīn fī sharḥ Iḥyāʾ ʿulūm ad-dīn.* Cairo: n.p., 1311.

Zaman, Muhammad Qasim. *Religion and Politics under the Early ʿAbbasids.* Leiden: E.J. Brill, 1997.

Zargar, Cyrus Ali. *Sufi Aesthetics: Beauty, Love, and the Human Form in the Writings of Ibn ʿArabī and ʿIrāqī.* Columbia, S.C.: University of South Carolina Press, 2011.

Ziriklī, Khayr ad-Dīn -al. *al-Aʿlām: Qāmūs tarājim li-ashhar ar-rijāl wa'n-nisāʾ min al-ʿarab wa'l-mustaʿribīn wa'l-mustashriqīn.* Beirut: Dār al-ʿIlm li'l-Malāyīn, 1992.

Index